# REAL WORLD
# GLOBALIZATION

## NINETEENTH EDITION

### A READER IN ECONOMICS, BUSINESS, AND POLITICS FROM

EDITED BY ARMAĞAN GEZICI, ELIZABETH T. HENDERSON,

JEANETTE MITCHELL, JAWIED NAWABI,

AND THE *DOLLARS & SENSE* COLLECTIVE

# REAL WORLD GLOBALIZATION, 19th edition

ISBN: 978-1-939402-47-9

Published by:  Economic Affairs Bureau, Inc. d/b/a *Dollars & Sense*

P.O. Box 209, Portsmouth, NH 03802

617-447-2177; dollars@dollarsandsense.org; www.dollarsandsense.org.

*Real World Globalization* is edited by the *Dollars & Sense* collective, which also publishes *Dollars & Sense* magazine and the classroom books *Real World Macro, Real World Micro, The Economics of the Environment, Introduction to Political Economy, Labor and the Global Economy, Real World Banking and Finance, Current Economic Issues, Real World Latin America, Real World Labor, Unlevel Playing Fields,* and *The Wealth Inequality Reader.*

The 2020 *Dollars & Sense* Collective:  Betsy Aron, Will Beaman, Sarah Cannon, Ed Ford, Elizabeth T. Henderson, Peter Kolozi, Tom Louie, John Miller, Jawied Nawabi, Zoe Sherman, Bryan Snyder, Abhilasha Srivastava, Chris Sturr, Jeanne Winner.

Editors of this volume: Armağan Gezici, Elizabeth T. Henderson, Jeannette Mitchell, and Jawied Nawabi

Production: Elizabeth T. Henderson and Chris Sturr

Cover design: Chris Sturr

Cover photo: Aydin Mutlu, via iStock.com

Printed in U.S.A.

# CONTENTS

# INTRODUCTION

When we survey the world today, there are indeed many positive developments—from new technological conveniences and life-saving medical advances which could treat routine illnesses to developing vaccines for viruses such as Covid-19. For all of these advances, the capitalist system, which drives globalization, receives great praise. Yet, capitalism is still an economic system in which a small minority of people owns the principal means of production, employs others as wage workers, and offers the goods and services the workers produce for sale with the goal of private profits. There is abundant historical evidence that this system expands relentlessly, spreading individualism, competition, and the exploitation of labor and the environment to the point of increasing the rate of climate change and generating more pandemics. It is a socioeconomic force that tears down the walls of other social systems, whatever their particular traditional beliefs and their organization of economic activity. The results are often devastating for entire groups and regions.

For the past several decades, the dominant set of ideas promoting corporate-led globalization has been neoliberalism, or "free market" economics. Neoliberalism advocates policies implemented through powerful governments, especially the U.S. government, and international institutions such as the World Bank, the International Monetary Fund, and the World Trade Organization. These governments and institutions frustrate attempts by nation states to regulate economic activity for wide social benefit. Neoliberalism strives for the elimination of restrictions on the mobility of capital or the penetration of local economies by foreign-based business. Regulations, which smaller and less-developed nation states attempt to erect in order to promote their local industries, are derided as anachronistic and "inefficient." In the doctrine of neoliberalism, the notion of competition is central. Competition among nations, regions, firms, and of course among workers, is supposed to allocate all resources—whether physical, natural, human, or financial—with the greatest possible efficiency. The result of this sort of competition is to increase economic inequality and transform human relations into conflictual economic relations.

It is the aim of this book to explain and critically analyze the basic contours of globalization, this continual spread of unfettered capitalist relations around the world, as it is currently taking place. The articles are written from a progressive perspective which critically analyzes the fanfare surrounding the positive and beneficial aspects of globalization. The articles focus on the disruptive and dis-equalizing aspects of corporate-led globalization. They also aim to outline alternatives to this current form of globalization. These alternatives have the aim of eliminating poverty and hunger and the continuing growth of inequality within and between nations. They would eliminate the coexistence of extreme poverty juxtaposed with the heights of luxury, environmental destruction, and growing religious and ethnic tensions.

Note: Most of the articles in this volume were originally published in *Dollars & Sense* magazine. The date of original publication is indicated, and some articles include an update. Also, some of these *Dollars & Sense* articles were in a column called "Ask Dr. Dollar," in which readers' questions are answered. With these, the questions are included at the beginning of the articles. When articles are form other sources, those sources and dates of original publication are listed.

## What's in This Book

The book is made up of thirteen chapters, each focusing on a particular aspect of the global economy.

## Chapter 1: Critical Perspectives on Globalization

This chapter starts off the volume with several key questions about globalization today: What is Globalization? Is the corporate-controlled version of globalization inevitable? How is the world economy changing today? Are there possibilities of a more inclusive and sustainable globalization? Are the trends of growing inequality inevitable? Has globalization increased the potential for economic freedom and social mobility, while safeguarding our rights and opportunities for a dignified life?

## Chapter 2: Inherent Crisis of Capitalism

Many mainstream economists and business news reports separate the causal explanations behind the Covid-19 pandemic. Instead, Covid-19 and other socioeconomic crises are explained as problems generated due to countries with questionable and weak institutions. The first three articles in this chapter reveal that perhaps the causes and the persistent problems of the rising death tolls resulting from the Covid-19 crisis are better understood by focusing on the vast global value chains in the capitalist system's agribusiness networks and the priority of profits over peoples' lives in this system. The remaining articles in this chapter cover generalized "secular stagnation" besetting the economies of the developed world, as well as the economies of middle and low-income countries; the wage repression of German workers; and the ongoing economic crisis in Greece. All of these articles illustrate how the capitalist economic system prioritizes the profits of private corporations and banks over the health of the public and the livelihoods of workers.

## Chapter 3: Corporate Power and the Global Economy

The articles in this chapter focus on the power of multinational corporations (MNCs). Mainstream ("neoclassical") economics textbooks assume that markets are competitive, with thousands of sellers offering consumers what they want at competitively determined prices. In other words, firms wield no real power and the consumer is "sovereign." In the real world, we find a handful of giant companies controlling an enormous share of world trade in each major industry. MNCs have immense power and are able to influence the terms of trade in the world's food system, the monetary and fiscal policies of countries, the corporate tax rate, the legal language of international agreements, and the power structures of international institutions.

## Chapter 4: International Trade and Investment

Despite differences among neoclassical economists on many theoretical and practical questions, one issue where there is virtual unanimity is the gospel of free trade. The theory of comparative advantage, or at least the contemporary textbook version, purports to show that "free trade" will benefit all countries regardless of size and level of economic development. The articles in this chapter offer critical perspectives about both trade itself and the use of "free trade" as a justification for the elimination of barriers to international movements of capital. It considers just what circumstances—specifically what forms of integration into the world economy—are required for trade between countries to be genuinely beneficial to their populations.

## Chapter 5: International Finance

The world of international finance may appear in standard textbooks as a benign sphere where men in suits and ties buy and sell the currencies of various countries, mainly for the purpose of buying and selling the goods and services of those countries. However, the currency policy of countries whose economies are large have deep consequential effects on large and small countries alike. U.S. government policies that maintain the dollar as the primary reserve currency in the world, for example, generate financial pressures on developing countries to put away a large part of their savings—sometimes hundreds of billions of dollars—in dollars or securities denominated in dollars. The deregulation of international finance, meanwhile, means that countries are exposed to destabilizing short-run, speculative movements of capital. Financial investment can rush into a country during a boom (making its currency more valuable), only to stampede out just as fast at the first hint of a downturn (potentially causing the currency to crash). As a result, instead of being able to engage in large-scale productive investment, developing countries have to use their savings to defend their currency's stable exchange rate from possible speculative "attack." Instead of productive investment that could benefit lower-income people in developing countries, this structure concentrates wealth in the financial sectors of the United States and other high-income countries, a form of invisible imperialism, as the articles in this chapter describe.

## Chapter 6: International Institutions

The world needs international institutions as much as we need domestic institutions. Institutions regulate matters like product safety, resource-depletion, environmental pollution, and conditions and compensation for labor. They create formal channels through which disputes between contracting parties can be resolved. Mainstream accounts often assume that existing international institutions are designed to bring about fair resolutions for these and other matters, based on what is best for the global community. However, the articles in this chapter—on the International Monetary Fund (IMF), the World Bank, the World Trade Organization (WTO), the European Union (EU), and Donald Trump's withdrawal from the World Health Organization (WHO)—reveal the elite-controlled nature of the international institutional architecture. These international institutions are of the wealthy, by the wealthy, and for the wealthy.

## Chapter 7: Labor in the Global Economy

Where do the cheap goods which fill our malls and online stores come from? When we see commercials for the products that we eat or wear, should we wonder about the working conditions of the workers who make them? The articles in this chapter describe the condition of workers in an array of countries in the Global South and their economic interconnections to workers in the Global North. They give a wide variety of examples, throughout the world, showing that globalization does not inevitably result in a "race to the bottom" on wages and working conditions. The power of workers' organizations, and the laws and policies that set conditions for labor organization in different countries, sectors, and occupations, also matter.

## Chapter 8: Migration

In the past 10 years immigration has been a sensitive topic for the U.S. public, partly because of the controversial act of deporting millions of undocumented migrants from the United States. Around the world, there are nearly 272 million migrants living outside of their home countries, primarily for economic reasons. As the articles in this chapter reveal, immigrants bring their creative talents and immense productive energy, from which their new adopted countries and most native-born and longtime resident workers benefit. Although the articles in this chapter focus primarily on migration from the Global South to the United States and to Europe, it should be noted that a substantial percentage of migration—between 36%–40%—is "South to South" migration.

## Chapter 9: Development and "Underdevelopment"

Does the development of one country or region come at the expense of other countries or regions? What does "development" actually measure? Why have the economic policies of the "Washington Consensus," formulated by the best trained economists from the top universities in the world, not been able to the reduce poverty and misery that is so pervasive in much of the world? What are the roles of the control of land and access to credit in economic development? These are some of the central questions in development economics that are addressed in this chapter, each in a concrete, present-day context.

## Chapter 10: The State, Globalization, and Development

This chapter focuses on a very contentious issue in economics: What is the role of the state in the economy? The economic literature includes much misunderstanding about, and bias concerning, the role of the state in economic development. However, as these articles reveal, by giving examples from Latin America, East Asia, and China, the difference between successful development—or lack of it—has often hinged on whether state intervention has been sufficient and effective. The role of government, as these articles reveal, is indispensable in managing the monetary system, capital controls, and even the larger transformational process of economic development by coordinating the industrial policies of developing countries.

## Chapter 11: The Political Economy of Empire

This chapter, which focuses on the unequal relations of power (military, political, and economic) among countries, flows logically from the previous one. What is the relationship of colonialism and neocolonialism to "underdevelopment" in today's world economy? How does Puerto Rico's political status affect its economy? What about Haiti's relationship to the United States? Why does foreign aid from high-income countries have such a poor record in affecting the economies of low-income countries? Does U.S. prosperity have to come at the expense of impoverishing the so-called developing countries?

## Chapter 12: Natural Resources and the Environment

This chapter addresses key controversies regarding natural-resource depletion and environmental degradation. Are low-income countries "havens" for polluting industries, or are some high-income countries also serious polluters? Is it a good or bad idea to move away from nuclear power production? Are environmental protections "luxuries" that only high-income countries can afford, or would people in developing countries benefit from such policies as well? Do we need to abandon economic growth—or even deliberately pursue "de-growth"—to tackle the threat of climate change?

## Chapter 13: Resistance and Alternatives

What are the alternatives to the present corporate-controlled globalization, and how do we build those alternatives? The articles in this chapter focus on movements and ideas which point to ways that the international economic system can be reorganized to bring about better conditions for labor, learning from Cuba's successful policies with tackling the Covid-19 crisis, reducing inequality, and achieving greater economic security and environmental sustainability. They offer not pie-in-the-sky fantasies but concrete and practical alternatives to corporate globalization. People around the world are advocating, demanding, and organizing in support of such alternatives and are confident in the belief that, contrary to what dominant elites tell them, another world is indeed possible!

—*Jawied Nawabi*

# Chapter 1

# CRITICAL PERSPECTIVES ON GLOBALIZATION

*Article 1.1*

## THE GLOBAL ECONOMY TODAY
*How we got here and where we need to go.*

**BY ARTHUR MacEWAN**
*January/February 2017*

Globalization has run into a backlash. There has long been opposition to the efforts of governments and large corporations in the high-income countries—especially the United States—to establish new rules of global commerce. This opposition appeared in the protests against the North American Free Trade Agreement (NAFTA) in the early 1990s and against the World Trade Organization (WTO) in the later 1990s. Remember the Zapatistas in 1994 and Seattle in 1999?

In 2016, however, the backlash against globalization became especially formidable. It emerged as a dominant theme in Donald Trump's ascendency to the U.S. presidency, and also was a major factor in Sen. Bernie Sanders' strong campaign for the Democratic nomination. In the United Kingdom, the Brexit vote to take the country out of the European Union was also in part a reaction against globalization, as has been the growing strength of right-wing politicians elsewhere in Europe. Globalization has become the focal point for the reaction of many to a wide range of social and economic ills, a reaction that has also been fueled by latent—and not so latent—xenophobia and racism.

Whatever other factors are involved, the backlash against globalization is based on the very real damage that has been done to economic equality, security, and the overall well-being of many people by the way international commerce has been organized. How did we get here—what's the history of our current situation? Could international commerce be organized differently? Are there alternatives?

## Not a New Phenomenon

At least since people began walking out of Africa tens of thousands of years ago, humans have been expanding the geographic realm of their economic, political, social, and cultural contacts. In this broad sense, globalization is nothing new, and it might reasonably be viewed as an inexorable process. To oppose it would be little different than trying to stop the ocean tides.

Globalization, however, is not one, well-defined phenomenon. It has taken different forms in different periods and has been connected to political power in different ways. It will certainly take new and different forms in the future. Colonialism, for example, has been a predominant form of globalization for thousands of years, and only disappeared—well, not entirely (consider Puerto Rico)—in the second half of the 20th century. Neo-colonialism, a system in which major powers exercise *de facto* control over the policies of lesser powers but without the formal, *de jure* controls of colonialism, often came into force as colonialism waned. From the 16th through the 18th century, under the ideology of mercantilism, European powers explicitly regulated their own countries' foreign commerce through import restrictions and export promotion. Mercantilism often went along with colonialism, and colonial powers also put economic restrictions on the countries they controlled. In the second half of the 20th century, the increasing integration of countries in Western Europe, leading to the formation of the European Union and creation of a common currency, is still another example of the varied forms of globalization.

Virtually everywhere among the now high income countries—the United Kingdom and the United States are prime cases—early industrialization was accomplished with high levels of government protection for manufacturing. At the same

### NAFTA and the Zapatistas

The Zapatista Army of National Liberation (Ejército Zapatista de Liberación Nacional, EZLN), popularly known as the "Zapatistas," is a revolutionary leftist political militant group based in Chiapas, the southernmost state of Mexico.

On the morning of January 1, 1994, the day that NAFTA went into effect, the Zapatistas issued their First Declaration and Revolutionary Laws from the Lacandon Jungle, and an estimated 3,000 armed Zapatista insurgents seized several towns and cities in Chiapas. They freed the prisoners in the jail of San Cristóbal de las Casas and set fire to several police buildings and military barracks in the area. The guerrillas enjoyed brief success, but the next day Mexican army forces counterattacked, and fierce fighting broke out in and around the market of Ocosingo. The Zapatista forces took heavy casualties and retreated from the city into the surrounding jungle.

The Zapatistas' initial goal was to instigate a revolution throughout Mexico. As this did not happen, they used their uprising as a platform to protest the signing of NAFTA, which the EZLN believed would increase the gap between rich and poor people in Chiapas—a prediction that has been vindicated by subsequent developments.

The Zapatistas have continued to exist into the 2000s, operating principally from their base in Chiapas (though also making unarmed forays around Mexico), issuing several further declarations, and organizing for social justice.

time, these countries' governments used their power to extend their global economic engagement, to seek resources or markets or both. For example, Britain developed a far-flung empire, and also employed its powerful navy to assure that, in regions outside the empire, markets and resources were available for British commerce—for the sale of textiles in Latin America, opium in China, etc. The United States, late to the era of colonialism, extended its realm of control, over land and other resources, by expanding westward across the continent. But the United States became a colonial power at the end of the 19th century, taking Puerto Rico, the Philippines, Hawaii, and Guam (and Cuba for a two-and-a-half-year period). At the same time, this country increasingly became a neo-colonial power, using military strength especially in the Caribbean and Central American to protect U.S. financial and other interests.

## Interruption and Reassertion

Globalization was severely interrupted in the first half of the 20th century by two world wars and the Great Depression. Furthermore, after the wars, two major areas of the world—the Soviet Union and its "satellite" countries, as well as China—were largely outside of the international capitalist system. In this context, the United States—with only 6% of the world's population, but some 27% of the world's output—became the undisputed leader of the "free world." With this economic prowess, its extreme military strength, and the relative devastation of other economically advanced countries, it was virtually able to dictate the terms, the rules of operation, in the international economic system.

The goal of the U.S. government in this regard was that U.S. firms would have access—indeed, they should have the right of access—to resources and markets throughout the international system. As one step toward accomplishing this end, the United States, with the acquiescence of other countries, established the dollar as the central currency of international commerce. Both directly and through its influence over international institutions (the World Bank, the International Monetary Fund, and the General Agreement on Tariffs and Trade), the U.S. government pushed for the minimization of countries' barriers to foreign trade and investment—that is,

### The Battle in Seattle

On November 30, 1999, the World Trade Organization (WTO) convened a Ministerial Conference to launch a new round of trade negotiations. The negotiations were quickly overshadowed by massive and controversial street protests outside the hotels and the Washington State Convention and Trade Center, in what became the known as "The Battle of Seattle." (A Hollywood movie with this title and based on the 1999 events was released in 2007.)

The large scale of the demonstrations, estimated at no less than 40,000 protesters, dwarfed any previous demonstration in the United States against a world meeting of any of the organizations generally associated with economic globalization (such as the WTO, the International Monetary Fund, or the World Bank).

"free trade." Trade barriers were, however, slow to come down as other advanced countries sought to rebuild their industries after the war and many lower-income countries sought to protect their nascent industries. Nonetheless, governments and business interests in these other countries also wanted foreign investment, resulting in the great expansion of U.S.-based multinational firms from the 1950s onward.

But trade barriers would eventually come down. The United States, which had built its own industrial capacity behind tariff walls in the 19th century, now insisted in the latter half of the 20th century that low-income countries abandon similar walls. Having reached the top, the United States was pulling the ladder up. The International Monetary Fund (IMF) played a major role in pushing low income countries to lower their import restrictions. When these countries turned to the IMF for financial assistance (especially during the debt crisis of the 1980s), the condition for that assistance was "structural adjustment," which included lowering import restrictions.

The efforts of the U.S. government began to achieve notable success in the 1990s, with NAFTA, which removed many trade barriers among the United States, Mexico, and Canada (and did a good deal more, as discussed below). Then it promoted the formation of the World Trade Organization (WTO), which, according to its own website, "is the only global international organization dealing with the rules of trade between nations." (The U.S. government, however, failed in its effort to establish the Free Trade of the Americas Agreement (FTAA)—about which negotiations took place through the 1990s and which would have included virtually all countries in the Western Hemisphere.)

The U.S. government has established either bilateral or small group (e.g., NAFTA) "free trade" agreements with 20 countries, most put into effect since 2000. Even without such agreements, access to the U.S. market and U.S. access to foreign markets have expanded considerably. There are still regions of the world, China and Russia, for example, where significant restrictions on foreign trade and investment still apply and with which the United States has no general trade agreements. Yet U.S. firms are nonetheless heavily involved in these countries as well. Compared to the situation after World War II, to say nothing of the 19th century, tariffs and other trade restrictions are now quite low.

The changes are illustrated, in Table 1, with data from the world's twelve largest economies. It is not simply tariff changes, however, that have brought about a burgeoning of international commerce. Other sorts of restrictions on trade (e.g., quantitative import restrictions, or "import quotas") have come down. And major advances in transportation and communications technology have also played a role. All in all, the rising role of international trade and investment has been huge—making the current age truly an era of economic globalization (at least in the broad sense).

In the decade of the 1960s, world exports averaged 12% of world GDP, but in the recent ten-year span of 2006-2015, the figure was 30%. The international trade of the U.S. economy also grew over the same period, though at a much lower level. (Larger countries tend to have lower imports and exports, relative to the size of their economies, than small countries.) Foreign direct investment (FDI) has grown especially rapidly in recent decades, with annual net inflows of FDI in the world rising 100 fold between the 1970s, when the average was $21 billion, and the period 2006-2015, with an average of over $2.1 trillion. (FDI includes investment that establishes control or substantial influence over the decisions of a foreign business—such as a wholly owned subsidiary—plus purchases of foreign real assets such as land and buildings.)

## Financialization and Crisis

There is also the international financialization phenomenon—the rising role of financial markets and financial institutions in the operation of the economy. The global amount of debt outstanding grew from $45 trillion in 1990 to $175 trillion in 2012, increasing from almost 2¼ times global GDP to almost 2½ times. (The most rapid growth took place before the Great Recession, followed by a slow-down in subsequent years.)

The economic instability associated with financialization became apparent in the Asian financial crisis of 1997. The rapid exodus of capital from countries where economic problems were developing greatly exacerbated the downturn. The financial crisis that emerged in the United States in 2008 and 2009, then spread to Europe and elsewhere, exposed the full and devastating force of global financial activity. The great size and extensive web of connections among financial institutions created a severe threat to the world economy. "Free market" ideology was put aside, and the U.S. government intervened heavily—with a huge bailout of the banks—to keep the economy from imploding.

Financialization created, and continues to create, a vast increase in debt levels in many counties. "Debt … is an accelerator," notes University of Massachusetts economist Gerald Epstein, "that enables the financial system to generate a credit bubble." The bubble allows financial institutions (banks, hedge fund, private equity firms, etc.) to extract wealth from non-financial firms and individuals, and can also quicken the pace of economic activity more generally. Bubbles, however, burst, leading to economic distress, deflation, and bankruptcies.

Beyond instability and crises, financialization appears to impede economic growth by diverting resources from productive activity into financial speculation. Also, financialization harms economic growth by contributing to extreme income inequality, which is increasingly recognized to have a negative impact on growth. Furthermore, though perhaps in a more extreme form, large financial firms present the same problems that arise with other large firms operating internationally, namely that the many options created by their global operations— to say nothing of their political influence—make them difficult to tax and regulate.

## Free Trade? Only in the Rhetoric

Even with U.S. trade-and-investment agreements, reduction in restrictions on international commerce, technological changes, and the WTO rules of operation, many

## TABLE 1: TARIFF RATE CHANGES FOR TWELVE LARGEST ECONOMIES FROM LATE 1980S OR EARLY 1990S TO 2014 (WEIGHTED MEAN, ALL PRODUCTS)

| Country | Late 1980s or Early 1990s | 2014 |
|---|---|---|
| United States | 4.0% (1989) | 1.4% |
| China | 32.2% (1992) | 3.2% |
| Japan | 3.8% (1988) | 1.2% |
| Germany | 3.6% (1988) | 1.5% |
| United Kingdom | 3.6% (1988) | 1.5% |
| France | 3.6% (1988) | 1.5% |
| India | 54.0% (1992) | 6.8% (2009) |
| Brazil | 31.9% (1989) | 7.8% |
| Canada | 7.2% (1989) | 0.8% |
| Rep. of Korea | 13.8% (1988) | 5.2% |
| Russia | 6.2% (1993) | 4.9% |

Source: World Bank (data.worldbank.org).

Note: The twelve largest economies are selected on the basis of 2016 nominal GDP in U.S. dollars, International Monetary Fund data (see statisticstimes.com/economy/countries-by-progectedgdp.php). The date in the "Late 1980s or Early 1990s" is the earliest date for which figures are available in the World Bank souce.

aspects of world commerce remain contested terrain. U.S. financial and nonfinancial firms, along with firms from other countries, want not only trade and investment access, but also as much assurance as they can get for the right to access. So under the banner of "free trade" the United States pushed forward to establish the Trans-Pacific Partnership Agreement (TPP), with eleven other countries along the Pacific Rim, and the Transatlantic Trade and Investment Partnership (TTIP), with the European Union. These agreements would expand the share of U.S. trade and investment taking place within realms where the "rules of the game" are firmly established—and those rules would essentially be rules promoted by large U.S. firms and the U.S. government, but of course with the cooperation of large firms and governments elsewhere. With the ascendancy of Donald Trump to the presidency, however, the TPP now seems dead, and the future of the TTIP and other agreements is unclear. A key to understanding these and earlier trade-and-investment pacts is to recognize that they are not "free trade" agreements. These agreements, while removing some barriers to international trade and investment, have focused on creating protections. This is most clear in regard to patents and copyrights—so-called "intellectual property rights." As Dean Baker, the co-director of the Center for Economic and Policy Research has written:

> The TPP is not about free trade. It does little to reduce tariffs and quotas for the simple reason that these barriers are already very low. ...In fact,

the TPP goes far in the opposite direction, increasing protectionism in the form of stronger and longer patent and copyright protection. These forms of protection for prescription drugs, software and other products, often raise the price by a factor of a hundred or more above the free market price. This makes them equivalent to tariffs of several thousand percent.

Patents and copyrights are alleged to encourage innovation, but there is no reason to think that the particular—especially high—U.S. system of protections promoted in these agreements is a good way to accomplish this end. There are more effective ways to promote innovations, but few more effective ways to promote profits for large pharmaceuticals and software firms.

Furthermore, while these agreements assure the unrestrained movement of capital—establishing rights for foreign investment in the participating countries—they do not provide for the movement of labor. People are inherently less mobile than capital, regardless of immigration restrictions. Yet, removing restrictions on capital mobility and doing nothing to facilitate the movement of labor or protect labor increases the power of firms over workers. Power depends on the availability of options. These agreements give greater options—and therefore greater power—to businesses. This power shows up in the stagnation, and in many cases the decline, of workers' wages, as their jobs are shifted to lower-wage countries and they are forced to accept lower wages in other employment. Even when firms do not actually move abroad, the threat of movement is sufficient to weaken workers' bargaining power.

Power to businesses is also provided—in these agreements, in NAFTA and the more recently proposed agreements—through provisions that give foreign investors the right to sue governments in private international arbitration (not the courts). These provisions are known as "investor-state dispute settlement," or ISDS. ISDS allows a firm to sue, claiming that new financial regulations, environmental laws, worker protections, food and health safety standards, or other laws and regulations threaten their profits. A recent example of the use of ISDS is the case filed in 2016 by TransCanada, claiming that the U.S. government's blocking construction of its Keystone XL pipeline violated its rights under NAFTA and seeking $15 billion in compensation. The danger of these agreement provisions is not only that the suits will be costly, but that they will inhibit the establishment of important laws and regulations. (There is, by the way, no provision for workers to sue when new laws or regulations harm their livelihoods.) The ISDS provisions and the patent and copyright protections in these various international agreements belie the rhetoric that they are free trade agreements.

In reality, there is no such thing as free trade, if the term is taken to mean international commerce without any impact from government actions. Governments' involvement in economic activity is ubiquitous and their impact on their countries' international commerce is affected by far more than tariffs, import quotas, and direct subsidies for export activity. Perhaps the best example is government expenditures on education and research. If these expenditures are high relative to other countries', the country has a trade advantage in goods and services that rely on highly skilled labor. These expenditures are, in effect, an indirect, though important, subsidy to certain kinds of exports. A particular and historically important case is that of government support of agricultural research and extension activity, which has long-placed U.S. agriculture in a strong position in international trade. More recent examples are the U.S. Defense Department's grants for information technology development and the National Science Foundation's support for activity biotechnology. Clearly, such expenditures, as well as the broad government support of public education, have profound effects on countries' international commerce.

The point here is not that governments should stop all economic engagement that affects international commerce, an impossible task that even celebrants of free trade themselves do not advocate. Instead, we should recognize that choices must be and are being made regarding the nature of a country's trade. Those choices are

### The Bretton Woods Arrangements

In July 1944, the U.S. government convened a conference at the Mount Washington Hotel in Bretton Woods, N.H., to set the rules for the international economy in the period after World War II.

Representatives from 44 governments, all of them U.S. allies in the war, attended the Bretton Woods Conference. A principal outcome of the conference was the establishment of the U.S. dollar's central role in international commerce. Other countries agreed to maintain the values of their currencies in a fixed relation to the dollar, and to change that value only under extreme circumstances. The United States, in turn, would maintain the value of the dollar in relation to gold at $35 per ounce—i.e., the U.S. government agreed to exchange other countries' dollars for gold at this rate. This arrangement was intended to maintain international economic stability and to serve as a foundation for open markets in the world economy.

The arrangement worked well for the U.S. government and U.S. firms. With global transactions taking place in dollars, most dollars were never traded in for gold. It was a bit like a person writing checks to pay for purchases and knowing that most of those checks would never be cashed; they would simply be used like money among other people. The stability this arrangement created also worked well for many other countries.

The dollar system, however, ended in 1971. A combination of heavy private and government (largely military) spending abroad and inflation and recession at home meant that the U.S. government could no longer maintain the $35 per ounce of gold relationship and abandoned the system (closed the "gold window"). The dollar continued to play a central role in global commerce, but through a series of changing arrangements, which were accompanied by greater instability in currency relationships.

The Bretton Woods agreements also created the International Monetary Fund, the World Bank, and the General Agreement on Tariffs and Trade (precursor to the World Trade Organization). These institutions, dominated by the U.S. and allied governments, have played major roles in affecting both the organization of the global economy and of many national economies.

The Bretton Woods conference was very much dominated by the United States. This country's great economic power—largely unscathed by war devastation experienced elsewhere—placed it in position to insist on rules and regulation for the international economy that would decisively establish it as the one superpower in the capitalist world, demoting Britain to the status of junior partner. As a wartime ally of the United States, the Soviet Union took part in the Bretton Woods conference, but—perhaps needless to say—did not sign the agreements.

bound up with all sorts of other choices about governments' engagement with their economies. The matter of how international commerce should be organized cannot hidden behind the rhetoric of free trade.

## Global Commerce and Political Power

The rhetoric of free trade, in any case, is simply one of the tools that the U.S. government, its allies, international agencies, and large firms use in shaping the world economy. Economic and political-military power is the foundation for this shaping. Following World War II, when the U.S. accounted for more than a quarter of world output, it had tremendous economic power—as a market, an investment source, and a source of new technology. U.S. firms had little competition in their global operations and were thus able to penetrate markets and control resources over a wide range (outside of the U.S.S.R., the rest of the East Bloc, and China). Along with this economic power, the military power of the United States was immense. In the context of the Cold War and the rise of democratic upsurges and liberation movements in many regions, the role of the U.S. military was welcomed in many countries—especially by elites facing threats (real or imagined) from the Soviet Union, domestic liberation movements, or both.

This combination of economic and military power, far more than the rhetoric of free trade, allowed the U.S. government to move other governments toward accepting openness in international commerce. The Bretton Woods conference was a starting point in this process; U.S. representatives at the conference were largely able to dictate the conference outcomes. In terms of international commerce, things worked quite well for the United Sates for about 25 years. Then, however, various challenges to the U.S. position emerged. In particular, the war in Indochina and its costs, competition from firms based in Japan and Europe, and the rise of OPEC and increase in energy costs began to disrupt the dominant U.S. role by the early 1970s.

Still, while the period after the 1970s saw slower economic growth, both in the United States and in several other high-income countries, the United States continued to hold its dominant positon. In part, this was due to the Cold War—the Soviet threat, or at least the perceived threat, providing the glue that attached other countries to U.S. leadership. Yet, by the 1990s, the U.S.S.R. was no more, and China was becoming a rising world power.

---

### GDP Comparisons: Market Exchange Rates and Purchasing Power Parity

To understand the difference between comparing countries' GDP using market exchange rates and based on purchasing power, suppose that the market exchange rate between the U.S. dollar and the peso in another country is one dollar equals one peso, and with this 1-to-1 exchange rate, this other country has a GDP that is one-half as large as the U.S. GDP. However, assume it turns out that one peso in this other county can buy as much as two dollars in the U.S. That is, in term of purchasing power, two dollars is equal to one peso. Based purchasing power, the two counties have the same GDP.

In spite of the changes in the world economy, the United States at first appears to have almost the same share of world output in 2016, 24.7%, as it had in the immediate post-World War II period, and is still considerably ahead of any other country. Yet this figure evaluates output in the rest of the world's countries at market exchange rates. When the figures are recalculated, using the real purchasing power of different currencies, the U.S. share drops to 15.6%, behind China's 17.9% of world output. Of course, as China has a much larger population than the United States, even using the purchasing power figures, per person GDP in the U.S. is almost four times greater than in China; it would be almost 7 times greater using the market exchange rates.

The rise of China has not moved the United States off its pedestal as the world's dominant economic power. Moreover, U.S. military strength remains dominant in world affairs. Yet the challenge is real, even to the point that China has recently created an institution, providing development loans to low-income countries, to be an alternative to the (U.S.-dominated) World Bank. Investment by Chinese firms, too, is spreading worldwide. Then there are the military issues in the South China Sea.

At the same time, the United States is engaged in seemingly intractable military operations in the Middle East, and has continued to maintain its global military presence as widely as during the Cold War. Having long taken on the role of providing the global police force, for the U.S. government to pull back from these operations would be to accept a decline in U.S. global power. But, further, the extensive and far flung military presence of U.S. forces is necessary to preserve the rules of international commerce that have been established over decades. The rules themselves need protection, regardless of the amount of commerce directly affected. The real threat to "U.S. interests" posed by the Islamic State and like forces in the Middle East, Africa, and parts of East Asia is not their appalling and murderous actions. Instead, their threat lies in their disruption and disregard for the rules of international commerce. From Honduras and Venezuela to Saudi Arabia and Iraq, if U.S. policy were guided by an attempt to protect human rights, the role of U.S. military and diplomatic polices would be very different.

Continuing to operate on a global level to halt threats to the "rules of the game"—in a world were economic power is shifting away from the United States—this country is threatening itself with imperial overreach. Attempting to preserve its role in global affairs and to maintain its favored terms of global commerce, the U.S. government may be taking on financial and military burdens that it cannot manage. In the Middle East in particular, the costs of military operations during the 21$^{st}$ century have run into the trillions of dollars. Military bases and actions are so widespread as to limit their effectiveness in any one theater of operations.

The potential danger in this situation is two-fold. On the one hand, the costs of these operations and the resulting strain on the U.S. government's budget can weaken the operation of the domestic economy. On the other hand, in the context of the rising challenges to the U.S. role in global affairs and the rising role of other powers, especially China but also Russia, U.S. forces may enter into especially dangerous attempts to regain U.S. power in world affairs—the treacherous practice of revanchism.

## Are There Alternatives?

Although globalization in the broad sense of a geographic expansion of economic, political, social, and cultural contacts may be an inexorable process, the way in which this expansion takes place is a matter of political choices—and political power. Both economic and political/military expansion are contested terrain. Alternatives are possible.

The backlash against globalization that appeared in 2016, especially in the U.S. presidential campaign, has had both progressive and reactionary components. The outcome of the election, having had such a reactionary and xenophobic foundation, is unlikely to turn that backlash into positive reforms, which would attenuate economic inequality and insecurity. Indeed, all indications in the period leading up to Trump's inauguration (when this article is being written) suggest that, whatever changes take place in the U.S. economic relations with the rest of the world, those changes will not displace large corporations as the principal beneficiaries of the international system.

Nonetheless, the Sanders campaign demonstrated the existence of a strong progressive movement against the current form of globalization. If that movement can be sustained, there are several reforms that it could push that would alter the nature of globalization and lay the foundation for a more democratic and larger changes down the road (Sanders' "revolution"). Two examples of changes that would directly alter U.S. international agreements in ways that would reduce inequality and insecurity are:

*Changing international commercial agreements so they include strong labor rights and environmental protections.* Goods produced under conditions where workers' basic rights, to organize and to work under reasonable health and safety conditions, are denied would not be given unfettered access to global markets. Goods whose production or use is environmentally destructive would likewise face trade restrictions. (One important "restriction" could include a carbon tax that would raise the cost of transporting goods over long distances.) Effective enforcement procedures would be difficult but possible.

*Establishing effective employment support for people displaced by changes in international commerce.* Such support could include, for instance, employment insurance funds and well funded retraining programs. Also, there would need to be provisions for continuing medical care and pensions. Moreover, there is no good reason for such support programs to be limited to workers displaced by international commerce. People who lose their jobs because of environmental regulations (such as coal miners), technological change (like many workers in manufacturing), or just stupid choices by their employers should have the same support.

Several other particular reforms would also be desirable. Obviously, the elimination of ISDS is important, as is cessation of moves to extend U.S. intellectual property rights. The reforms would also include: global taxation of corporations; taxation of financial transactions; altering the governance the IMF, World Bank, and WTO to reduce their role as instruments of the United

States and other high income countries; protections for international migrants and protection of their rights as workers. The list could surely be extended. Changes in international economic relations, however, cannot be separated from political changes. The ability of the United States and its allies to shape economic relations is tied up with military power. Military interventions and the threat of military interventions have long been an essential foundation for U.S. power in the global economy. These interventions and threats are often cloaked in democratic or humanitarian rhetoric. Yet, one need simply look at the Middle East to recognize the importance of the interests of large U.S. firms in bringing about these military actions. It will be necessary to build opposition to these military interventions in order to move the world economy in a positive direction—to say nothing of halting the disastrous humanitarian impacts of these interventions.

No one claims that it would be easy to overcome the power of large corporations in shaping the rules of international commerce in agreements or to reduce (let alone block) the aggressive military practices of the U.S. government. The prospect of a Trump presidency certainly makes the prospect of progressive change on international affairs—or on any other affairs—more difficult. There is, however, nothing inevitable about the way these central aspects of globalization have been organized. There are alternatives that would not undermine the U.S. economy (or other economies). Indeed, these alternatives would strengthen the U.S. economy in terms of improving and sustaining the material well-being of most people.

The basic issues here are who—which groups in society—are going to determine basic economic policies and by what values those policies will be formulated. ❑

*Sources:* The World Bank, Global Monitoring Report 2014/15, "Ending Poverty and Sharing Prosperity" (worldbank.org); Oxfam Briefing Paper, "An Economy for the 1%," 18 January 2016 (oxfam.or)g; Statistics Times, List of Countries by Projected GDP, Data from the International Monetary Fund, 21 October 2016 (statisticstimes.com; US Share of World GDP in market prices ycharts.com; Dean Baker, "The TPP and Free Trade: Time to Retake the English Language" (cepr. net); The Canadian Press, "TransCanada Makes Good On NAFTA Lawsuit Against U.S. Over Keystone Rejection" Huffington Post, June 27, 2016 (huffingtonpost.ca); Joseph Stiglitz, "Beware of TPP's Investor–State Dispute Settlement Provision," March 28, 2016 (rooseveltinstitute.org); World Bank data (data.worldbank.org); Gerald Epstein, "Financialization: There's Something Happening Here," PERI Working Paper 394, August 2015 (peri.umass.edu); "Financial Globalization: Retreat or Rest?" McKinsey Global Institute, March 2103.

*Article 1.2*

# INEQUALITY IN THE WORLD

## BY ARTHUR MacEWAN
*November/December 2014*

> Dear Dr. Dollar:
> I had thought that neoliberal globalization was making the world more unequal. But recently I have seen claims that the distribution of income in the world has become more equal. Is this true?
> —*Evan Swinerton, Brookline, Mass.*

The answer to these questions depends on what you mean by "in the world." In many countries in the world—including most of the high-income countries and the most populous lower-income countries—the distribution of income has become more unequal. If we look at the income differences among countries, however, the situation has become more equal because per capita income has generally increased more rapidly in lower-income countries than in higher-income countries—though with important exceptions. And if we look at income distribution among all the people in the world—accounting for inequality both within and between countries—it seems that in recent decades the very high degree of inequality has remained about the same. (Before proceeding, please see the warning in the box below.)

---

## Warning!

There are many problems in determining the extent of income inequality. The results can differ depending on which measure of inequality we use. Also, there are data difficulties. While some of these difficulties arise from poor reporting, plenty arise from the complexity of the issues. Also, different countries collect income data in different ways and do so in different years. With one exception (explained below), I will not detail the difficulties here, but readers should keep in mind that such difficulties exist.

How we compare incomes in different countries, where relative prices differ, currencies differ, and exchange rates (e.g., the number of Mexican pesos it takes to buy a dollar) often do not tell us accurately the buying power of income in different countries. The income data here are reported in terms of purchasing power parity (PPP) and reported in relation to the U.S. dollar. Comparing incomes in different countries using the PPP method gives us a comparison of the real buying power of income in the different countries. Calculating PPP data is complex and not precise, but the PPP figures are the best we have.

---

## FIGURE 1: INCOME RATIO, TOP 10% TO BOTTOM 10%, SELECTED HIGH-INCOME COUNTRIES

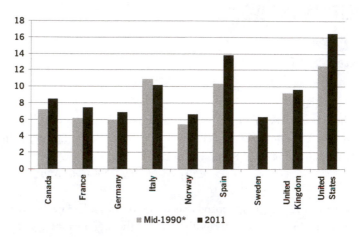

■ Mid-1990* ■ 2011

*Source:* OECD. *For the U.K. the figure is for 1999; for Spain the figure is for 2004; for France the figure is for 1996. For all others the earlier figures are for 1995. The later U.S. figure is for 2012.

## Distribution *Within* Countries

Take a look at Figures 1 and 2, which show the changes in the distribution of income within selected countries, several high-income and several low- or middle-income, over roughly the last two decades. The measure of income distribution used in these graphs is the ratio of the total income of the highest-income tenth of the population to the total income of the lowest-income tenth of the population.

The first thing that stands out in Figure 1 is that the U.S. income distribution is substantially more unequal than those of any of the other countries. Also, the absolute increase by this measure of inequality is greatest in the United States. However, with the sole exception of Italy, all the countries in Figure 1 experienced *rising income inequality*.

Things are different in Figure 2, which includes the ten most populous lower-income countries (ten of the twelve most populous countries in the world, the United States and Japan being the other two). The degree of inequality is quite high in some of the countries in the graph. Brazil is the extreme case. However, Brazil and most of the other countries in Figure 2 experienced a *reduction of inequality* in this period—though several are still highly unequal. The most populous countries in Figure 2—China, India, and Indonesia—though, experienced rising inequality. These countries are the first, second, and fourth most populous countries in the world (with the United States third).

The data in Figures 1 and 2 illustrate the widespread rise of income inequality *within* countries, especially among high-income countries. Among lower-income countries, the picture is mixed. Although Brazil remains highly unequal, the reduction of inequality in Brazil is important because it has been achieved, at least in part, by policies directed at reducing poverty. Brazil's redistributive policies represent a trend in many Latin American countries—a backlash against the neoliberal policies of preceding decades.

## FIGURE 2: INCOME RATIO, TOP 10% TO BOTTOM 10%, MOST POPULOUS LOW- AND MIDDLE-INCOME COUNTRIES

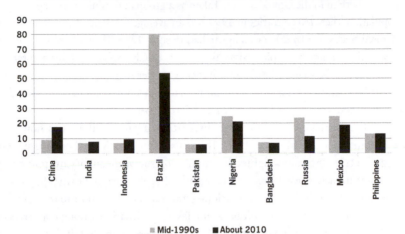

■ Mid-1990s   ■ About 2010

*Source:* World Bank. *Note:* These countries along with the United States and Japan are the twelve most populous countries in the world. The combined population of these ten accounts for 55% of the world's population in 2014.

## FIGURE 3: PER CAPITA GDP, MOST POPULOUS LOW- AND MIDDLE-INCOME COUNTRIES, AS PERCENTAGE OF U.S. GDP (PPP)

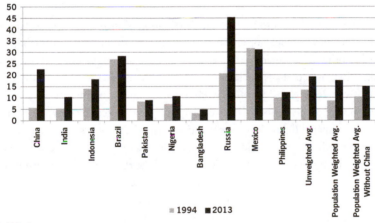

■ 1994   ■ 2013

*Source:* World Bank.

## Distribution *Among* Countries

Figure 3 illustrates what has been happening to income distribution *among* countries and indicates that the situation has become more equal because, in general, lower-income countries have grown more rapidly during the last two decades than have higher-income countries. For 1994 and 2013, the two columns in Figure 3 show Gross Domestic Product (GDP) per capita in the ten most populous low- and middle-income countries (listed by population) compared to GDP per capita in the United States. The comparison is in terms of purchasing power parity (PPP).

For nine of these ten countries—Mexico is the exception—GDP per capita rose more rapidly than in the United States. Taken as a group and using an average weighted by population, these ten countries in 1994 had an average GDP per capita 9% of that in the United States, but by 2013 this figure had risen to 17%. The basic result is not due simply to the remarkably rapid economic growth in China. When China is removed from the group, the weighted average still increases over this time period, from 10% to 15%. (This general phenomenon is certainly not a universal phenomenon; several very low-income countries have fallen further and further behind.)

So, if countries are our units of observation, Figure 3 illustrates how things have become more equal since the early 1990s. Going back further in time, comparing countries' incomes weighted by population shows inequality dropping pretty much continuously since 1960, and especially sharply since the early 1990s. But if the average is not weighted by population—thus removing the dominance of China, India, and some other very populous countries—the situation among countries only started to become more equal from 2000. Nonetheless, many low-income countries have been left behind in this period, most notably several countries of Africa. The dominant trend is not the exclusive trend.

## Global Distribution Among People

To obtain a truly global estimate of the distribution of income, it is necessary to compare the incomes of people (or families or households) in the world. Availability of data (as well as other data problems) makes such an estimate rough, but useful nonetheless. Branko Milanovic, perhaps the leading expert on these issues, has shown that, from the mid-1980s to 2011, global inequality remained roughly constant, with a slight decline toward the end of this period—likely explained by the greater slowdown of high-income countries compared to low-income countries in the Great Recession. The relative stability of income distribution would seem to result from a rough balance between the reduction of inequality among countries (Figure 3) and the rise of inequality within countries (Figure 1 and the most populous countries of Figure 2).

Milanovic's estimate uses the Gini coefficient, a standard measure of income inequality. The Gini takes account of incomes of the whole population, unlike the measure used in Figures 1 and 2, which focuses on extremes. The Gini can vary from 0 (everyone has the same income) to 1 (all the income goes to one person). For income distribution in almost all countries, the Gini ranges from about 0.27 (Norway) to about 0.65 (South Africa).

For the global population, over the period of Milanovic's estimates, the Gini varies around 0.70—a higher figure, showing a more unequal distribution, than for any single country. However, if inequality were measured by a comparison of extremes, it is likely that inequality would be rising. There remains a large share of the world's population that continues to live in extreme poverty, while incomes at the very top have sky-rocketed in recent years. But whether the measure is the Gini or a comparison of extremes, the distribution among people in the world is very unequal.

## What Matters?

Each of these measures of income inequality "in the world" matters in one way or another. For example, to understand political conflicts within countries, the changes in the distribution within countries is probably most important. To understand how the changing structures of the global economy have affected people's lives in various parts of the world, it is useful to consider all of these measures. And to understand the dynamics of international politics, the measures that focus on inequalities among countries are probably paramount.

The measurements show both some positive and negative changes in the world. On the one hand, the rapid growth of several low-income and middle-income countries has, in spite of the high (and sometimes rising) level of inequality in these countries, pulled many people out of abject poverty. On the other hand, we know that rising inequality within a country tends to undermine social cohesion and generate stress at virtually all levels of society—with damaging effects on health, education, the natural environment, and crime. Even in this era of increased globalization, it is in the national context that inequality has the primary impact on people's behavior and how they judge their well-being.

And no matter how we look at the situation, the world has long been and remains a very unequal place. ❑

*Sources:* Branko Milanovic, *Worlds Apart: Measuring International and Global Inequality*, Princeton University Press, 2005; Branko Milanovic, *Global Income Inequality by the Numbers: in History and Now—An Overview*, The World Bank, Development Research Group, Poverty and Inequality Team, November 2012; Christoph Lakner and Branko Milanovic, *Global Income Distribution: From the Fall of the Berlin Wall to the Great Recession*, The World Bank, Development Research Group, Poverty and Inequality Team, December 2013, WPS6719; Richard Wilkinson and Kate Pickett, *The Spirit Level: Why Greater Equality Makes Societies Stronger*, Bloomsbury Press, 2009.

*Article 1.3*

# MAXIMUM "ECONOMIC FREEDOM": NO CURE-ALL FOR OUR ECONOMIC ILLS

## BY JOHN MILLER
*March/April 2005, updated November 2015*

> We are the party of maximum economic freedom and the prosperity freedom makes possible.
>
> Our vision of an opportunity society stands in stark contrast to the current Administration's policies that expand entitlements and guarantees, create new public programs, and provide expensive government bailouts. That road has created a culture of dependency, bloated government, and massive debt.
>
> —2012 Republican Platform, "We Believe in America"

> The decline in economic freedom in the United States has been more than three times greater than the average decline found in the OECD [Organisation for Economic Cooperation and Development]. ... Unless policies undermining economic freedom are reversed, the future annual growth of the US economy will be only about half its historic average of 3%.
>
> —James Gwartney, Robert Lawson, and Joshua Hall, *Economic Freedom of the World: 2015 Annual Report*, The Fraser Institute

The Republican Party no doubt will once again in 2016 claim that it is the "party of maximum economic freedom" and that the presidential election will once again offer a choice between free enterprise, an opportunity society, and prosperity versus "a culture of dependency, bloated government, and massive debt."

Just in case the boilerplate of their platform is not enough to convince you that maximum "economic freedom" is the key to prosperity, two free-market think tanks, the Canada-based Fraser Institute and the Washington, D.C.-based Cato Institute, have the numbers to prove it—or so they say.

Their Economic Freedom Index of the World (EFW), its latest edition published just this fall, purports to show that economic freedom in the United States is on the decline, and as economic freedom has plummeted, economic growth has slowed, inequality has worsened, and political rights and civil liberties have been curtailed. The same, according to the EFW report, holds true for countries across the globe—those that are "more free" economically enjoy better economic outcomes and more civil liberties and political rights.

But even a quick glance at the EFW country rankings makes clear that there is something seriously amiss with its numbers.

# That Can't Be Right—and It Isn't

The EFW provides an objective-looking list that ranks 157 countries and territories from the "most free" (Hong Kong and Singapore) to the "least free" (The Republic of the Congo and Venezuela). Their assessment of economic freedom uses 24 separate measures to score each country on five major areas: the size of government, the legal system and property rights, sound money, freedom to trade internationally, and regulation.

So what's wrong with the numbers? To begin with, the rankings seem to have little to do with political freedom. Consider the two city-states, Hong Kong and Singapore, which have repeatedly topped their list of free countries. Freedom House, which the *Wall Street Journal* has called "the Michelin Guide to democracy's development," classifies Hong Kong and Singapore as only "partially free." Freedom House, however, classifies some 89 other countries, almost half of the countries in its rankings, as "free." Hong Kong receives low marks from Freedom House for its restrictions on press freedom and freedom of assembly, especially limiting protests, and for the Chinese government's limits on the candidates who can be nominated for Hong Kong's executive elections. Likewise, the organization reports that Singapore's press is "not free," while the Internet is only "partially free" there. Also, in Singapore, rights to demonstrate are limited; films, TV, and the like are censored; and preventive detention is legal.

In addition to its rankings, the EFW report comes with accompanying charts. They purport to show that the "most free" quartile of the countries in their rankings average higher levels of per capita income, faster economic growth rates, less inequality, longer life expectancies, and more political rights and civil liberties than the other three "less free" quartiles of countries.

But these correlations are too facile to be credible. For instance, instead of arranging countries by their EFW ranking, let's group them by their score on just one of the five major areas of the index, the size of government. Because the EFW size-of-government index never recognizes that government programs such as Social Security have improved the life chances of citizens and enlarged the choices available to them, countries with the smallest government and lowest tax rates score the highest on "freedom." If the correlations between the EFW and prosperity, well-being, and political freedom have meaning, then the countries with the smallest governments should be associated with better outcomes than those being crushed by an outsized public sector.

But that's not case. The economies of the EFW's ten best-scoring countries on size of government (Hong Kong, Bangladesh, Honduras, Madagascar, the Philippines, Nepal, Haiti, Guatemala, Nicaragua, and Pakistan), on average, did grow more quickly than those of the ten countries that did worst by that measure (Algeria, Netherlands, Denmark, Belgium, France, Timor-Leste, the Republic of Congo, Burundi, and Finland). But the average income per capita for the EFW's worst ten countries was more than four times as great as for the EFW's best ten countries on the government-size measure. Also, the overall levels of income inequality (according to the standard measure, the Gini coefficient) were lower and the income share of the poorest 10% of the population was larger. In addition, the average life-spans in the countries the EFW

## SIZE OF GOVERNMENT AND ECONOMIC PERFORMANCE: THE ECONOMIC FREEDOM INDEX OF THE WORLD

| Size of gov't (EFW rank) | Growth rate 1992-2014 | GDP per capita | Gini coefficient | Income share, bottom 10% | Life expectancy at birth | Political rights, civil liberties |
|---|---|---|---|---|---|---|
| Top ten (smallest gov't) | 3.14% | $8,633 | 43.4 | 2.36% | 70.8 | 3.9 |
| Bottom ten (largest gov't) | 2.60% | $26,946 | 30.8 | 3.42% | 73.8 | 2.6 |

Note: The conventional preferable score (higher growth, higher GDP, greater equality/lower inequality, higher life expectancy, greater political rights and civil liberties) is shaded in the table.

Definitions and Sources: Size of government: *Economic Freedom of the World: 2015 Annual Report*; Economic growth rates: Annual average 1992-2014, source: UNCTADstat; Gross Domestic Product per capita: Purchasing Power Parity, constant 2011 dollars, source: World Bank, 2014; Gini coefficient: lower number means greater equality, source: World Bank, latest year available 2009-2013; Income share of bottom or poorest 10% of the population: larger share means greater equality, source: World Bank, latest year available 2006-2013; Life expectancy: number of years a person can expect live at birth, source: World Bank, 2013; Political rights and civil liberties: average of Freedom House civil liberties and political rights scores, lower score indicates greater political rights and civil liberties, source: *Freedom of the World 2015*, Freedom House.

ranked worst were three years longer than for those living in the countries the EFW ranked best. Finally, according to Freedom House, political rights and civil liberties are greater in the countries with the largest-size governments than in those with the smallest-size governments.

If the goal is a more prosperous nation with greater equality, longer life-spans, and more political rights and civil liberties, then a proper reading of EFW is that quite a large government is called for. That's hardly the message the EFW is intending to send, and one more likely to appear on the Bernie Sanders website than in the Republican Party platform.

## U.S. Stagnation and "Unfreedom"

The EFW report also claims to show that that deteriorating economic freedom is at the heart of U.S. economic stagnation and worsening inequality. Since 2000, the United States has fallen in the EFW rankings from third to sixteenth. In addition, the drop in the U.S. economic freedom score was more than three times that of the OECD average score. (The Organisation for Economic Cooperation and Development (OECD) includes most high-income countries.) "Unless policies undermining economic freedom are reversed," warns the EFW report, "the future annual growth of the U.S. economy will be only about half its historic average of 3%."

But before you dust off your copy of Ayn Rand's *Atlas Shrugged* and join some "maximum economic freedom" movement, consider this: As the U.S. EFW score dropped three times faster than that of the average OECD country, the U.S. economy grew more quickly (1.6% a year) than the OECD average (1.4% a year) from 2000 to 2014. Last year, the U.S. economy grew at an annual rate of 2.4%—considerably above the OECD average of 1.8%, but still well below its 3.0% historical average. But the specific factors driving the decline of the U.S. EFW rating don't support the case that deteriorating economic freedom is what lies behind continued economic stagnation in the United States.

Since 2000, the U.S. ratings have fallen in all five areas of the EFW index. For instance, the U.S. size of government score got worse as government spending, consumption, and transfers increased, especially in the wake of the Great Recession. The U.S. score on "sound money" also slipped after the Great Recession, as the Federal Reserve (the "Fed") pushed interest rates to near zero by accelerating the growth of the money supply. But the additional government spending, though falling far short of what was needed, did more to revive economic growth than to inhibit it. Likewise, without the Fed's lax monetary policy, the less-than-robust economic growth since the Great Recession would have been yet more feeble.

But the largest declines in the U.S. EFW score came in three other areas: the legal system and the protection of property rights, freedom to trade internationally, and regulation. The EFW report allows that several factors could lie behind the drop in the U.S. scores in these areas, including some serious infringements on civil liberties.

But the EFW report goes on to ask if Sarbanes-Oxley (a 2002 law that seeks to improve corporate accounting practices and to make CEOs responsible for their corporations' profit reports), or the Affordable Care Act (which expands healthcare coverage), or Dodd-Frank (which attempts to curb some of the worst practices of a reckless financial industry), or the auto-industry bailout (that revived a failing industry and saved millions of jobs) "could be seen as a threat to property rights." The fact that the EFW report would single out those government interventions makes clear that what counts in their index is the economic freedom of only a tiny segment of the U.S. population, not that of workers, consumers, or even, in some cases, stockholders.

Despite its objective appearance, the EFW fails to make the case that a lack of economic freedom is the root cause of our economic ills, or that its brand of maximum "economic freedom" will cure them. Rather the EFW stands in the way of policies that might resolve our economic problems and improve the life chances of most people, as it protects the economic freedom and prerogatives of elites. ❑

*Sources:* "We Believe in America: 2012 Republican Platform"; James Gwartney, Robert Lawson, and Joshua Hall, *Economic Freedom of the World: 2015 Annual Report* (Fraser Institute, 2015); Freedom House, "Discarding Democracy: Return to the Iron Fist—Freedom in the World 2015" (freedomhouse.org); Robert Lawson, "Economic Freedom in the United States and Other Countries," in Donald Boudreaux, ed., *What America's Decline in Economic Freedom Means for Entrepreneurship and Prosperity* (Fraser Institute, 2015); James Gwartney, Randall Holcombe, and Robert Lawson, "Institutions and the Impact of Investment on Growth," *Kyklos*, 59(2), 2006; Greg Leichty, "'Economic Freedom?' Professor, Your Bias Is Showing," Progress Louisville, Oct. 15, 2015; Daniel Mitchell, "Economic Freedom in America is Declining Mostly Because of Creeping Protectionism and the Loss of Rule of Law and Property Rights," Aug. 25, 2015 (finance.townhall.com).

*Article 1.4*

# THE PANDEMIC AND THE GLOBAL ECONOMY

**BY JAYATI GHOSH**
*April 2020,* Dissent

There are still many uncertainties about the Covid-19 pandemic: about the extent of its spread, its severity in different countries, the length of the outbreak, and whether an initial decline could be followed by a recurrence. But some things are already certain: we know that the economic impact of this pandemic is already immense, dwarfing anything that we have experienced in living memory. The current shock to the global economy is certainly much bigger than that of the 2008 global financial crisis, and is likely to be more severe than the Great Depression. Even the two world wars of the 20th century, while they disrupted supply chains and devastated physical infrastructure and populations, did not involve the restrictions on mobility and economic activity that are in place in the majority of countries today. This is therefore an unprecedented global challenge and requires unprecedented responses.

This very severe economic impact has been exacerbated by measures that have been adopted across the world to contain it, which have ranged from relatively mild restrictions on mobility and public gatherings to complete lockdowns (and clampdowns) that have brought to a halt most economic activity. This has meant a simultaneous attack on demand and supply. During lockdowns, people (especially those without formal work contracts) are deprived of incomes and joblessness increases drastically, causing huge declines in consumption demand that will continue into the period after the lockdown is lifted. At the same time, production and distribution are halted for all but essential commodities and services—and even for these sectors, supply is badly affected because of implementation issues and inadequate attention to the input-output linkages that enable production and distribution. Previous regional and global crises have not entailed this near-cessation of all economic activity. The deadly combination of collapses in both demand and supply is why this time is truly different and has to be dealt with differently.

World trade in both goods and services is already collapsing. The World Trade Organization (WTO) expects trade to fall anywhere between 13% and 32% in 2020. But even these dismal projections could well be underestimates, because they implicitly rely on relatively rapid containment of the virus and the lifting of lockdown measures by late summer of 2020. Exports of goods—other than those deemed "essential"—have effectively ceased; travel has declined to a tiny fraction of what it was, and tourism has also stopped for the time being; various other cross-border services that cannot be delivered electronically are contracting sharply. Trade prices have collapsed and will continue to decline. In the month leading up to March 20, 2020, primary commodity prices fell by 37%, with energy and industrial metals prices falling by 55%.

Within countries, economic activity is contracting at hitherto unimaginable rates, bringing about not only a dramatic immediate collapse but the seeds of future contraction as negative multiplier effects start playing out. In the United States alone, around 22 million people lost their jobs in four weeks, with GDP estimated to contract by 10% to 14% from April to June. Elsewhere the pattern is no different, probably worse, as most countries are facing multiple forces of economic decline. The International Monetary Fund (IMF) predicted on April 14 that global output will fall by 3% in 2020, and as much as 4.5% in per capita terms—and this is based on the most optimistic projections.

These collapses in economic activity necessarily affect global finance, which is also in disarray. The classic point about financial markets being imperfect not only because of asymmetric but also incomplete information is being borne out in practice: these markets are all about time, and now we must painfully accept that no one can know the future, even a few months ahead. Financial bets and contracts made just a few months ago now appear completely implausible to sustain. Most debts are clearly unpayable; insurance claims will be so extreme as to wipe out most insurers; and stock markets are collapsing as investors realize that none of the assumptions on which earlier investments were made are valid anymore. These negative forces together amount to humongous losses that could threaten the very viability of the global capitalist order (an order that was already struggling to show any dynamism over the past decade).

## Unequal Effects

In an already very unequal world, this crisis already has and will continue to sharply increase global inequality. A large part of this is because of the very different policy responses in most developing countries (other than China, the origin of the pandemic, which has managed to contain its spread and revive economic activity relatively quickly) as compared to advanced economies. The sheer enormity of the crisis has apparently registered with policymakers in the developed world, who have (probably temporarily) abandoned all talk of fiscal austerity and suddenly appear to have no problem simply monetizing their government deficits. It is likely that the global financial system would have collapsed in the panic that arose in the third week of March without massive intervention by the major central banks of the developed world—not just the U.S. Federal Reserve but the European Central Bank, the Bank of Japan, the Bank of England, and others.

The "exorbitant privilege" of the United States as the holder of the world's reserve currency obviously gives it greater freedom to prop up its own economy. But other developed countries are also putting forward fairly large fiscal packages, from 5% of GDP in Germany to 20% in Japan, in addition to various other expansionary and stabilizing measures through their central banks.

By contrast, most developing countries have much less leeway to engage in such policies, and even those larger developing economies that could do so appear to be constrained by the fear of financial markets punishing them further. This is terrible: their economic challenges are already much greater than those in the developed world. Developing countries—many of which have yet to experience the full force of the spread of the virus—have been hit by a perfect storm of collapsing global trade, falling remittances, sharp reversals of capital flows, and currency depreciation. In just the month of March, capital flight from emerging market assets was an estimated $83 billion, and since January nearly $100 billion has flown out—compared to $26 billion after the 2008 financial crisis. Portfolio investment is down by at least 70% from January to March 2020, and spreads on emerging market bonds have risen sharply. Currencies of developing countries have mostly depreciated sharply, other than in China. The foreign exchange crunch is generating serious problems in servicing external debt, which is harder to do because of shrinking foreign exchange inflows and rising domestic costs for servicing them. By early April, 85 countries had approached the IMF for emergency assistance because of severe problems in meeting foreign currency payment obligations, and that number is likely to rise.

These external pressures, which are already together much greater than anything experienced during the Great Depression, have come to bear on economies that are already struggling with the terrible domestic economic consequences of their virus-containment strategies. The burden of these processes has fallen massively upon informal workers and self-employed people, who are being deprived of their livelihoods and falling into poverty at very rapid rates. Informal workers make up 70% of the labor force in developing countries, and they are unlikely to be paid at all during lockdowns in which they are forced to be inactive. Workers with formal contracts have also started losing their jobs. The International Labour Organization estimated in early April that more than four out of every five workers in the world are facing the adverse impacts of the pandemic and associated policy responses, and most of them reside in the developing world. Women workers are more likely to be disproportionately adversely affected: more likely to lose jobs and experience major pay cuts, more likely to be rationed out of labor markets when jobs do become available, more likely to suffer during lockdowns because of enhanced possibilities of domestic abuse, and more likely to suffer from inadequate nutrition in a time of household food shortages.

In many countries, livelihood losses are associated with dramatic increases in the extent of absolute poverty and growing hunger, even among those previously not classified as poor. Indeed, the re-emergence of hunger on a global scale is likely to be an unfortunate legacy of the pandemic and the containment measures that resulted. To add to all of this depressing news, most states in developing countries will not be able to indulge in the necessary levels of deficit financing (by borrowing from central banks) to enable the required increases in public expenditure, because of foreign exchange constraints and greater surveillance of financial markets over their deficits.

## The Aftermath

This, unfortunately, is just the beginning. What of the aftermath, when the pandemic is brought under control? It bears reiterating that after a seismic shock of this magnitude, economies across the world will not simply be able to carry on as before, picking up where they had left off before this crisis. Over the coming year, many things are likely to change, including global reorganization of trade and capital flows. International trade will remain subdued for a while. Most commodity prices will also remain low, because global demand will take some time to pick up. This will affect commodity exporters' revenues, but it need not provide much advantage for commodity importers because of the overall deflationary pressures stemming from depressed demand.

On the other hand, the breaking of supply chains could well lead to specific shortages, including of some essential items, generating cost-push inflation especially in developing countries. Cross-border capital flows will be volatile and unstable, and most developing countries will struggle to attract sufficient secure capital on terms that would make it beneficial to add to domestic savings and meet trade financing costs. The steep currency depreciations that have already occurred are unlikely to get completely reversed and could even accelerate further, depending upon what strategies are pursued in both developed and developing countries. These falling currency values, higher margins on interest paid, and rising yields on bonds will all continue to make debt servicing a massive problem. Indeed, most developing country debt will be simply unpayable.

In addition to problems in domestic banks and non-bank lenders because of likely large-scale defaults, there will be massive problems in insurance markets, with the failure of some insurance companies and rising premiums that could be a disincentive for most medium and small enterprises to be insured at all. Travel and tourism revenues will also be significantly curtailed over the medium term, as the earlier confidence underlying such travel will have eroded. Similarly, many migrants will have lost employment. Demand for foreign labor is likely to decline in many host countries, so remittances will also decline. All of this will continue to put pressure on government finances especially (but not only) in the developing world.

## Averting Catastrophe

This litany of horrors is well within the realm of the possible. The saving grace is that these outcomes are not inevitable: they depend crucially on policy responses. The terrible consequences described above are predicated on international institutions and national governments not taking the measures that could ameliorate the situation. There are both national and global policies that could help, but they must be implemented quickly, before the crisis generates even more humanitarian catastrophe. It is essential to ensure that the policy responses do not (as they currently do) increase national and global inequalities. This means that recovery strategies must be reoriented away from handouts to large corporations without adequate regulation of their activities, and toward enabling the survival, employment, and continued consumption demand of poor and middle-income groups, and the survival and expansion of tiny, small, and medium enterprises.

There are some obvious steps that the international community needs to take immediately. These steps rely on the existing global financial architecture—not because this architecture is just, fair, or efficient (it is not), but because, given the need for a speedy and substantial response, there is simply no possibility of constructing meaningful alternative institutions and arrangements quickly enough. The existing institutions—especially the IMF—have to deliver, which requires that they shed their pro-capital bias and their promotion of fiscal austerity.

The IMF is the only multilateral institution that has the capacity to create global liquidity, and this is the moment when it must do so at scale. An immediate issue of Special Drawing Rights (SDRs), which are supplementary reserve assets (determined by a weighted basket of five major currencies), would create additional international liquidity at no extra cost. Since a fresh issue of SDRs must be distributed according to each country's quota in the IMF, it cannot be discretionary and cannot be subject to other kinds of conditionality or political pressure. At least 1 to 2 trillion SDRs must be created and distributed. This will have a huge impact in ensuring that global international economic transactions simply do not seize up even after the lockdowns are lifted, and that developing countries are able to engage in international trade. Advanced economies with international reserve currencies are much less likely to need to use them, but they can be a lifeline for emerging markets and developing economies, providing additional resources to fight both the pandemic and the economic disaster. They are much better than depending on the IMF to provide loans, which often require conditionalities. (Insofar as additional emergency loans from the IMF are required, they must also be provided without conditionality, as purely compensatory financing for this unprecedented shock.) The issuance of more SDRs is also preferable to allowing the U.S. Federal Reserve to play the role of sole stabilizer of the system. The Fed's swap lines are currently providing central banks of a few chosen countries with dollar liquidity as it becomes scarce in this crisis. But this is not a norm-based multilateral allocation; these swaps reflect the strategic national interests of the United States, and therefore reinforce global power imbalances.

One reason why there has been only limited issue of SDRs so far (the last increase was after the 2008 crisis, but to the tune of only around 276 billion SDRs) is the fear that such an increase in global liquidity would stoke inflation. But the world economy has just experienced more than a decade of the largest increases in liquidity ever due to "quantitative easing" by the U.S. Fed without inflation, because global demand remained low. The current situation is only different because it is more acute. If additional liquidity is used to invest in activities that would ease the supply shortages likely to come up because of lockdowns, then it could also ease any cost-push inflation that might emerge.

The second important international measure is dealing with external debt problems. There should immediately be a moratorium or standstill on all debt repayments (both principal and interest) for at least the next six months as countries cope with both the spread of the disease and the lockdown effects. This moratorium should also ensure that interest payments do not accrue over this period. It is obvious that very few developing countries will be in any position to service their loans when foreign exchange inflows have effectively stopped. But in any case, if everything else is on hold in the global economy today, why should debt payments be any different?

A moratorium is a temporary move to tide these countries over during the period when the pandemic and the closures are at their peaks. But eventually substantial debt restructuring is likely to be necessary, and very substantial debt relief must be provided especially to low-income and middle-income countries. International coordination would be much better for all concerned than the disorderly debt defaults that would otherwise be almost inevitable.

Within nation-states, the institution of capital controls would enable developing countries to deal at least partly with these global headwinds by stemming the volatility of cross-border financial flows. Such capital controls must be explicitly allowed and encouraged, in order to curtail the surge in outflows, to reduce illiquidity driven by sell-offs in emerging markets, and to arrest declines in currency and asset prices. Ideally, there should be some cooperation among countries to prevent any one country from being singled out by financial markets.

The aftermath of this crisis is also going to require a revival of planning—something that had almost been forgotten in too many countries in the neoliberal era. The collapse of production and distribution channels during lockdowns means that defining and maintaining the supply of essential commodities is of critical importance. Such supply chains will have to be thought through in terms of the input-output relationships involved, which in turn requires coordination between different levels and departments in governments as well as across provinces—and possibly at the regional level as well.

The pandemic is likely to bring about a change in attitudes to public health in almost all countries. Decades of neoliberal policy hegemony have led to drastic declines in per capita public health spending in rich and poor countries alike. It is now more than obvious that this was not just an unequal and unjust strategy but a stupid one: It has taken an infectious disease to drive home the point that the health of the elite ultimately depends on the health of the poorest members of society. Those who advocated reduced public health spending and privatization of health services did so at their own peril. This is true at a global scale as well. The current pathetically nationalist squabbles over access to protective equipment and drugs betray a complete lack of awareness of the nature of the beast. This disease will not be brought under control unless it is brought under control everywhere. International cooperation is not just desirable but essential.

While pushing for these major strategies for national governments and international organizations, we need to be conscious of some concerns. One is the fear that governments across the world will use the opportunity presented by the pandemic to push for the centralization of power, with significantly increased monitoring and surveillance of citizens, and increased censorship and control over information flows to reduce their own accountability. This has already started in many countries, and fear of infection is causing many people across the world to accept invasions of privacy and forms of state control over individual lives that months ago would have been seen as unacceptable. It will be harder to sustain or revive democracy in such conditions. Much greater public vigilance is required both at present and after the crisis has ended.

There is also a fear that the increased inequalities thrown up by this crisis will reinforce existing forms of social discrimination. In principle, a virus does not respect class or other socio-economic distinctions. But there are well-known negative feedback loops between the squalor associated with income poverty and infectious diseases. In our unequal societies, poor and socially disadvantaged groups are more likely to be exposed to Covid-19 and are more likely to die from it, because people's ability to take preventive measures, their susceptibility to disease, and their access to treatment all vary greatly according to income, assets, occupation, and location. Perhaps even worse, Covid-19 containment policies within countries show extreme class bias. "Social distancing" (better described as physical distancing) implicitly assumes that both residences and workplaces are not so crowded and congested that the prescribed norms can be easily maintained, and that other essentials like access to soap and water are not limited. The fear of infection during the pandemic has brought out some more unpleasant forms of social discrimination and prejudice in many countries, from antipathy to migrants to differentiation on the basis of race, caste, religion, and class. At a time when the universality of the human condition is highlighted by a virus, responses in too many countries have been focused on particularistic divisions, which bode ill for future progress.

Despite these depressing possibilities, it is also true that the pandemic, and even the massive economic crisis it has brought in its wake, could also bring about some changes in attitudes that point to a more hopeful future. Three aspects of this deserve comment.

The first is the recognition of the essential nature and social significance of care work and the greater respect and dignity accorded to paid and unpaid care workers. This could result in societies increasing the number of paid care workers, providing required training for them because of greater appreciation of the skills involved in such labor, and offering these workers better remuneration, more legal and social protection, and greater dignity.

Second, the wider realization among the public of the real possibility that unthinkable events can occur and unimaginably dreadful processes can be unleashed by our ways of life may also bring home the reality of climate change and the disasters it will bring in its wake. This could make more people conscious of the need to change how we live, produce, and consume, before it is too late. Some of the less rational aspects of global supply chains, especially in the multinational food industry (which has encouraged produce from one part of the world to be shipped to another part of the world for processing, before coming back to places near its origin to be consumed), will be questioned and could decline in significance. Other changes in lifestyle and consumption and distribution patterns could follow.

Finally, on a more philosophical level, existential threats like pandemics encourage more recognition of the things that really matter in human existence: good health, the ability to communicate and interact with other people, and participation in creative processes that bring joy and satisfaction. These realizations could encourage the first steps toward civilizational shifts that lead to the reorganization of our societies. There is an opportunity to move away from dominant assumptions about individualistic utility maximization and the profit motive to more caring and cooperative social frameworks. ❑

# Chapter 2

# INHERENT CRISES OF CAPITALISM

*Article 2.1*

## COVID-19 AND CATASTROPHE CAPITALISM

**BY JOHN BELLAMY FOSTER AND INTAN SUWANDI**
**AS EDITED AND ABRIDGED BY THE *DOLLARS & SENSE* COLLECTIVE**

*January/February 2021*

*Editors' note: This is an abridged and edited version of an article written by John Bellamy Foster and Intan Suwandi that originally appeared in the June 2020 issue of* Monthly Review *magazine.*

The global pandemic that emerged with the sudden appearance of the coronavirus has shown how the current global system of capitalism has left the world vulnerable to catastrophe. Public services and the institutions of public health—eroded with decades of budget cuts—have been unable to cope with the pandemic. Like most of the corporate world, pharmaceutical companies were incentivized to reward shareholders through stock-buyback schemes instead of investing in research and development, which would have made a significant difference in their ability to quickly deliver a vaccine for the disease. However, what's often overlooked is the underlying structural reasons for why this global economic and health crisis is happening. It is true that, in our globalized economy, travel has increased exponentially in the past couple of decades both for business and pleasure, and that this can contribute to the global spread of communicable diseases. Yet that alone does not explain why we have seen a series of infectious disease outbreaks over the same time period, especially zoonotic diseases (or zoonoses), that is, diseases that are caused by pathogens transmitted to humans from wild or domesticated animals, such as SARS, MERS, Ebola, H1N1, and now, Covid-19. This article focuses on the role of the global economy in general, and agribusinesses in particular, in causing ecological degradation, emergent diseases, and potential global pandemics.

During the last decade, a holistic One Health-One World approach to the causes and origins of diseases arose in response to these outbreaks. The One Health model is a multidisciplinary approach that recognizes the connection between human and animal health and their shared environment. With the involvement of the World Bank, the World Health Organization (WHO), and the Centers for Disease Control and Prevention (CDC) in the United States, this approach makes it possible for people who are involved in protecting the health of humans, animals, and the environment—including public health providers, private medicine, agribusinesses, and pharmaceutical companies—to work together to develop a holistic approach to preventing the spread of zoonotic diseases. However, over time the original ecological framework that motivated the One Health approach has become dominated by agribusinesses, which have systemically downplayed the connections between epidemiological crises and the capitalist world economy.

While the One-Health framework still dominates the national and international agencies' approach to public health issues, a critical perspective that comes out of the Marxist tradition, known as Structural One Health, has been proposed as an alternative way of understanding the causes and origins of disease. For proponents of Structural One Health, the key is to ascertain how pandemics in the contemporary global economy are connected to the rapidly changing environmental conditions that are driven by the need of global capitalism for continuous growth. Instead of concentrating on certain locales in which novel viruses emerge as random events, this approach aims to understand local developments in the context of how these localities are connected to the global capitalist economy. Specifically, Structural One Health scientists explicitly recognize the role of global agribusiness in the destruction of natural ecosystems and focus on commodity chains as the global economic conduits of disease transmission.

In one of the most prominent works illustrating this approach, *Big Farms Make Big Flu,* Rob Wallace states that the breeding of monocultures of genetically similar animals, including massive hog feedlots and vast poultry farms, coupled with rapid deforestation and the chaotic mixing of wild birds and other wildlife with industrial animal production, have created the conditions for the spread of deadly diseases such as SARS, MERS, Ebola, H1N1, H5N1, and now Covid-19. "Agribusinesses," Wallace writes, "are moving their companies into the Global South to take advantage of cheap labor and cheap land," and "spreading their entire production line across the world." As a result, increased interactions between birds, hogs, and humans produce more new diseases. "Influenzas," Wallace tells us, "now emerge by way of a globalized network of corporate feedlot production and trade, wherever specific strains first evolve. With flocks and herds whisked from region to region multiple strains of influenza are continually introduced into localities filled with populations of susceptible animals." Large-scale commercial poultry operations have been shown to have much higher odds of hosting these virulent zoonoses. Value-chain analysis has been used to trace the origin of new influenzas such as H5N1 along the poultry production commodity chain. The interconnected global commodity chains of agribusinesses, which provide the basis for the appearance of novel zoonoses, ensure that these pathogens move rapidly from one place to another, with human hosts moving in days, even hours, from one part of the globe to the other. Wallace and his colleagues write, "Some pathogens emerge right out of centers of production. … But many like Covid-19 originate on the frontiers of capital production. Indeed, at least 60% of novel human pathogens emerge by spilling over from wild animals to local human communities (before the more successful ones spread to the rest of the world)."

## Commodity Chains & Covid-19

Since the late 20th century, capitalist globalization has increasingly adopted the form of interlinked commodity chains controlled by multinational corporations, connecting various production zones, primarily in the Global South, with the center of world consumption, finance, and accumulation, primarily in the Global North. In this system, exorbitant profits are made not only from *global labor arbitrage*, through which multinational corporations overexploit industrial labor, but also increasingly through *global land arbitrage*, in which agribusiness multinationals expropriate cheap land in the Global South so as to produce export crops mainly for sale in the Global North. In the past decade, more than 81 million acres of land worldwide—an area the size of Portugal—have been sold off to foreign investors. Some of these deals are what's known as "land grabs": land deals that happen without the free, prior, and informed consent of communities. These conditions have been promoted by various development banks in the context of what is euphemistically known as "territorial restructuring," which involves removing subsistence farmers and small producers from the land at the behest of multinational corporations, primarily agribusinesses, as well as rapid deforestation and ecosystem destruction.

The 2008 spike in food prices—and the ensuing food shortages—triggered a rush in land deals in order to expand production. While these large-scale land deals were supposedly being struck to grow food, the crops grown on the land rarely feed local people. Instead, the land is used to grow profitable crops—like sugarcane, palm oil, and soy—often for export. In fact, more than 60% of crops grown on land bought by foreign investors in developing countries are intended for export, instead of for feeding local communities. Worse still, two-thirds of these agricultural land deals are in countries with serious hunger problems. The result is the mass migration of these communities, with people being thrown off the land. As subsistence farmers and small producers, and their practices, disappear, the agricultural ecology of whole regions is altered, replacing traditional agriculture with monocultures, and pushing rural populations into urban slums.

These urban slums contribute to the transmission of zoonotic diseases in multiple ways. The unequal distribution of health services, clean food and water, and sanitation lead to hotspots of diseases within cities. Cities also promote the increased movement of people, animals, and wildlife products between rural and urban locations—migrants may introduce zoonotic diseases to cities if they travel with animals or may also arrive in cities already infected with pathogens.

Buildings and impervious surfaces in urban areas, which prevent rainwater from soaking into the ground, may increase the prevalence of water-borne viruses and disease-carrying mosquitos. And as human settlements increasingly encroach on wild areas, human-wildlife interactions increase. As a result, humans and their domesticated animals (including livestock) are increasingly exposed to diseases that previously only impacted wild animals.

Covid-19, like other dangerous diseases that have emerged or reemerged in recent years, is closely related to a complex set of factors, including: 1) the focus of global agribusiness on breeding monocultures of genetically similar animals, which increases the likelihood of transmitting zoonotic diseases from wild to domestic animals to humans; 2) the destruction of wild habitats and disruption of the activities of wild species; and 3) the fact that human beings are living in closer proximity to wild areas. There is little doubt that global commodity chains and the kinds of connectivity that they have produced have become vectors for the rapid transmission of disease, throwing this whole globally exploitative pattern of development into question.

Nor are new viruses the only emerging global health problem. The overuse of antibiotics within agribusinesses, as well as modern medicine, has led to the dangerous growth of bacterial superbugs causing increasing numbers of deaths, which by mid-century could surpass annual cancer deaths, leading the WHO in 2018 to declare a "global health emergency." As the Structural One Health approach has suggested, the origin of the new pandemics can be traced to the overall problem of ecological destruction brought on by capitalism. Since communicable diseases, due to the unequal conditions created by capitalism, fall heaviest on the working class and the poor, the system that generates such diseases in the pursuit of wealth can be charged with social murder. The future of humanity in the 21st century lies not in the direction of increased economic and ecological exploitation and expropriation, imperialism, and war. Rather, attaining what Karl Marx called "freedom in general" and the preservation of a viable "planetary metabolism" are the most pressing necessities today in determining the human present and future, and even human survival. ❑

*Article 2.2*

# CORONAVIRUS: A CAPITALIST CRISIS

**BY RICHARD D. WOLFF**
*March/April 2020*

Consider the gross failure of the U.S. private, profit-driven, capitalist medical-industrial complex (four industries: doctors, hospitals, drug and device makers, and medical insurance firms). They decided not to prepare for a serious virus problem. Will so huge a failure finally tip U.S. ideology and politics in favor of socializing health care? Will the parallel preparatory failure of the U.S. government, long captured by its corporate donors in general and those in the medical-industrial complex in particular, boost a resurgent U.S. socialism? Or will a traumatized, socially distanced population turn rightward instead to a dictator for salvation from a clearly out-of-control crisis?

President Donald Trump, his government, and the system he serves need to blame the coronavirus catastrophe in the United States on something other than U.S. capitalism. Enter the Trump/GOP nationalism that generally scapegoats foreigners (immigrants, trading partners, etc.). Official blame targets what Trump calls "the Chinese virus."

Yet such blaming is racist, divisive, and ignorant. Viruses have always been part of our natural world. Ongoing mutations have repeatedly produced strains that have caused widespread human sickness and death. That is why medical science has long studied viruses. In the 1918 flu epidemic, an H1N1 virus killed almost 700,000 in the United States, plus many millions more around the world. It began in Kansas, yet no one since called it "the U.S. virus." H1N1 resurfaced in 2009 as "swine flu." Other recent viruses include SARS (2002–2004) and MERS (since 2012).

Given this history of viruses, systematic preparation for future outbreaks of seriously dangerous viruses was an obvious social need. Availability of sufficient (many millions of) tests was needed for the crucial role of identifying and separating the infected from the uninfected. Producers of ventilators, masks, hospital beds, etc. should have stockpiled them. Training should have been routinized to equip more than enough volunteers to help cope with outbreaks. To block disease transmission, plans should have been made to accommodate social distancing: securing suitable locations, appropriate supervision, distribution of supplies, etc. Likewise, the consequences of social distancing— lost jobs, closed businesses, disrupted supply chains, crippled purchasing power, chaotic credit markets, etc.—should have been planned for. The newly unemployed could and should have been re-employed to manage social distancing. Yet no remotely adequate planning occurred.

U.S. capitalism failed at everything on this partial list of "shoulds." Capitalist industries failed to serve public health because private profits were an inadequate incentive for them to do so. The government failed to compensate for private capitalism's failures, as usual, because government leaders (drawn heavily from corporate CEO ranks) share similar mentalities.

Knowledge of the dangerous new coronavirus emerged clearly from China in December 2019. CDC documents from this past January show full awareness of the huge threat of the virus and of the extreme social-distancing measures China had undertaken to control it. China's massive coordination of public and private resources saw profits displaced by public health as the prioritized goal or "bottom line." South Korea acted similarly. In contrast, neoliberalism has arisen and prevailed in many countries since the 1970s, undermining the state by privatization and deregulation. Such steps blocked the kinds of social mobilization achieved in China and South Korea. Social mobilization was and remains more partial, fragmentary, and slower in Italy, the United States, and beyond.

When infections and deaths mounted quickly, panic followed. Political leaders saw threats to their positions. Most people began to grasp how misled and underprepared their nations were, that their jobs, income, and lives were in danger. They saw their leaders floundering atop an out-of-control situation. As debt-ridden economies collapsed into sharp recessions or worse, corporate leaders turned, as usual, to the state for bailouts even as global capitalism still shook from the results of the 2008–2009 bailouts.

Crisis moods overtake most of us as we watch desperate leaders' evident failures to cope. Schools are shut, but without plans to handle consequences: children not taken care of, taught, or often not even fed; parents with children now at home who cannot continue their jobs; emotional strains on families thrown together. No plan exists to train mental health counselors to help work on these problems. Panicked leaders foresee a possible unemployment rate of 20% (it was 25% in 1933) yet also propose cash distributions of $1,000–$2,000 per taxpayer. That laughably inadequate response typifies what one has come to expect from a government that failed to stockpile tests, masks, and hospital beds.

Either public health—including preparedness for viruses—dominates private profit for capitalists or it does not. The coronavirus catastrophe demonstrates the results when public health is subordinate to private profit and to a governmental apparatus that adulates the superiority of private over public administration.

History's latest virus has threatened and challenged U.S. society. But it has been our political economy that failed to meet the challenge, to defeat the threat. The catastrophe we are living through was caused by a capitalist system that could not anticipate, plan for, or cope with the coronavirus. To "get through" this catastrophe (as we did with the Great Depression of the 1930s) while leaving the system intact will guarantee the next catastrophe. The lesson to be learned now is that we desperately need a basically different economic system that will better and more democratically determine the state and its social interventions. Moving in that direction now can yield something positive amid the mammoth negatives raining down on us. ❑

*Article 2.3*

# STRINGENT, STINGY, AND SEVERE
*The Covid-19 crisis in Modi's India.*

## BY SMRITI RAO
*July/August 2020*

Some months ago, *The Economist* magazine called the Indian government's response to the Covid-19 crisis one of the most "stringent" in the world. The two-month long national lockdown imposed by the Indian central government from March 24 to May 30 involved a ban on all internal and international travel, including a complete suspension of all public transportation services, something no other country did. Most retail and production facilities were closed, with the list of "essential activities" exempted from this suspension being much narrower than in other countries.

But the economic pain and sacrifice of the Indian people throughout this lock-down seems to have been for nothing. Four months later, India is number three in the world when it comes to the country's number of Covid-19 cases—right behind the United States and Brazil. Daily new cases are still increasing exponentially. The official death count is low, at around 2.5% of confirmed cases, but only around 75% of deaths are ever officially registered in India, a problem compounded by testing shortages in the case of Covid-19 deaths. The relative youth of India's population might save it from the six-digit fatality rate of the United States, but the magnitude of the tragedy unfolding in the world's second most populous country is still immense.

How did India go from one of the world's most stringent lockdowns, to one of the world's most severe outbreaks? Based on the evidence thus far, one important explanation lies in what *The Economist* called the relative "stinginess" of the state's response. Whether we look at fiscal relief to Indian citizens during and after the initial lockdown, public investment in Covid-19 testing and treatment facilities, or federal assistance to the state governments trying to manage local Covid-19 outbreaks, the Indian government's response has been amongst the least generous in the world. This failure to appropriately use macroeconomic policy tools in a crisis is compounded by a more long-term failure of "social provisioning" in India. Successive Indian governments have failed to adequately invest in public programs that could ensure Indians' ability to fulfill their basic needs of healthcare, food security, water, and sanitation, all of which have become more vital in the wake of the Covid-19 crisis. The combination of "stringent and stingy" that characterizes the Indian government's response has contributed to its failure to control the spread of Covid-19.

Most importantly, this particular policy response was a choice, rather than something the government was pushed into. As the leader of a right-wing national-ist government that was just re-elected with an expanded electoral majority—and the backing of a very powerful right-wing grassroots movement—India's prime minister Narendra Modi had the political space to respond with much more spending on economic relief, which would have reduced the economic pressure to ease the lockdown. The much larger relief programs announced by other emerging-country governments, not to mention the United States and Europe, could have provided international cover for such a move, if such cover was needed. By the time India's lockdown was announced, the International Monetary Fund (IMF), the World Bank, and mainstream economists across the world were calling for expansions of basic income guarantee programs, wage subsidies, large-scale deficit spending, and a host of other measures once considered far too radical. The fact that there were so few of these programs in India tells us something about the class bias of the government and about its understanding of its social contract with the Indian people.

## India's "Stringent" Lockdown

India's first Covid-19 case was confirmed on January 30. Throughout early February clusters of infection were small, limited to international travelers, and managed by quarantines, public service announcements, and screening at international ports of entry. Unlike in the case of Brazil or the United States, the national leadership seemed to take the scientific evidence about Covid-19 seriously. In the Indian case, the inability to effectively manage the health and economic crises generated by Covid-19 stems from the ideological basis and design of the central government's response in light of that knowledge.

Evidence of limited community transmission in India emerged by early March as the United States and Europe began to go into lockdowns. However, Prime Minister Modi's own announcement of a nationwide lockdown was made without consulting state governments or relevant national authorities, and gave Indians barely four hours to prepare for a complete shutdown of all transportation and non-essential economic activity. No one outside of Modi's inner circle had an opportunity to plan for the economic impact of the lockdown. Modi's surprise announcement was drawing upon a colonial legacy of undemocratic law-and-order pronouncements from the Indian central government. His announcement was perhaps subconsciously reflecting the fact that the Indian state's coercive powers are still much greater than its ability to deliver welfare to its citizens. But the nature of the announcement also reflected Modi's own authoritarian instincts, something he shares with leaders like Donald Trump and Jair Bolsonaro of Brazil. Each has worked to cultivate the image of an "I-alone-can-fix-it" leader, and in Modi's case this has meant operating like a president despite being part of a parliamentary system.

Once the lockdown was announced, the coercive machinery of the state swung into action, unleashing the dreaded lathi charge (police hitting people with batons) to keep people off the streets. This was a tremendous hardship for the millions of Indians in rural and urban India who earn their living as small traders, street vendors, drivers of taxis or auto-rickshaws, and wage workers on construction sites and in factories. Farmers and home-based piece-rate workers were cut off from access to raw materials, supplies, and markets. But the defining images of the lockdown will be the heartbreaking pictures of millions of destitute migrants, children in tow, setting off on foot to walk hundreds of miles from cities like Delhi, Mumbai, or Chennai to their homes in distant states. They had never been able to access clean water, decent housing, or sanitation in the work-site camps they lived in. Now there was no income, either. If they were going to die, they told reporters across the country, whether of hunger or of the coronavirus, they would rather do so with their families, in their hometowns. As they set off on their journeys, did they encounter a government that was organizing transportation, rest stops, and food for them? Did they find well-stocked quarantine camps at their destinations where they could receive food and access to Covid-19 testing? "Darling, this is India," as the Bollywood movie title goes. They were on their own, well and truly "doubly free," as Marx famously called workers to whom capitalism grants a freedom to choose between work and starvation.

## Why the Lockdown Didn't Work

Given that 90% of India's workforce consists of informal-sector workers with almost no benefits or savings, it was always obvious that a Covid-19 lockdown would be economically devastating for most Indian households. Furthermore, Covid-19 arrived as the Indian economy was already slowing down. This slowdown reflected an overall decrease in the growth of developing country economies after commodity price declines in 2015. But it was made worse by Prime Minister Modi's inexplicable decision to demonetize the Indian economy in 2016. India's GDP per capita growth had fallen even before the Covid-19 crisis, from an average of 7% in 2016 to below 5% in the last quarter of 2019.

And yet, the cumulative relief package announced by India during this period is among the least generous in the world. While the prime minister has claimed that government economic relief amounts to 10% of GDP, analysts ranging from investment bankers to public policy experts have concluded that actual new spending is closer to 1.5% of GDP. As the Table indicates, of this new spending, a third consists of transfers targeted to formal sector workers. The remaining expenditure, about 1% of GDP, consists primarily of an expansion in the entitlement of food provided through the country's Public Distribution System, and increased expenditure on the country's National Rural Employment Guarantee Scheme. These are much-needed expansions, but in accounting for barely 1% of GDP, they fall far short of the scale required to combat this crisis. For comparison, the United States has already spent 10% of its GDP on Covid-19 fiscal relief.

The Indian government is clearly aware of the need to sound like it is providing generous relief. It arrived at its (inflated) 10% of GDP Covid-19 relief package figure by 1) including welfare program adjustments that were already scheduled to go into effect this year and were merely advanced to count as Covid-19 relief, and 2)

**TABLE: THE COMPOSITION OF INDIA'S COVID-19 RELIEF: ACTUAL NEW SPENDING**

| | Expenditure (Billions of Rupees) | Expenditure (Millions of Dollars) | % of total |
|---|---|---|---|
| Investment in healthcare | ₹ 1.5 | $20 | 5% |
| Payroll tax cuts (primarily affecting formal sector workers) | ₹ 5.7 | $76 | 21% |
| Other transfers to formal sector workers | ₹ 4 | $53 | 14% |
| Expansion of the National Rural Employment Guarantee Scheme | ₹ 4.4 | $59 | 16% |
| Expansion of the Public Distribution System for food | ₹ 4 | $53 | 14% |
| Other Transfers to informal worker households | ₹ 8 | $107 | 29% |
| **Total:** | **₹ 27.6** | **$368** | **100%** |

*Source*: Suhasish Dey and Anirban Kundu, "Atmanirbhar Bharat Abhiyan: Putting the Cart Before the Horse," Ideas for India, July 6, 2020 (ideasforindia.in).

monetary easing and liquidity boosting measures. The latter are actions by India's Central Bank that lower interest rates and make it easier for banks to lend. While helpful for larger businesses and corporations who have existing relationships with banks in India, bank loans (and the burden of ultimately repaying those loans) are not what daily wage workers who cannot feed their families most immediately need.

There is the basic humanitarian imperative of trying to save lives through tangible transfers of the food, medical services, and cash that they need. There is also the economic case for such transfers: Macroeconomics teaches us that direct transfers to poorer consumers translate more directly into spending, and are thus a bigger boost for the economy, than changes to interest rates. This is something that even powerful central bankers, including the Chairman of the U.S. Federal Reserve, have been pointing out since the beginning of the crisis, as they have urged legislators to provide direct fiscal relief.

The Indian government claims that concerns about a downgrading of its credit rating prevent it from spending more; that it worries about its ability to attract foreign investment. This is ironic, given that at the beginning of the lockdown capital outflows from India (and indeed the rest of the developing world) had already exceeded those after the Great Recession, as capitalists fled to the "safety" of advanced capitalist countries running historic levels of deficits. As with most attempts to placate financial capital, this one also failed. Credit rating agencies recently downgraded India's credit rating anyway—from stable to negative—citing the increased likelihood of an extended economic recession, which is of course compounded by insufficient economic stimulus.

In the end, the actual management of India's health and economic crises has been left to state governments, as have the bulk of test-and-trace efforts. India's federal system means that states have some leeway when it comes to health and social welfare policy, but the central government very firmly controls the purse strings. State governments in Indian states such as Kerala, which has a communist state government, have been much more responsive and responsible, but restrictions on their ability to borrow means that they are ultimately constrained by the central government's willingness to fund them.

## A Failure of Social Provisioning

India's inability to effectively deal with the Covid-19 crisis is also the result of a more long-standing failure of social provisioning. That is, a failure to invest in the public provision of goods and services—such as water, housing, food security, and healthcare—that are essential to human well-being. When India began IMF- and World Bank-mandated programs of structural adjustment and liberalization in 1991, the country had a minimal social safety net. The main nationwide program with any systematic impact was the Public Distribution System (PDS), which was created in the 1940s to manage food scarcity, and currently provides 800 million people with subsidized grains through more than 500,000 fair price shops. Through the 1990s, the government was required to cut its already limited funding for such programs in order to address its balance of payments deficit.

However, as in other parts of the Global South, there was some expansion of the social safety net from 2004–2014 in response to grassroots struggles. As a result, the PDS became stronger in some states, and, at the national level, there was an expansion of mid-day meal programs for school children, pensions for the elderly and, in particular, the institution of the National Rural Employment Guarantee Scheme in 2005, which guarantees 100 days of minimum wage employment every year to rural Indians. Interestingly, both programs have been particularly accessible to, and inclusive of, women. On the other hand, even after the expansion in the 2000s, social provisioning remained inadequate. Total spending by the Indian state on all social provisioning programs, including on public health, was around 3% of GDP in 2018, in comparison to 20% for the United States and Brazil, or 7% for China and Mexico.

The electoral win of the right-wing Bharatiya Janata Party (BJP) in 2014 had some elements of a backlash to these advances, and these social provisioning programs stagnated after the BJP took power. The government has attacked and attempted to weaken the grassroots movements that pushed for these programs. Since 2014, the BJP has also focused on so-called public-private partnerships as a means to expand basic social services. For example, right before the Covid-19 crisis hit, India's health care system, which was already almost fully privatized, was going to be pushed even further in that direction by a proposal to privatize district-level community health centers. The consequences of this push to privatize are being felt right now, as private hospitals turn away Covid-19 patients and charge exorbitant prices to those they allow in.

## Power, Inequality, and Covid-19 in India

Sociologist Ananya Roy has written about informality as an idiom of state power in India. The fickleness of the state allows it the ability to create zones of exception and exclusion that operate to marginalize on the basis of class, caste, and gender. With the Covid-19 crisis, it is revealing to see how the absence of a substantive plan for governmental intervention has played out. The existence of around 100 million internal migrants living precariously on work sites across India is not a surprise to the Indian state or the Indian people—the urban boom of the last two decades has been built upon their labor. Yet during the lockdown, the state suspended all public transportation without organizing food, water, and health care for these migrants at their work sites. When it announced the first round of Covid-19 relief, it ignored the fact that eligibility for welfare programs in India is based upon your place of residence, and India's precarious migrants do not have proof of residence in the cities in which they live. And in its continuing refusal to extend sufficient support to state governments, it is disproportionately hurting the ability of poorer states—the home states of most internal migrants—to provide food and health care to their residents.

The state's failure to act has also accentuated the gendered character of the crisis. Inadequate access to non-market provisioning of basic food and health care hurts all Indians, but women are bearing the brunt of increases in the intensity of reproductive labor performed within the home during social distancing. Families are also sites of inter-generational and gendered violence—up to one in three Indian women are estimated to suffer from some form of domestic violence—and many women and children are now trapped inside abusive homes. Last, but not least, we know that during food and health care shortages in India, women are more likely to be excluded from access, as families concentrate their scarce resources upon feeding and caring for male breadwinners. Thus, the secondary health and economic effects of this crisis are likely to be worse for women, even as rates of mortality and job loss are currently higher for men.

While the actual relief delivered to Indian citizens has been inadequate, the central government has seized the opportunity to announce further pro-capital liberalization measures. Apart from cheaper credit, which disproportionately benefits larger capitalists, the government has approved the previously controversial privatization of state-owned enterprises and announced measures that would make it easier for corporations to expand into Indian agriculture. When some state governments went further and announced the rollback of labor laws such as those restricting the length of the workweek, they did so with the support of the central government.

It is feeling increasingly like the state understands the class character of the pandemic all too well. The urban working class lives in crowded conditions with even less access to India's minimal safety net or public health systems than the rural poor. Urban daily wage workers tend to have high rates of tuberculosis, HIV/AIDs and, in the case of women in particular, malnutrition, all of which make them more vulnerable to Covid-19. Many of the most destitute urban migrants are meanwhile drawn from the ranks of land-poor and landless families who live in rural India, who are in similarly poor health. If past epidemics are any guide, deaths are also likely to be concentrated among these groups—since they are at once the most marginalized and also, importantly, the most disposable subjects of a state that is much more concerned with representing the interests of economic elites.

## Some Reasons for Hope

India's failure to provide food and housing to the majority of Indians in need increased the pressure to end the lockdown order. Those same failures now make prolonged social distancing economically unviable. The refusal to invest in a threadbare public health system, even in the midst of a crisis as severe as this one, makes it unlikely that the health care system will be able to save lives, a proposition that will be tested now that the virus is rapidly spreading. The sharp increase in cases in India is proof, if we needed it, that stringent lockdowns fail when they are also stingy.

The Indian government's response to this crisis appears to be of a piece with a backlash against the progress made by social movements in India in the 2000s. Apart from the pushback against programs expanding social provisioning in India, the government had also intensified attempts to marginalize Muslims and other religious minorities in India pre-Covid-19. These attempts included a draconian lockdown in the contested region of Kashmir, a change to citizenship laws that has the potential to exclude religious minorities, and a refusal to intervene to stop religious riots in the capital city of Delhi. Unsurprisingly, the Covid-19 crisis has also been communalized, with gatherings of Muslims singled out for blame when it came to spreading the virus. Efforts to censor the free press have also increased. This current Indian government does have the ability and inclination to seize even more coercive power under the cover of the crisis, and it will certainly try.

But there are at least three reasons for optimism. One is that the excellent performance of some state governments, such as Kerala, is bolstering the case for greater federalism and decentralization of state power. Second, the destitution of the urban poor has been exposed as never before. This may lead to greater mobilization of marginalized urban classes and castes to demand universal social provisioning. It may also imply more popular legitimacy for any such protest movement. Third, right before the Covid-19 crisis, we were seeing the emergence of popular resistance to Hindu nationalism from Muslim groups allied with other minority religious and lower-caste groups. The BJP's response to the coronavirus crisis has only further accentuated the insecurity felt by such groups. If this resistance reemerges, and it is able to ally with other marginalized urban groups, India may still see a popular movement that can push for better and more equally distributed social provisioning by the state as well as a retrenchment of the Hindu nationalist agenda. ❑

*Sources*: "Emerging-market lockdowns match rich-world ones. The handouts do not," *The Economist*, April 4, 2020 (economist.com); Blavatink School of Government and University of Oxford, "Coronavirus Government Response Tracker," (bsg.ox.ac.uk); Henrik Pettersson, Byron Manley, and Sergio Hernandez, "Tracking coronavirus' global spread," CNN, as of July 18, 2020 (cnn.com); Subhasish Dey and Anirban Kundu, "Atmanirbhar Bharat Abhiyan: Putting the cart before the horse," Ideas for India, July 6, 2020 (ideasforindia.in); William A. Galston, "Heed Powell's Call for Fiscal Stimulus," *Wall Street Journal*, May 19, 2020 (wsj.com); International Labour Organization website (ilostat.ilo.org); Jagdish Rattanani, "Coronavirus: Time to commandeer private hospitals?," *Deacan Herald*, June 14, 2020 (deacanherald.com); Payal Mohta, "India's coronavirus lockdown is forcing women to do all the work," *South China Morning Post*, May 10, 2020 (scmp.com); Sheikh Saaliq, "Every Third Woman In India Suffers Sexual, Physical Violence at Home," News 18, Feb. 8, 2018 (news18.com); D. P. K. Pillay and T.K. Manoj Kumar, "Food Security in India: Evolution, Efforts and Problems," *Strategic Analysis*, Issue 6, 2018; Kabir Agarwal, "Six Charts Show That India Needs to (and Can Afford to) Universalise PDS," *The Wire*, April 18, 2020 (thewire.in).

*Article 2.4*

# THE "EMERGING ECONOMIES" TODAY

**AN INTERVIEW WITH JAYATI GHOSH**
*May/June 2016*

The terms *"emerging markets"* and *"emerging economies"* have come into fashion, especially to refer to countries supposedly poised to make the leap from *"developing"* to *"developed"* economies. There's no definitive list, but Brazil, India, Indonesia, Mexico, Russia, South Africa, Turkey, and China are among the large countries that often headline articles on *"emerging economies."* Economic growth rates—as well as the drop-off in growth during the global Great Recession and the recovery since—vary widely between countries typically placed in this group.

China is by far the most prominent of the emerging economies—the most populous country in the world, with an extraordinary period of industrial growth since the 1980s, and with an enormous impact (not only as an exporter of manufactured goods but also as an importer of raw-material and intermediate inputs to manufacturing) on the world economy. The "secular stagnation" of the high-income capitalist economies and resulting growth slowdown in China, therefore, has much wider implications for the developing world. In this interview, economist Jayati Ghosh addresses the current challenges for China and other countries—and possible paths toward inclusive and sustainable development. —Eds.

**Dollars & Sense:** You've written about the "retreat" of emerging-market economies, which until recently had been held up as examples of robust growth, in contrast to the stagnant economies of the so-called capitalist "core." What's driving the slowdown of economic growth in the emerging economies today?

**Jayati Ghosh:** The emerging economies are really those that have integrated much more into the global financial system, not just the global trade system. And I think what happened during the period of the economic boom is that many people forgot that their growth was still ultimately driven by what was happening in the North. That is, the engine of demand was still the northern economies. So whether you're talking about China in particular or the range of emerging economies that was seen as more prominent in the first half of the 2000s, all of them depended on exports to the North and particularly to the United States.

It was the U.S. boom that drew in more and more of the exports from developing countries. When it came to an end—as it inevitably had to—these economies had to look for other sources of demand. There are two ways of doing this. One is to try and do a domestic demand-driven expansion based on higher domestic incomes because of wage and employment growth. And the other is the model which unfortunately seems to be the more popular one, which is to have a debt-driven kind of growth, based on both consumption and accumulation that is essentially led by taking on more and more debt. This is, of course, also what the U.S. did in the 2000s, which unraveled in 2007 and 2008. But it's also what a number of European economies did, and they're paying the price now.

Remarkably, developing countries that don't need to take this path, and can see all the problems associated with it, also took this path in the wake of the global financial crisis. In China there was a doubling of the debt-to-GDP ratio between 2007 and 2014. This reflected increases in debt to every single sector, but it was dominantly for investment. In a range of other important developing countries, from Mexico to Indonesia, Malaysia, South Korea, etc., there was a dramatic expansion of household debt, particularly real estate and housing debt. We all know that these real-estate and housing bubbles that are led by taking on more debt, these end in tears. And that's really what has been happening.

In these "emerging" economies, financial integration allowed them to break the link between productive investment and growth. It fueled a debt-driven pattern of expansion, which inevitably has to end. It's ending now. The problem is that it's ending at a time when demand from the North is slowing dramatically. So there is a double whammy for these emerging economies. The slowdown in northern markets means that China—which had become the major driver of expansion—can no longer continue to export at the same rate. That means its imports have also come down. In the past year, China's exports fell by 5%, but its imports fell by 20%. That has affected all the other developing countries. And that's in combination with this end of the debt-driven expansion model.

*D&S:* A number of economists have argued for quite some time that China's export-oriented growth model would inevitably reach its limits. Are we seeing it finally reach an impasse now, and if so, is there a prospect for China to make a transition from a low-wage export-oriented model to a domestic demand-driven model that would necessarily require higher wages?

**JG:** I think it's indisputable that the export-driven model is over for the time being, for sure, certainly for the next five years, probably the next decade. That's not a bad thing, because one of the problems with that export-driven model is that it persists in seeing wages as costs rather than as a source of internal demand that you can use to your benefit. It encourages massive degradation of nature and taking on environmental costs that are now recognized to be completely unsustainable and socially undesirable. And, overall, we know that these can't last—these export-driven models can't last.

So, yes, it has ended. It does mean that the Chinese government and authorities have to look for an alternative. Many of us have been arguing that the alternative necessarily requires much more emphasis on increasing consumption, not through debt, but by increasing real incomes. And that means encouraging more employment of a desirable type—"decent work" as it's been called—and increasing wages. Now, this doesn't mean that the rates of growth will continue as high as they have been, but that doesn't matter.

In fact, the obsession with GDP growth is becoming a real negative now in the search for alternatives. The Chinese authorities, like all the financial analysts across the world who are constantly looking at China, are obsessed with GDP: Is it going to be 6.5% annual growth? Is it going to be 6.1%? Is it going to fall below 6%? As if that's all that matters. What they should really be looking at is the incomes of, let us say, the bottom 50 or 60%. Are these growing? If these are growing at about 4 or 5%, that's fantastic. That's wonderful. And that's really what the economy needs in a sustainable way. If these are growing in combination with patterns of production and consumption that are more sustainable, that are environmentally friendly, that are less carbon-emitting, then that is of course even more desirable.

But that means the focus has to shift away from GDP growth, and away from just pushing up GDP by any means whatsoever—to one which looks at how to improve the real incomes and the quality of life of the majority of the citizens. Unfortunately, the Chinese government doesn't seem to be choosing that path just yet. There have been some moves—in terms of increasing health spending, in terms of some attempts to increase wages and social protection for some workers—but overall the focus is still once again on more accumulation, on more investment, usually driven by more debt.

**D&S:** When you say the export-oriented model is "over," does that mean you think sticking to this approach will no longer deliver what policymakers and elites are aiming for, in terms of growth and accumulation? (And perhaps that this will lead to an elite-driven restructuring in the near term?) Or is it that this approach just cannot plausibly deliver in terms of inclusive development—the improvement in the quality of life for the majority?

**JG:** Both, really. The conditions of the global economy at present are such that an economy as large as that of China (and many other smaller economies as well) cannot expect much stimulus from external demand Significant increases in exports would only be possible by increasing markets share; that is, eating into some other country's exports. So the past pattern of accumulation based on external demand is unlikely to work in the near future.

But in addition, this approach has not delivered in terms of inclusive growth over the past decade except to some extent in China, which has been able to use it to generate a "Lewisian" process (theorized by economist Arthur Lewis in the 1950s) of shifting labor out of lower productivity activities. Even in China it was successful because wages increased much less than productivity and so export prices could fall or remain low. In many other countries, export-led expansion has actually been associated stagnant or lower wages and greater fragility of incomes, along with very substantial environmental costs that are typically not factored in.

**D&S:** Is it possible that that kind of transition is not going to happen in China until we see the development of a robust labor movement that's capable of winning a higher share of the national income in the form of wages, and pushing up mass consumption in that way?

**JG:** There is probably much greater public concern about all this in China than is often depicted in the media, certainly in the Chinese media, but even abroad. We know that there are thousands, literally, tens of thousands of protests in China—often about land grabs and so on in the peasantry, but also many, many workers' protests, and many other protests by citizens about environmental conditions. They have mostly been suppressed, but I don't think you can keep on suppressing these.

I do believe the Chinese elite has recognized that there are a couple of things that are becoming very important for them to maintain their political legitimacy. One is, of course, inequality and, associated with that, corruption. That is why the anti-corruption drive of President Xi Jinping retains a lot of popularity. Then there is the fact of the environmental unsustainability. Both India and China have created monstrosities in urban areas, in terms of the pollution, congestion, degradation, which are really making many of our cities and towns unlivable. There is widespread protest about that, and about the pollution of water sources, of the atmosphere, of land quality. And there is real concern that ordinary Chinese citizens are not continuously experiencing the better life that they have grown accustomed to expect.

So I think, even without a very large-scale social mobilization, there is growing awareness in China—among officialdom, as well—that they can't carry on as before. It is likely that there's a tussle at the very higher echelons of the leadership and in the Communist Party, between those who are arguing for the slower but more sustainable and more wage-led path, and those who just want to keep propping up growth by more financial liberalization, by encouraging investors to jump in and invest even in projects that are unlikely to continue, and somehow keep that GDP growth going. It's a political tussle but of course that will determine the direction of the economy as well.

**D&S:** In the midst of this period of stagnation of the very high-income capitalist economies, and a resulting slowdown of growth in the so-called emerging economies, we also have an effect on countries that had primarily remained raw-material (or "primary-product") exporters. Is that boom in commodities exports now also over for the foreseeable future, and do you see those countries as now reinventing their economic development models?

**JG:** I think that the period of the boom was really a bit of an aberration. Since the early 20th century, these periods of relatively high commodity prices have always been outliers, and they don't last very long. They last for about five, six, maybe eight years at most, and then they you come back to this more depressed situation relative to other prices. I have a feeling this is now going to continue, and that boom is, for the time being, over. It definitely means that the manna from heaven that many countries experienced has reduced, and therefore you have to think of other ways of diversifying your economies.

Many countries actually tried to do this but, you know, when you're getting so much income from the primary product exports it's very hard to diversify. It's actually easier to diversify when primary product prices are lower. So, once again, I think it's important for these countries to stop thinking of this as a huge loss, and start thinking of it as an opportunity—as an opportunity to use cheap primary commodities as a means of industrializing for domestic and regional markets. So it means a different strategy. The export-led obsession has to end. Without that, we're not going to get viable and sustainable strategies.

I'd like to make one other point, though, about the slowdown in China and the impact on developing countries, which is that it's also going to affect manufacturing exporters. China had become the center of a global production chain that was heavily exporting to the North but was drawing in more and more raw material and intermediate products from other developing countries. So almost every country had China become their main trade partner in both imports and exports. Many of these manufacturing economies are now going to face, once again, a double whammy. They will face a reduction, from China, in terms of lower Chinese imports of raw materials and intermediate goods for final export, and they're going to face greater competition from China in terms of their own export markets and their own domestic markets. Because China is now devaluing its currency, even though thus far it has been minor. It is looking to cheapen its exports even further, and this will definitely impact on both export markets and internal markets in developing countries.

So I think both primary exporters and manufacturing exporters are in for a bit of a bad time. They need to think of creative ways of dealing with the situation. It is not helped by believing that integration into global value chains is the only option, because these global value chains basically reduce the incomes of the actual producers. If you look at it, the emergence of global value chains and the associated trade treaties—not just the World Trade Organization (WTO) but the proliferation of regional trading agreements and things like the Trans-Pacific Partnership (TPP)—increase competition and reduce the value of the actual production stage of all commodities and goods. And they simultaneously increase the pre-production and post-production value. That is, all of the aspects that are driven by intellectual property monopolies—their values increase. So whether it is design elements or it is the marketing and branding and all of that—the intellectual property rights over which are retained by companies in the North—all of those are getting more and more value. And the actual production is getting less value because of the greater competitive pressure unleashed by these various trade agreements.

Developing countries that are seeking to get out of this really have to think of alternative arrangements—possibly regional arrangements, more reliance on domestic demand and South-South trade, which is more possible today than it has ever been—and moving away from a system that allows global and northern-led multinationals to capture all the rents and most of the profits of production everywhere.

**D&S:** So, in the course of this discussion, I think two major questions emerge about the way forward in so-called developing economies. One is how to square economic development—in terms of raising the quality of life for the majority—with environmental sustainability. The other is how to ensure the economic development of some countries isn't at odds with development in others. Are there ways of mutually fostering development—and in particular sustainable development—across the developing economies?

**JG:** Yes, I think we need to really move away from the traditional way of looking at growth and development, which is ultimately still based on GDP. As long as we keep doing that, we're going to be caught in this trap. We have to be focusing much more on quality of life and ensuring what we would call the basic needs or minimum requirements for a civilized life among all the citizenry. If we do that, then we're less in competition with one another and we're less obsessed with having to be the cheapest show in town. We then see wages and employment growth as a means of expansion of economic activity. We will see social policies as delivering not just better welfare for the people but also more employment, and therefore a better quality of life.

If we look for regional trading arrangements that recognize this, if we look to increase the value of domestic economic activity by encouraging the things that matter for ordinary people (especially, let's say, the bottom half of the population), if we focus on new technologies that are adapted to specific local requirements—in terms of being more green, more environmentally sustainable, as well as recognizing the specific availability of labor in these economies—I think we can do a lot more. It may be slower in terms of GDP growth, but really that doesn't mean anything. So we have to move away from GDP growth as the basic indicator of what is desirable. I think that's the ultimate and most essential issue. ❑

*Article 2.5*

# "SECULAR STAGNATION" CONTINUES

## BY JOHN MILLER
*September/October 2018*

> So much for "secular stagnation." With Friday's report of 4.1% growth in the second quarter, the U.S. economy has now averaged 3.1% growth for the last six months and 2.8% for the last 12.
>
> The acceleration has been driven by business investment, which increased 6.3% in 2017 and has averaged 9.4% in the first half of 2018.
>
> The same people who said this growth revival could never happen are now saying that it can't last.
>
> But there are reasons to think that a 3% growth pace can continue. The investment boom will drive productivity gains and job creation that will flow to higher wages and lift consumer spending.
>
> —The Editorial Board, "The Return of 3% Growth: Tax reform and deregulation have lifted the economy out of the Obama doldrums," *Wall Street Journal*, July 28, 2018.

The *Wall Street Journal* editors may think that Trump's "amazing" growth rates, as the president refers to them, have vanquished secular stagnation from the U.S. economy.

But "secular stagnation," a long-term (or "secular") slowdown in economic growth, is not behind us. Rather, healthy economic growth and financial stability remain incompatible in today's economy—a tell-tale sign of secular stagnation. On top of that, the Trump economy has failed to lift wages as it has showered riches on those who need them the least, making today's gaping inequality yet worse.

## Secular Stagnation Continues

Economic growth rates have indeed picked up in the last year. But those growth rates are neither unprecedented nor as stellar as the editors and the president make them out to be. For instance, in 2014, during the Obama administration, the economy posted two consecutive quarters of economic growth that topped Trump's second-quarter 4.1% growth rate— yet the editors did not declare the end of secular stagnation. And the 2.8% economic growth rate the economy averaged over 12 months in 2017 and 2018 is hardly something to crow about. That is slower than the 2.9% growth rate the U.S. economy has averaged of over the last seven decades, and far slower than the 4.3% and 3.6% average growth rates of the long economic expansions of the 1960s and 1990s, respectively. Finally, the current pick-up in economic growth began in the second half of 2016, before Trump came to office, and that upward trend has not accelerated in the last year and a half. On top of that, real private investment during the Trump administration has grown more slowly than it had from 2010 to 2016, during the Obama administration.

Nor does the secular stagnation hypothesis suggest that economic growth rates would never accelerate. Rather, secular stagnation occurs when a chronic lack of demand—a shortfall of spending—has slowed long-term economic growth to the point where "it may be impossible to achieve full employment, satisfactory growth and financial stability simultaneously simply through the operation of conventional monetary policy [that lowers interest rates]," as economist (and former treasury secretary and World Bank chief economist) Lawrence Summers, who has championed the secular stagnation hypothesis, has put it.

Today unsustainable finances and extraordinary economic stimulus are masking the inability of the economy to maintain faster growth rates. Under the Trump administration, the federal government has slashed taxes for corporations and the rich, boosted spending on the military, and driven up the federal budget deficit. The deficit is on course to reach $1 trillion or 5.1% of GDP by fiscal year 2019 according to the White House, unprecedented levels for an economy in the midst of a long-running economic expansion. Along with that fiscal stimulus, interest rates (which determine the cost of borrowing) remain low by historic standards, despite the Fed's multiple increases of its benchmark interest rate, the Fed Funds rate, since December 2015. The Fed Funds rate is still just under 2%, well below its 5.0% rate in 2007 on the eve of the Great Recession.

Growing signs of financial instability also haunt today's economy. A spate of corporate borrowing enabled by low interest rates has more than doubled U.S. corporate debt (total debt of nonfinancial corporations) from 2007 to the end of 2017, according to the McKinsey Global Institute. With higher interest rates that corporate borrowing becomes more costly and unsustainable for some corporations with a high debt burden.

In addition, increased volatility returned to the stock market this year after a long period of nearly uninterrupted rising stock prices. The editors dismissed the increased volatility as little more than the "return of normal risk." But stock-market prices have stagnated since then, no higher in the beginning of August (measured by the S&P 500) than they had been in the end of January.

## Economic Malnourishment

Trump insists that the more recent economic growth is "very sustainable," but most economists disagree. Even the *Wall Street Journal* survey of 60 economists, which does foresee the economy growing at a 3.0% rate in the second half of this year, has economic growth slowing to 2.4% for 2019. And former Fed Chair Ben Bernanke believes that by 2020 Trump's overstimulated economy "is going to go off the cliff," much like the cartoon character Wile E. Coyote. If the current trade conflict worsens, it could push the economy into a recession before that.

Beyond concerns about financial fragility and whether the current fiscal and monetary stimulus can be sustained, economists have seized upon one-time factors that pushed up the second-quarter economic growth rate. The most important of those is the surge in exports, which accounted for one quarter of the growth during the second quarter. Much of the surge came from importers snapping up U.S. exports before their countries imposed tariffs in retaliation to Trump's tariffs. Chinese pre-tariff purchases of U.S. soybeans alone added 0.6 percentage points to the economic growth rate, according to Pantheon Macroeconomics.

The other is the strong consumer spending that pushed up the second-quarter growth rate. The largely pro-rich Trump tax cut added some money to the take-home pay of even less-than-well-to-do taxpayers, which helped to boost consumer spending. That level of consumer spending, however, is unlikely to continue. U.S. consumer debt has now reached $13.3 trillion, more debt than on the eve of last decade's financial crisis, and higher interest rates will increase that debt burden. Finally, the net worth of all but the richest 10% of households remains below its level prior to the 2008–2009 financial crisis.

One-off increases in exports and consumer spending goosed the quarterly economic growth rate, but putting an end to secular stagnation requires a steady diet of increased investment and consumer spending. That's not being served up by the Trump economy.

Slashing corporate taxes has not generated an investment boom. During the second quarter of 2018, housing investment continued to slump, and spending on new equipment, the largest component of investment, grew only half as quickly as it had at the end of 2017, prior to the tax cut. Business investment in structures such as office buildings and factories did increase far more quickly than before the tax cut. But most of that spending went into oil and gas drilling spurred on by higher world energy prices.

The majority of the profits freed up by cutting corporate taxes have gone to buying back stocks, dividends, and other payments to investors. The current torrent of stock buybacks, according to Goldman Sachs estimates, is on track to reach $1 trillion and surpass the buyback bonanza in 2007 on the eve of the Great Recession by year's end. That's $1 trillion that will not go to domestic investment that might have created jobs, lifted wages, and boosted productivity. Nor will those stock buybacks help most workers, who own little or no stock.

Workers' wages have continued to stagnate during the Trump administration. Trump's Council of Economic Advisors promised that an "immediate jump in wage growth" would follow their tax giveaway to the rich adding more than $4,000 of income to the typical family. But corrected for inflation, average hourly earnings of all private nonfarm employees were just 0.6% higher in June 2018 than when Trump took office. Six months after the tax cut, workers' purchasing power is no higher, and consumers are less wealthy and deeper in debt than they were a decade ago. That's hardly a formula for generating a sustained increase in consumer spending.

## Not Just Economics

In the last analysis, the secular stagnation problem is a political problem rather than an economic one. With sufficient political will—and political might—we could enact a program that would put an end to secular stagnation, reduce inequality, and improve the lot of most people.

Large-scale public investment could make up for the persistent shortfall of private investment. The People's Budget of the Congressional Progressive Caucus (CPC) proposes a $2 trillion program of much needed public investments—about the cost of the Trump tax cut and his increase in military spending. That infrastructure spending could clean up drinking-water pipes, update our energy grid to support renewable power resources, support public transportation, expand broadband, and rebuild public schools.

Nor is wage-stagnation an economic phenomenon alone. The National Labor Relations Board has undermined unionization at the same time the federal government has failed to enforce existing labor laws. Trump has put a freeze on pay increases for federal workers. State governments have overturned local pro-labor regulations, from raising minimum wages to mandating paid leave to establishing fair scheduling. Undoing those anti-labor policies and facilitating unionization is key to improving the bargaining power of workers and overcoming wage stagnation.

Those measures, unlike the Trump policies endorsed by the *WSJ* editors, could truly put an end to secular stagnation. ❑

*Sources:* Steve Rattner, "Testimony the House Ways and Means Committee," May 16, 2018; Lawrence Summers, "What to do About Secular Stagnation," *World Economic Forum*, Oct. 31, 2014; *Budget of the U.S. Government, Fiscal Year 2019: Mid-Session Review*, Office of Management and Budget, July 13, 2018, Table S-1; Susan Lund, et al., "Rising corporate debt: Peril or promise?" Discussion Paper, McKinsey Global Institute, June 2018; "The Return to Normal Risk," *Wall Street Journal*, February 5, 2018; *Wall Street Journal* Economic Forecasting Survey; Craig Torres, "Bernanke Says U.S. Economy Faces a 'Wile E. Coyote' Moment in 2020," *Bloomberg Businessweek*, July 7, 2018; Paul Kiernan, "U.S. Soybean Exports Surged Last Quarter," *Wall Street Journal*, July 6, 2018; "Household Debt and Credit Report (Q2 2018)," Center for Microeconomic Data, Federal Reserve Bank of New York; Josh Zumbrun, "Household Borrowing Hits High," *Wall Street Journal*, Aug. 15, 2018; "Feel That Post-Recession Bounce," *New York Times*, Sept 27, 2017; Grep Ip, "A Solid Economy With Room to Run," *Wall Street Journal*, July 28, 2018; "Stock Prices Defy Surge in Buybacks," *Wall Street Journal*, July 9, 2018; Lu Wang, "Forget Apple, Goldman Says, Flagging New $1 Trillion for S&P 500," *Bloomberg Businessweek*, August 6, 2018; Heather Long, "The average American family will get $4,000 from tax cuts, Trump team claims," *Washington Post*, Oct. 16, 2017; "Worker Rights Preemption in the US," Economic Policy Institute, September 2017; "The People's Budget: A Progressive Path Forward FY 2019," The Congressional Progressive Caucus.

*Article 2.6*

# GERMAN WAGE REPRESSION
*Getting to the Roots of the Eurozone Crisis*

**BY JOHN MILLER**
*September/October 2015*

> Germany has been insistent that the so-called peripheral countries increase their competitiveness through slower wages [sic] rises or even wage cuts. Wage increases in Germany are an equally important, and symmetrical, part of this necessary adjustment process. ...
>
> The wage increases are steps in the right direction, but relatively small steps. More gains for German workers in the future would be both warranted and a win-win proposition for Germany and its trade partners.
>
> — Ben Bernanke, "German wage hikes: A small step in the right direction," Brookings Institution, April 13, 2015.

Ben Bernanke not only supports recent [2015] German wage increases, he also thinks further wage increases for German workers are "warranted and a win-win proposition for Germany and its trade partners"?

Now that's a jaw-dropper. Has the former head of the Federal Reserve Board—the guardian of "price stability" that makes policy designed to keep U.S. wages in check—switched sides in the class war, now that he is retired?

Hardly. Rather, it's that catering to the demands of German high finance and other elites has been so disastrous that even the former chair of the Fed cannot deny the undeniable: unless Germany changes course and boosts workers' wages, the euro crisis will only worsen.

Let's look more closely at just how German wage repression and currency manipulation pushed the eurozone into crisis, ignited a conflict between northern and southern eurozone countries (with Germany as the enforcer of austerity), and left Greece teetering on the edge of collapse.

## From "Sick Man" to Export Bully

In the year 2000, Germany was widely considered "the sick man of Europe." Through much of the previous decade, the German economy grew more slowly than the European Union average, its manufacturing base shrunk, and its unemployment rate rose to near double-digits levels. Nor was Germany an export powerhouse, with its current account (the mostly widely used and most comprehensive measure of a nation's financial balance with the rest of the world) showing a modest deficit in 2000.

Adopting the euro as its sole currency, in January 2002, was no panacea. For the next two years, Germany's economy continued to stagnate. But converting to the euro—whose value was more or less an average of that of the stronger and weaker former currencies of the member countries—soon did improve Germany's competitive position internationally. German exports, no longer valued in strong deutschmarks, but in weaker euros, became cheaper to buyers in other countries. At the same time, the exports of countries that used to have weaker currencies, such as the Greek drachma and the Spanish peseta, became more expensive. That alone transformed Germany's current account deficit into a surplus.

China is widely accused of "currency manipulation," keeping the renminbi weak to boost its exports. But few see that the eurozone—the now 19-country bloc sharing the euro as its common currency—has functioned for Germany as a built-in currency manipulation system. And much like China, Germany used a lethal combination of wage repression and an undervalued currency to boost its exports and output at the expense of its trading partners.

Following the adoption of the euro, Germany instituted a set of "labor-market flexibility" policies intended to further improve its international competitiveness. Known as the Agenda 2010 Reforms, the new policies reduced pensions, cut medical benefits, and slashed the duration of unemployment benefits from nearly three years to just one. They also made it easier to fire workers, while encouraging the creation of part-time and short-term jobs. Employers increasingly divided formerly full-time jobs into state-subsidized, low-paying, insecure "mini-jobs." A decade later, one in five German jobs was a mini-job.

Germany's repressive labor policies kept a lid on wage growth. In every year from 2000 through the onset of the financial crisis in 2009, German compensation per employee increased more slowly than the eurozone average, and less even than in the United States.

During the 1990s, German workers' real (inflation-adjusted) wages rose along with productivity gains, meaning that employers could pay the higher wages without facing higher labor costs per unit of output. After 1999, wage gains no longer kept pace with productivity, and the gap between the two widened. As wages stagnated, inequality worsened, and poverty rates rose. Total labor compensation (wages and benefits) fell from 61% of GDP in 2001 to just 55% of GDP in 2007, its lowest level in five decades.

German wage repression went even further than necessary to meet the 2% inflation target mandated by the eurozone agreement, and insisted upon by German policymakers. Unit labor costs (workers' compensation per unit of output) is perhaps the most important determinant of prices and competitiveness. Unit labor costs rise with wage increases but fall with gains in productivity. From 1999 to 2013, German unit labor costs increased by just 0.4% a year. The reason was not German productivity growth, which was no greater than the eurozone average over the period; rather, it was that German labor market policies kept wage growth in check.

This combination of a built-in system of currency manipulation afforded by the euro and labor-market policies holding labor costs in check turned Germany into the world's preeminent trade-surplus country. As its competitive advantage grew, its exports soared. Germany's current account surplus became the largest in the world relative to the size of its economy, reaching 7.6% of the country's GDP, more than twice the size of China's surplus compared to its GDP.

## Beggar Thy Neighborhood

Germany's transformation into an export powerhouse came at the expense of the southern eurozone economies. Despite posting productivity gains that were equal or almost equal to Germany's, Greece, Portugal, Spain, and Italy saw their labor costs per unit of output and prices rise considerably faster than Germany's. Wage growth in these countries exceeded productivity growth, and the resulting higher unit labor costs pushed prices up by more than the eurozone's low 2% annual inflation target (by a small margin).

The widening gap in unit labor costs gave Germany a tremendous competitive advantage and left the southern eurozone economies at a tremendous disadvantage. Germany amassed its ever-larger current account surplus, while the southern eurozone economies were saddled with worsening deficits. Later in the decade, the Greek, Portuguese, and Spanish current account deficits approached or even reached alarming double-digit levels, relative to the sizes of their economies.

In this way, German wage repression is an essential component of the euro crisis. Heiner Flassbeck, the German economist and longtime critic of wage repression, and Costas Lapavistas, the Greek economist best known for his work on financialization, put it best in their recent book *Against the Troika: Crisis and Austerity in the Eurozone*: "Germany has operated a policy of 'beggar-thy-neighbor' but only after 'beggaring its own people' by essentially freezing wages. This is the secret of German success during the last fifteen years."

While Germany's huge exports across Europe and elsewhere created German jobs and lowered the country's unemployment rate, the German economy never grew robustly. Wage repression subsidized exports, but it sapped domestic spending. And, held back by this chronic lack of domestic demand, Germany's economic growth was far-from-impressive, before or after the Great Recession. From 2002 to 2008, the German economy grew more slowly than the eurozone average, and over the last five years has failed to match even the sluggish growth rates posted by the U.S. economic recovery. With low wage growth, consumption stagnated. German corporations hoarded their profits and private investment relative to GDP fell almost continuously from 2000 on. The same was true for German public investment, held back by the eurozone budgetary constraints.

At the same time, Germany spread instability. Germany's reliance on foreign demand for its exports drained spending from elsewhere in the eurozone and slowed growth in those countries. That, in turn, made it less likely that German banks and elites would recover their loans and investments in southern Europe.

## Wage Repression and the Crisis

No wonder Bernanke now describes higher German wages as an important step toward reducing Europe's trade imbalances. More spending by German workers on domestic goods and imports would help Germany and its trading partners grow, and improve the lot of working people throughout the eurozone.

Of course, much more needs to be done. Putting an end to the austerity measures imposed on Greece and the other struggling eurozone economies would boost their demand as well. In fact, it would also better serve the interests of Germany and the profitmaking class, by helping to stabilize a system from which they have benefited so greatly at the expense of much of the region's population.

Still, raising the wages of German workers to match productivity gains is, as Bernanke recognizes, surely a step in the right direction. Raising U.S. wages to match productivity gains would help defuse U.S. wage repression and boost economic growth here as well. If Bernanke throws his weight behind that proposition, we'll truly wonder which side is he on. ❑

*Sources*: Kaja Bonesmo Fredrikson, "Income Inequality in the European Union," OECD Economic Department Working Papers, No. 952, April 16, 2012; Brian Blackstone, "Germany's Rising Wages Bode Well for Global Economy," *Wall Street Journal*, April 12, 2015; Heiner Flassbeck and Costas Lapavistas, *Against the Troika: Crisis and Austerity in the Eurozone* (Verso, 2015); Real News Network, Interview with Heiner Flassbeck: "Germany's Collective Denial," Feb. 22, 2015; Ben Bernanke, "Greece and Europe: Is Europe Holding up its end of the Bargain?" Ben Bernanke's Blog, July 17, 2015; Philippe Legrain, "Germany's Economic Mirage," Project Syndicate, Sept. 23, 2014.

*Article 2.7*

# THE HUMAN TOLL OF GREEK AUSTERITY

**BY EVITA NOLKA**
*March/April 2016*

Giannis and Lena, both in their early 30s and with MBA degrees, consider themselves lucky to be employed. Living in Thessaloniki, Greece's second largest city, located in the heart of Macedonia, Giannis is a merchandise buyer at a company that imports household items. Lena works in the export department of a pasta-producing enterprise.

"Every Greek family is experiencing the crisis their own way," Lena tells me. "Unemployment, wage and pension cuts, taxes, and increases in prices of basic goods have caused despair to millions of people."

Giannis shares a bit more. His family's income has taken a real hit. His father's wages have been reduced by one third and his mother got laid off three years ago. She used to work at a ready-made garments factory that went bankrupt soon after. For a year and a half, she hasn't been paid and she is still claiming the money she is owed.

Like so many others, Giannis had been unemployed for years. There was nothing he could do other than hope to get accepted at one of the five-month temporary work programs in the country funded by the European Union (EU). "You're being deprived of the opportunity to work during the most productive years of your life," Giannis tells me as he explains the psychological burden of unemployment. "There's a feeling that you're standing still even though the whole world keeps moving and after a while you feel numb. You accept that's how things are and you are unable to get out of the rut."

## Sticking with Austerity

For six years now [since 2008], Greece has lived under unprecedented austerity policies demanded by its lenders and accepted by a succession of governments. The social and political reality created by austerity was demonstrated sharply by two events on the same day in October 2015.

First, Eurostat, the European statistical service, released a report on poverty and social exclusion in Greece. The report showed that, in 2014, 22.1% of the Greek population lived in conditions of poverty, 21.5% were severely materially deprived, and 17.2% lived in families with very low work intensity. (Economists define "work intensity" as the total number of months that all working-age household members have worked as a percentage of the total number of months they theoretically could have worked. Households under 20% are considered to have "very low" work intensity.) Altogether, 36% of the population faced one or more of these terrible conditions. That figure was 7.9% percentage points higher than in 2008.

Second, the Greek parliament approved a new piece of legislation imposing further austerity measures as demanded by its creditors—primarily the EU and the International Monetary Fund (IMF)—to meet the terms of Greece's most recent (third) bailout agreement. The new package involves cutting public spending by 14.32 billion euros, while raising taxes by 14.09 billion euros, over the next five years. The measures will primarily affect privately owned businesses, homeowners, and employees close to retirement.

Austerity policies were first adopted in 2010 as a "solution" to the economic crisis that erupted in 2009–10. Severe cuts in public spending, deep reductions in wages and pensions, enormous tax increases, and a stripping back of labor protections were imposed—ostensibly—to stabilize the economy and gain the confidence of financial markets. In practice, the measures have plunged the Greek economy into a prolonged recession that has led to the disastrous results outlined by Eurostat. Unfortunately, the current Greek government, formed by the left-wing SYRIZA party, appears determined to keep the country on the same path.

## The Crushing Burden of Unemployment

In the course of the recession, the Greek economy has shrunk by more than 25%. At present, more than one out of four workers is unemployed (one out of two among the nation's youth), and more than one million jobs have disappeared. The prospects for improvement, given the austerity policies imposed under the third bailout agreement, are dim at best. "No legislation can guarantee even the most basic labor rights," Lena says in describing the way employers have used the specter of unemployment to further reduce wages. "It's no wonder," she adds, "that so many well-educated young people choose to leave the country."

Since the unemployment rate for people with higher education is nearly 20%—the highest in the world—more than 200,000 young Greeks have left the country in search of better opportunities abroad. I discussed Greece's brain drain with Victoria, 18, a first-year electrical and computer engineering student at the University of Thessaly. "Don't be mistaken," she says, "all those young people that seek a better life abroad care deeply for Greece and won't hesitate to return once things have improved." Victoria herself is already considering leaving Greece once she finishes her studies. Who can blame her? She is highly unlikely to find a job in her field after graduation.

## Collapse of Production

Austerity policies have also led the country's productive sector to near collapse, with industrial production in 2015 down by a staggering 35% compared to its level in 2008. Industrial production currently represents less than 10% of Greece's GDP, an exceptionally low level historically for the country, as well as for the eurozone today.

To be sure, the deindustrialization of the Greek economy started a lot earlier, in the early 1980s. The country's new development model, after its integration into the

European Community and the emerging Single Market, systematically favored the tertiary (services) sector and ignored the primary (agriculture, mining, etc.) and secondary (manufacturing) sectors. Greek industries, accustomed to the heavy protectionist measures of the post-war period and poorly prepared for the requirements of market integration and the liberalization of trade, failed to adapt. The massive influx of European funds to the tertiary sector (mainly tourism) shaped a services-centered economy (the services sector contributes over 80% to the country's GDP), while weakening the country's competitiveness and contributing decisively to the dismantling of its industrial base.

Things got immeasurably worse after 2009. During the recession, about 250,000 small and medium-sized enterprises closed down. Many more have been forced to the verge of closure due to reduced revenues and increased financial obligations to social security funds, tax offices, and banks. Thousands of small business owners have opted to relocate to neighboring Balkan countries, which offer lower labor costs and corporate tax breaks.

"Reality has shown that the austerity measures applied across Europe are not the most effective response to the crisis," says Costas, a civil engineer from Patra, Greece's third largest city, in the southern region of the Peloponnese. Costas is 45 years old and a former member of SYRIZA, the current governing party. "No other country in the eurozone has had to impose such far-reaching austerity programs," he says, "and I just don't see how Greek society can sustain the burden of yet another bailout."

The policy is simply not working, even on its own terms. After five years of austerity and three bailout agreements, Greece's national debt of 320 billion euros is right where it was in 2010. But its debt-to-GDP ratio has shot up to 175% (compared to 150% in 2010), and the European Commission projects that it will rise to 200% in 2016. The country's destroyed economy will never be able to repay this huge volume of debt.

## SYRIZA U-Turn, Popular Disillusionment

Originally elected in January 2015 on a vehement anti-austerity platform, Greek Prime Minister Alexis Tsipras subsequently made a complete U-turn. Ignoring the popular outcry against austerity, loudly expressed in a referendum on July 5, 2016, he has given in to the creditors' demands. In August, SYRIZA and the creditors signed a new bailout agreement, including not only another round of austerity measures but also neocolonial restrictions on Greece's national sovereignty. No legislation related to the objectives of the bailout, however minor, can be taken by Greece's political institutions without the prior approval of its creditors. The creditors thus have the right to monitor the Greek government and to wield veto power over virtually all policy measures in Greece.

And yet, on September 20, 2016, Tsipras won a new election, again forming a government. The result seemed to vindicate his capitulation. It appears that Greek voters, confronted with a narrative presenting the new agreement as inescapable, opted to give the governing party a second chance. "This wasn't a vote of hope," says Costas, the civil engineer from Patra, "but a vote for the 'lesser evil' within the limits of a 'nothing can really change' mentality."

Costas is even convinced that if there were another general election soon, the governing party would still emerge victorious. Greek voters appear to think that there is no credible alternative to austerity. "Ever since the PM marginalized any voices in SYRIZA that tried to show a different way and declared there was no alternative," he says, "Greek society, having lost its morale, has come to accept its fate."

## Defeat and Apathy

To fully understand the popular mood, one must look at the abstention rates in the recent election. Turnout plummeted, with a record-high abstention rate of 45%. In addition, blank ballots reached an extraordinary 2.5%. The message is quite clear: the Greek people's disappointment has led to a massive rejection of the political process altogether. Victoria tells me that most of her friends either cast a blank ballot or didn't bother to vote at all since "they didn't believe any of the existing political parties could actually make a difference."

The low turnout was not an isolated incident. During the past few years, social unrest and frustration over the austerity measures have given rise to widespread discontent and large-scale demonstrations. But the decline of the struggle as unemployment began to bite and, especially, SYRIZA's betrayal of popular hopes have led to a wholesale rejection of politics by broad layers of the population. The sense of defeat and indifference is pronounced among workers, and especially the young.

"Wishful thinking," says Costas about SYRIZA's hopes to overturn austerity by creating a domino effect in the countries of the European periphery. The balance of power has proven not that easy to change and now people feel that Greece is being punished for daring to question Europe's neoliberal policies.

European Union officials have categorically ruled out any possibility of a debt write-down. Restructuring in the form of a lengthening of maturity or perhaps a lowering of interest rates is still on the table, but it would have very debatable long-term results. Greece would probably be given more time to get back on its feet, but this would not eliminate short-term financing problems. Besides, even though Greek aid loans are very long-term (over thirty years) and interest rates have already been lowered several times (lower than 1%), the country's national debt is still considered unsustainable.

As for the SYRIZA government's current promise to implement a "parallel" social program that would ease the burden of harsh new austerity policies on poorer Greeks, it has already been forced to withdraw the intended bill following severe objections by the country's creditors. Many of the proposed measures lacked required budget-impact estimates. There were also concerns about the program's compatibility with the conditions of the third bailout agreement. "Parallel" programs running alongside austerity measures are not what the EU has in mind, nor would they be possible to implement within the strict framework of the latest bailout.

## The Prospect of Change

The only real question for Greece at the moment is: Could there be an alternative path?

Not everyone has given in to despondency and apathy. In a school building in central Athens, I meet Georgia, a young teacher and mother of three, who offers extra classes to underprivileged students free of charge. "People would take to the streets because they hoped they could make an actual difference," she says. "Now it is clear that our hopes were false." Nonetheless, she tells me, the economic crisis has made her more politically aware. She now chooses to spend much of her time and energy in political and social movements and social solidarity structures, where she can actually feel useful.

Popular Unity, a new political front including SYRIZA's left wing, which split from the party by refusing to accept the new bailout, has so far offered the only coherent argument about how Greece could adopt an anti-bailout strategy. Its radical program includes the introduction of a new national currency, a deep national debt write-off, a lifting of austerity measures, and a restructuring of the productive sector and the welfare state. However, Popular Unity has so far failed to convince Greek voters, and did not gain parliamentary representation in the last elections.

Social injustice has spurred new modes of resistance far from political parties and trade unions. As the state becomes ever more hostile to the Greek people, many choose to self-organize by forming neighborhood assemblies and solidarity networks that support basic human rights, organizing micro-economies without middle-men, and setting up "solidarity clinics" providing free health care.

This is a period of reflection and finding alternative forms of resistance that could potentially be the basis for something new to emerge in the future. All hope is not yet lost that Greece may regain some economic stability and find a development policy in the interest of its people. "People feel exhausted, defeated and betrayed," says Georgia, "but many refuse to give up." ❑

*Sources:* Eurostat news release 181/2015 (ec.europa.eu/eurostat/documents); Eurostat dataset (ec. europa.eu/eurostat), "Youth unemployment rate," "Long-term unemployment rate," "Production in industry—manufacturing," "Production in industry—total (excluding construction)," "Production in industry—annual data, percentage change," "General government gross debt—annual data"; "Young, gifted and Greek: Generation G—the world's biggest brain drain," *The Guardian* (theguardian.com); C. Pitelis & N. Antonakis (2003), "Manufacturing and competitiveness: the case of Greece," *Journal of Economic Studies*, Vol. 30, Issue 5, pp. 535—547; H. Louri and I. Pepelasis Minoglou (2002), "A hesitant evolution: industrialisation and de-industrialisation in Greece over the long run," *Journal of European Economic Studies*, Vol. 31, No. 2, pp. 321-348; M. Nence, "Greek entrepreneurship after crisis—investment abroad, the easiest solution" (pecob.eu); Kathimerini, "Crisis wipes out a quarter of Greece's SMEs" (ekathimerini.com); September 2015 official election results (ekloges.ypes.gr).

# Chapter 3

# CORPORATE POWER AND THE GLOBAL ECONOMY

*Article 3.1*

## MONOPOLY EVERYWHERE
*Outsized market share isn't limited to big tech.*

**BY ARMAĞAN GEZICI**
*January/February 2020*

In October 2019, 47 attorneys general joined a New York-led antitrust investigation of Facebook with the concern that, according to New York's attorney general, "Facebook may have put consumer data at risk, reduced the quality of consumers' choices, and increased the price of advertising." Earlier the same year, a similar state investigation was launched into Google's advertising practices. At the federal level, the Justice Department is now investigating Facebook and Google, while the Federal Trade Commission is reported to have started an investigation of Facebook and Amazon.

However, concerns about tech companies' market power go beyond issues of data privacy and the way they handle disinformation and hate speech. The increased market power of tech companies and corporations in many other industries have also recently received great attention.

Many U.S. markets and industries are dominated by large corporations. According to data released in 2019 by the Open Markets Institute, Amazon dominates e-commerce, which was a $525.9 billion market in 2018 (around 10% of all retail sales in the U.S.). Google's Android and Apple's iOS hold a 99% share of the market for smart phone operating systems. In retail, Walmart controls 72% of all warehouse clubs and supercenters in the United States. The market shares of Home Depot and Lowe's in home improvement stores add up to a whopping 81%. Combined, Walgreens, and CVS comprise 67% of all pharmacy sales.

Many large corporations have international operations and sizeable global market shares. In a world of high mobility for capital, large corporations are multinational. The locations of their headquarters seem irrelevant to their activities, except for regulatory and tax purposes. Global markets for agricultural seeds and chemicals, for instance, have long been dominated by three companies: Germany's Bayer, which bought U.S. giant Monsanto in 2018; DowDupont, which was the biggest chemical conglomerate in the world until 2019; and Syngenta, a Swiss-based company, which bought agricultural branches of two other global companies, Novartis and Zeneca, in the last decade, and is currently owned by a Chinese state-owned enterprise. Even in industries with a large variety of brands that seem to offer consumers a choice of many companies, many of those brands can be owned by just one company. For example, Anheuser-Busch Inbev, a holding company that was created in 2008 through the mergers of various American, Brazilian, British, and Belgian beer companies, holds a 41% share of the beer market in the United States and owns 55 different brands.

That capitalism would be dominated by monopolies has long been viewed as inevitable by most radical political economy traditions in general and the "monopoly capital school" of Marxism in particular. But the process of monopolization has accelerated in the last couple of decades. Recent research shows that more than 75% of U.S. industries have become more concentrated and the average size of publicly traded firms has tripled since the mid-1990s. Studies also find that, during this period, profitability has risen for firms in industries that have experienced increases in concentration levels. Many of these larger and more profitable firms, such as those mentioned above, are found to be in the retail, information, transportation, and warehousing sectors of the economy. Thanks to their dominant positions in their respective markets, these companies can easily increase the prices of products or reduce the cost of production. Before giving examples of how they achieve higher price-cost margins and profitability, let us first take a look at one big change that allowed the current monopolization in the U.S. economy to occur.

## Behind the Recent Wave of Monopolization

An increased number of mergers and acquisitions are visible in almost all industries. The lax enforcement of antitrust laws has much to do with the uptick in mergers and acquisitions. The Sherman Antitrust Act of 1890 and other legislation in the decades that followed outlawed any "restraints of trade" that reduce competition and any concentrations of market power that restrict interstate commerce. The Clayton Antitrust Act of 1914, for instance, explicitly blocked mergers that would result in more consolidated industries, and it also forbade interlocking directorates (membership on the board of directors of two or more firms by the same individual). Until the 1980s, these two acts and other industry-specific regulatory laws continued to keep the monopolization of U.S. industries in relative control.

However, after the 1980s, the Department of Justice adopted an entirely new framework for evaluating mergers and acquisitions: instead of considering

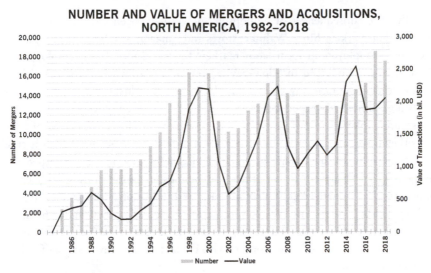

NUMBER AND VALUE OF MERGERS AND ACQUISITIONS, NORTH AMERICA, 1982–2018

the effects on smaller businesses and entrepreneurship, the focus solely shifted to whether a deal would promote "efficiency" and "consumer welfare," with a promise of lower prices. Yet, as seen in the figure above, it was not until the "new economy" boom" of the mid-1990s that the current spate of mergers and acquisitions took off. Over the last two decades, the number of mergers and acquisitions nearly tripled, surpassing the merger wave of the late 1960s and early 1970s. Rising pressures from shareholders in a rapidly financializing economy, coupled with low interest rates and high stock market valuations for mergers and acquisitions, were also responsible for creating the conditions for this expansion. Over the same period, the lack of intervention from regulatory agencies created incentives for firms to engage in mergers and acquisitions, which further reduced competition. A Supreme Court case in 2004 on Verizon's refusal to share its telephone network with its competitor, AT&T, was the perfect example of this paradigm shift. The court unanimously ruled in favor of Verizon, holding that the telecommunications company's "monopoly power" was "an important element of the free-market system," a display of "business acumen," and resulted in "the incentive to innovate."

## Dire Consequences of Monopsony and Monopoly Power

As antitrust legislation became more focused on pricing and how it affects consumer welfare, the regulatory control over monopolies has become further irrelevant for certain industries due to globalization. For the last two decades, the availability of cheap imports and the opportunity to produce globally in low-cost locations has allowed large companies to keep consumer prices relatively low. In particular, retail giants like Walmart have been able to dictate their own terms and prices with suppliers, acting as monopsonies as well as monopolies (for a definition of monopsony, see the sidebar in Article 3.3).

The dire consequences of monopsony power have been particularly notice-able in labor markets. Since Walmart stores and Amazon warehouses are typically the largest employers in local labor markets for low-skilled labor, employees in these areas can be forced into low-paying jobs or precarious working conditions because they don't have any alternatives. In high-tech industries that rely on rela-tively high-skilled labor, non-compete agreements, where employers contractually constrain employees from joining competing companies for some period of time after they leave, are an important component of the U.S. labor market. It is true that monopsony cannot always be equated with monopoly power. Yet, especially in industries with low consumer prices, the monopsony power of these large com-panies in the labor market is as important as the use of cheap foreign inputs in keeping their prices low. While specific monopsonistic practices in the labor market vary greatly across industries, recent studies find that industries with a growing concentration of large firms are also those that pay a lower share of indus-try incomes to their employees.

A stronger case can be made for antitrust regulation in industries with monopolies that can charge extraordinarily high prices. The U.S. pharmaceutical industry is a case in point. Americans spend more on prescription drugs—aver-age costs are about $1,200 per person per year—than people anywhere else in the world. What really sets the United States apart from most other countries is high prices. Unlike other nations, the United States doesn't directly regulate medicine prices. In Europe, the second-largest pharmaceutical market after the United States, governments negotiate directly with drug manufacturers to limit what their state-funded health systems pay. The U.S. pharmaceutical industry's response to demands for price regulation has been that it will kill innovation. U.S. drug companies claim that they need higher prices than those that prevail elsewhere so that the extra profits can be used to augment research and develop-ment (R&D) spending to continue to innovate and patent new drugs. This is far from the reality. A recent academic study shows 18 big pharmaceutical companies listed in the S&P 500 spent more on share buybacks and dividends ($516 billion) in a recent 10-year period than they did on R&D ($465 billion). As these com-panies spend their profits on boosting their stock performance, there has been a prominent productivity decline in drug discovery in the U.S. pharmaceutical industry. According to a working paper by William Lazonick for the Institute for New Economic Thinking, the overall clinical approval success rate declined from approximately one-in-five to approximately one-in-eight during the 2000s. In addition to allocating their profits to activities that maximize shareholder value, pharmaceutical companies also contribute to the decline in the diversity of ideas and research potential through mergers and acquisitions, since there are increas-ingly fewer companies to carry out research.

With Verizon, AT&T, T-Mobile, and Sprint as the only operators, the industry of wireless carriers in the United States is another distinctly high-price industry. U.S. mobile data pricing has been found to be four times more expensive than prices in many European Union countries, which have four wireless carriers instead of three. Economics textbooks tell us about how utilities, such as telecommunications, are "natural monopolies," yet the striking difference between the United States and the European Union need to be understood by differences in regulatory policy. While E.U. governments have forced companies to lease their networks to competitors at cost, U.S. regulators have not done so, allowing a formidable barrier against competitors. In October 2019, the U.S. Federal Communications Commission approved a merger between Sprint (owned by the Japanese conglomerate Softbank) and T-Mobile (owned by Germany's Deutsche Telekom), suggesting that the merger would "enhance competition." Those in opposition to this move estimate that the merger will result in the loss of potentially thousands of jobs in the short term and in the long term, according FCC commissioner Geoffrey Starks, "it will establish a market of three giant wireless carriers with every incentive to divide up the market, increase prices, and compete only for the most lucrative customers." When it comes to shopping for internet services, most Americans typically have just two choices. The first choice is internet providers, many of which—including CenturyLink, Frontier, and AT&T—started out as, or bought, phone companies, giving them control of one of the only physical lines that serve each household. Typically, the second is cable TV providers who, in turn, own the cables that enter almost every home. It appears that the telecommunications companies carve up territory to avoid competing with more than one other provider, effectively creating local monopolies.

Companies gaining market power through mergers and acquisitions claim they benefit consumers by providing better technologies and higher quality products at lower prices thanks to the synergies expected of mergers and acquisitions. This argument fits perfectly within the paradigm of neoliberal economics, which tends to see rising market power as the inevitable result of top firms gaining market share by adopting new technologies that increase their efficiency. In this view, monopolistic companies are "super-star firms" competing either on the merits of their innovations or superior efficiency; the important driver of the monopolization is technological change, not anticompetitive practices. These claims are hard to reconcile with the aggregate economic trends of the last two decades. Since the beginning of the 2000s, despite relatively high corporate profits, the U.S. economy has been in a period of slower capital accumulation marked by weak investment, declining labor share of income, and lower aggregate productivity growth, signaling a slowing down in technological progress and dynamism. This is the same period where a considerable rise of market concentration has occurred in most U.S. industries.

While the causes of increasing concentration and monopolization might be different across industries, there is good reason to doubt the claims of corporations and their advocates, and to look deeper into the negative consequences of increasing monopoly power for workers, suppliers, and consumers in the United States and across the globe. ❑

*Sources*: Letitia James, "Attorney General James Gives Update On Facebook Antitrust Investigation," press release, New York State Attorney General's office, Oct. 22, 2019 (ag.ny.gov); Gustavo Grullon, Yelena Larkin, Roni Michaely , "Are US Industries Becoming More Concentrated?" *Review of Finance*, July 2019; William Lazonick, Matt Hopkins, Ken Jacobson, Mustafa Erdem Sakinç, and Öner Tulum, "US Pharma's Financialized Business Model," Institute for New Economic Thinking Working Paper Series No. 60., July 13, 2017; Standish Fleming, "Pharma's Innovation Crisis, Part 2: How to Fix It," *Forbes*, Sept. 11, 2018; "FCC Clears T-Mobile/Sprint Merger Deal" National Public Radio, Nov. 5, 2019 (npr.org); Chris Zubak-Skees and Allan Holmes, "How broadband providers seem to avoid competition," The Center for Public Integrity, April 1, 2015 (publicintegrity.org).

*Article 3.2*

# IF CORPORATIONS ARE PEOPLE, WHAT KIND OF PEOPLE ARE THEY?

## BY GEOFF SCHNEIDER

*June 2016*

In 1886, the U.S. Supreme Court ruled, in *Santa Clara County v. Southern Pacific Railroad*, that corporations have the same legal status as persons. The legal rights of corporations gradually have been expanded in the United States since that time to include the right to free speech and to contribute unlimited amounts to political campaigns (a product of the Supreme Court's 2010 *Citizens United* ruling). A key question that emerges from U.S. corporate personhood is: If corporations are people, what kind of people are they?

One of the key characteristics of a corporation is that, by its very legal structure, it is an amoral entity. It exists for the sole purpose of making profits, and it will do whatever is necessary to increase profits, without considering ethical issues except insofar as they impinge on the bottom line. A crucial reason for this behavior is that chief executive officers (CEOs) and other executives have a legal "fiduciary duty" to act in the best financial interests of stockholders. As conservative economist Milton Friedman stated in his book *Capitalism and Freedom*, "there is one and only one social responsibility of business—to use its resources and engage in activities designed to increase its profits so long as it stays within the rules of the game, which is to say, engages in open and free competition without deception or fraud." Thus, those who control corporations are obligated to do whatever they can within the law to make as much money as possible.

This can lead to behavior that some have called psychopathic. In the provocative 2003 film, "The Corporation," the filmmakers argue that corporations meet these diagnostic criteria used by psychiatrists to determine if a person is psychopathic:

- Callous disregard for the feelings of others;
- Reckless disregard for the safety of others;
- Incapacity to maintain enduring relationships;
- Deceitfulness: repeated lying and conniving others for profit;
- Incapacity to experience guilt; and
- Failure to conform to social norms with respect to lawful behaviors.

Although at first blush the claim that corporations are psychopaths seems incredible, if we consider the worst behaviors of corporations over the last few decades, and the disturbing frequency with which such behaviors seem to recur, it is possible to see why so many people hold corporations in such low esteem. Below, we describe briefly some of the most horrific behaviors of large corporations in recent years.

## Rana Plaza Building Collapse, 2013:
### *An Example of Corporate Abuses of Subcontracting and Sweatshops*

For decades, U.S. and European clothing manufacturers have been moving their operations overseas to countries with extremely low wages and with few safety or environmental regulations. One of their favorite destinations in recent years has been Bangladesh, where wages for clothing workers are the lowest in the world (only $0.24 per hour until the minimum wage was raised to $0.40 per hour in 2014), and where few safety standards are enforced. Bangladesh now has more than 5,000 garment factories handling orders for most of the world's top brands and retailers, and is second in garment manufacturing output behind China.

In 2013, the Rana Plaza building that housed several clothing factories collapsed, killing 1,134 people in the worst disaster in garment-industry history. It was later discovered that the building was constructed with substandard materials in violation of building codes. Even more disturbing was the fact that the owners of the factories insisted that employees return to work even after an engineer inspected the building the day before the collapse and deemed it unsafe due to cracks in the walls and clear structural deficiencies. The factories were making clothes for Walmart, Benetton, and many other large, multinational companies.

Disasters like this one, along with the torture and killing of a Bangladeshi labor activist in 2012, are a product of the subcontracting system used by large clothing manufacturers. The corporations issue specifications for the garments that they want to have manufactured, and contractors around the world bid for the right to make the garments. The lowest bidder wins. But what kind of factory is likely to have the lowest bid? Given the regular occurrence of disasters and labor abuses in garment factories, it appears that the contractors who win bids are those who are the most likely to pay workers the least under the most unsafe conditions. Huge multinational clothing companies are only too eager to participate, while at the same time claiming that they are not responsible for the deaths and abuses because they themselves were not the factory owners. The factory owners in Bangladesh were charged with murder, but there were no major consequences for the clothing companies. The callous disregard for the feelings and safety of others and incapacity to experience guilt that many clothing manufacturers display is certainly consistent with the definition of a psychopath.

## BP Oil Spill in the Gulf of Mexico, 2010:
### *Taking Chances with People's Lives and the Environment*

The 2010 BP oil spill in the Gulf of Mexico was the worst in U.S. history. The Deepwater Horizon oil rig exploded on April 20, 2010, killing 11 people and spilling 210 million gallons of oil into the Gulf. Investigations into the causes of the spill indicated significant negligence.

- Deepwater drilling procedures were adapted from shallow-water techniques, without adequate consideration of the differences of the deep-water environment.
- Federal regulators relaxed requirements for environmental reviews, tests, and safety plans at the request of BP, and encouraged but did not require key backup systems.
- BP used well casings, cement, and other equipment that violated company safety guidelines and industry best practices, despite concerns raised by BP engineers.
- Warning signs were ignored, and safety tests delayed despite the warning signs.

The human and environmental costs of the spill were devastating. In addition to the human deaths, millions of birds, turtles, dolphins, and fish were killed. The Gulf tourism industry was devastated for several years, costing businesses $23 billion in lost revenue. And the Gulf still has not recovered, with ongoing problems cropping up related to the environment and wildlife.

The primary culprit here was BP's relentless pursuit of lower costs. Poor quality materials plus skimping on safety measures created conditions for the explosion and meant that BP was unable to deal with the disaster once it happened. Although BP was found guilty of negligence and fined a record $18.7 billion, that amount was only about 8% of their annual revenue, and no BP official went to prison.

## ExxonMobil and Climate Change Denial, 1981–2008:
### *Lying to People for Profit*

In 1981, a team of researchers at Exxon conclusively established the connection between thew burning of fossil fuels, the spewing of greenhouse gases into the air (especially carbon), and climate change. Their research was supported by dozens of other studies by climate scientists. These studies have been so convincing that over 97% of climate scientists agree that climate change is occurring and that human activity is a significant cause. As anyone who studies scientific research will know, it is rare to have near-universal agreement on something as complex as climate change, which helps us to understand that the evidence for climate change is overwhelming.

Despite this evidence, Exxon, which merged with Mobil in 1999, spent millions of dollars on a public-relations effort to deny the existence of climate change so that they could continue to sell as much of their oil as possible. As documented in the book *Merchants of Doubt* (later adapted as a film of the same name), Exxon funded foundations who paid a small group of scientists and public-relations professionals to cast doubt on the idea of climate change in order to prevent action from being taken. And their impact in the United States was dramatic. While much of the world was taking climate change seriously and enacting policies to begin reducing greenhouse gas emissions, the United States was increasing its use of fossil fuels and its emissions.

ExxonMobil now states publicly that it accepts the idea that climate change is occurring, and the company has stopped formally funding climate change denialism. However, ExxonMobil's reduction in public funding of denialism has coincided with a dramatic increase in untraceable "dark money" being used to fund climate change denialism. One cannot help but wonder who is funding such efforts.

Thanks to ExxonMobil and others who have prevented progress on climate change, we are now faced with the prospect of dramatic climate events that will cost many people their lives. We are likely to see increasing droughts, food shortages, heat waves, sea-level rise, floods, and other disasters that threaten our very existence. All so that ExxonMobil and other giant companies could sell more barrels of oil. As is so often the case, there have been no criminal prosecutions related to these incidents.

## Enron's Fraudulent Use of Derivatives and Shell Companies, 1990–2002:
*Financial Deregulation Plus Executive Stock Options are a Toxic Mix*

One of the arguments in favor of corporations is that, thanks to the profit motive, they tend to innovate in order to make money. But, what kind of innovations might result from the profit motive? Enron executives Kenneth Lay and Jeffrey Skilling used the deregulated environment in financial markets in the 1990s and early 2000s (the same environment that also produced the financial crisis) to create an innovative financial model build on fraud and subterfuge.

Enron was the world's largest energy trading company, with a market value of $68 billion. But its real innovation was in shady accounting practices. Enron would start by undertaking a legitimate investment, such as building a power plant. They would then immediately claim all of the expected profit from the power plant on their books, even though they had yet to make any money on the investment, making them appear to be an incredibly profitable company. If the power-plant profits ever came in below expectations, Enron would transfer the unprofitable assets to a shell company—a company that did not really exist formally, other than as a vehicle for Enron to dispose of losses—thereby hiding Enron's losses from its investors. Shell-company investors were given shares of Enron common stock to compensate them for the shell-company losses. Thus, Enron appeared to be incredibly profitable even while it was incurring losses, which caused its stock price to soar.

Much of the reason for this behavior was the incentive system created by financial markets. At the time, most CEOs and highly placed executives were paid most of their salaries in stock options. This meant that they could make more money if they could get the company's stock price to increase, which would allow them to cash in their stock options at a higher value. In theory, paying CEOs in stock options gave them an incentive to run the company in the most profitable way possible, which would then cause the stock price to go up. But stock options also gave executives an incentive to artificially prop up stock prices in order to cash in, which is what the Enron executives did. Meanwhile, the accounting auditors who were supposed to flag questionable and illegal financial transactions looked the other way in order to keep Enron's business.

As Enron's losses mounted, the executives cashed in all of their stock options and left the company bankrupt. More than 5,000 employees lost their jobs and millions of investors lost their savings. Lay, Skilling and 15 other Enron executives were found guilty of fraud. But these sordid events didn't stop an even bigger financial market manipulation from dragging down the entire global economy less than a decade later.

## Goldman Sachs, CMOs, and the Financial Crisis of 2007–2008:
*Betting Against Your Own Clients*

The global financial crisis of 2007–2008 was a product of a number of corporate misdeeds, fueled by greed and the deregulation of financial markets. To increase their profits in the early 2000s, banks started loaning money to extremely risky, subprime borrowers with very poor credit scores to purchase houses. The banks then bundled large groups of these subprime mortgage loans into securities called collateralized mortgage obligations (CMOs). The banks did not care about the creditworthiness of borrowers because they immediately sold these securities to investors.

As more and more subprime borrowers took out mortgage loans, the real-estate market boomed, forming a huge bubble. At the peak of the bubble in 2006-2007, default rates on mortgages started to increase rapidly. Realizing that subprime loans were likely to fail, Goldman Sachs and several other big investment banks began to do something highly unethical: they sold bundles of subprime mortgages (as CMOs) to investors, and they used financial instruments called credit default swaps to bet that the mortgages in the CMOs they sold were going to default and that the CMOs would become worthless. In other words, they sold investors CMO securities that they believed were going to fail, and they even made bets in financial markets that the CMOs they sold would fail. Goldman Sachs was not the only investment bank to do this. Deutsche Bank and Morgan Stanley also engaged in similar transactions to profit at the expense of their own investors.

As in so many other cases of corporate malfeasance, the consequences amounted to little more than a slap on the wrist. Goldman Sachs paid a $550 million fine in 2010 to settle the fraud case brought by the Securities and Exchange Commission (SEC), an amount that was just 4% of the $13.4 billion in profits Goldman Sachs made in the previous year. In 2016, Goldman Sachs agreed to an additional $5.1 billion fine for misleading investors about the quality of the CMOs they sold them. However, not a single Goldman Sachs official went to jail.

## VW Programs Cars to Cheat on Emissions Tests, 2009–2015:
*The Things a Company Will Do to Become #1*

Martin Winterkorn, Volkswagen's chief executive officer from 2007 to 2015, established the goal of making VW the largest car company in the world, and he embarked on an ambitious plan to achieve that goal. Much of his plan hinged on developing fuel-efficient, clean diesel cars as an alternative to hybrids. But, when VW discovered that it could not develop an inexpensive technology to remove pollution without compromising the car's gas mileage and overall performance, they turned to a fraudulent approach. VW programmed 10.5 million cars so that the cars would detect when they were being tested for emissions, and during testing the cars' engines would run in a way that they would meet emissions standards. But when the cars were driven normally, they would spew pollutants at a rate much higher than allowed by law.

A nonprofit group, the International Council on Clean Transportation, discovered the problem when they tested numerous diesel cars in 2013. They alerted the Environmental Protection Agency (EPA), which launched an investigation in 2014. As is so often the case, VW responded to the investigation aggressively, accusing regulators and testers of being incompetent. But additional testing established conclusively that VW cars had been programmed to reduce emissions when tested, and to spew large amounts of pollutants when driven normally. The EPA told VW that it would no longer allow the company to sell diesel cars in the United States in 2015, and accused them of violating the Clean Air Act. Particularly problematic was the fact that VW diesels spewed large amounts of nitrogen oxide, in amounts up to 40 times the legal limit. Nitrogen oxide is a pollutant that causes emphysema, bronchitis, and contributes to many other respiratory diseases. The EPA estimates that the additional pollution from VW diesel cars will cause as many as 34 deaths and sicken thousands of people in the United States. Other studies predicted up to 200 premature deaths.

VW did briefly become the largest car company in the world in July of 2015 when they surpassed Toyota, but since the scandal became public the company has fallen back. On June 27, 2016, VW agreed to pay $14.7 billion in fines to the government and compensation for VW diesel car owners. A criminal inquiry is also underway.

## General Motors' Faulty Ignition Switches, 2005-2007:
### *Why Would Anyone Sell a Product That They Knew Could Kill People?*

Imagine yourself as a CEO or vice president of a major corporation. An engineering report comes across your desk, noting that a part in one of your products is faulty, and that the consequences of that part failing could be the injury or even deaths of some of your customers. Would you still sell the faulty product, even knowing that it might kill people? This is what General Motors (GM) did with its faulty ignition switch.

This particular sordid story starts in 2010, when a 29-year-old nurse named Brooke Melton died in a car crash after losing control of her car. Her parents, who knew that she was a safe driver and that her car had been behaving oddly, sued GM and hired engineering experts to try to determine the cause of the crash. They discovered that the problem was the ignition switch that had been installed on over 22 million GM cars manufactured from 2001 to 2007. The ignition switch could turn from "On" to "Acc" just by being bumped lightly or if the key was on a particularly heavy keychain. The shift from "On" to "Acc" could disable the power steering, anti-lock braking, and airbags and cause the car to stall.

As the investigation progressed, the full scale of GM's deceit became apparent. In 2001, GM engineers initially detected the defective part, labelling it the "switch from hell." Problems with the switch cropped up repeatedly over the next several years. In 2005, internal documents show that GM acknowledged the problem but chose not to fix it because it would be too costly. Instead, they sent a note to GM dealerships telling them to urge customers to use lighter key chains. Each year, people died as ignition switches failed and air bags failed to deploy, but GM continued to hide the problem and refused to recall cars and repair the problem.

Finally, thanks to the Melton lawsuit and government investigations that followed, GM recalled the vehicles and repaired the faulty switch. But not before at least 124 people died in crashes related to the faulty part. GM paid a $900 million fine in 2015, and other settlements with victims brought the total cost of the debacle to $2 billion. While this put a dent in the company's 2015 profits of $9.7 billion, no individuals faced criminal charges for their actions.

## Are Corporations Psychopaths?

Above, we highlighted seven examples of horrific corporate behavior. In each case, corporations exhibited many of the behaviors characteristic of psychopaths, especially a callous disregard for the feelings and safety of others, deceitfulness, avoidance of admitting guilt and taking responsibility for their actions, and failure to respect social and ethical norms and the law. But, are these behaviors typical of powerful, profit-hungry corporations, or are they exceptions?

As we all know, many corporations behave ethically, and many invent useful and innovative products that improve our lives. Yet, every year a certain number of corporations cast ethics and morality to the side and engage in unscrupulous behavior, resulting in economic harm, injury, and even deaths. There appear to be aspects of the corporate structure that encourage such behavior, including the relentless quest for maximum profits, the lack of personal responsibility for any illegal actions taken by the corporation, and the power corporations have to manipulate the legal system and government regulators.

Regarding the last point, one of the elements to every story above was the inadequate efforts of government regulators. The push for deregulation by various politicians directly facilitated many of the above corporate misdeeds. And government regulators are often overmatched by corporate legal teams with almost unlimited resources, which allows many corporations to avoid serious consequences even in cases where they have done something horrible. Even when corporations have been caught red handed in clear violation of the law, the penalties are usually little more than a slap on the wrist and are often far less than the profits from the offense in question. Corporate wealth and power appear to allow them to avoid significant checks on their behavior. Thus, instead of engaging in "open and free competition without deception or fraud," as Milton Friedman hoped that they would, some corporations use deception and fraud with near impunity in order to outdo the competition.

Such problems could be fixed. We need a regulatory system with teeth, where corporate lobbyists don't have undue influence over how they are regulated. And we need real consequences for corporate crime. When corporations find out that their actions or products may harm people, if they refuse to take action and to inform the public and regulators of the problem, the people who make those decisions should go to prison.

Finally, like real people, corporations should face real consequences when they break the law. A corporation that engages in particularly egregious behavior, especially a corporation that does so repeatedly, should face sanctions that have a real impact on executives and stockholders. For cases in which a corporation causes deaths, the corporation should face the "death penalty": having its charter revoked and its assets seized by the public. If stockholders could potentially lose all of their investment in a company that behaved illegally, they would begin checking up on companies and we would see much less illegal and unethical behavior.

Of course, all of these solutions require us to get corporate money out of politics. As long as corporations can buy off politicians, they can continue to act as psychopaths and face very little in the way of consequences. ❑

*Selected Sources:* Julfikar Ali Manik and Nida Najar, "Bangladesh Police Charge 41 With Murder Over Rana Plaza Collapse," *New York Times*, June 1, 2015 (nytimes.com); Julfikar Ali Manik and Jim Yardley, "Building Collapse in Bangladesh Leaves Scores Dead," *New York Times*, April 24, 2013; "One Year After Rana Plaza" (editorial), *New York Times*, April 27, 2014; Lauren McCauley, "Workers Decry Multinationals' Greed Following Disaster in Bangladesh," Common Dreams, April 25, 2013 (commondreams.org); Ian Urbina, "In Gulf, It Was Unclear Who Was in Charge of Rig," *New York Times*, June 5, 2010; Ben Bryant, "Deepwater Horizon and the Gulf Oil Spill—the Key Questions Answered," *The Guardian*, April 20, 2011 (theguardian.com); Douglas Fischer, "'Dark Money' Funds Climate Change Denial Effort," *Scientific American*, Dec. 23, 2013 (scientificamerican.com); Oliver Milman, "Oil Industry Knew of 'Serious' Climate Concerns More Than 45 Years Ago," *The Guardian*, April 13, 2016; Suzanne Goldenberg, "Exxon Knew of Climate Change in 1981, Email Says—but it Funded Deniers for 27 More Years," *The Guardian*, July 8, 2015; Bill Keller, "Enron for Dummies," *New York Times*, Jan. 26, 2002; Gretchen Morgenson and Louise Story, "Banks Bundled Bad Debt, Bet Against It and Won," *New York Times*, Dec. 23, 2009; "Senate Panel Says Goldman Misled Clients, Lawmakers on CDOs," Bloomberg News, April 13, 2011 (bloomberg.com); Guilbert Gates, Jack Ewing, Karl Russell, and Derek Watkins, "How Volkswagen's 'Defeat Devices' Worked," *New York Times*, March 16, 2017.

*Article 3.3*

# NO FRIENDSHIP IN TRADE
*Farmers face modern-day robber barons.*

## BY SASHA BREGER BUSH
*March/April 2015*

Presiding over monopolies in shipping and railroads, U.S. robber baron Cornelius Vanderbilt once said that "there is no friendship in trade." During the 19th century, railroad magnates like Vanderbilt used their concentrated power to increase the price of freight, creating financial hardships for farmers who needed to ship their produce. Likewise, bankers like J.P. Morgan squeezed farmers, who were reliant on credit to get through the growing season, with high interest rates. By the latter part of the century, farmers "found the prices for their produce going down, and the prices of transportation and loans going up," wrote historian Howard Zinn, "because the individual farmer could not control the price of his grain, while the monopolist railroad and the monopolist banker could charge what they liked." The market dynamics set in motion by the robber barons ushered in decades of conflict between farmers and the railroad magnates, motivating populist movements and calls for government regulation of monopolies.

Biographer T.J. Stiles notes that a "blood-chilling ruthlessness infused all [of Vanderbilt's] actions." He continues, "Although Vanderbilt habitually dressed in the simple black-and-white outfit of a Protestant clergyman, his only religion was economic power." This religion of economic power is alive and well in today's global food system and farmers trade with the new robber barons of the global food system at their peril.

The small farmers and laborers who grow and process most of the world's food—who provide one of the few things we cannot live without—are themselves often hungry and poor. That is the simple, central paradox of the global food system.

Much of the explanation for this state of affairs focuses on processes of "unequal exchange." Unequal exchange results from trading relationships between parties with unequal levels of power, between powerful monopolies on the one hand and people who struggle in more competitive markets on the other. Unequal exchange is a mechanism for *exploitation* in the food system; that is, it siphons wealth away from farmers and workers and enriches multinational food and finance corporations.

## Power, Inequality, and Unequal Exchange

Beginning in the 16th century, colonization, industrialization, and globalization have worked to undermine locally self-sufficient systems of food production, gradually replacing them with a system of global food interdependence. In this new system, food production, processing, distribution, and consumption are divided up among lots of different people and communities performing different food-related tasks, often in different parts of the world. In other words, there is now a "global division of labor" in food, and the people within this division of labor (who, these days, represent most of the global population) are dependent upon one another for the food they need to survive.

This new system is hierarchically ordered, with large multinational food and agriculture corporations controlling many aspects of production, processing, distribution, and consumption. Multi-national corporations' (MNCs) dominance over the global food system owes in large part to their *market power*. "Market power" refers to a firm's ability to influence the terms of trade—such as prices, but also quality and production standards—in a given market.

Today's food monopolies have consolidated their power thanks both to changes in national and international laws and regulations and to the policies of international institutions like the World Trade Organization (WTO), World Bank, and International Monetary Fund (IMF), among others. Of course, the capital- and technology-intensive nature of food processing, distribution, and retail these days—a key part of the process of food industrialization—also results in high barriers to entry in these markets. These barriers reduce competition for companies in the food industry.

The global food system is riddled with monopolistic markets, markets in which, on one side, stand only one or a few multinational corporate juggernauts, while on the other side there are many people jockeying for position. Inequalities in market power are magnified by geographical inequalities (e.g., between the global North and the global South), gender inequalities, racial inequalities, and inequalities in standards of living.

## The U.S. Poultry Economy

The U.S. poultry chain is a good example. In the United States, three companies—Tyson, Perdue, and Pilgrim's Pride—control more than 50% of the market in broiler chickens. These large, industrial poultry companies are called "integrators," a reference to the "vertically integrated" poultry chain where big companies own and control almost every stage of the poultry production process. One recent commentator notes: "In fundamental ways, the meat business has returned to the state where it was 100 years ago, a time when just four companies controlled the market with a shared monopoly."

Poultry producers working in Arkansas, Mississippi, Georgia, or Kentucky compete with one another like dogs for scraps from the integrator's table, and thus end up with low incomes, low standards of living, and large debts. Poultry producers are largely "contract growers," meaning that they produce at the behest of the integrators and must accept whatever price the integrators offer for their chickens. In fact, the chickens themselves are actually owned by the integrator, with the "integrated out growers" (poultry producers) owning only the expensive chicken houses that chicks are raised in. The chicken houses are often purchased from the integrators on credit, burdening producers with large debts. Poultry producers also risk injury on the job, income losses associated with dead birds, antibiotic resistance and allergy (stemming

---

### Monopolies, Monopsonies, Oligopolies, Oligopsonies: A Note on Terminology

In a **perfectly competitive** marketplace, no single participant can influence prices because there are so many buyers and sellers, each of which represents only a very small portion of the total marketplace.

By contrast, a **monopoly** is a type of uncompetitive market in which there is only one seller. The classic textbook example is the post-WWII diamond monopoly held by the DeBeers company.

A **monopsony** is a type of uncompetitive market in which there is only one buyer. The classic example is a labor market in a one-factory town; the relationship Walmart has with many of its suppliers is another good example.

An **oligopoly** is an uncompetitive market with only a few sellers (like the U.S. markets for airline tickets), while an **oligopsony** is an uncompetitive market with only a few buyers (like the U.S. market for published books which is dominated by Amazon and Barnes & Noble, or the global market for unroasted coffee beans).

As a shorthand, I refer to all of types of uncompetitive markets as "monopolies," and those companies that enjoy market power as "monopolists." Some economics textbooks technically define an "oligopoly" as a market in which the 50% of the market is controlled by four or fewer firms, while others employ the looser definition noted above.

---

from their regular contact with the antibiotics used to treat sick birds), among other serious risks. While the most risky and costly stage of the process—growing out the birds—is left to poultry producers, the integrators enjoy absolute control, massive profits and minimal competition in virtually every other stage of production. The integrators even operate under a "gentlemen's agreement" of sorts, with each integrator agreeing not to employ the growers contracted by the others, limiting competition among integrators and constraining poultry producers even further.

This trading relationship—between monopolistic integrators on the one hand and poultry producers facing high competition, serious risk, and large production costs on the other—is a stark example of unequal exchange and has concrete implications for the well-being of producers.

In an interview with the *American Prospect* magazine, Mike Weaver, who heads up a West Virginia poultry producer association, describes the tenuous financial position of producers in the United States. Weaver notes that "chicken farmers in his area are settling for almost an entire cent less per pound of meat *than they did in 1975*—when the median household income [in the United States] was around $11,800. ... The number of companies buying livestock from farmers has declined, and the surviving companies have grown bigger by acquiring the smaller firms. For growers, that often means doing business with only one firm."

The inequalities and injustices apparent in the poultry chain are replicated within the corporate hierarchy of integrators like Tyson: there is a dangerous division of labor between those who must compete to survive and those who do not need to do so. Highly paid executives, who are engaged in management work and are secure in their positions, lord over low-paid, interchangeable employees who work with their hands capturing chickens one-by-one at night in the chicken houses or performing dangerous work in slaughterhouses. Most of these managers are white men, while many of the workers that actually capture and slaughter the chickens are people of color, often with insecure immigration status. The Food Empowerment Project notes that workers in meat processing are mostly people of color from low-income communities. Historically populated by African Americans, this workforce has recently witnessed an influx of Latin American workers, with some 38% of workers in meat processing today hailing from outside of the United States.

## The Global Coffee Economy

The power dynamics, inequalities and unequal exchanges apparent in the U.S. poultry chain are replicated in a variety of global food production systems. Take, for example, the global coffee economy, a chain connecting different parts of the global division of coffee labor to one another, taking us downstream from the green coffees harvested in the field by farmers, through various traders and processors, to the cups of roasted coffee consumed by final consumers.

International traders and roasters operate in a very uncompetitive market setting—they are monopolists. The six largest coffee trading companies control over 50% of the marketplace at the trading step along the coffee chain (Neumann Kaffee Gruppe from Germany and ED&F Man based in London are the largest international traders). The roasting stage of coffee production is even more concentrated, with only two companies (Nestle and Phillip Morris) controlling almost 50% of the market. Market power gives these modern-day robber barons influence over prices and other terms of trade, allowing them to place downward pressure on prices they pay to farmers, and upward pressure on the prices they charge to consumers.

This inequality in market power introduces inequalities in incomes and standards of living between different actors in the coffee economy. Unsurprisingly, farmers operating in the shadow of the big traders and roasters have relatively low incomes and standards of living. By contrast, owners, managers, and some workers

---

### Coffee: A Story of Market Power

The global coffee economy is marked by severe inequalities in wealth and power.

Coffee farmers along with small-scale traders and processors, operate in a competitive market environment. Located primarily in the global South, they sell their coffees onward, down the supply chain, to international traders and roasters. The traders and roasters operate in a relatively uncompetitive market environment and are located primarily in the global North. These inequalities in market power result in lower standards of living for coffee farmers and other marginalized actors in producing countries.

Consumers (most of whom are from the global North) also have little negotiating power, when it comes to purchasing coffee from big retailers (supermarkets and corporate café chains like Starbucks). By contrast, the northern monopolies in trading, roasting, and retail earn high profits associated with their disproportionate market power.

Monopolists thus push prices for growers down and prices for consumers up, capturing the super-profits generated in between.

at the big coffee monopolies enjoy relatively high incomes and standards of living. There are also race and gender dimensions to consider: coffee farmers are disproportionately women of color, while owners and managers in the big coffee monopolies are generally white men. There is also a strong North-South dimension to this power inequality—coffee farmers from Latin America, Africa, and Asia compete fiercely with one another, their incomes undermined by the pricing power of monopolies headquartered in Europe and the United States.

Twenty-five million coffee farming families from Latin America, sub-Saharan Africa, South Asia, and Southeast Asia compete globally with one another to sell coffee to a handful of international coffee trading companies. Similar to the situation of poultry producers, there are in practice usually only one or two potential buyers for a farmer's coffee crop. Lacking the transport and information resources to effectively market their crops, many coffee farmers sell to whomever comes to the farm gate. Unsurprisingly, things do not usually go well for our coffee farmers.

The graph below illustrates the distribution of income in the global coffee economy. Only a small percentage of total income is retained by those—growers, small-scale traders who transport coffee from the farm gate, and petty processors who transform dried coffee cherries into green beans in producing countries—who operate in competitive markets. Most of the income is appropriated in consuming countries, mainly by the coffee monopolists in trading and roasting, but also

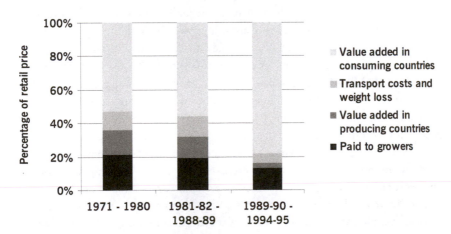

## DISTRIBUTION OF INCOME IN THE GLOBAL COFFEE ECONOMY (% OF INCOME)

*Source*: John M. Talbot, "Where Does Your Coffee Dollar Go? The Division of Income and Surplus along the Coffee Commodity Chain," *Studies in Comparative International Development*, Vol. 32, No. 1 (1997), Tables 1 and 2.

*Note*: Data for 1971–1980 are for calendar years. Data for 1981–82 to 1988–89 and for 1989–90 to 1994–95 are for "coffee years" (Oct. 1–Sept. 30). Percentages of total retail price (reported by Talbot (1997)) for calendar years (1971–1980) or coffee years (1981–82 to 1988–89 and 1989–90 to 1994–95) were used to calculate means for intervals shown. Figures calculated did not add exactly to 100.0% due to rounding (in all cases between 99.9% and 100%). Bar graphs show each income category as percentage of sum of four income categories.

by large retailers (e.g., supermarkets and corporate café chains like Starbucks). The position of coffee growers deteriorated between the 1970s and 1990s. Expanded global trade in coffee since the late 1980s, with "free trade" increasing the market leverage of multinational traders and roasters over coffee farmers and final consumers, has led to decreasing relative income of growers.

## Promoting Justice and Equity in the Global Food System

As the coffee and chicken examples suggest, unequal exchange is commonplace between farmers and producers on the one hand, and multinational, monopolistic middlemen (food traders, processors, and supermarkets) on the other. While larger corporate coffee farms may have some leverage in negotiating prices with these big middlemen, smaller and peasant farms have virtually no negotiating power. If a coffee farmer does not want to sell to the Neumann Kaffee Gruppe (NKG) at the price NKG offers, then NKG will simply move on until it finds a farmer who will. Similarly, if a poultry producer does not want to sell to Tyson at the company's offered price, the producer risks being cut out of the chain all together. Tyson will just move on to the next farm. In both cases, the market power of the monopolists also allows them to set conditions such as product quality and the specific technologies used in the production process. The same basic relationship holds for cattle ranchers and cocoa farmers selling to Cargill, pork producers selling to Smithfield (now owned by the China-headquartered WH Group), soy farmers selling to Archer Daniels Midland, vegetable producers selling to Walmart and Tesco, and orange producers selling to Coca-Cola Co. (to make Fanta Orange and Minute Maid juices), among many other global examples.

Unequal exchange helps to explain inequalities in wealth and power in the global food system, and how trade relationships work to facilitate exploitation—the unjust redistribution of wealth from people with less to people with more market power, from poor to rich, from black and brown to white, from women to men, from the global South to the global North. In answer to the question posed at the outset—how is it that the people who produce our food are themselves so often poor and hungry?—I answer simply: Because they engage in unequal exchange with powerful food monopolies, and there is no friendship in this trade.

A variety of policies, programs, and alternatives could help to make the global food system more equitable and fair. These include, but are certainly not limited to, anti-trust enforcement, public commodity price management, and producer unionization. In 1890, the U.S. Congress passed the Sherman Anti-Trust Act, a piece of legislation aimed at breaking up some of the large monopolies that dominated the U.S. economy at the time. Among the targets of the new anti-trust enforcers were the big meatpackers. The Supreme Court's 1905 decision in *Swift & Co. v. United States* found the Chicago "meat trust" to be engaging in price-fixing for meat and shipping rates. The case set the stage for more stringent government regulation of monopolies. Since the early 1980s, starting with the Reagan administration, anti-trust enforcement in the U.S. has waned. According to Barry Lynn, the author of

*Cornered: The New Monopoly Capitalism and the Economics of Destruction*, this is partly due to increasingly pro-big business ideologies and political interests of public officials, like Reagan. Yet, the Sherman Act remains on the books and could be revived as a tool to break up the new meat trusts in the U.S. food system.

Historically, governments have also intervened in food markets to set and stabilize prices. While the system was not perfect, the International Coffee Agreement that regulated global coffee trading from 1962 to 1989 did indeed help many coffee farmers obtain better prices for their crops. A system of import and export quotas at the international level was complemented by public institutions at the national level that were responsible for purchasing coffee from producers at fixed prices and then exporting the coffee into the global market according to the quota arrangement. While the system was a mechanism for exploiting farmers in some cases (as in Uganda in the 1970s), in other cases (like in Mexico) public commodity price management helped farmers earn more money and stabilize their incomes. With the eruption of the global food crisis in 2006–2007, global interest in such institutions has been revived, perhaps creating a political opening for new public price management programs.

As with most economic cases in which individuals are overpowered by large companies—be they integrators, coffee roasters, or employers—organization and unionization can help them increase their market leverage and bargaining power. In Colombia, some three quarters of the country's coffee farmers are organized under the umbrella of a single union. The union advocates for farmers in various political forums, and negotiates coffee prices with exporters and traders, often securing higher prices for farmers than they could obtain on their own. Support for such organizations, as well as related farmer cooperatives and producer associations, could help to empower and organize producers.

Such policies and programs are not mutually exclusive. Further, anti-trust enforcement, public price management, and producer unionization could be complemented by a wide variety of other mechanisms for promoting justice and equity in the global food system. For example, programs that support national and local food self-sufficiency, crop and income diversification, and organic farming techniques can potentially reduce producer reliance on global monopolists for income, financing and production inputs, among many other benefits. ❑

*Sources:* Oscar Farfan, "Understanding and Escaping Commodity Dependency: A Global Value Chain Perspective," World Bank, 2005; Food Empowerment Project, "Slaughterhouse Workers," Food Empowerment Project, 2015 (foodispower.org); Michael Kazin, "Ruthless in Manhattan," *New York Times*, May 7, 2009; Christopher Leonard, "How the Meat Industry Keeps Chicken Prices High," March 3, 2014 (slate.com); Barry Lynn, "Killing the Competition: How the New Monopolies are Destroying Open Markets," *Harper's Magazine*, February 2012; National Chicken Council, "Vertical Integration," 2015 (nationalchickencouncil.org); Stefano Ponte, "The Latte Revolution," *World Development*, 2002; Monica Potts, "The Serfs of Arkansas," *The American Prospect*, March 5, 2011; Vandana Shiva, "From Seeds of Suicide to Seeds of Hope," Huffington Post, May 29, 2009; Howard Zinn, *A People's History of the United States* (Harper, 2005).

*Article 3.4*

# ENSURING FAIRER INTERNATIONAL CORPORATE TAXATION

**BY ANIS CHOWDHURY AND JOMO KWAME SUNDARAM**
*September 2019, Inter Press Service*

Large transnational corporations (TNCs) are widely believed to be paying little tax. The ease with which they avoid tax and the declining corporate tax rates over the decades have deprived developing countries of much needed revenues besides undermining public faith in the tax system.

The rise of digital giants, such as Google, Facebook, Amazon and Apple, is an additional concern for all countries. Digitalization makes it hard to establish where "production" takes place. Hence, digital tech TNCs' revenues typically bear little relation to reported profits and tax bills.

## Corporate Tax Rules Favor Rich Countries

Through the Organization for Economic Cooperation and Development (OECD), developed economies have long set corporate tax rules, without much consideration for the effects on developing countries' revenues. United Nations initiatives on profit shifting and tax avoidance have been largely resisted by developed countries. At the Third UN Financing for Development Conference in Addis Ababa in mid-2015, developing countries failed to "elevate" the UN Tax Committee into an inter-governmental body. Even more modest efforts to strengthen it failed, due to opposition from developed countries.

On-going efforts—under the OECD's Base Erosion and Profit Shifting (BEPS) project to reform international corporate tax rules, mandated by the G20—suffer from legitimacy deficits, as developing countries continue to be marginalized, with only consultative roles.

BEPS Actions were decided by a group of 44 OECD, OECD accession countries and G20 members. Although the UN set up a subcommittee to facilitate inputs into the BEPS process from developing countries, the UN Committee of Tax Experts remains marginalized.

The so-called BEPS Inclusive Framework (IF) tries to ensure that OECD-set standards are enforced in developing countries even though their legitimate concerns remain unresolved, while unilateral actions by developed countries continue to harm them.

The OECD designed BEPS still allows companies to move their profits anywhere legally via "transfer pricing" to take advantage of low-tax jurisdictions which some OECD countries such as Ireland provide. This favours developed countries which can better afford lower corporate tax rates.

Therefore, the latest report of the Independent Commission for the Reform of International Corporate Taxation (ICRICT) argues that BEPS has achieved all it can. Instead, it proposes new tasks, dubbed "BEPS 2.0," urging the OECD to reject transfer pricing.

## Digital Economy Challenge

Recent, highly profitable, "highly digitized," "technology-driven" business models—which rely heavily on intangible assets, such as patents or software, that are hard to value—are another reason for rethinking international corporate taxation.

Assuming links between income, profits, and physical presence now seems irrelevant, triggering new concerns. Countries with many users or consumers of digital services have little or no tax revenue from these companies which insist they have no physical presence there. Current tax systems are unable to prevent egregious tax avoidance by digital TNCs. With their marginal cost of production at zero, all revenue can be taxed effectively without negatively affecting the supply of digital services.

The OECD has been addressing this issue within the BEPS Framework over the past half-decade without reaching consensus. "With no consensus on taxation of the digital economy, some countries have resorted to unilateral measures," notes the UN Committee of Experts on International Cooperation in Tax Matters.

The recent unilateral action by France to tax tech giants invoked the U.S. threat of new tariffs on French exports. Clearly, the overriding priority now is to establish an international corporate tax system for the digital economy benefiting both developing and developed countries.

## Unitary Taxation

The ICRICT has proposed that the international taxation system should move toward unitary taxation of multinationals, which would deter their abuse of transfer pricing as global income would need to be consolidated.

Global profits and taxes could then be allocated geographically according to objective criteria such as sales, employment, resources, even digital users in each country. A global minimum effective corporate tax rate of 20-25% of all profits earned by TNCs would be an advance.

The ICRCT also recommended four measures to tackle harmful international tax competition, namely putting a floor under tax competition, eliminating all tax breaks on profits, establishing a level playing field and ensuring participation.

Recent International Monetary Fund (IMF) research has proposed various options and three criteria for consideration: better addressing profit-shifting and tax competition; overcoming legal and administrative obstacles to reform; and fully recognizing the interests of emerging and developing countries.

However, as the UN Committee of Experts emphasized, "the solution should be simple to administer ... and easy to comply with" as "developing countries often neither have the capacity to administer complex solutions nor are they equipped to handle costly international dispute settlement processes."

## IMF and UN Roles

The IMF claims near-universal membership, which enables better understanding of developing countries' problems. It also provides technical support on tax issues to over a hundred countries yearly. But as Fund governance is stacked against developing countries, only the UN can better ensure that developing country interests receive due recognition.

The Platform for Collaboration on Tax (PCT), a joint effort by the IMF, World Bank, OECD and UN, has tried to enhance co-operation on tax issues. As the PCT is not a political body, there is need to recognize the UN Tax Committee as the principal PCT decision-making body to ensure its decisions fairly serve both developed and developing countries.

Countries must work together so that more inclusive, equitable and progressive multilateral coordination can accelerate progress. Clearly, a new approach to international corporate taxation is urgently needed. ❑

*Article 3.5*

# MULTINATIONALS AND OIL COMPANIES ARE IMPOSING THEIR GREED ON THE PEOPLE OF MOZAMBIQUE

BY VIJAY PRASHAD
*September 2020, Independent Media Institute*

Three years ago, on October 5, 2017, fighters with the Al Sunnah wa Jama'ah (ASWJ) entered the town of Mocímboa da Praia in northern Mozambique. They attacked three police stations, and then withdrew. Since then, this group—which has since proclaimed its allegiance to the Islamic State—has continued its battle, including capturing the port of Mocímboa da Praia in August 2020.

Mozambique's military has floundered. Under pressure from the International Monetary Fund (IMF), Mozambique's government has cut the salaries of government employees, including the military. It now relies on private security companies hired by multinational corporations to do its fighting; this outsourcing of defense is permitted by the IMF and wealthy creditors. That is why Mozambique's Ministry of the Interior has hired the South African Dyck Advisory Group (DAG), the Russian Wagner Group, and Erik Prince's Frontier Services Group. Colonel Lionel Dyck, the head of the Dyck Group, recently told Hannes Wessels, who runs the website Africa Unauthorized, that "The Mozambican Defence [Armed] Forces are unprepared and under-resourced."

Dyck, Wagner, and Frontier Services Group are joined in northern Mozambique by a range of other mercenary security forces (such as Arkhê Risk Solutions and GardaWorld) hired by the French energy company Total and the U.S. energy company ExxonMobil. Both firms have interests in the gas fields in Area 1 and Area 4 of Mozambique's Rovuma Basin, which increases the country's natural gas reserves to 100 trillion cubic feet (third only to Nigeria and Algeria in Africa). These firms plan to invest more than $55 billion in the extraction of natural gas and in the construction of liquefaction plants.

Total, the French firm, and Mozambique's government signed a deal to create a joint force to provide security to these gas fields. Mozambique's Minister of Mineral Resources and Energy—Max Tonela—said that this deal "reinforces security measures and efforts to create a safe operating environment for partners like Total."

The narrative fed by Total, Mozambique's government, and the private security firms is that the conflict in northern Mozambique is authored by the Islamists, and that all measures must be taken to thwart this three-year-old insurgency.

## The Forgotten Cape

This area of northern Mozambique—Cabo Delgado—is known colloquially as the "forgotten cape" or Cabo Esquecido. A study of government statistics shows that the people of this part of Mozambique—where the anti-colonial war against the Portuguese broke out on September 25, 1964—experience all of the traps of poverty: low income, high illiteracy, and low morale. The lack of opportunities alongside social aspirations led to the emergence of various forms of economic activity, including artisanal mining for rubies and trafficking of Afghan heroin toward South Africa. The arrival of Islamism simply provided another outlet for the deep frustrations of sections of the population.

It is called the "forgotten cape" because not much of Mozambique's social wealth has come into the communities of the region; though it has not escaped the scourge of the oil and gas companies. These companies—and their predecessors such as Texas-based Anadarko—as well as the other large multinationals such as Montepuez Ruby Mining (owned by the U.K.-based Gemfields) have participated in the eviction of thousands of people from their homes and livelihoods. Given permission by the government in Maputo to settle the land to remove the rubies and the natural gas, these firms have returned little to the people of the north.

## The Phantom of ISIS

There's nothing like the appearance of Islamist groups that fly the flag of ISIS to allow Western firms to set aside their own role in the creation of poverty. Everything becomes about terrorism. In June 2019, two Mozambican scholars—Mohamad Yassine of the Higher Institute of International Relations (ISRI) and Saíde Habibe, who co-authored a 2019 study on Islamic radicalization in northern Mozambique—said that ISIS will not find fertile ground in northern Mozambique; this is largely because the Muslim population in that region is small. These so-called Islamists, Habibe said, are better known for their role in the illicit trades than in the creation of an Islamic State.

A French NGO—Les Amis de la Terre France—published a report in June 2020 that made the point that the insurgency "was built on a tangle of social, religious, and political tensions, exacerbated by the explosion of inequalities and human rights violations linked to gas projects." The militarization of the conflict to protect the gas installations, the NGO argued, "contribute[s] [sic] to fuel the tensions." Indeed, "Human rights violations are on the increase in [these] communities, caught between insurgents, private military and paramilitary forces, multinationals or their subcontractors," the report stated.

South Africa's Institute for Security Studies published a report in October 2019 called "The Genesis of Insurgency in Northern Mozambique." The institute is known to be quite hawkish when it comes to security issues. But reality is too difficult to avoid. This report cautions that "a lasting solution to the extremist violence in Cabo Delgado cannot be brought about by hard power and military might." Social inequality is the main problem. The introduction of the energy firms, rather than bringing prosperity to the people, says the institute, "appears to have brought discontent."

# Interventions

Just off the coast of Mozambique is the island of Mayotte, which is a French possession with a French military base (and which is facing unrest). The governments of France and Mozambique are considering a maritime cooperation agreement, which could eventually allow direct French intervention to protect Total's investments.

At a briefing on drug trafficking in Africa, U.S. Deputy Assistant Secretary of State Heather Merritt said that the issue of the heroin trade is very significant, and that the United States is willing to assist the government in Mozambique in any way.

South Africa's Intelligence Chief Ayanda Diodlo has said that her government is "taking very, very seriously" the threat in northern Mozambique. South Africa is considering a military intervention, despite a warning from ISIS that it would open up a new front inside South Africa if this happens.

Such interventions—by France, the United States, and South Africa—will not solve the problem of northern Mozambique. But they will certainly provide a reason for Western countries to create a military foothold on the continent.

Meanwhile, for the people of Mocímboa da Praia, it would be business as usual. ❑

**Sources**: *OPais*, "Ministry of Higher and Technical-Professional Education passes to the Secretary of State," November 17, 2020 (opais.co.mz); Carta de Mozambique, "How Wagner's Russian mercenaries lost the war against terrorists in northern Mozambique," April 20, 2020 (cartamz.com); e-Global News, "Mozambique: Frontier Services Group to have "closed" agreement with Mozambican company ENHL for security services in Cabo Delgado," August 2, 2018 (e-global.pt); Joseph Hanlon, "Mozambique: Mercenaries to the Fore as Dyck Contract Extended," All Africa, July 27, 2020 (allafrica.com); U.S. Energy Information Administration, "Mozambique—Analysis," July 2020 (eia.gov); Sylvie Rantrua, "Mozambique: this future gas El Dorado," *Le Point*, February 26, 2020 (lepoint.fr); Lusa, "Mozambique / Attacks: Government and Total sign agreement for security of natural gas project in Cabo Delgado," *Visão*, August 24, 2020 (visao.sapo.pt); Carta de Mozambique, "Who is behind the violence in Cabo Delgado?," February 13, 2020 (cartamz.com); João Feijó and Jerry Maquenzi, "Poverty, Inequality, and Conflict in Northern Cabo Delgado," *Observador Rural*, July 2019 (omrmz.org); Jean-Christophe Servant, "In Cabo Delgado, fog of war, drums of internationalization," *Le Monde Diplomatique*, August 13, 2020 (blog.mondediplo.net); Saide Habibe, Salvador Forquilha, and João Pereira, "Radical Islam in Northern Mozambique," *Cadernos IESE*, September 2019 (iese.ac.mz); Carta de Mozambique, "Mohamad Yassine says that Mozambique is not a natural or desirable stage for the Islamic State," June 6, 2019 (cartamz.com); Les Amis de la Terre France, "Mozambique: From Gas El Dorado to Chaos," June 15, 2020 (amisdelaterre.org); David M. Matsinhe and Estacio Valoi, *The genesis of insurgency in northern Mozambique*, Institute for Security Studies, October 2019 (issafrica.org); Ministry of the Armed Forces, "A new naval base in Mayotte," September 19, 2016 (defense.gouv.fr); Nicolas Goinard, "Violence: Mayotte is plagued by gangs of young people who sow terror," *Le Parisien*, August 21, 2020 (leparisien.fr); Adrian Frey, "Mozambique: Military maritime cooperation agreement with France under discussion," Club of Mozambique, July 17, 2020 (clubofmozambique.com); Heather

Merritt, "Telephonic Press Briefing on Drug Trafficking in Africa," U.S. Department of State, July 21, 2020 (state.gov); Qaanitah Hunter, "'We are taking it very, very seriously': Dlodlo on ISIS threat," news24, July 19, 2020 (news24.com); Aymenn Jawad Al-Tamimi, "Islamic State Editorial on Mozambique," Pundicity, July 3, 2020 (aymennjawad.org).

# Chapter 4

# INTERNATIONAL TRADE AND INVESTMENT

Article 4.1

## THE GOSPEL OF FREE TRADE
*The New Evangelists*

**BY ARTHUR MacEWAN**
*November 1991, updated July 2009*

Free trade! With the zeal of Christian missionaries, for decades the U.S. government has been preaching, advocating, pushing, and coercing around the globe for "free trade."

As the economic crisis emerged in 2007 and 2008 and rapidly became a global crisis, it was apparent that something was very wrong with the way the world economy was organized. Not surprisingly, as unemployment rose sharply in the United States, there were calls for protecting jobs by limiting imports and for the government to "buy American" in its economic stimulus program. Similarly, in many other countries, as unemployment jumped upwards, pressure emerged for protection—and some actual steps were taken. Yet, free trade missionaries did not retreat; they continued to preach the same gospel.

The free-traders were probably correct in claiming that protectionist policies would do more harm than good as a means to stem the rising unemployment generated by the economic crisis. Significant acts of protectionism in one country would lead to retaliation—or at least copying—by other countries, reducing world trade. The resulting loss of jobs from reduced trade would most likely outweigh any gains from protection.

Yet the argument over international economic policies should not be confined simply to what should be done in a crisis. Nor should it simply deal with trade in goods and services. The free-traders have advocated their program as one for long-run economic growth and development, yet the evidence suggests that free trade is not a good economic development strategy. Furthermore, the free-traders preach the virtue of unrestricted global movement of finance as well as of goods and services. As it turns out, the free flow of finance has been a major factor in bringing about and spreading the economic crisis that began to appear in 2007—as well as earlier crises.

## The Push

While the U.S. push for free trade goes back several decades, it has become more intense in recent years. In the 1990s, the U.S. government signed on to the North American Free Trade Agreement (NAFTA) and in 2005 established the Central American Free Trade Agreement (CAFTA). Both Republican and Democratic presidents, however, have pushed hard for a *global* free trade agenda. After the demise of the Soviet Union, U.S. advisers prescribed unfettered capitalism for Eastern and Central Europe, and ridiculed as unworkable any move toward a "third way." In low-income countries from Mexico to Malaysia, the prescription has been the same: open markets, deregulate business, don't restrict international investment, and let the free market flourish.

In the push for worldwide free trade, the World Trade Organization (WTO) has been the principal vehicle of change, establishing rules for commerce that assure markets are open and resources are available to those who can pay. And the International Monetary Fund (IMF) and World Bank, which provide loans to many governments, use their financial power to pressure countries around the world to accept the gospel and open their markets. In each of these international organizations, the United States—generally through the U.S. Treasury—plays a dominant role.

Of course, as with any gospel, the preachers often ignore their own sermons. While telling other countries to open their markets, the U.S. government continued, for instance, to limit imports of steel, cotton, sugar, textiles, and many other goods. But publicly at least, free-trade boosters insist that the path to true salvation—or economic expansion, which, in this day and age, seems to be the same thing—lies in opening our market to foreign goods. Get rid of trade barriers at home and abroad, allow business to go where it wants and do what it wants. We will all get rich.

Yet the history of the United States and other rich countries does not fit well with the free-trade gospel. Virtually all advanced capitalist countries found economic success through heavy government regulation of their international commerce, not in free trade. Likewise, a large role for government intervention has characterized those cases of rapid and sustained economic growth in recent decades—for example,

Japan after World War II, South Korea in the 1970s through the 1990s, and China most recently.

Free trade does, however, have its uses. Highly developed nations can use free trade to extend their power and control of the world's wealth, and business can use it as a weapon against labor. Most important, free trade can limit efforts to redistribute income more equally, undermine social programs, and keep people from democratically controlling their economic lives.

## A Day in the Park

At the beginning of the 19th century, Lowell, Massachusetts became the premier site of the U.S. textile industry. Today, thanks to the Lowell National Historical Park, you can tour the huge mills, ride through the canals that redirected the Merrimack River's power to those mills, and learn the story of the textile workers, from the Yankee "mill girls" of the 1820s through the various waves of immigrant laborers who poured into the city over the next century.

During a day in the park, visitors get a graphic picture of the importance of 19th-century industry to the economic growth and prosperity of the United States. Lowell and the other mill towns of the era were centers of growth. They not only created a demand for Southern cotton, they also created a demand for new machinery, maintenance of old machinery, parts, dyes, *skills*, construction materials, construction machinery, *more skills*, equipment to move the raw materials and products, parts maintenance for that equipment, *and still more skills*. The mill towns also created markets—concentrated groups of wage earners who needed to buy products to sustain themselves. As centers of economic activity, Lowell and similar mill towns contributed to U.S. economic growth far beyond the value of the textiles they produced.

The U.S. textile industry emerged decades after the industrial revolution had spawned Britain's powerful textile industry. Nonetheless, it survived and prospered. British linens inundated markets throughout the world in the early 19th century, as the British navy nurtured free trade and kept ports open for commerce. In the United States, however, hostilities leading up to the War of 1812 and then a substantial tariff made British textiles relatively expensive. These limitations on trade allowed the Lowell mills to prosper, acting as a catalyst for other industries and helping to create the skilled work force at the center of U.S. economic expansion.

Beyond textiles, however, tariffs did not play a great role in the United States during the early 19th century. Southern planters had considerable power, and while they were willing to make some compromises, they opposed protecting manufacturing in general because that protection forced up the prices of the goods they purchased with their cotton revenues. The Civil War wiped out the planters' power to oppose protectionism, and from the 1860s through World War I, U.S. industry prospered behind considerable tariff barriers.

## Different Countries, Similar Experiences

The story of the importance of protectionism in bringing economic growth has been repeated, with local variations, in other advanced capitalist countries. During the late 19th century, Germany entered the major league of international economic powers with substantial protection and government support for its industries. Likewise, in 19th-century France and Italy, national consolidation behind protectionist barriers was a key to economic development.

Britain—which entered the industrial era first—is often touted as the prime example of successful development without tariff protection. Yet, Britain embraced free trade only after its industrial base was well established; as in the U.S., the early and important textile industry was erected on a foundation of protectionism. In addition, Britain built its industry through the British navy and the expansion of empire, hardly prime ingredients in any recipe for free trade.

Japan provides an especially important case of successful government protection and support for industrial development. In the post-World War II era, when the Japanese established the foundations for their economic "miracle," the government rejected free trade and extensive foreign investment and instead promoted its national firms.

In the 1950s, for example, the government protected the country's fledgling auto firms from foreign competition. At first, quotas limited imports to $500,000 (in current dollars) each year; in the 1960s, prohibitively high tariffs replaced the quotas. Furthermore, the Japanese allowed foreign investment only insofar as it contributed to developing domestic industry. The government encouraged Japanese companies to import foreign technology, but required them to produce 90% of parts domestically within five years.

The Japanese also protected their computer industry. In the early 1970s, as the industry was developing, companies and individuals could only purchase a foreign machine if a suitable Japanese model was not available. IBM was allowed to produce within the country, but only when it licensed basic patents to Japanese firms. And IBM computers produced in Japan were treated as foreign-made machines.

In the 20th century, no other country matched Japan's economic success, as it moved in a few decades from a relative low-income country, through the devastation of war, to emerge as one of the world's economic leaders. Yet one looks back in vain to find a role for free trade in this success. The Japanese government provided an effective framework, support, and protection for the country's capitalist development.

Likewise, in many countries that have been late-comers to economic development, capitalism has generated high rates of economic growth where government involvement, and not free trade, played the central role. South Korea is a striking case. "Korea is an example of a country that grew very fast and yet violated the canons of conventional economic wisdom," writes Alice Amsden in *Asia's Next Giant: South Korea and Late Industrialization,* widely acclaimed as perhaps the most important analysis of the South Korean economic success. "In Korea, instead of the market mechanism allocating resources and guiding private entrepreneurship, the government made most of the pivotal investment decisions. Instead of firms operating in a competitive market structure, they each operated with an extraordinary degree of market control, protected from foreign competition."

Free trade, however, has had its impact in South Korea. In the 1990s, South Korea and other East Asian governments came under pressure from the U.S. government and the IMF to open their markets, including their financial markets. When they did so, the results were a veritable disaster. The East Asian financial crisis that began in 1997 was a major setback for the whole region, a major disruption of economic growth. After extremely rapid economic growth for three decades, with output expanding at 7% to 10% a year, South Korea's economy plummeted by 6.3% between 1997 and 1998.

## Mexico and Its NAFTA Experience

While free trade in goods and services has its problems, which can be very serious, it is the free movement of capital, the opening of financial markets that has sharp, sudden impacts, sometimes wrecking havoc on national economies. Thus, virtually as soon as Mexico, the United States and Canada formed NAFTA at the beginning of 1994, Mexico was hit with a severe financial crisis. As the economy turned downward at the beginning of that year, capital rapidly left the country, greatly reducing the value of the Mexican peso. With this diminished value of the peso, the cost of servicing international debts and the costs of imports skyrocketed—and the downturn worsened.

Still, during the 1990s, before and after the financial crisis, free-traders extolled short periods of moderate economic growth in Mexico —3% to 4% per year—as evidence of success. Yet, compared to earlier years, Mexico's growth under free trade has been poor. From 1940 to 1990 (including the no-growth decade of the 1980s), when Mexico's market was highly protected and the state actively regulated economic affairs, output grew at an average annual rate of 5%.

Most important, Mexico's experience discredits the notion that free-market policies will improve living conditions for the masses of people in low-income countries. The Mexican government paved the way for free trade policies by reducing or eliminating social welfare programs, and for many Mexican workers wages declined sharply during the free trade era. The number of households living in poverty rose dramatically, with some 75% of Mexico's population below the poverty line at the beginning of the 21st century.

## China and Its Impact

Part of Mexico's problem and its economy's relatively weak performance from the 1990s onward has been the full-scale entrance of China into the international economy. While the Mexican authorities thought they saw great possibilities in NAFTA, with the full opening of the U.S. market to goods produced with low-wage Mexican labor, China (and other Asian countries) had even cheaper labor. As China also gained access to the U.S. market, Mexican expectations were dashed.

The Chinese economy has surely gained in terms of economic growth as it has engaged more and more with the world market, and the absolute levels of incomes of millions of people have risen a great deal. However, China's rapid economic growth has come with a high degree of income inequality. Before its era of rapid growth, China was viewed as a country with a relatively equal distribution of income. By the beginning of the new millennium, however, it was much more unequal than any of the other most populace Asian countries (India, Indonesia, Bangladesh, Pakistan), and more in line with the high-inequality countries of Latin America. Furthermore, with the inequality has come a great deal of social conflict. Tens of thousands of "incidents" of conflict involving violence are reported each year, and most recently there have been the major conflicts involving Tibetans and Ouigers.

In any case, the Chinese trade and growth success should not be confused with "free trade." Foundations for China's surge of economic growth were established through state-sponsored infra-structure development and the vast expansion of the country's educational system. Even today, while private business, including foreign business, appears to have been given free rein in China, the government still plays a controlling role—including a central role in affecting foreign economic relations.

A central aspect of the government's role in the county's foreign commerce has been in the realm of finance. As Chinese-produced goods have virtually flooded international markets, the government has controlled the uses of the earnings from these exports. Instead of simply allowing those earnings to be used by Chinese firms and citizens to buy imports, the government has to a large extent held those earnings as reserves. Using those reserves, China's central bank has been the largest purchaser of U.S. government bonds, in effect becoming a major financer of the U.S. government's budget deficit of recent years.

China's reserves have been one large element in creating a giant pool of financial assets in the world economy. This "pool" has also been built up as the doubling of oil prices following the U.S. invasion of Iraq put huge amounts of funds in the pockets of oil-exporting countries and firm and individuals connected to the oil industry. Yet slow growth of the U.S. economy and extremely low interest rates, resulting from the Federal Reserve Bank's efforts to encourage more growth, limited the returns that could be obtained on these funds. One of the consequences—through a complex set of connections—was the development of the U.S. housing bubble, as financial firms, searching for higher returns, pushed funds into more and more risky mortgage loans.

It was not simply free trade and the unrestricted flow of international finance that generated the housing bubble and subsequent crisis in the U.S. economy. However, the generally unstable global economy—both in terms of trade and finance—that has emerged in the free trade era was certainly a factor bringing about the crisis. Moreover, as is widely recognized, it was not only the U.S. economy and U.S. financial institutions that were affected. The free international flow of finance has meant that banking has become more and more a global industry. So as the U.S. banks got in trouble in 2007 and 2008, their maladies spread to many other parts of the world.

# The Uses of Free Trade

While free trade is not the best economic growth or development policy and, especially through the free flow of finance, can precipitate financial crises, the largest and most powerful firms in many countries find it highly profitable. As Britain preached the loudest sermons for free trade in the early 19th century, when its own industry was already firmly established, so the United States—or at least many firms based in the United States—find it a profitable policy at the beginning of the 21st century. The Mexican experience provides an instructive illustration.

For U.S. firms, access to foreign markets is a high priority. Mexico may be relatively poor, but with a population of 105 million it provides a substantial market. Furthermore, Mexican labor is cheap relative to U.S. labor; and using modern production techniques, Mexican workers can be as productive as workers in the United States. For U.S. firms to obtain full access to the Mexican market, the United States has to open its borders to Mexican goods. Also, if U.S. firms are to take full advantage of cheap foreign labor and sell the goods produced abroad to U.S. consumers, the United States has to be open to imports.

On the other side of the border, wealthy Mexicans face a choice between advancing their interests through national development or advancing their interests through ties to U.S. firms and access to U.S. markets. For many years, they chose the former route. This led to some development of the Mexican economy but also—due to corruption and the massive power of the ruling party, the PRI—huge concentrations of wealth in the hands of a few small groups of firms and individuals. Eventually, these groups came into conflict with their own government over regulation and taxation. Having benefited from government largesse, they came to see their fortunes in greater freedom from government control and, particularly, in greater access to foreign markets and partnerships with large foreign companies. National development was a secondary concern when more involvement with international commerce would produce greater riches more quickly.

In addition, the old program of state-led development in Mexico ran into severe problems. These problems came to the surface in the 1980s with the international debt crisis. Owing huge amounts of money to foreign banks, the Mexican government was forced to respond to pressure from the IMF, the U.S. government, and large international banks which sought to deregulate Mexico's trade and investment. That pressure meshed with the pressure from Mexico's own richest elites, and the result was the move toward free trade and a greater opening of the Mexican economy to foreign investment.

Since the early 1990s, these changes for Mexico and the United States (as well as Canada) have been institutionalized in NAFTA. The U.S. government's agenda since then has been to spread free trade policies to all of the Americas through more regional agreements like CAFTA and ultimately through a Free Trade Area of the Americas. On a broader scale, the U.S. government works through the WTO, the IMF, and the World Bank to open markets and gain access to resources beyond the Western Hemisphere. In fact, while markets remain important everywhere, low-wage manufacturing is increasingly concentrated in Asia—especially China—instead of Mexico or Latin America.

The Chinese experience involves many of the same advantages for U.S. business as does the Mexican—a vast market, low wages, and an increasingly productive labor force. However, the Chinese government, although it has liberalized the economy a great deal compared to the pre-1985 era, has not abdicated its major role in the economy. For better (growth) and for worse (inequality and repression), the Chinese government has not embraced free trade.

## Who Gains, Who Loses?

Of course, in the United States, Mexico, China and elsewhere, advocates of free trade claim that their policies are in everyone's interest. Free trade, they point out, will mean cheaper products for all. Consumers in the United States, who are mostly workers, will be richer because their wages will buy more. In Mexico and China, on the one hand, and in the United States, on the other hand, they argue that rising trade will create more jobs. If some workers lose their jobs because cheaper imported goods are available, export industries will produce new jobs.

In recent years this argument has taken on a new dimension with the larger entrance of India into the world economy and with the burgeoning there of jobs based in information technology—programming and call centers, for example. This "out-sourcing" of service jobs has received a great deal of attention and concern in the United States. Yet free-traders have defended this development as good for the U.S. economy as well as for the Indian economy.

Such arguments obscure many of the most important issues in the free trade debate. Stated, as they usually are, as universal truths, these arguments are just plain silly. No one, for example, touring the Lowell National Historical Park could seriously argue that people in the United States would have been better off had there been no tariff on textiles. Yes, in 1820, they could have purchased textile goods more cheaply, but in the long run the result would have been less industrial advancement and a less wealthy nation. One could make the same point with the Japanese auto and computer industries, or indeed with numerous other examples from the last two centuries of capitalist development.

In the modern era, even though the United States already has a relatively developed economy with highly skilled workers, a freely open international economy does not serve the interests of most U.S. workers, though it will benefit large firms. U.S. workers today are in competition with workers around the globe. Many different workers in many different places can produce the same goods and services. Thus, an international economy governed by the free trade agenda will tend to bring down wages for many U.S. workers. This phenomenon has certainly been one of the factors leading to the substantial rise of income inequality in the United States during recent decades.

The problem is not simply that of workers in a few industries—such as auto and steel, or call-centers and computer programming—where import competition is an obvious and immediate issue. A country's openness to the international economy affects the entire structure of earnings in that country. Free trade forces down the general level of wages across the board, even of those workers not directly affected by imports. The simple fact is that when companies can produce the same products in several different places, it is owners who gain because they can move their factories and funds around much more easily than workers can move themselves around. Capital is mobile; labor is much less mobile. Businesses, more than workers, gain from having a larger territory in which to roam.

## Control Over Our Economic Lives

But the difficulties with free trade do not end with wages. In both low-income and high-income parts of the world, free trade is a weapon in the hands of business when it opposes any progressive social programs. Efforts to place environmental restrictions on firms are met with the threat of moving production abroad. Higher taxes to improve the schools? Business threatens to go elsewhere. Better health and safety regulations? The same response.

Some might argue that the losses from free trade for people in the United States will be balanced by gains for most people in poor countries—lower wages in the United States, but higher wages in Mexico and China. Free trade, then, would bring about international equality. Not likely. In fact, as pointed out above, free trade reforms in Mexico have helped force down wages and reduce social welfare programs, processes rationalized by efforts to make Mexican goods competitive on international markets. China, while not embracing free trade, has seen its full-scale entrance into global commerce accompanied by increasing inequality.

Gains for Mexican or Chinese workers, like those for U.S. workers, depend on their power in relation to business. Free trade or simply the imperative of international "competitiveness" are just as much weapons in the hands of firms operating in Mexico and China as they are for firms operating in the United States. The great mobility of capital is business's best trump card in dealing with labor and popular demands for social change—in the United States, Mexico, China and elsewhere.

None of this means that people should demand that their economies operate as fortresses, protected from all foreign economic incursions. There are great gains that can be obtained from international economic relations—when a nation manages those relations in the interests of the great majority of the people. Protectionism often simply supports narrow vested interests, corrupt officials, and wealthy industrialists. In rejecting free trade, we should move beyond traditional protectionism.

Yet, at this time, rejecting free trade is an essential first step. Free trade places the cards in the hands of business. More than ever, free trade would subject us to the "bottom line," or at least the bottom line as calculated by those who own and run large companies. ❑

*Article 4.2*

# COMPARATIVE ADVANTAGE

## BY RAMAA VASUDEVAN
*July/August 2007; revised November 2018*

Dear Dr. Dollar:

When economists argue that the outsourcing of jobs might be a plus for the U.S. economy, they often mention the idea of comparative advantage. Free trade, they say, would create higher-paying jobs than the ones that would be outsourced. But is it really true that free trade leads to universal benefits?
—*David Goodman, Boston, Mass.*

You're right: The purveyors of the free-trade gospel do invoke the doctrine of comparative advantage to dismiss widespread concerns about the export of jobs. Attributed to 19th-century British political-economist David Ricardo, the doctrine says that a nation always stands to gain if it exports the goods it produces *relatively* more cheaply in exchange for goods that it can get *comparatively* more cheaply from abroad. Free trade would lead to each country specializing in the products it can produce at *relatively* lower costs. Such specialization allows both trading partners to gain from trade, the theory goes, even if in one of the countries production of *both* goods costs more in absolute terms.

For instance, suppose that in the United States to produce one car requires 40 hours of labor time and to produce one ton of rice also requires 40 hours of labor time. Suppose, further, that in the Philippines, 80 hours of labor time are required to produce a car and 60 hours of labor time are required to produce a ton of rice. So the in the United States both goods, cars and rice, are produced at less cost than in the Philippines. Since both goods are produced at lower costs in the states, it might seem that there is no point in trading with the Philippines.

Yet, both countries could gain from trade. The United States has a *comparative advantage* in the production of cars, as it cost half as much to produce a car while it costs two-thirds as much to produce rice, as compared to the Philippines. And the Philippines has a *comparative advantage* in the production of rice.

For example, if the United States had not specialized in car production, it could use 4,000 hours of labor time to produce 50 cars and 50 tons of rice. Similarly, if the Philippines did not specialize in rice production, it could prod 7,600 hours of labor time to produce 50 cars and 50 tons of rice. Between the two countries, there would then be 100 cars and 100 tons of rice.

However, if the United States specializes in car production, it can use the 4,000 hours to produce 100 cars; and if the Philippines specializes in rice production, it can use the 7,600 hours to produce 126.7 tons of rice. It is then possible for trade between the two countries to leave them both better off—though which will gain the most depends on the price at which cars and rice are exchanged.

The real world, unfortunately, does not always conform to the assumptions underlying comparative-advantage theory. One assumption is that trade is balanced. But many countries are running persistent deficits, notably the United States, whose trade deficit is now at nearly 7% of its GDP. A second premise, that there is full employment within the trading nations, is also patently unrealistic. As global trade intensifies, jobs created in the export sector do not necessarily compensate for the jobs lost in the sectors wiped out by foreign competition.

The comparative advantage story faces more direct empirical challenges as well. Nearly 70% of U.S. trade is trade in similar goods, known as *intra-industry trade*: for example, exporting Fords and importing BMWs. And about one third of U.S. trade as of the late 1990s was trade between branches of a single corporation located in different countries (*intra-firm trade*). Comparative advantage cannot explain these patterns.

Especially important, comparative advantage is a static concept that identifies immediate gains from trade but is a poor guide to economic development, a process of structural change over time which is by definition dynamic. If, in the example above, the Philippines does produce its own cars, workers will learn by doing and become more productive over time. The skills they develop can be transferred to other activities, leading to more rapid economic growth and changes in the country's comparative advantage. Moreover, manufacturing activity such as car production is often important for its far reaching simulative impacts on an economy, creating supply chains and generating innovation. Thus the comparative advantage tale is particularly pernicious when preached to developing countries, consigning many to "specialize" in agricultural goods or be forced into a race to the bottom where cheap sweatshop labor is their sole source of competitiveness.

The irony, of course, is that none of the rich countries got that way by following the maxim that they now preach. These countries historically relied on tariff walls and other forms of protectionism to build their industrial base. And even now, they continue to protect sectors like agriculture with subsidies. The countries now touted as new models of the benefits of free trade—South Korea and the other "Asian tigers," for instance—actually flouted this economic wisdom, nurturing their technological capabilities in specific manufacturing sectors and taking advantage of their lower wage costs to *gradually* become effective competitors of the United States and Europe in manufacturing.

The fundamental point is this: contrary to the comparative-advantage claim that trade is universally beneficial, nations as a whole do not prosper from free trade. Free trade creates winners and losers, both within and between countries. In today's context it is the global corporate giants that are propelling and profiting from "free trade": not only outsourcing white-collar jobs, but creating global commodity chains linking sweatshop labor in the developing countries of Latin America and Asia (Africa being largely left out of the game aside from the export of natural resources such as oil) with ever-more insecure consumers in the developed world. Promoting "free trade" as a political cause enables this process to continue.

It is a process with real human costs in terms of both wages and work. People in developing countries across the globe continue to face these costs as trade liberalization measures are enforced; and the working class in the United States is also being forced to bear the brunt of the relentless logic of competition. ❑

*Sources:* Arthur MacEwan, "The Gospel of Free Trade: The New Evangelists," *Dollars & Sense*, July/August 2002; Ha-Joon Chang, *Kicking Away the Ladder: The Real History of Fair Trade*, Foreign Policy in Focus, 2003; Anwar Shaikh, "Globalization and the Myths of Free Trade," in *Globalization and the Myths of Free Trade: History, Theory, and Empirical Evidence*, ed. Anwar Shaikh, Routledge 2007.

*Article 4.3*

# OUTSIZED OFFSHORE OUTSOURCING

*The scope of offshore outsourcing gives some economists and the business press the heebie-jeebies.*

**BY JOHN MILLER**
*September/October 2007*

At a press conference introducing the 2004 *Economic Report of the President*, N. Gregory Mankiw, then head of President Bush's Council of Economic Advisors, assured the press that "Outsourcing is probably a plus for the economy in the long run [and] just a new way of doing international trade."

Mankiw's comments were nothing other than mainstream economics, as even Democratic Party-linked economists confirmed. For instance Janet Yellen, President Clinton's chief economist, told the *Wall Street Journal*, "In the long run, outsourcing is another form of trade that benefits the U.S. economy by giving us cheaper ways to do things." Nonetheless, Mankiw's assurances were met with derision from those uninitiated in the economics profession's free-market ideology. Sen. John Edwards (D-N.C.) asked, "What planet do they live on?" Even Republican House Speaker Dennis Hastert (Ill.) said that Mankiw's theory "fails a basic test of real economics."

Mankiw now jokes that "if the American Economic Association were to give an award for the Most Politically Inept Paraphrasing of Adam Smith, I would be a leading candidate." But he quickly adds, "the recent furor about outsourcing, and my injudiciously worded comments about the benefits of international trade, should not eclipse the basic lessons that economists have understood for more than two centuries."

In fact Adam Smith never said any such thing about international trade. In response to the way Mankiw and other economists distort Smith's writings, economist Michael Meeropol took a close look at what Smith actually said; he found that Smith used his invisible hand argument to favor domestic investment over far-flung, hard-to-supervise foreign investments. Here are Smith's words in his 1776 masterpiece, *The Wealth of Nations*:

> By preferring the support of domestic to that of foreign industry, he [the investor] intends only his own security; and by directing that industry in such a manner as its produce may be of the greatest value, he intends only his own gain, and he is in this, as in many other cases, led by an invisible hand to promote an end, which was no part of his intention.

Outsized offshore outsourcing, the shipping of jobs overseas to take advantage of low wages, has forced some mainstream economists and some elements of the business press to have second thoughts about "free trade." Many are convinced that the painful transition costs that hit before outsourcing produces any ultimate benefits may be the biggest political issue in economics for a generation. And some recognize, as Smith did, that there is no guarantee unfettered international trade will leave the participants better off even in the long run.

## Keynes's Revenge

Writing during the Great Depression of the 1930s, John Maynard Keynes, the pre-eminent economist of the twentieth century, prescribed government spending as a means of compensating for the instability of private investment. The notion of a mixed private/government economy, Keynes's prosthesis for the invisible hand of the market, guided U.S. economic policy from the 1940s through the 1970s.

It is only fitting that Paul Samuelson, the first Nobel Laureate in economics, and whose textbook introduced U.S. readers to Keynes, would be among the first mainstream economist to question whether unfettered international trade, in the context of massive outsourcing, would necessarily leave a developed economy such as that of the United States better off—even in the long run. In an influential 2004 article, Samuelson characterized the common economics wisdom about outsourcing and international trade this way:

> Yes, good jobs may be lost here in the short run. But …the gains of the winners from free trade, properly measured, work out to exceed the losses of the losers. … Never forget to tally the real gains of consumers alongside admitted possible losses of some producers. … The gains of the American winners are big enough to more than compensate the losers.

Samuelson took on this view, arguing that this common wisdom is "dead wrong about [the] *necessary* surplus of winning over losing" [emphasis in the original]. In a rather technical paper, he demonstrated that free trade globalization can sometimes give rise to a situation in which "a productivity gain in one country can benefit that

---

### Offshored? Outsourced? Confused?

The terms "offshoring" and "outsourcing" are often used interchangeably, but they refer to distinct processes:

*Outsourcing*—When a company hires another company to carry out a business function that it no longer wants to carry on in-house. The company that is hired may be in the same city or across the globe; it may be a historically independent firm or a spinoff of the first company created specifically to outsource a particular function.

*Offshoring* or *Offshore Outsourcing*—When a company shifts a portion of its business operation abroad. An offshore operation may be carried out by the same company or, more typically, outsourced to a different one.

country alone, while permanently hurting the other country by reducing the gains from trade that are possible between the two countries."

Many in the economics profession do admit that it is hard to gauge whether intensified offshoring of U.S. jobs in the context of free-trade globalization will give more in winnings to the winners than it takes in losses from the losers. "Nobody has a clue about what the numbers are," as Robert C. Feenstra, a prominent trade economist, told *BusinessWeek* at the time.

The empirical issues that will determine whether offshore outsourcing ultimately delivers, on balance, more benefits than costs, and to whom those benefits and costs will accrue, are myriad. First, how wide a swath of white-collar workers will see their wages reduced by competition from the cheap, highly skilled workers who are now becoming available around the world? Second, by how much will their wages drop? Third, will the U.S. workers thrown into the global labor pool end up losing more in lower wages than they gain in lower consumer prices? In that case, the benefits of increased trade would go overwhelmingly to employers. But even employers might lose out depending on the answer to a fourth question: Will cheap labor from abroad allow foreign employers to out-compete U.S. employers, driving down the prices of their products and lowering U.S. export earnings? In that case, not only workers, but the corporations that employ them as well, could end up worse off.

## Bigger Than A Box

Another mainstream Keynesian economist, Alan Blinder, former Clinton economic advisor and vice-chair of the Federal Reserve Board, doubts that outsourcing will be "immiserating" in the long run and still calls himself "a free-trader down to his toes." But Blinder is convinced that the transition costs will be large, lengthy, and painful before the United States experiences a net gain from outsourcing. Here is why.

First, rapid improvements in information and communications technology have rendered obsolete the traditional notion that manufactured goods, which can generally be boxed and shipped, are tradable, while services, which cannot be boxed, are not. And the workers who perform the services that computers and satellites have now rendered tradable will increasingly be found offshore, especially when they are skilled and will work for lower wages.

Second, another 1.5 billion or so workers—many in China, India, and the former Soviet bloc—are now part of the world economy. While most are low-skilled workers, some are not; and as Blinder says, a small percentage of 1.5 billion is nonetheless "a lot of willing and able people available to do the jobs that technology will move offshore." And as China and India educate more workers, offshoring of high-skill work will accelerate.

Third, the transition will be particularly painful in the United States because the U.S. unemployment insurance program is stingy, at least by first-world standards, and because U.S. workers who lose their jobs often lose their health insurance and pension rights as well.

How large will the transition cost be? "Thirty million to 40 million U.S. jobs are potentially offshorable," according to Blinder's latest estimates. "These include scientists, mathematicians and editors on the high end and telephone operators, clerks and typists on the low end."

Blinder arrived at these figures by creating an index that identifies how easy or hard it will be for a job to be physically or electronically "offshored." He then used the index to assess the Bureau of Labor Statistics' 817 U.S. occupational categories. Not surprisingly, Blinder classifies almost all of the 14.3 million U.S. manufacturing jobs as offshorable. But he also classifies more than twice that many U.S. service sector jobs as offshorable, including most computer industry jobs as well as many others, for instance, the 12,470 U.S. economists and the 23,790 U.S. multimedia artists and animators. In total, Blinder's analysis suggests that 22% to 29% of the jobs held by U.S. workers in 2004 will be potentially offshorable within a decade or two, with nearly 8.2 million jobs in 59 occupations "highly offshorable."

Mankiw dismissed Blinder's estimates of the number of jobs at risk to offshoring as "out of the mainstream." Indeed, Blinder's estimates are considerably larger than earlier ones. But these earlier studies either aim to measure the number of U.S. jobs that will be outsourced (as opposed to the number at risk of being outsourced), look at a shorter period of time, or have shortcomings that suggest they underestimate the number of U.S. jobs threatened by outsourcing.

## Global Arbitrage

Low wages are the reason U.S. corporations outsource labor. Computer programmers in the United States make wages nearly *ten times* those of their counterparts in India and the Philippines, for example. Today, more and more white-collar workers in the United States are finding themselves in direct competition with the low-cost, well-trained, highly educated workers in Bangalore, Shanghai, and Eastern and Central Europe. These workers often use the same capital and technology and are no less productive than the U.S. workers they replace. They just get paid less.

This global labor arbitrage, as Morgan Stanley's chief economist Stephen Roach calls it, has narrowed international wage disparities in manufacturing, and now in services too, by unrelentingly pushing U.S. wages down toward international norms. ("Arbitrage" refers to transactions that yield a profit by taking advantage of a price differential for the same asset in different locations. Here, of course, the "asset" is wage labor of a certain skill level.) A sign of that pressure: about 70% of laid-off workers in the United States earn less three years later than they did at the time of the layoff; on average, those reemployed earn 10% less than they did before.

And it's not only laid-off workers who are hurt. A study conducted by Harvard labor economists Lawrence F. Katz, Richard B. Freeman, and George J. Borjas finds that every other worker with skills similar to those who were displaced also loses out. Every 1% drop in employment due to imports or factories gone abroad shaves 0.5% off the wages of the remaining workers in that occupation, they conclude.

Global labor arbitrage also goes a long way toward explaining the poor quality and low pay of the jobs the U.S. economy has created this decade, according to Roach. By dampening wage increases for an ever wider swath of the U.S. workforce, he argues, outsourcing has helped to drive a wedge between productivity gains and wage gains and to widen inequality in the United States. In the first four years of this decade, nonfarm productivity in the United States has recorded a cumulative increase of 13.3%—more than double the 5.9% rise in real compensation per hour over the same period. ("Compensation" includes wages, which have been stagnant for the average worker, plus employer spending on fringe benefits such as health insurance, which has risen even as, in many instances, the actual benefits have been cut back.) Roach reports that the disconnect between pay and productivity growth during the current economic expansion has been much greater in services than in manufacturing, as that sector weathers the powerful forces of global labor arbitrage for the first time.

## Doubts in the Business Press?!

Even in the business press, doubts that offshore outsourcing willy-nilly leads to economic improvement have become more acute. Earlier this summer, a *BusinessWeek* cover story, "The Real Cost of Offshoring," reported that government statistics have underestimated the damage to the U.S. economy from offshore outsourcing. The problem is that since offshoring took off, *import* growth, adjusted for inflation, has been faster than the official numbers show. That means improvements in living standards, as well as corporate profits, depend more on cheap imports, and less on improving domestic productivity, than analysts thought.

Growing angst about outsourcing's costs has also prompted the business press to report favorably on remedies for the dislocation brought on by offshoring that deviate substantially from the non-interventionist, free-market playbook. Even the most unfazed pro-globalization types want to beef up trade adjustment assistance for displaced workers and strengthen the U.S. educational system. But both proposals are inadequate.

More education, the usual U.S. prescription for any economic problem, is off the mark here. Cheaper labor is available abroad up and down the job-skill ladder, so even the most rigorous education is no inoculation against the threat of offshore outsourcing. As Blinder emphasizes, it is the need for face-to-face contact that stops jobs from being shipped overseas, not the level of education necessary to perform them. Twenty years from now, home health aide positions will no doubt be plentiful in the United States; jobs for highly trained IT professionals may be scarce.

Trade adjustment assistance has until now been narrowly targeted at workers hurt by imports. Most new proposals would replace traditional trade adjustment assistance and unemployment insurance with a program for displaced workers that offers wage insurance to ease the pain of taking a lower-paying job and provides for portable health insurance and retraining. The pro-globalization research group McKinsey Global Institute (MGI), for example, claims that for as little as 4% to 5% of the amount they've saved in lower wages, companies could cover the wage losses of all laid-off workers once they are reemployed, paying them 70% of the wage differential between their old and new jobs (in addition to health care subsidies) for up to two years.

While MGI confidently concludes that this proposal will "go a long way toward relieving the current anxieties," other globalization advocates are not so sure. They recognize that economic anxiety is pervasive and that millions of white-collar workers now fear losing their jobs. Moreover, even if fears of actual job loss are overblown, wage insurance schemes do little to compensate for the downward pressure offshoring is putting on the wages of workers who have not been laid off.

Other mainstream economists and business writers go even further, calling for not only wage insurance but also taxes on the winners from globalization. And globalization has produced big winners: on Wall Street, in the corporate boardroom, and among those workers in high demand in the global economy.

Economist Matthew Slaughter, who recently left President Bush's Council of Economic Advisers, told the *Wall Street Journal*, "Expanding the political support for open borders [for trade] requres making a radical change in fiscal policy." He proposes eliminating the Social Security-Medicare payroll tax on the bottom half of workers—roughly, those earning less than $33,000 a year—and making up the lost revenue by raising the payroll tax on higher earners.

The goal of these economists is to thwart a crippling political backlash against trade. As they see it, "using the tax code to slice the apple more evenly is far more palatable than trying to hold back globalization with policies that risk shrinking the economic apple."

Some even call for extending global labor arbitrage to CEOs. In a June 2006 *New York Times* op-ed, equity analyst Lawrence Orlowski and New York University assistant research director Florian Lengyel argued that offshoring the jobs of U.S. chief executives would reduce costs and release value to shareholders by bringing the compensation of U.S. CEOs (on average 170 times greater than the compensation of average U.S. workers in 2004) in line with CEO compensation in Britain (22 times greater) and in Japan (11 times greater).

Yet others focus on the stunning lack of labor mobility that distinguishes the current era of globalization from earlier ones. Labor markets are becoming increasingly free and flexible under globalization, but labor enjoys no similar freedom of movement. In a completely free market, the foreign workers would come here to do the work that is currently being outsourced. Why aren't more of those workers coming to the United States? Traditional economists Gary Becker and Richard Posner argue the answer is clear: an excessively restrictive immigration policy.

## Onshore and Offshore Solidarity

Offshoring is one of the last steps in capitalism's conversion of the "physician, the lawyer, the priest, the poet, the man of science, into its paid wage laborers," as Marx and Engels put it in the *Communist Manifesto* 160 years ago. It has already done much to increase economic insecurity in the workaday world and has become, Blinder suggests, the number one economic issue of our generation.

Offshoring has also underlined the interdependence of workers across the globe. To the extent that corporations now organize their business operations on a global scale, shifting work around the world in search of low wages, labor organizing must also be global in scope if it is to have any hope of building workers' negotiating strength.

Yet today's global labor arbitrage pits workers from different countries against each other as competitors, not allies. Writing about how to improve labor standards, economists Ajit Singh and Ann Zammit of the South Centre, an Indian non-governmental organization, ask the question, "On what could workers of the world unite" today? Their answer is that faster economic growth could indeed be a positive-sum game from which both the global North and the global South could gain. A pick-up in the long-term rate of growth of the world economy would generate higher employment, increasing wages and otherwise improving labor standards in both regions. It should also make offshoring less profitable and less painful.

The concerns of workers across the globe would also be served by curtailing the ability of multinational corporations to move their investment anywhere, which weakens the bargaining power of labor both in advanced countries and in the global South. Workers globally would also benefit if their own ability to move between countries was enhanced. The combination of a new set of rules to limit international capital movements and to expand labor mobility across borders, together with measures to ratchet up economic growth and thus increase worldwide demand for labor, would alter the current process of globalization and harness it to the needs of working people worldwide. ❑

*Sources:* Alan S. Blinder, "Fear of Offshoring," CEPS Working Paper #119, Dec. 2005; Alan S. Blinder, "How Many U.S. Jobs Might Be Offshorable?" CEPS Working Paper #142, March 2007; N. Gregory Mankiw and P. Swagel, "The Politics and Economics of Offshore Outsourcing," Am. Enterprise Inst. Working Paper #122, 12/7/05; "Offshoring: Is It a Win-Win Game?" McKinsey Global Institute, August 2003; Diane Farrell et al., "The Emerging Global Labor Market, Part 1: The Demand for Talent in Services," McKinsey Global Institute, June 2005; Ashok Bardhan and Cynthia Kroll, "The New Wave of Outsourcing," Research Report #113, Fisher Center for Real Estate and Urban Economics, Univ. of Calif., Berkeley, Fall 2003; Paul A. Samuelson, "Where Ricardo and Mill Rebut and Confirm Arguments of Mainstream Economists Supporting Globalization," *J Econ Perspectives* 18:3, Summer 2004; Alan S. Blinder, "Free Trade's Great, but Offshoring Rattles Me," *Wash. Post,* 5/6/07; Michael Mandel, "The Real Cost of Offshoring," *BusinessWeek,* 6/18/07; Aaron Bernstein, "Shaking Up Trade Theory," *BusinessWeek,* 12/6/04; David Wessel, "The Case for Taxing Globalization's Big Winners," *WSJ,* 6/14/07; Bob Davis, "Some Democratic Economists Echo Mankiw on Outsourcing," *WSJ;* N. Gregory Mankiw, "Outsourcing Redux," gregmankiw.blogspot.com/2006/05/outsourcing-redux; David Wessel and Bob Davis, "Pain From Free Trade Spurs Second Thoughts," *WSJ,* 3/30/07; Ajit Singh and Ann Zammit, "On What Could Workers of the World Unite? Economic Growth and a New Global Economic Order," from *The Global Labour Standards Controversy: Critical Issues For Developing Countries,* South Centre, 2000; Michael Meeropol, "Distorting Adam Smith on Trade," *Challenge,* July/Aug 2004.

*Article 4.4*

# THE UNITED STATES HAS GIVEN PROTECTIONISM A BAD NAME

*Tariffs and subsidies to support infant industries can be key for economic development in the Global South.*

## BY WILLIAM G. MOSELEY
*September/October 2018*

While it might not seem like it now, President Donald Trump is a gift to free-market oriented economists and policymakers. His clumsy approach to protectionism has ignited a trade war that will inevitably harm the U.S. economy. When the pendulum inexorably swings the other way after the Trump fiasco, free-trade ideology will return with a vengeance. This is a potential tragedy for left-leaning policy analysts who have long been concerned about the excesses of neoliberalism and argued for a more measured use of tariffs to foster local economic development. As such, it is critical that we distinguish between Trump's right-wing nationalist embrace of tariffs and the more nuanced use of this tool to support infant industries.

As a development geographer and an Africanist scholar, I have long been critical of unfettered free trade because of its deleterious economic impacts on African countries. At the behest of the World Bank and the International Monetary Fund, the majority of African countries were essentially forced, because of conditional loan and debt-refinancing requirements, to undergo free-market oriented economic reforms from the early 1980s through the mid-2000s. One by one, these countries reduced tariff barriers, eliminated subsidies, cut back on government expenditures, and emphasized commodity exports. With the possible exception of Ghana, the economy of nearly every African country undertaking these reforms was devastated.

This is not to say that there was no economic growth for African countries during this period, as there certainly was during cyclical commodity booms. The problem is that the economies of these countries were essentially underdeveloped as they returned to a colonial model focused on producing a limited number of commodities such as oil, minerals, cotton, cacao, palm oil, and timber. Economic reforms destroyed the value-added activities that helped diversify these economies and provided higher wage employment, such as the textile, milling, and food processing industries. Worse yet, millions of African farmers and workers are now increasingly ensnared in a global commodity boom-and-bust cycle. Beyond that cycle, they are experiencing an even more worrying long-term trend of declining prices for commodities.

One of the consequences of the hollowing out of African economies has been the European migration crisis. While some of this migration is clearly connected to politics, war, and insecurity in the Middle East and Africa, a nontrivial portion is related to grim economic prospects in many African countries.

After the global financial crisis of 2007, as well as the global food crisis of 2008, even mainstream economists and policy analysts began to realize that unfettered free markets were a problem for the development of African economies, not to mention other areas of the world. As a consequence, some in the development policy community began to reconsider the strategic use of limited tariffs and subsidies to protect and support infant industries. After being demonized for 30 years, import substitution—the idea that some goods could be produced at home rather than imported from abroad—was beginning to have a renaissance.

For example, the middle-income African nation of Botswana has long mined and exported diamonds. In fact, Botswana was and continues to be the largest exporter of gem-quality diamonds in the world. Nearly all of these were exported as rough diamonds, with the actual cutting and polishing done in countries like India and the Netherlands. Beginning in 2013, Botswana made a concerted attempt to onshore some of these value-added activities by subsidizing a domestic diamond cutting and polishing industry. Such industries take time to develop, since you need to cultivate a highly skilled labor pool. But the payoff is more and better-paid employment for a country's population.

While the Botswana example is still unfolding, it is worth noting that both South Korea and Taiwan also skillfully protected industries in the 1960s and 1970s before breaking onto the world stage as export-oriented manufacturers.

Now the recent Trump fiasco with tariffs is threatening to tar and feather the whole idea of fostering local economic development for decades to come unless the left pushes back with a more nuanced perspective. After the inevitable crash of the American economy—not to mention the collateral damage—the global policy community, and the broader public, will likely reembrace free-market policies because they appear to be the opposite of Trump's racist, nationalist, and nativist stance.

This potential scenario is eerily reminiscent of what unfolded in South Africa in the early 1990s. With the African National Congress (ANC) and President Nelson Mandela coming to power, one would have expected that they would have adopted left-leaning, redistributive economic policies given their socialist history and the economic divisions in the country. Instead, what ensued was the full embrace of free-market policies. This remarkable shift has been attributed to a global policymaking community that deftly associated any use of tariffs, subsidies, and protection with the apartheid regime and South Africa's National Party. This sleight of hand allowed them to position free-market policies as the foe of apartheid and the friend of the rainbow nation. Sadly, while these policies initially spawned economic growth, they also deepened inequality, creating a problem that continues to plague the ANC and South Africa today. We need to be sophisticated enough to disentangle policies that promote local economic development from the horrific antics of the Trump regime. Import substitution and the fostering of infant industries are critical aspects of economic development for many countries in the global South. These policies must not forever be associated with the right-wing nationalism of Trump. ❑

*Sources*: Cadman Atta Mills, "Structural Adjustment in Sub-Saharan Africa," Economic Development Institute of the World Bank, October 1989 (worldbank.org); "A hopeful continent," *The Economist*, March 2, 2013 (economist.com); Gumisai Mutume, "Loss of textile market costs African jobs," *Africa Renewal*, April 2006 (un.org); William G. Moseley, Judith Carney, and Laurence Becker, "Neoliberal policy, rural livelihoods, and urban food security in West Africa," *Proceedings of the National Academy of Sciences*, March 2010 (pnas.org); Mark J. Perry, "Julian Simon: Still More Right Than Lucky On Commodities In 2013," Seeking Alpha, January 13, 2013 (seekingalpha.com); "Africa: International migration, emigration 2015," African Studies Centre Leiden (openaccess.leidenuniv.nl); Andrew England, "Botswana seeks to reap more than diamond dollars," *Financial Times*, December 27, 2015 (ft.com); Dani Rodrik, "Getting Interventions Right: How South Korea and Taiwan Grew Rich," *Economic Policy*, April 1995 (nber.org); Richard Peet, "Ideology, Discourse, and the Geography of Hegemony: From Socialist to Neoliberal Development in Postapartheid South Africa," *Antipode*, January 2002 (wiley.com); Jason Beaubien, "The Country With the World's Worst Inequality Is...," *Goats and Soda*, April 2, 2018 (npr.org).

*Article 4.5*

# LOCAL, OR FAR AWAY?

**BY ARTHUR MacEWAN**
*July/August, 2020*

> Dear Dr. Dollar:
> *I have always been skeptical of the argument that it is better for economies to specialize, importing what they cannot produce as cheaply as someone else. Doesn't the Covid-19 pandemic show that it's not a good way to obtain medical supplies and equipment? And what about food and energy? Wouldn't there be more resilience in the economy and in the society it is supposed to support if there were a higher degree of local self-reliance coupled with selective regional or national specialization?*
> —Katharine Rylaarsdam, by email

Here's the problem—and it is a general problem among economists—economists tend to assume that the sole goal of our economic activity is to get things as cheaply possible. It follows automatically, then, that if things from far away can be obtained more cheaply than they can be obtained locally, they should be obtained from far away.

The as-cheaply-as-possible outlook of economists has provided support for the interests of many firms, which profit from using labor and obtaining raw materials from wherever they are least expensive. Low-cost supplies mean higher profits.

But outside the narrow world of economists and away from firms' balance sheets, getting things as cheaply as possible is not people's sole goal in their economic activity. We also care about, for example, security, resilience, fairness, and environmental sustainability.

Yes, it is nice to get things cheaply. But do we care that cheap goods often come from areas—in southern U.S. states, Bangladesh, or China—where repressive labor regulations keep wages low? Or from factories just across the border in Mexico, where health-damaging pollution is rampant?

And, as the Covid-19 crisis has brought out, by the United States obtaining much of our medical equipment from far away, we have undermined the resilience of our health care system—which, of course, means more loss of life. (There is something a bit grotesque in advocates of free trade arguing that an exception should be made for "national security," but not mentioning health care equipment. "People security" does not seem to merit the same exception.)

Part of the reliance on goods from distant countries is a result of the fact that the real cost of transporting those goods to consumers is higher than the price that those consumers pay out of pocket. For example, when fresh flowers are flown from Colombia to the U.S. market or from Kenya to the European market, the cost of

---

### Trade-related Environmental Damage in the Netherlands

In preparing this article, I corresponded with a friend, David Sogge, in the Netherlands. Here are some further comments that David offered:

> With the airplane and truck freight involved in re-export via the distribution hub [of the Netherlands], but especially with the production and transport of the stuff produced on home ground, the carbon requirements of flowers, bulbs, and other "ornamentals" are clearly substantial. A carbon tax would have a major impact on the price. Dutch greenhouses are heated year-round by gas, most of which is pumped from beneath the North Sea, in Dutch waters.
>
> The Dutch "ornamentals" industry also has terrible consequences for the quality of underground and surface water, thanks to the intensive use of liquid manure and ag-richemicals. Cleaning that up no doubt also brings costs in carbon in the longer run. But now that you've got me started on the environmental effects of greenhouse agriculture (flowers and vegetables) there's the awful light pollution of those gas-warmed/illuminat-ed greenhouses. At night in much of the West of the Netherlands, you can see barely any stars. Then biodiversity has also taken a big hit. Insect populations, and the birds that lived on them, have declined here dramatically in the past three decades, largely thanks to intensive (and much more economically concentrated) agribusiness.

---

environmental damage from the planes' use of fossil fuel doesn't show up in the market price. Many of the flowers destined for Europe go through the Netherlands, which is a hub for distribution to the rest of Europe—which results in more fossil fuel use.

And the Netherlands also produces a large amount of flowers for export. While much of the Netherlands' production is in open fields (tulips), there is also production of higher priced flowers (e.g., roses, lilies, chrysanthemums) in greenhouses, which use heat and light from fossil fuels. Again, there is no accounting for these environmental costs in the price of the flowers. (And there is also the light pollution from the greenhouses. A friend in the Netherlands reports, "At night in much of the West of the Netherlands, you can see barely any stars." See sidebar for more.)

If the prices of flowers and other goods transported over long distances included the cost of the environmental damage generated by that transportation, the prices would be higher and there would be less long-distance transport. Complex international supply chains would be reduced. And reliance on local sources of supply would increase. A carbon tax and regulations that protect the environment would also help.

Regardless of the problems of "free trade" (minimal taxes and regulations) and the consequent reliance on distant sources of supply, it should also be recognized that there are some very positive results of international commerce. International exchange in the arts, sciences, and intellectual pursuits generally can be highly beneficial. Also, many fruits and vegetables cannot be grown, for example, in New England. We should not expect to get them at low prices because of the repression of workers or because environmental costs are ignored, but it would be nice to be able to get them; and wheat is probably best produced on the Great Plains. As to energy, if we are going to move our energy system to solar and wind power, those of us in the Northeast will need a way to get energy from the Southwest (where the sun shines the most) and the Great Plains (where the wind blows the most).

International commerce based only on getting goods as cheaply as possible should not define our economic policies. But this does not mean a retreat into nationalism and isolation. The need is to regulate our commerce in ways that serve the large set of economic goals to which most people aspire, including security, resilience, fairness, and environmental sustainability. ❑

# Chapter 5

# INTERNATIONAL FINANCE

*Article 5.1*

## DOLLAR DOMINANCE

**BY ARTHUR MacEWAN**
*January/February 2015*

> Dear Dr. Dollar:
> What does it mean that the dollar is the "dominant" global currency? Why does this situation exist? And how does it matter? —*Anonymous*

Suppose that, when you paid for things with checks, all the recipients of those checks believed that you were a very responsible person, that you would keep plenty of money in the bank to honor those checks. Moreover, not only did the check recipients believe in you, but people in general had this same opinion.

Under these circumstances, the people holding your checks wouldn't have to cash them in. Those checks could simply be used as money. The checks themselves would be acceptable in transactions among all those people who believed you were so responsible.

This situation would be nice for you because you could write plenty of checks and not worry about those checks being cashed in against your account. Extra buying power for you. At the same time, the people who used your checks as money would have an easier time with transactions, having your checks as a widely acceptable form of currency—i.e., they would have more "liquidity." Also, holding onto your checks—keeping them "in reserve"—would be a safe way for people to store money for when they needed it.

### Fiction and Reality

To a large extent, this fictional situation with your checks is analogous to the real situation of the U.S. dollar in global commerce. With people and banks around the world using dollars and holding dollars, not "cashing them in" for U.S. goods, the United States— primarily its government and businesses—is able to spend more abroad without giving up so much in goods and services produced in the United

States. Governments, businesses, and people around the world have more liquidity than they would otherwise, and they have more confidence than they would otherwise in the value of the currency (dollars) they are using and holding in reserve

Like you in the fictional scenario, the U.S. government in the real scenario is viewed as "responsible." An important part of the U.S. government being viewed as "responsible" is that it would keep the value of the dollar relatively stable—i.e., not much inflation (at least compared to other currencies). This organization of the global finance system, with the dollar in this special, or dominant, position has an interesting history—and some powerful implications.

## Where Did This System Come From?

The crucial formal step in creating the dollar-dominated system came at the end of World War II, with the United States in an extremely strong economic position. Indeed, the high level of government spending on the war had brought the U.S. economy out of the Great Depression, while other high-income countries (and many low-income countries) had had their economies physically decimated by the war. Combined with this economic power, the United States had extreme military power. Thus, the era following World War II came to be called "The American Century" (Of course it was not really a full century, but let's not quibble.)

As the end of the war was coming into sight, in July 1944, representatives of the U.S. government and of 43 allied governments (over 700 delegates in all) met over three weeks at the Mt. Washington Hotel in Bretton Woods, N.H. The purpose of this conference was to set up the arrangements for the operation of the global economy in the postwar era. Although the Soviet Union and China were both represented at the Bretton Woods conference, in subsequent years they did not take part in the arrangements. (Today you can go to Bretton Woods and, at the entrance to the hotel's driveway, see the sign commemorating this conference, but you have to pay an entrance fee to actually get onto the hotel grounds.)

Unsurprisingly, given the relative economic and political power of the allied governments, the U.S. government basically dictated the conference outcomes, arrangements by which commerce among capitalist countries would be organized in the decades following World War II—the "Bretton Woods era." The central feature of these arrangements was that the dollar would be at the core of global commerce. Other countries' currencies would be "pegged" to the dollar, which meant that each government would set the value of its currency in terms of the dollar. For example, in 1949 the French franc was pegged at $0.37 and the British pound at $2.80. The dollar itself was set in relation to gold: $34 to the ounce. Other countries' banks could redeem their dollars for gold at this rate, but, as with your checks, they generally didn't do so. When the gold-redemption promise was terminated in 1971, it turned out not to make much difference—more on that in a moment.

Of course, economies change in relation to one another. In the postwar era, different rates of inflation and different rates of productivity growth meant that the values of the currencies in terms of the dollar had to be changed from time to time. For example, if France was running a trade deficit with the rest of the world (importing more than it was exporting), this meant that the value of its franc was too high in relation to the dollar—i.e., in terms of dollars, the cost of French goods was too high and France's exports would be low, while the cost for France of goods from elsewhere would be too low and France's imports would be high. Moreover, with French exports not paying for its imports, France would necessarily build up a foreign debt to pay for the excess imports.

One could look at this franc-dollar relationship another way: instead of the franc being too high, one could say that the dollar was too low. But the rules that were established at Bretton Woods excluded the dollar from having to adjust. In this example, it was the French who would have to adjust the value of their currency—i.e., France would have to devalue its currency. And, importantly, it would have to borrow to cover the foreign debt it had built up. The U.S. economy, on the other hand, was protected from the disruption that would have been caused by changing the value of the dollar.

The International Monetary Fund (IMF) was established at Bretton Woods to provide countries in this kind of situation with the loans they needed. The IMF provided these loans, but with various conditions—in particular that the county taking the loans would have to take steps to reorganize their economies, generally in ways that opened them to more foreign commerce, trade and investment.

While the IMF did play a role in European adjustments, its actions became especially important in lower-income countries, where it used its loan conditions to push countries towards a greater openness to international investment and trade—very much in the interests of multinational firms based in the richer countries. (The World Bank was also created at Bretton Woods, but its role is not a central part of the story here.)

## Change Without Change

The Bretton Woods rules of the game worked fairly well for twenty-five years. In fact, from the perspective of the United States one might say they worked too well. While the Bretton Woods system promoted U.S. commerce, opening up trade and investment opportunities around the (capitalist) world, it also provided a stability in global affairs in which firms based elsewhere—in Japan and Europe—were able to also expand and ultimately challenge the dominant position of U.S firms.

A critical juncture in global commercial arrangements then came in 1971: the Bretton Woods system fell apart. A combination of heavy spending abroad by the U.S. government (on the Vietnam War), the economic challenge from other rich countries, and inflation in the United States led the U.S. government to drop its promise of redeeming dollars for gold. Yet, while the system fell apart, there was surprisingly little change in international trade and investment. The relative economic and military power of the United States, though not as extreme as it had been in the immediate post-World War II era, continued. And the perceived threat of the Soviet

Union served as a glue, binding the world's major capitalist powers in Europe and Asia to the United States, and leading them to accept continued U.S. economic, as well as military, dominance.

After 1971, various new arrangements were put in place—for example, a system of partially managed "pegs" was established. Yet the dollar remained the central currency of global commerce. Prices of internationally traded goods—most importantly oil—continued to be set in dollars, and countries continued to hold their reserves in dollars.

Although 1971 marked the beginning of a new era in international financial arrangements, the dollar retained its dominant position. Regardless of the various economic problems in the United States, the dollar has remained both relatively stable and in sufficient supply to grease the wheels of international commerce. Indeed, an ironic example of the continuing role of the dollar came in the Great Recession that began in 2008. Even while the U.S. economy was in the doldrums, businesses and governments elsewhere in the world were buying U.S. government bonds—a principal means of holding their reserves in dollars—since they still considered these the safest assets available.

## Power and a Symbol of Power

In years leading up to the Great Recession, China had entered the global for-profit economy and was exporting at a high rate, exceeding its imports. The Chinese government used the extra money that China was obtaining from its trade surplus to heavily invest in U.S. government bonds. That is, China built up extensive reserves in dollars. In effect, China was loaning money to the United States—loans which filled both the federal budget deficit and the U.S trade deficit. What many observers decried as a dangerous situation—We are becoming indebted to the Chinese! Horror!—in fact served both the U.S. and Chinese governments quite well.

The international role of the dollar is a symbol of U.S. power and is based on that power. At the same time, the dollar's role works to enhance that power, giving the U.S. government and U.S. business the liquidity needed for carrying out global operations—everything from wars to benign commerce.

There are problems with the system. The continued role of the dollar depends to a large extent on the avoidance of significant inflation in the United States. Yet restraints on inflation—e.g., the Federal Reserve raising interest rates—generally work against expanding employment. So maintaining the role of the dollar can come at the expense of most people in the country.

Also, there is always the risk of change. Just as the position of the dollar supports U.S. power in world affairs, if that position is undermined, U.S. power would suffer. In recent years, there has been some threat that other governments would challenge the dollar with their own currencies. China, in particular, has attempted to establish its own positon in world affairs, which, if successful, could ultimately undercut the dominance of the dollar. Indeed, the fear associated with China holding reserves in dollars (i.e., as U.S. government bonds) is to some extent based on concern about the potential implications of China shifting out of dollars (or threatening to do so). Yet, especially with the recent weakening of the Chinese economy, this particular challenge does not appear likely in the near future.

Over the last several decades, the role of the dollar in world affairs has become like the role of the English language. Both developed as a consequence of the extreme power of the United States. in the global economy, and both give advantages to the U.S. government, to U.S. firms, and to any individuals engaged in international activities. Most important, the roles of both the dollar and the English language have become thoroughly entrenched. Even as the power of the United States weakens, then, those roles are likely to continue for some time to come. ❑

*Article 5.2*

# INFLATION TARGETING AND NEOLIBERALISM

## BY GERALD EPSTEIN
*May 2016*

*I*n recent decades, central banks in both high-income ("developed") and lower-income ("developing") countries have turned increasingly towards "inflation targeting" monetary policy—the emphasis on very low inflation, to the exclusion of other policy objectives. In this interview, Gerald Epstein, a professor of economics at UMass-Amherst and a founding co-director of the Political Economy Research Institute (PERI) explains the causes behind the rise of inflation targeting, its effects in practice, and possible alternative approaches. —Eds.

**Dollars & Sense:** When we talk about central banks and monetary policy, what precisely is meant by the phrase "inflation targeting"? And how does that differ from other kinds of objectives that central banks might have?

**Gerald Epstein:** Inflation targeting is a relatively new but very widespread approach to central bank policy. It means that the central bank should target a rate of inflation—sometimes it's a range, not one particular number, but a pretty narrow range—and that should be its only target. It should use its instruments—usually a short-term interest rate—to achieve that target and it should avoid using monetary policy to do anything else.

So what are some of the other things that central banks have done besides try to meet an inflation target? Well, the United States Federal Reserve, for example, has a mandate to reach two targets—the so-called "dual mandate"—one is a stable price level, which is the same as an inflation target, and the other is high employment. So this is a dual mandate. After the financial crisis there's a third presumption, that the Federal Reserve will look at financial stability as well. Other central banks historically have tried to promote exports by targeting a cheap exchange rate. Some people have accused the Chinese government of doing this but many other developing countries have targeted an exchange rate to keep an undervalued exchange rate and promote exports. Other countries have tried to promote broad-based development by supporting government policy. So there's a whole range of targets that, historically, central banks have used.

**D&S:** Has inflation targeting gone hand-in-hand not only with prioritizing price stability over other kinds of objectives, but also an emphasis on very low rates of inflation?

**GE:** That's right. In practice, what inflation-targeting advocates have argued for is an extremely low rate of inflation. For example, the European Central Bank has a 2% target, or to keep inflation in fact just below 2%, and typically what is called for is inflation in the low single digits. In developing countries, targets have ranged from 4% to 8%. So these are targets for inflation that are very low compared to broad historical experience. These days, very low inflation and indeed the threat of deflation in some countries have raised all kinds of issues about this inflation targeting approach.

I see this as part of a whole neoliberal approach to central banking. That is, the idea that the economy is inherently stable, it will inherently reach full employment and stable economic growth on its own, and so the only thing that the macro policymakers have to worry about is keeping a low inflation rate and everything else will take care of itself. Of course, as we've seen, this whole neoliberal approach to macroeconomic policy is badly mistaken.

**D&S:** Why have we seen inflation targeting become more prevalent in monetary policy making, both in high-income and lower-income countries, in recent years? What are the key arguments that are made by advocates of inflation targeting in favor of that approach? And what might be some underlying political and economic causes, even apart from those arguments?

**GE:** It's been a real revolution in central bank policy and, as I said earlier, it's in my view part and parcel of the whole neoliberal trend in macroeconomic policy. The essential thing underlying this, in my view, is to try to reduce the power of government and social forces that might exercise some power within the political economy—workers and peasants and others—and put the power primarily in the hands of those dominating in the markets. That's often the financial system, the banks, but also other elites.

The idea of neoliberal economists and policymakers is that you don't want the government getting too involved in macroeconomic policy. You don't want them promoting too much employment because that might lead to a raise in wages and, in turn, to a reduction in the profit share of the national income. So, sure, this might increase inflation, but inflation is not really the key issue here. The problem, in their view, is letting the central bank support other kinds of policies that are going to enhance the power of workers, people who work in agricultural areas, and even sometimes manufacturing interests. Instead, they want to put power in the hands of those who dominate the markets, often the financial elites.

That is, of course, not what the advocates of inflation targeting say publicly. What the advocates say is, "Look, inflation is harmful. We've got to keep a low and stable rate of inflation in order to promote economic growth." They build on the neoclassical, New Keynesian, or even New Classical approaches to macroeconomic policy that say the market economy is stable in and of itself, so government intervention can only mess things up. So there's only one thing left to do—there's only one thing on the "to do" list for macroeconomic policy—and that is to keep a stable inflation rate, so let's assign the central bank to do that and not to do anything else, and the capitalist economy will take care of itself.

This approach, I think, really has contributed to enormous financial instability. Notice that this inflation targeting targets commodity inflation. But what about asset bubbles, that is, asset inflation? There's no attempt to reduce asset bubbles like we had in subprime or in real estate bubbles in various countries. That is another kind of inflation that could have been targeted.

Of course, we know that the capitalist economy does not achieve full employment on its own. So why not target higher employment? In South Africa, for example, they have unemployment rates of 25 or 26%. They have an inflation-targeting regime to keep inflation in the low single digits, rather than targeting employment. It makes no sense at all.

The other argument that inflation-targeting advocates make is a government failure argument. Even if you concede that the economy won't do perfectly on its own, any time the government gets involved in the market economy they just mess it up. So, they argue, let's just have a minimalist kind of government intervention and at least the government will do no harm. I think this is a common argument as well. But as we know, there have been many successful government interventions in South Korea and China and elsewhere where governments working with a financial system and other actors in the economy have played a crucial role in economic development. The government-failure arguments, I think, have now been shown to be pretty fallacious. Olivier Blanchard, who was the chief economist at the IMF said we had this beautiful illusion that all we needed is one target, that is low inflation, and one interest rate, that is a short-term interest-rate, and everything would be OK. Well, after the crisis, we now know that we need multiple targets and we need multiple tools to achieve our goals.

**D&S:** Hasn't it been a central concern on the part of elites in capitalist countries, at least in those where there is representative government, that the majority could impose its will and force policymakers to prioritize full employment and wage growth (as opposed to, say, "sound money")? Has the transition toward inflation targeting been accompanied by institutional changes to "wall off" monetary policy from those kinds of popular pressures?

**GE:** Yeah, I think that's a very important point here. Inflation targeting ideas have also been often accompanied by the idea that central banks should be "independent"—that is, independent from the government. I think you'll find that these two things go hand-in-hand.

If you look at the whole list of central bank rules that the International Monetary Fund (IMF) and others have advocated for developing countries, the argument goes like this: You want to have an independent central bank. Well, what should this independent central-bank do? It should target inflation. Well, isn't this anti-democratic? No, what we're really saying is that central bankers should have instrument independence, that is, the ability to decide how they'll achieve their target. The government should set the target, but what should target be? Well, the consensus is that the target should be a low rate of inflation. So that's a nice little package designed to prevent the central bank from doing such things as helping to finance government infrastructure investment or government deficits. It's designed to prevent the central bank from keeping interest rates "too low," which might actually contribute to more rapid economic growth or more productivity growth, but might lead to somewhat higher inflation.

Where do they get this low inflation rate from? There's no economic evidence, in fact—and there have been lots of studies—to demonstrate that an inflation rate in the low single digits is optimal for economic growth in most countries, certainly not in developing countries. Some early studies—and this has been replicated many times—have suggested that inflation rates of up to 15%, even 20%, as long as they're relatively steady, don't harm economic growth. They might even contribute to it. So this is a kind of straitjacket that these forces are trying to put the central bank in, in order to prevent them from making policies in the interest of a broader part of the economy. And it's just one plank in the macroeconomic neoliberal straitjacket. The other plank, of course, is no fiscal deficits. So you limit what government can do—no fiscal deficits or low fiscal deficits—you limit what the central bank can do—only target low inflation—and you've pretty much made it impossible for the government to engage in macroeconomic policy that's going to have a broad-based supportive effect on the economy.

**D&S:** What is the record of inflation targeting policy in practice, in terms of economic outcomes we can actually observe, in both developing and so-called developed countries?

**GE:** The first thing to realize, I think, is that inflation-targeting approaches have been devastating in the reaction to the financial crisis of 2007-2008, particularly in Europe. There you had, an extreme case where the European Central Bank (ECB) mandate was to target inflation—period—and nothing else. And indeed to keep inflation in the low single digits, less than 2%. And what this did—along with other rules, other problems in Europe, not just this—was give the ECB the cover to do very little in terms of fighting the crisis when it hit, to in fact raise interest rates within the first year after the crisis hit. And it took the ECB several years before it finally realized the disaster that had befallen Europe and, when Mario Draghi finally came in as president of the ECB in 2011, to do whatever it takes to keep the euro going. It took a break from this kind of orthodoxy for them to begin to turn around Europe. (As we can now see Europe is still in terrible shape.)

Second, the single-minded focus on inflation in Europe and in other countries made them ignore the financial bubble, the asset bubbles that were occurring. Central bankers said, "Well, you know, that's not my department. I'll just worry about commodity inflation. I won't worry about other kinds of inflation because that's not my mandate." They had this tunnel vision, not seeing what else was going on around them in the economy.

In developing countries, there's pretty strong evidence that real interest rates have been higher than they would have been otherwise. There's some evidence that economic growth is lower in a number of developing countries than it would have been otherwise, because real interest rates have been so high. And there is some evidence that this has contributed to a redistribution of income towards the rentiers, that is, to the bankers and the financiers, and away from others because real interest rates have been so high and inflation has been relatively low. Most of the evidence suggests that it has had a negative consequence for working people and others in developing countries as well.

In the end, the negative impacts have been mitigated to some extent by the fact that a lot of central banks, in developing countries particularly, claim to be following a very strict inflation-targeting regime but in fact they've been "cheating." Almost all of them target exchange rates to some extent because they know they can't let their exchange rates get too overvalued or otherwise that is going to hurt their exports and cause other problems. They've been fiddling with the inflation data, or exactly what kind of inflation target they use, etc. In some ways it's a bit of a ruse. For developing countries, it's saying to the IMF, "OK, we're doing what you're telling us." Saying to the global financial markets, to the global investors, "OK we're doing this orthodox thing, but (wink wink) if we really did this all the time in a strict way it would be suicide so we're not going to really do this completely." So they're finally is a recognition, I think, that inflation targeting is a very destructive practice.

*D&S:* In your view, then, what would be a preferable approach to central bank policy—what priorities should central banks have and how should they go about achieving these aims?

**GE:** Central banks should be free and open, in conjunction with their governments, to identify the key problems facing their own countries, the key obstacles to social and economic development, and developing tools and targets that are appropriate to dealing with those problems. And these are going to differ from country to country. So, for example, in South Africa, my colleagues Bob Pollin, James Heintz, Leonce Ndikumana, and I did a study a number of years ago: We proposed an employment-targeting regime for the central bank. The Reserve Bank of South Africa, in conjunction with the government of South Africa, would develop a set of policies and tools—such as credit allocation policies, subsidized credit, lower interest rates, capital controls to keep the capital in the country, more expansionary and targeted fiscal policy—so that monetary policy and fiscal policy would work hand-in-hand to lower the massively high unemployment rate in South Africa. That's an example of an alternative structure for monetary policy and one that has worked for other developing countries. So, for example, in South Korea in the 1950s ,1960s, and 1970s, the central bank supported the government's industrial policy—by lending to development banks that would lend to export industries, by subsidizing credit for export industries, and they would do this as part of the government plan to develop the economy. I call this developmental central banking, that is, central banking that in combination with the government is oriented to developing the country using a variety of tools—interest rates, credit allocation tools, etc.

Not all countries would do the same thing. It not only depends on the country, but also on the problems of the historical conjuncture. So take the United States for example. Right now we do have for the Federal Reserve a dual mandate, which some Republicans are trying to get rid of, for high employment and stable prices. But the financial intermediation system is broken because of what happened in the crisis. Interest rates are down to zero but banks aren't lending to the real economy. People aren't able to borrow from banks for small businesses and so forth. The Federal Reserve, through quantitative easing, bought a lot of financial assets but it's probably time for the Fed to develop new tools, to give direct credit to small businesses, for infrastructure development, etc.

It is the case now, with the crisis and with negative interest rates, or very low interest rates, central banks are being much more experimental trying to develop new tools, new approaches. But they're all doing it under the guise of inflation targeting. European central bankers were doing all these wild monetary experiments, but their goal was really just to get inflation up to 2%. In fact, what's happening is that this inflation targeting is no longer the guiding post for central banks. They need to have much broader sets of tools and targets to get out of this terrible slump that most of these economies are in. ❑

*Article 5.3*

# LESSONS FROM ICELAND'S FINANCIAL CRISIS

## BY NINA EICHACKER
*March/April 2016*

In a span of just three days in 2008—between October 7 and October 9—Iceland's three largest banks, Landsbanki, Glitnir, and Kaupthing, all failed. The banks' debts amounted to over 15 times Iceland's GDP at the time. Iceland residents, British and Dutch account holders, bank shareholders, and, soon, the rest of the world learned that those banks were completely insolvent, and that the Icelandic government could not afford to bail them out (at an estimated price tag of $300 billion).

Following these events, the people of Iceland began the "Kitchenware Revolution," gathering in front of parliament while banging pots and pans. They successfully demanded the resignation of the ruling right-wing Independence Party, which had implemented the financial deregulation that had led to the implosion of Iceland's financial system. In addition, they laid the groundwork for the rejection in a national referendum of the next government's plan to pay loan guarantees, for one of the country's three big banks, to the governments of the UK and the Netherlands. In December 2008, the Icelandic government created the Special Inquiry Commission, which produced an exhaustive report of the causes and consequences of the financial crisis. The government authorized a special prosecutor to investigate and bring charges against guilty parties—including prominent political figures such as the former minister of finance, financial figures including the president and CEO of Glitnir, the president and chairman of Kaupthing, and the president and managing director of Landsbanki.

The crisis, years in the making, was a consequence of the Icelandic government's rapid deregulation and privatization of Iceland's banking system back in the 1990s and early 2000s, and of the banks' embrace of large-scale and risk-heavy investment banking. With little or no supervision, and relying on the widespread belief globally in the integrity of Iceland's government and financial system, bankers got away with murder—until the fall of the U.S. investment bank Lehman Brothers in 2008, after which Iceland's banks could no longer rely on cheap and easy credit from U.S. investment banks.

## Foreseeable, But Not Foreseen

Policymakers, academics, and business reporters should have seen it coming. By 2006, Icelandic banking and economic data described an overheating financial sector and overall economy. Foreign banks' lending to Iceland increased from just over 50% of Icelandic GDP in 1999 to nearly 80% in 2003 to over 400%

in 2007. Icelandic credit intermediation—the share of loans held by financial corporations compared to borrowing by non-financial firms, the general government, households, and non-profits—also increased in this period, from 64% in 2004 to 80% in 2007. This trend of a rapidly growing financial sector relative to the "real" sector of the economy was by no means unique to Iceland, but the scale was. Financial firms' debt rose from less than four times Iceland's GDP in 2003, to over nine times in 2007, to over 15 times in 2008. The net negative financial worth of Iceland's financial corporations rose from 4% of GDP in 2003, to 147% in 2007, to 649% in 2008.

Economist Anne Sibert and finance expert Gudrun Johnsen have written about "love-letters"—debt securities issued by Icelandic banks and then used as collateral for borrowing from other Icelandic banks, the Central Bank of Iceland, and even the European Central Bank. Icelandic banks' developed this fraudulent practice as they found it more difficult to borrow in global capital markets from 2006 onward. Economist and former banking regulator William K. Black has argued that the rapid acceleration of the banks' debts just before the collapse of Iceland's banking system was the result, not of desperate attempts to resurrect the banks, but of fraud: bank officers were trying to loot as much money as possible while they still could. In the years that Icelandic banks engaged in these practices, Frederic Mishkin (Columbia University), Richard Portes (London Business School), and Fridrik Baldursson (Reykjavik University) all wrote reports celebrating the integrity of the Icelandic financial system.

Perhaps as a consequence of these reports, top Icelandic officials, like the then prime minister and head of the central bank, were still surprised by the onset of the country's financial crisis, as were reporters with major media outlets like the *New York Times*, *Fortune*, and *BusinessWeek*. Top economists who had promoted the Icelandic strategy of financial deregulation, like Arthur Laffer (formerly economic advisor in the Reagan administration), Mishkin, Portes, and Baldursson were quiet in the immediate aftermath.

These events point to the dominance of neoliberal theories about the necessity of financial deregulation, and an assumption that a northern European country would have the institutional sophistication to avoid financial crises like those observed in developing countries that had rapidly deregulated. Neoclassical economists with outsize faith in the efficiency of financial markets and integrity of the Icelandic state believed that little could go wrong in Iceland—the crisis in October of 2008 proved otherwise. A wider understanding of the theories of economists John Maynard Keynes and Hyman Minsky would have helped policymakers and other observers foresee Iceland's crisis, and to prevent future such episodes. Keynes and Minsky understood—as Icelandic government officials, academic economists, and the financial press did not—that financial actors will engage in risky behavior in the pursuit of profits, making financial crises inevitable in the absence of regulation to prevent such behavior. Governments therefore must regulate financial sectors for the greater economic good.

## Underproduction of Criticism, Overproduction of Praise

The lack of financial-market transparency was one integral reason that Iceland's crisis went unforeseen. Organizations that could have reported on the conditions of the Icelandic financial marketplace and the state of the Icelandic economy simply did not. The Icelandic state threatened to defund public institutions and agencies that published reports contradicting the narrative of a robust financial infrastructure and growth.

Iceland's Chamber of Commerce paid economists, like Columbia University's Mishkin, hundreds of thousands of dollars to write favorable reports—including one titled "Financial Stability in Iceland"—about the country's financial sector and overall economic growth prospects. Mishkin would later become infamous, in the documentary "Inside Job," for that report and for changing its title to "Financial Instability in Iceland" on his curriculum vitae after Iceland's collapse.

The Icelandic news media consistently underpublicized reports critical of the Icelandic financial sector, while publishing many stories that praised Iceland's big three banks. Iceland's center-right party historically had large ownership stakes in several Icelandic media companies; the shared interest of Iceland's right and center-right parties in promoting the financial sector explains some of the media's lack of coverage of financial malfeasance.

Another cause of this disparity was the cross-ownership of media company shares by Icelandic financial actors and institutions, and financial-corporation shares by Icelandic media institutions. The chair of the board of directors of Baugur Group, a large stakeholder in Kaupthing Bank, also owned 365—parent company of *Frettabladid*, Iceland's largest-circulation daily newspaper—as well as DV, another large media company. Björgólfur Guðmundsson, the former majority owner and chairman of Landsbanki, acquired Arvakur, the company that publishes *Morgunbladid*, the other major Icelandic newspaper, only to sell in 2009 after declaring bankruptcy. The interconnectedness of these industries created conflicts of interest for all involved.

Credit-rating agencies, meanwhile, also contributed to the notion that Iceland's financial markets were safer than they were. The sub-prime mortgage crisis of 2007 revealed a host of problems with how the three largest global credit-rating agencies—Moody's, Standard & Poor's, and Fitch—operate. It used to be that parties interested in investing in a particular class of assets paid for reports evaluating their riskiness. Since the 1970s, however, the setup as shifted, to one in which institutions issuing securities paid for ratings. This gave the agencies an incentive to rate securities as safer than they were. In other words, it created huge conflicts of interest.

In 2007, Fitch, the smallest of the big three rating agencies, downgraded Iceland's credit rating on the basis of its overextension. But Moody's, one of the two bigger agencies, upgraded it, on the premise that Iceland was so financially leveraged that its central bank would, as the lender of last resort, bail out the big three banks. This move paradoxically increased broad confidence in Icelandic financial stability, despite the fact that the rationale for the improved rating was the excessive leverage of Iceland's financial sector. This further lulled international investors and retail banking customers into trusting Icelandic financial actors with their money and spurred still greater leverage and risky behavior. The feedback effects increased the scale of the financial system relative to the Icelandic economy as a whole, placed more and more actors throughout Iceland at risk in the likely event of failure, and increased the severity of the imminent collapse of Iceland's financial system.

In short, the underproduction of criticism and the overproduction of praise for Iceland's banks skewed public understanding of the country's financial sector.

## Governments and International Institutions

The Icelandic Central Bank's decision to change from stability-promoting to inflation-targeting monetary policy led to rising interest rates, precipitous increases in capital inflows, and asset bubbles in the housing market.

Prior to the early 1990s, the Icelandic Central Bank had pursued economic stability above all else. It charged very low interest rates in order to promote lending to local banks, and to hedge against possible bank failures at the local level. Bank employees at all levels were compensated in ways that would not encourage risky behavior.

The shift to inflation-targeting monetary policy resulted in a rapid increase in Icelandic interest rates. Inflation targeting is designed to prevent an increase in the price level, typically through high interest rates, which make it more difficult for banks and other institutions to borrow. High interest rates, however, attracted capital flows from investors in the United States and Western Europe, two financial markets with low interest rates in the early 2000s. This, in turn, had the perverse consequence of raising the value of the Icelandic krona relative to other global currencies. As the krona grew stronger, Iceland's exports fell and its imports rose, leading to a large trade deficit. The financial inflows also provided Icelandic bankers with a ready source of funding for financial speculation. The government's promotion of non-financial firms' and households' purchase of shares in the banks created perverse incentives for them to raise share prices, and increased the scope of losses in the event of the banks' failure. Bank employees now had motivation to boost share prices by whatever means; households with little understanding of the activities of the banking sector would be increasingly vulnerable to the fate of the banks' performance.

Global financial institutions, meanwhile, seemed to forget that Argentina and Chile had liberalized their financial markets in the 1970s and 1980s with bad results: banks became more risk-taking, without becoming more efficient. Argentina's Central Bank offered guarantees on bank deposits, which encouraged more capital inflows. Though Chile's government initially stated that it would not insure deposits, its Central Bank ultimately guaranteed them after several panics early in the liberalization process. The big banks that had been privatized in the 1970s had to be re-nationalized during the crisis of the early 1980s, despite the "free market" views of the University of Chicago economists (or "Chicago Boys") who made economic policy for Chile's military dictatorship.

Foreign governments' economic and political pressure for governments and central banks to insure their investments guaranteed what economists call "moral hazard" problems: if businesses and banks trust that a government will bail them out in times of crisis, they will likely engage in riskier behavior, since they will profit more in the event of success, and not pay as much (or perhaps not pay anything) in the event of failure. Private financial institutions around the world, but particularly in Europe, trusted in Iceland's supposedly robust financial governance, despite Iceland's short history of financial liberalization. Many followed the advice of economists like Mishkin and Portes, who argued that Iceland should not be assumed to have the same financial risks as developing economies, despite the newness of its supercharged financial system. Outside investors' continued willingness to lend to Iceland increased the leveraged state of Icelandic banks and the scope of the eventual financial crisis.

## Heading Off the Next Crisis

Iceland's crisis reveals the inherent instability created by rapid financialization. When a country deregulates banks, encourages international capital inflows, and promotes wide-scale acquisition of those financial institutions' securities (by households, non-financial firms, government, and other banks), financial firms appear to be artificially profitable. Conflicts of interest develop that weaken the stability of the financial sector and the economy as a whole.

Mainstream economists failed to recognize this. However, this was well understood by heterodox figures like Keynes and Minsky, who argued that financial systems without adequate regulatory apparatuses are inherently prone to crisis. A number of current scholars, absorbing the lessons of Keynes and Minsky, argued that Iceland's financial sector was due for a collapse given the changes that had occurred in banking practices and economic orientation of the country. These processes increased Icelandic instability and the costs of the inevitable crisis.

Irrational exuberance and moral hazard overcame the ample evidence that Iceland was dangerously over-leveraged. Investors had access to data demonstrating the risks of investing in Iceland's financial system and economy, yet turned headlong into the storm. National and international unwillingness to compare Iceland's policy actions and history to that of developing economies like Argentina and Chile reflected the faulty assumption that Icelandic institutions were ready for the job of supervising a radically transformed financial sector. The Icelandic government's repression of data demonstrating instability, and the Icelandic media's unwillingness to publish unflattering stories, gave the lie to the notion that western European states' financial institutions and governments were robust enough for highly liberalized financial sectors. Iceland's crisis demonstrates the need for radically different policies: States and social movements must promote widespread financial literacy, so that ordinary people are aware of changes in the financial landscape and better able to protect themselves. If it is to be undertaken, financial deregulation, like cigarette packages, should come with large and impossible-to-miss warnings about its inherent dangers. These warnings should alert the public to the risks of purchasing large shares in globally active banks or other under-regulated financial products, and should warn less sophisticated financial intermediaries like pension funds about the riskiness of different financial assets. In Iceland, as in the United States, the financial system's default setting was to push households into excessive risk-taking; a public counterweight that prioritizes stability over risk would be valuable. "Nudges" encouraging safer approaches to personal wealth management—like insured deposits, defined-benefit retirement plans, and manageable mortgage loans—would still allow financially savvy or risk-loving individuals to engage in riskier transactions, while protecting the broader public. Stability-minded monetary policy is another means to ensuring greater financial and economic well-being. Greater regulatory vigilance against the excesses of financialization and shadow banking, too, would benefit most.

More broadly, given Iceland's experiences and those of other countries before it, states should reject financial deregulation and finance-led growth strategies. The costs of financialization, in the presence of moral hazard and irrational exuberance, expand rapidly in the absence of meaningful oversight. Iceland's experience illustrates this to the rest of the world. The country's policy responses to the crisis—starting with a systematic inquiry and prosecution of guilty bankers—also provide a worthy model for the world. Other countries would be wise to follow its example: The renationalization of banks that could have bankrupted the Icelandic government and central bank, implementation of capital controls (regulations on international capital flows) to stabilize an out-of-control financial system, and enforcement of new financial regulations to protect banks, firms, and households from the consequences of another financial bubble. ❑

*Sources:* Robert Aliber, "Monetary Turbulence and the Icelandic Economy," in Robert Aliber and Gylfi Zoega, eds., *Preludes to the Icelandic Financial Crisis* (Palgrave MacMillan, 2011); Anna Andersen, "The Watchdog That Didn't Bark," Reykjavik Grapevine, October 2010 (grapevine.is); Daniel Chartier, *The End of Iceland's Innocence: The Image of Iceland in the Foreign Media During the Financial Crisis* (University of Ottawa Press, 2011); V. Corbo and J. De Melo, "Lessons from the Southern Cone Policy Reforms." *The World Bank Research Observer,* 2(2), 1987; Jon Danielsson and Gylfi Zoega, "The Collapse of a Country," Working Paper 09:03, Institute of Economic Studies (hhi.hi.is); C. Diaz-Alejandro, "Good-Bye Financial Repression, Hello Financial Crash." *Journal of Development Economics,* 19(1), 1985; Gudrun Johnsen, Bringing Down the Banking System (Palgrave MacMillan, 2014); John Maynard Keynes, "National Self-Sufficiency," *The Yale Review* 22, 1933; Charles Kindleberger and Robert Aliber, *Manias, Panics, and Crashes: A History of Financial Crises* (Wiley, 2005); E. G. Mendoza and M.E. Terrones, *An Anatomy of Credit Booms and Their Demise* (No. w18379), National Bureau of Economic Research, 2012 (nber.org); Hyman Minsky, *Stabilizing An Unstable Economy* (McGraw-Hill, 2008); Hyman Minsky, "The Financial Instability Hypothesis," The Levy Institute, Working Paper No. 74, May 1992 (levyinstitute. org); Hyman Minsky, *Can 'It' Happen Again? Essays on Instability and Finance* (M.E. Sharpe, Inc., 1982); Frederic Mishkin and Tryggvi Herbertsson, "Financial Stability in Iceland," Iceland

Chamber of Commerce Publication, 2006 (vi.is); F. S. Mishkin, *Inflation Targeting in Emerging Market Countries* (No. w7618), National Bureau of Economic Research (nber.org); D. Rodrik, "Growth Strategies," in P. Aghion and S.N. Durlauf, eds., *Handbook of Economic Growth*, Volume 1 (Elsevier, 2005); Throstur Sigurjonsson, "Privatization and Deregulation: A Chronology of Events," in Robert Aliber and Gylfi Zoega, eds., *Preludes to the Icelandic Financial Crisis* (Palgrave Macmillan, 2011); Robert Wade, "Iceland as Icarus," *Challenge* 52, 2009; Robert Wade and Silla Sigurgeirsdottir, "Lessons from Iceland," *New Left Review* 65, 2010; Robert Wade and Silla Sigurgeirsdottir, "Iceland's Rise, Fall, Stabilization, and Beyond," *Cambridge Journal of Economics* 36, 2011; Gylfi Zoega, "A Spending Spree," in Robert Aliber and Gylfi Zoega, eds., *Preludes to the Icelandic Financial Crisis* (Palgrave Macmillan, 2011).

*Article 5.4*

# NO BLANK CHECK FOR DEVELOPMENT BANKS

## BY KEVIN P. GALLAGHER AND JÖRG HAAS
*April 2018, Project Syndicate*

Global financial leaders convened in Washington, DC, last month for the annual spring meetings of the World Bank Group and the International Monetary Fund. This year, they asked the world's taxpayers to grant the World Bank and other multilateral development banks (MDBs) more capital to fill global infrastructure gaps.

Increasing the capital—and optimizing the existing capital—of the world's MDBs is of the utmost importance. But doing so makes sense only if that financing is used to move the world economy in a direction consistent with the United Nations Sustainable Development Goals (SDGs) and the 2015 Paris climate agreement.

According to researchers at the Brookings Institution, the world needs to invest an additional $3 trillion per year in sustainable infrastructure in order to keep global warming below 2°C relative to pre-industrial levels—the target enshrined in both the SDGs and the Paris agreement. Today, however, infrastructure contributes heavily to global warming, with about 70% of all greenhouse-gas emissions coming from its construction and operation.

That means that the infrastructure we build—or cease to build—can determine whether we will achieve global climate goals. It will also determine whether safe and affordable infrastructure services (for example, water, sanitation, electricity, and health care) can be scaled up to meet other SDGs, such as eliminating poverty.

Here, MDBs can play an essential role, given that the private sector and national governments often shy away from such investment. Private capital markets are inherently biased toward short-termism, and tend not to finance long-term investments in infrastructure. Although global economic growth is accelerating, private-sector financing of infrastructure has been falling, according to the World Bank, from $210 billion in 2010 to $38 billion in 2017.

And while national governments provide more than 75% of financing for infrastructure, they tend to avoid massive expenditures for new projects, particularly sustainable infrastructure. Moreover, many governments have come to prefer public-private partnerships that allow them to keep liabilities off-budget. And, as the IMF recently found, governments often launch infrastructure projects as a way to swing votes in the run-up to elections. Longer-term sustainability concerns (including infrastructure maintenance) thus usually take a back seat to political motives.

In light of these shortcomings, development banks have a unique role to play in harnessing expertise and bringing together stakeholders to finance the right kinds of infrastructure. To that end, in 2015, the World Bank and other MDBs launched a strategy to increase development financing "from billions to trillions," by using public finance to "crowd in" private investment, especially from large institutional investors like pension and insurance funds.

But, since then, the World Bank has rebranded its approach as "maximizing finance for development" (MFD), while failing to demonstrate how it will actually achieve the SDGs. This strategic uncertainty should serve as a reminder that, while MDBs have a critical role to play, they should not be given carte blanche.

At Boston University's Global Development Policy Center, we estimate that the MDBs could increase lending by up to $1.9 trillion. That said, a blank check would be disastrous, given that the current financing pattern of the MDBs—and particularly the World Bank Group—is highly carbon-intensive. Moreover, a recent study by the Inter-American Development Bank documents how MDB-financed projects under the current model have fueled social inequity and conflict in different parts of the world.

Taxpayer money for closing global infrastructure gaps should thus be conditioned on the MDBs' recalibration of their strategies toward the SDGs and the Paris climate agreement. This will require reforms to MDBs' board- and project-level governance. The goal should be to ensure that developing countries—especially those most vulnerable to climate change—have more say in development banks' board-level decisions. In addition, poorer and vulnerable communities need to be included in the process from the beginning, so that they can provide full prior consent. Affected communities should be sharing the benefits, not absorbing the costs, of new infrastructure investments.

To address climate change directly, all infrastructure investments should be subject to a "Paris test" to confirm that projects are being carried out in accordance with the goal of keeping global warming well below 2°C, or even below 1.5°C. The World Bank's pledge to end financial support for upstream oil and gas is a step in the right direction, but it should be expanded and become the norm for all MDBs. Moreover, more impact assessments are needed to ensure that road, rail, and waterway projects do not destroy livelihoods or nearby ecosystems, leading to further greenhouse-gas emissions and a loss of vital biodiversity.

Finally, we will need adequate monitoring and evaluation systems to enforce a new compact for MDBs. Without accountability and clear targets set by the SDGs and the Paris agreement, the MDBs will continue to operate according to their own taxpayer-financed discretion, to the detriment of the climate, the environment, and social equity worldwide. ❑

*Article 5.5*

# THE FINANCING NEEDS OF DEVELOPING COUNTRIES

## BY ESRA UĞURLU
*May 2020, Political Economy Research Institute*

Since the outbreak of the coronavirus, developing countries have been exposed to massive withdrawals of capital flows. In this article, I unpack the financial challenges these countries are facing and consider what role the Special Drawing Rights (SDRs) of the International Monetary Fund (IMF) can play in easing the burden.

According to the calculations by the Institute for International Finance (IIF), investors withdrew almost $80 billion over recent weeks from emerging markets. During periods of crisis, investors "fly to safety" by selling risky assets and purchasing safe assets such as U.S. dollars and U.S. Treasury Securities. As international investors flee to dollars amidst the financial turmoil caused by the coronavirus, there is an acute concern that low and middle-income countries will be short of dollars. Furthermore, the scale of the withdrawal suggests that these countries will face great difficulty in raising funds for their sovereign debt payments. Besides governments, firms based in developing countries are also expected to face difficulties in raising foreign currency-denominated debt in international capital markets. Meeting this growing demand requires a global lender of last resort that can provide dollars on request. Within the existing global financial order, the Fed and the IMF are two major organizations that are capable of meeting this demand.

The Fed can provide dollar liquidity through swap lines, which allows global central banks access to dollars in exchange for their own currency with the promise that the principal, as well as the interest, will be paid later. When engaging in a swap operation, the Fed provides dollars to the recipient central bank for an equivalent amount of their currency at a given market exchange rate. After a certain period, the two central banks resell to each other their respective currencies at the initial exchange rate. The recipient central bank provides the dollars to financial institutions in its jurisdictions at the same maturity and rate. This way, swap lines provide dollar liquidity to recipient countries' central bank and financial institutions.

To meet the rising demand for U.S. dollars, the Fed has recently extended its dollar swap lines. However, despite the extension, the scope of this operation is still minimal as it includes just 14 countries, out of which only two of them (Brazil and Mexico) are emerging economies (three if we count South Korea as an emerging market).

The IMF's emergency loans are another option for countries facing financial difficulties. According to Kristalina Georgieva, the managing director of the IMF, 103 countries have already approached the IMF for emergency financing. Besides deploying new emergency lending facilities, the IMF, together with the World Bank and the G-20 countries, has agreed to a debt standstill for the 76 poorest countries. Even though the introduction of new channels to disburse funding and the temporary debt relief are positive developments, it does not fully address the dire financing needs of many nations. For instance, economic historian Adam Tooze notes that the needs of low-income countries are small in economic terms as they owe just over $150 billion in public debt. However, the emerging markets owe about $7.69 trillion, of which $484 billion is long-term bonds held by private investors, $2 trillion is long-term debts owed to banks, and $2.1 trillion is short-term borrowing.

In the context of the urgent liquidity needs of developing countries and the insufficiency of other responses to address this gap, there have been several calls from academics, policymakers, and politicians, for a major issuance of SDRs to address the financial fallout caused by the coronavirus crisis.

## The Recent Proposals to Issue SDRs in Response to the Coronavirus Crisis

SDRs are interest-bearing international reserve assets that can be held by the IMF, its member countries, and designated official entities known as the prescribed holders. The IMF holds the authority to create unconditional liquidity through general SDR allocations to all its members in proportion to their quotas at the IMF, which reflect their relative economic standing in the global economy. Through SDR allocations, the Fund provides every member with on-demand access to freely usable currencies. Members can exchange these SDRs to meet their balance of payments needs or to adjust the composition of their reserves. Although the SDR market generally functions on a voluntary basis, in the event that there are not enough voluntary buyers, the IMF can designate members with a strong balance of payment position to provide freely usable currency in exchange for SDRs.

One of the proposals for a new SDR allocation, which was published in the *Financial Times* in mid-March, came from Kevin P. Gallagher, José Ocampo, and Ulrich Volz. This proposal called for the IMF to agree to an allocation of the equivalent of at least $500 billion as part of the global response to the coronavirus crisis. Larry Summers, former U.S. Treasury Secretary, and Gordon Brown, former British Prime Minister, similarly called for an SDR allocation of over $1 trillion.

Besides academics and policymakers, several political leaders including Abiy Ahmed, the prime minister of Ethiopia, Cyril Ramaphosa, the president of South Africa, French President Emmanuel Macron, and German Chancellor Angela Merkel urged the IMF to allocate more SDRs to provide additional liquidity that can be used for the procurement of basic commodities and essential medical supplies.

Even though the use of SDRs is not necessarily less costly for low-income countries than borrowing directly from the IMF, SDRs have the advantage of being unconditional, which allows countries to avoid following IMF programs. SDRs would also be more preferable to the Fed's swap lines because only a few countries have swap lines with the Fed, and the choice of countries that are included in swap lines often reflect the strategic national interests of the United States. As David Adler and Andrés Arauz, the former knowledge minister of Ecuador, puts it "Swap lines are the ventilators, allowing governments to keep their economies—and their citizens—alive. The Federal Reserve is the doctor, deciding which ailing patients it will choose to save from the mortal symptoms of economic crisis."

In theory, SDRs can allow developing countries that are in a dire financial situation to cover basic services, such as hospital care or medical supplies, without relying on the political will of the United States. However, journalistic reports suggest that the Trump administration does not want a new SDR issuance given that two enemies of the Trump administration, namely Iran and Venezuela, would benefit from a new allocation. SDR allocations require an 85% vote of all members, and with its 16.51% voting share, an approval by the United States is necessary for a new SDR allocation to take place. Therefore, the resistance by the United States to SDR proposals make the prospect of a partial financial relief for developing countries dependent on the political will of the United States.

If it is approved, close to two-fifths of the new SDR allocation would go to emerging and developing countries, which will be the primary users of SDRs. Given that about three-fifths of the SDRs will go to advanced economies, some critics, including the U.S. Treasury, find the proposals for a new SDR allocation as ill-targeted. However, what these critiques miss is that advanced economies will not have to use the SDRs if they do not need to, and two-fifths of the SDR allocation can still provide great help to some developing nations.

An increase in SDR allocations is particularly needed for countries like Colombia, Turkey, and South Africa who are left out from standstill agreements and the Fed's swap arrangements. Besides, the list of countries that do not have access to other kinds of financial safety nets, including many countries in Sub-Saharan Africa and Latin America, can be beneficiaries of a new SDR allocation. Even though an allocation of about $500 billion or $1 trillion may not be sufficient to fully address the financing gaps faced by emerging markets, it would nonetheless be an important step in the right direction. ❑

*Sources*: David Adler and Andres Arauz, "It's Time to End the Fed's 'Monetary Triage,'" *The Nation*, April 21, 2020 (thenation.com); Saleem Bahaj and Ricardo Reis, "Central Bank Swap Lines," VOX EU, Sept. 25, 2018 (voxeu.org); Gordon Brown and Lawrence H. Summers, "Debt Relief Is the Most Effective Pandemic Aid," Project Syndicate, April 15, 2020 (project-syndicate. org); Kevin P. Gallagher, José Antonio Ocampo, and Ulrich Volz, "IMF Special Drawing Rights: A Key Tool for Attacking a COVID-19 Financial Fallout in Developing Countries," Brookings Institute, March 26, 2020 (brookings.edu); Kristalina Georgieva, "A Global Crisis Like No Other Needs a Global Response Like No Other," IMF Blog, April 21, 2020 (blogs.imf.org); IMF, "Fact Sheet: Special Drawing Right (SDR)," April 16, 2020 (imf.org); Laurissa Mühlich, Barbara Fritz, William N. Kring, and Kevin P. Gallagher, "The Global Financial Safety Net Tracker: Lessons for the COVID-19 Crisis from a New Interactive Dataset," Boston University Global Development Policy Center, April 2020 (bu.edu/gdp); James Politi, "U.S. Holds off on IMF Plan to Boost

Emerging Economies' Finances," *Financial Times*, April 15, 2020 (ft.com); Adam Tooze, "The IMF Was Organizing a Global Pandemic Bailout—Until the Trump Administration Stopped It," *Foreign Policy*, April 17, 2020 (foreignpolicy.com); Edwin M. Truman, "The G20 Missed an Opportunity to Expand Financial Resources for Vulnerable Countries," Peterson Institute for International Economics (piie.com); Jonathan Wheatley, "Surging Dollar, Coronavirus and Oil Slump Hit Emerging Economies," *Financial Times*, March 19, 2020 (ft.com).

# Chapter 6

# INTERNATIONAL INSTITUTIONS

*Article 6.1*

## THE INTERNATIONAL MONETARY FUND AND WORLD BANK

BY THE *DOLLARS & SENSE* COLLECTIVE
*March/April 2000, last revised November 2020*

The basic structure of the postwar international capitalist economy was created in 1944, at an international conference in Bretton Woods, New Hampshire. While the Bretton Woods conference included high-level negotiations between representatives of the U.S. and British governments, the Americans dominated the outcome.

The British delegation (including the legendary economist John Maynard Keynes) argued for an international currency for world trade and debt settlements. The Americans insisted on the U.S. dollar being the de facto world currency, with the dollar's value fixed in terms of gold and the values of other currencies fixed in relation to the dollar. The British wanted countries that ran trade surpluses and those that ran trade deficits (and became indebted to the "surplus" countries) to share the costs of "adjustment" (bringing the world economy back into balance). The United States insisted on a system in which the "deficit" countries would have to do the adjusting, and a central aim would be making sure that the debtors would pay back their creditors at any cost.

Among the institutions coming out of Bretton Woods were the World Bank and the International Monetary Fund (IMF). For this reason, they are sometimes known as the "Bretton Woods twins." Both institutions engage in international lending. The IMF was established to lend to countries facing current-account deficit problems, so that they could continue international trade without interruption, and avoid defaulting on debts, which would disrupt world economic stability. So the IMF primarily acts as a "lender of last resort" to countries (usually, but not always, lower-income countries) that have become heavily indebted and cannot get loans elsewhere. The World Bank, officially called the International Bank for Reconstruction and Development, was initially tasked to help rebuild post-World War II Europe through infrastructure lending. In the years since, it has continued to engage primarily in longer-term "development" lending, though its focus has moved to the developing world.

At both the World Bank and the IMF, the number of votes a country receives is closely proportional to how much capital it contributes to the institution, so the voting power of rich countries like the United States is disproportionate to their numbers. Eleven rich countries, for example, account for more than 50% of the voting power in the IMF Board of Governors. At both institutions, eight powerful countries—the United States, China, France, Germany, Japan, Russia, Saudi Arabia, and the United Kingdom—get their own representatives on the institution's executive board, with the rest of the directors (16-17) elected by the rest of the 180-odd member countries. The president of the World Bank is elected by the Board of Executive Directors, and traditionally nominated by the U.S. representative. The managing director of the IMF is traditionally a European.

The IMF and the World Bank wield power vastly greater than the share of international lending they account for because private lenders follow their lead in deciding which countries are credit-worthy. The institutions have taken advantage of this leverage—and of debt crises in Latin America, Africa, Asia, and even Europe—to push a "free-market" (or "neoliberal") model of economic development.

## The IMF

The IMF was a key part, from the very start, of the "debtor pays" system the U.S. government had insisted on at Bretton Woods. When a country fell heavily into debt, and could no longer get enough credit from private sources, the IMF would step in as the "lender of last resort." This made it possible for the debtor to continue to pay its creditors in the short run. The typical IMF adjustment program, however, demanded painful "austerity" or "shock therapy"—elimination of price controls on basic goods (such as food and fuel), cuts in government spending, services, and employment, and "devaluation" of the country's currency. All of these austerity measures hit workers and poor people the hardest, the first two for fairly obvious reasons. The impact of currency devaluation, however, requires a little more explanation.

Devaluation meant that the currency would buy fewer dollars—and fewer units of every other currency "pegged" to the dollar. This made imports to the country more expensive. (Suppose that a country's peso had been pegged at a one-to-one ratio to the dollar. An imported good that cost $10 would cost 10 pesos. If the currency was devalued to a two-to-one ratio to the dollar, an imported good that cost $10 would now cost 20 pesos.) Devaluation caused domestic prices to rise, both because imports became more expensive and because domestic producers faced less import competition and so could more readily raise their own prices. Meanwhile, it made the country's exports less expensive to people in other countries. The idea was that the country would export more, earn more dollars in return, and—this is the key—be able to pay back its debts to U.S. and European banks. In other words, the people of the country (especially workers and the poor) would consume less of what they produced, and send more of it abroad to "service" the country's debt.

It is the poor who are hurt the most by devaluation. For instance, if a county's devalues its currency by 50%, then the poor will lose about half the purchasing power on their money savings (which they hold overwhelmingly in the national currency). However, the rich and ruling elite hold the bulk of their financial wealth abroad in other currencies. Once a devaluation has been carried out, they can use their foreign currency holdings to buy their country's currency, now at a more favorable rate due to the devaluation.

For many years, austerity measures like these were the core of IMF "adjustment" plans. Starting in the 1970s, however, the IMF broadened its standard program to include deeper "structural" changes to debtor countries' economies. "Structural adjustment programs" (SAPs) included not only the austerity measures described above, but also the elimination of trade barriers and controls on international investment, the privatization of public enterprises, and the "deregulation" of labor markets (including elimination of minimum wage laws, hours laws, occupational safety and health regulations, and protections for unions).

These were the basic ingredients for overturning "regulated" (or "interventionist") forms of capitalism in many lower-income countries, and replacing it with "free-market" (or "neoliberal") capitalism. Austerity, privatization, and deregulation kept the same elite-dominated government and bureaucratic institutions in place, while moving the epicenter of economic decisionmaking away from public institutions and into private hands. For years, the SAPs that have been implemented by the IMF and World Bank have been criticized for their intrusive economic policy conditions as they promoted policies which essentially put countries under financial surveillance, which narrowed their autonomy to formulate policy decisions and undermined their "ownership of national development strategies." Yet, despite efforts to "streamline" the number of conditions in the face of severe criticism, the IMF's 2018 Review of Program Design and Conditionality found that the number of structural conditions is on the rise. The results of these conditionalities is that a country's national economic development shifts under the control of private corporations (MNCs)—with their power over basic resources such as water, food, and energy. This increasing corporate power weakens the ability of populations in these countries to hold their elites accountable because now the "market" is in charge—and not the so-called elected officials.

Structural adjustment also prepared the ground for the system of globalized production—making it easier for multinational companies to locate operations in affected countries (thanks to the removal of restrictions on foreign investment), employ a relatively cheap and controllable workforce (thanks to the removal of labor regulations), and export the goods back to their home countries or elsewhere in the world (thanks to the elimination of trade barriers). Structural adjustment programs became the lance-point of "free-market" reform, especially in Latin America during the 1980s debt crisis, but also in other low-income regions.

## The World Bank

In its early years, just after World War II, the World Bank mostly loaned money to Western European governments to help rebuild their war-ravaged economies. This was an important factor in the postwar reconstruction of the world capitalist economy. European reconstruction bolstered demand for exported goods from the United States, and ultimately promoted the reemergence of Western Europe as a global manufacturing powerhouse.

During the long period (1968-1981) that former U.S. Defense Secretary Robert S. McNamara headed the World Bank, however, the bank turned toward "development" loans to lower-income countries. McNamara brought the same philosophy to development that he had used as a chief architect of the U.S. war against Vietnam: big is good and bigger is better. The World Bank came to favor large, expensive projects regardless of their appropriateness to local conditions, and with little attention to environmental and social impacts. The Bank became especially notorious, for example, for supporting large dam projects that flooded wide areas, deprived others of water, and uprooted the people living in affected regions. The Bank's support for large, capital-intensive "development" projects has also been a disguised way of channeling benefits to large global companies. Many of these projects require inputs—like high-tech machinery—that are not produced in the countries where the projects take place. Instead, they have to be imported, mostly from high-income countries. Such projects may also create long-run dependencies, since the spare parts and technical expertise for proper maintenance may only be available from the companies that produced these inputs in the first place.

While the Bank's main focus is long-term "development" lending, it has also engaged in "structural adjustment" lending. The Bank's structural adjustment policies, much like those from the IMF, have imposed heavy burdens on workers and poor people. In the 1980s and 1990s, during its "structural adjustment era," the Bank went so far as to advocate that governments charge fees even for public primary education. (Predictably, in countries that adopted such policies, many poor families could not afford the fees and school enrollment declined.) The Bank has since then publicly called for the abolition of school fees. Critics argue, however, that the shift is at least partly rhetorical. Katarina Tomasevski, founder of the organization Right to Education, argues that the Bank presents itself as opposing fees, but does not oppose hidden charges, as for textbooks, school uniforms, and other costs of attending school.

The World Bank has also made development loans conditional on the adoption of "free-market" policies, like privatization of public services. Most notoriously, the Bank has pushed for the privatization of water delivery. Where privatization of water or other public services has not been possible, the Bank has urged governments to adopt "cost-recovery" strategies—including raising fees on users. Both privatization and cost-recovery strategies have undermined poor people's access to water and other essentials.

## Recent Developments

Since the 1990s, opposition to World Bank and IMF policies have shaken the two institutions' credibility and economic policy influence—especially in Latin America, the world region to which "neoliberalism" came first and where it went furthest. This is part of a broader backlash against neoliberal policies, which opponents (especially on the Latin American left) blame for persistent poverty and rising inequality in the region. The 1990s and 2000s saw a so-called "pink tide" in Latin America, with "center-left" parties coming to power in Argentina, Bolivia, Brazil, Chile, Ecuador, and Venezuela. (The center-left has since lost and then regained the presidency in Chile, and has recently lost the presidencies of Argentina and Brazil.) Different governments have adopted different policies in power, some staying close to the neoliberal path, others veering sharply away from it. Venezuela has, along with several other countries, withdrawn from the World Bank-affiliated International Centre for the Settlement of Investment Disputes (ICSID). Several South American governments, including those of Argentina, Brazil, and Venezuela, have also jointly formed a new regional lending institution, the Bank of the South, which aims to act as an alternative lender (for both long-term development and short-term "liquidity crises") to the IMF and World Bank.

On the other hand, the IMF has emerged, surprisingly, as a powerful influence in Western Europe. For many years, acute debt crises seemed to be confined to lower-income economies, and most observers did not dream that they could happen in Europe or other high-income regions. (For this reason, the IMF was widely criticized as a hammer that high-income countries used on low-income countries.) During the current economic crisis, however, several Western European countries have fallen deeply into debt. The IMF has stepped in as part of "bailout" programs for Greece, Iceland, and Ireland. True to its origins, it has also pushed for austerity—especially cuts in public spending—in highly indebted countries. Many economists—especially proponents of "Keynesian" views—have argued that weakness in total demand is the main cause of the current economic crisis in Europe and the rest of the world. Under these conditions, they argue, cuts in government spending will only reduce total demand further, and likely cause the crisis to drag on. ❑

*Sources:* International Monetary Fund, "IMF Members' Quotas and Voting Power, and IMF Board of Governors" (www.imf.org); International Monetary Fund, "IMF Executive Directors and Voting Power" (www.imf.org); World Bank, "Executive Directors and Alternates" (www.worldbank.org); World Bank, "Cost Recovery for Water Supply and Sanitation and Irrigation and Drainage Projects (www.worldbank.org); Zoe Godolphin, "The World Bank as a New Global Education Ministry?" Bretton Woods Project, January 21, 2011 (www.brettonwoodsproject.org); Katerina Tomasevski, "Both Arsonist and Fire Fighter: The World Bank on School Fees," Bretton Woods Project, January 23, 2006 (www.brettonwoodsproject.org); Katerina Tomasevski, "Six Reasons Why the World Bank Should Be Debarred From Education," Bretton Woods Project, September 2, 2006 (www.brettonwoodsproject.org); Bretton Woods Project, "What are the main criticisms of the World Bank and the IMF?," June 4, 2019.

Article 6.2

# THE WORLD TRADE ORGANIZATION

## BY THE *DOLLARS & SENSE* COLLECTIVE
*March/April 2000, last revised November 2020*

If the World Trade Organization (WTO) is famous for one thing, it is the "Battle in Seattle." Over 50,000 people went to Seattle in 1999 to say no to the WTO's corporate agenda, successfully shutting down the first day of the ministerial meeting. African, Caribbean, and other least-developed country representatives, in addition, walked out of the meeting. But what is the WTO? Where did it come from? And what does it do?

## Where Did It Come From?

Starting in the 1950s, government officials from around the world began to meet irregularly to hammer out the rules of a global trading system. Known as the General Agreements on Trade and Tariffs (GATT), these negotiations covered, in excruciating detail, such matters as what level of taxation Japan could impose on foreign rice, how many American automobiles Brazil could allow into its market, and how large a subsidy France could give its vineyards. Every clause was carefully crafted, with constant input from business representatives who hoped to profit from expanded international trade.

The GATT process, however, was slow, cumbersome and difficult to monitor. As corporations expanded more rapidly into global markets they pushed governments to create a more powerful and permanent international body that could speed up trade negotiations as well as oversee and enforce provisions of the GATT. The WTO arose from the 1986-1994 GATT negotiations, known as the Uruguay Round. The new organization, formed out of the ashes of GATT, was formally established in 1995. It now occupies a central position in the world as an organization for trade negotiations.

Following the shocking demonstrations in Seattle, the WTO held its 2001 ministerial meeting in Doha, Qatar, safe from protest. The WTO initiated a new round of trade talks that it promised would address the needs of developing countries. The Doha Development round, however, continued the WTO's pro-corporate agenda. Two years later "the Group of 20 developing countries" at the Cancún ministerial refused to lower their trade barriers until the United States and EU cleaned up their unfair global agricultural systems. By the summer of 2006, five years after it began, the Doha round had collapsed and the WTO suspended trade negotiations. Since 2008 there have been attempts to revive talks but without major success. The most significant difference of contention is between the developed countries of the United States, the European Union,

Canada, and Japan and the developing countries led by Brazil, India, China, and South Africa revolving around the unfair global agricultural trade system that developed countries impose on the developing countries.

## What Does It Do?

The WTO functions as a sort of international court for adjudicating trade disputes. Since July 29, 2016, each of its 164 member countries has one representative, who participates in negotiations over trade rules. The heart of the WTO, however, is not its delegates, but its dispute resolution system. With the establishment of the WTO, corporations now have a place to complain to when they want trade barriers—or domestic regulations that limit their freedom to buy and sell—overturned.

Though corporations have no standing in the WTO—the organization is, officially, open only to its member countries—the numerous advisory bodies that provide technical expertise to delegates are overflowing with corporate representation. The delegates themselves are drawn from trade ministries and confer regularly with the corporate lobbyists and advisors who swarm the streets and offices of Geneva, where the organization is headquartered. As a result, the WTO has become, as an anonymous delegate told the *Financial Times,* "a place where governments can collude against their citizens."

Lori Wallach and Michelle Sforza, in their book *The WTO: Five Years of Reasons to Resist Corporate Globalization*, point out that large corporations are essentially "renting" governments to bring cases before the WTO, and in this way, to win in the WTO battles they have lost in the political arena at home. Large shrimping corporations, for example, got India to dispute the U.S. ban on shrimp catches that were not sea-turtle safe. Once such a case is raised, the resolution process violates most democratic notions of due process and openness. Cases are heard before a tribunal of "trade experts," generally lawyers, who, under WTO rules, are required to make their ruling with a presumption in favor of free trade. The WTO puts the burden squarely on governments to justify any restriction of what it considers the natural order of things. There are no amicus briefs (statements of legal opinion filed with a court by outside parties), no observers, and no public records of the deliberations.

The WTO's rule is not restricted to such matters as tariff barriers it's rule has expanded about 20 areas of trade. When the organization was formed, environmental and labor groups warned that the WTO would soon be rendering decisions on essential matters of public policy. This has proven absolutely correct. The organization ruled against Europe for banning hormone-treated beef and against Japan for prohibiting pesticide-laden apples. Also WTO rules prohibit selective purchasing laws, even those targeted at human rights abuses. In 1998 the WTO court lodged a complaint against the Massachusetts state law that banned government purchases from Burma in an attempt to punish its brutal dictatorship. Had the WTO's rules been in place at the time of the anti-Apartheid divestment movement, laws barring trade with or investment in South Africa would have violated them as well.

## Why Should You Care?

At stake is a fundamental issue of popular sovereignty—the rights of the people to regulate economic life, whether at the level of the city, state, or nation. The United States does not allow businesses operating within its borders to produce goods with child labor, for example, so why should we allow those same businesses—Disney, Gap, or Walmart—to produce their goods with child labor in Haiti and sell the goods here? ❑

*Sources:* World Trade Organization, "Understanding the WTO: The Organization" (wto.org); World Trade Organization, "The Doha Round" (wto.org).

*Article 6.3*

# BEYOND THE MYTH AND THROUGH THE MEXICAN LABYRINTH

*Labor under the "New NAFTA," the U.S.-Mexico-Canada Agreement*

**BY JAMES M. CYPHER AND MATEO CROSSA**
*May/June 2019*

President Trump has declared that Congressional approval of the U.S.-Mexico-Canada Agreement (the USMCA), signed by the three governments in November 2018, is his number one legislative priority for 2019. Full deployment of the legislative machine pushing for approval of the USMCA was put on hold until April 2019, in anticipation of a U.S. International Trade Commission (USITC) report on the economic impact of the agreement. The report, which was finally released in mid-April, asserted, predictably, that the USMCA would lower the trade deficit with Mexico, raise U.S. employment by creating 178,000 new jobs—including 76,000 in the auto sector in the next five years—and raise the U.S. GDP by $68 billion. The Office of the US. Trade Representative—which is part of the executive office of the U.S. president—simultaneously issued their own glowing analysis (see the sidebar "Lies, Damn Lies, and Models" for details). This effectively fired off the starting gun in the high-stakes, corporate-led negotiations intended to bring the USMCA across the finish line in the months to follow.

But in the United States, the powers that be had already jumped the gun, forming two vast organizations intended to create a public upsurge of support for ratification of the USMCA—particularly in states that will benefit from the antici-pated investment and employment effects from the redesign of NAFTA. Below we analyze this effort to "sell" the USMCA as well as the Mexican oligarchy's role in fomenting the agreement. The crux of the new treaty entails a realignment of auto-sector production, particularly in Mexico, as well as facing the challenge that Asian and European auto plants based in Mexico pose to this sector.

## Peak Business Associations in the North

"Peak" business associations—such as the U.S. Chamber of Commerce—play a major, often unnoted, role in shaping economic strategies; and at critical moments they use their vast organizational powers to shape national policies. Thus, to lead the charge in the frenzied race to ratification, the Pass USMCA Coalition (which was formed in February 2019 and has over 200 corporate members and numerous busi-ness associations, including the Business Roundtable and the American Petroleum Institute) has commenced an outsized public relations campaign to sell the new NAFTA to the U.S. Congress, the press, and the voting public. In March, the coalition launched its first mass television campaign, spreading the message that the USMCA is "a win for workers" into millions of otherwise uninformed households. Also in March, the Republican Party launched Trade Works for America, a self-described "grassroots" organization designed to finance a multi-million dollar media blitz on the voting public, employees in affected industries, and the U.S. Congress—targeting several legislators by urging district voters to call their Washington office. This effort will include a focus on right-wing senators who might otherwise bridle at some of the Agreement's labor provisions—particularly for Mexican workers (as discussed below). In their first two weeks, Trade Works for America spurred voters to place 50,000 phone calls and send emails targeting more than 24 key Congressional districts.

Framing a political and economic message is essential in any national debate. Trade Works for America and the Pass USMCA Coalition have now clearly framed their message; and these two groups, with nearly unlimited funds, have the advantage of being the "first movers" on the USMCA. So far, there has been almost no counter-narrative in broad circulation. Congressional representatives have had little to offer, the many Democratic Party candidates for the U.S. presidency in 2020 have stalled on the issue, and those who play inside baseball in Washington's legislative games—including unions and assorted NGOs—have been slow to hone a critical message.

## Peak Business Associations in the South

Mexico's economic oligarchy constantly seeks, and normally maintains, the policy high ground by using its clout to back advantageous trade policies as it steers Mexico's political class toward its own enrichment. This oligarchy works through several peak business organizations, the most important being the Business Coordinating Council, where a few billionaires (along with some CEOs) are perpetually fine-tuning their national policy initiatives. It synchronizes and directs public policy initiatives for the six largest business associations in Mexico. The Council was formed in 1976 in opposition to the state-led policies of the Mexican government and set the stage for Mexico's long, dark descent into neoliberalism beginning in the 1980s. Known in Mexico as the CCE, the firms represented in this Council employ an estimated 18 million workers and account for roughly 60% of all private sector investments in Mexico. Their wealth and socioeconomic power was significantly strengthened when NAFTA was implemented in 1994 and they are dedicated to assuring that its replacement will further facilitate Mexico's asymmetrical economic integration with the United States. As a result, the CCE was the main force in Mexico giving shape to the economic policies intended to set the stage for USMCA.

## The U.S.-Mexico CEO Dialogue

In this context it is important to take note of an extremely powerful cross-border summit of large corporate interests—the U.S.-Mexico CEO Dialogue—which promotes private-sector investment. Formed in 2013, this organization asserts that by uniting the forces of the U.S. Chamber of Commerce and those of the CCE it "has served as the primary private sector vehicle for input into the U.S.-Mexico High Level Economic Dialogue" through its biannual summit meetings. It functions under the auspices of the U.S.-Mexico Economic Council (USMXECO), the foremost cross-border business advocacy organization designed to set policy priorities. As the positioning dance over the approval of the USMCA accelerated in Washington, D.C., the April 2019 meeting of the CEO Dialogue occurred in Mexico at the regal Hacienda San Diego Cutz, whose website calls it the "most spectacular hacienda in the Yucatán Peninsula." The stunningly restored hacienda was built during the henequen boom in the 19th century when essentially enslaved peons rapidly created some of the greatest fortunes of the era for the 50 "henequen kings" of the Yucatán. (Before the Mexican Revolution, henequen, a fibrous plant used to make rope, cordage, and twine became a major export for Mexico.) High profits led to monopolistic economic consolidation—from 1902 to 1915 the U.S.-based International Harvester Company controlled 90% of the global henequen market.

Presiding over the meeting for the U.S. side was Department of Commerce Secretary Wilbur Ross. He is the billionaire vulture-capitalist whom President Trump chose as his number-one economic promoter of the "America First" doctrine. Ross served as the commander of the nationalist U.S. team of negotiators who gave form to the USMCA. Joining Ross was the president and CEO of the U.S. Chamber of Commerce, Thomas J. Donohue. The U.S. Chamber of Commerce represents more than three million business members—it constitutes the largest corporate interest group in the United States. Donahue's organization is the main force that assembled the Pass USMCA Coalition. Among the approximately two dozen CEOs in attendance, also representing the U.S. contingent was Larry Fink, CEO of the world's biggest hedge fund, the $6 trillion BlackRock company.

On the Mexican side—illustrating the perpetual asymmetry of power between the two nations—the President of Mexico, Andrés Manuel López Obrador (known by the acronym "AMLO") arrived with a vast political team that included most of his cabinet, as well as his Chief of Staff Alfonso Romo Garza.

In an administration that is largely understood in the United States as being progressive, Garza's presence signals the contradictory nature of AMLO's leadership: an ag-biotech billionaire who also owns 60% of Mexico's largest insurance company, he is related through marriage to the "old-money" Monterrey dynasty of the Garza Sada family. Garza stated, after López Obrador's election in July 2018, that "Mexico needs to become a paradise for private investment." He also proclaimed at another event that the private sector would be the "cornerstone" for a period of economic growth "unlike anything seen before."

The central focus of the meeting in the Yucatán was a presentation on the Council for the Promotion of Investment, Employment, and Economic Growth for the edification of the assembled U.S. plutocrats. Created in February 2019, the Council will operate under the direction of Garza. Viewed by AMLO as a crucial institutional innovation that will harmonize the interests of the public, private, and "social" sectors (i.e., all entities that are not part of the public or private sector, such as unions and collective farmers, or ejidatrios). Garza has stated that the Council will double the rate of economic growth by attracting direct foreign investment, thereby raising the rate of national investment. (This has been the argument for 25 years under NAFTA. Foreign investment did rise, but much of it arrived to buy out already existing Mexican firms. Meanwhile, the Mexican oligarchy was busy investing abroad. The continual outflow as Mexican corporations invested abroad was so strong that, in 2012 Mexico became—by a large margin—a net capital-exporting nation.)

Carlos Salazar Lomelín, the president of the CCE, represented Mexico's CEOs at the meeting. Given that the announced purpose of the forum was to identify areas for investment and collaboration between the United States and Mexico, the director of the CCE occupied the most important position possible with regard to the expansion of private sector activities in Mexico.

Salazar Lomelín assumed leadership of the CCE in February 2019. Previously, he was the CEO of FEMSA—the second largest Mexican company—and he came to the CCE directly from the ultra-conservative employers' association Coparmex, one of the six peak business organizations which comprise the CCE.

## AMLO: Yes to the USMCA, No to Neoliberalism, Yes to "Free" Trade?

In March, López Obrador stated that with Mexico under his new authority "neoliberalism has been left behind." As he then promoted his National Plan for Economic Development, it appeared that Mexico was poised to pivot 180 degrees away from the pro-globalization, anti-labor, market-fundamentalist policies that reigned supreme since 1988. However, he and his cabinet members have repeatedly proclaimed their support for the essentially neoliberal USMCA. And, AMLO stated in early April that "Mexico is in favor of free trade"—thereby seeming to ignore the economic straightjacket under which Mexico suffered under NAFTA (as documented in part one of this article, "Dancing on Quicksand: A Retrospective on NAFTA on the Eve of Its Replacement," D&S, March/April 2019).

President López Obrador's influential Foreign Relations Secretary, Marcelo Ebrard, noted that the USMCA would provide new opportunities for Mexico to grow within the secure barriers of the powerful economic bloc that NAFTA created for the United States, Mexico, and Canada. Nonetheless, he stressed that Mexico would pursue an industrial policy—a national economic policy designed to stimulate dynamic transformations in selected key economic sectors through subsidies, investment promotion, and public policies—in an attempt to rejuvenate the decrepit internal market through a program to promote "human capital" and cutting edge technologies. Ebrard failed to note that as early as November 1987 Mexico had agreed to forego all forms of industrial policy (while the United States continues to promote leading sectors of its economy through the sub-rosa industrial policies it had long pursued, especially through the Pentagon's Defense Advanced Research

Projects Administration) when Mexico agreed to the U.S.-Mexico Bilateral Agreement on Trade and Investment. Meanwhile, echoing Ebrard's advocacy of industrial policy to some extent, López Obrador made it clear that Mexico would preserve its national sovereignty over the energy sector even as foreign firms would have limited participation in the long-contested oil sector.

## Labor Law Changes for the USMCA

With AMLO and his cabinet declaring that they are fully behind the ratification of the USMCA, one matter of considerable weight remains to be resolved: the United States has called for the end of "protection" labor contracts which—for roughly three-quarters (some estimate 90%) of the unionized Mexican labor force—bind workers to an agreement determined by captive union administrators who collude with their employers. Workers under such contracts frequently do not know that they are actually in a union. Union leaders who administer these company-union contracts that protect the power of the employer to suppress wages and avoid strikes are understood to receive large side-payments—allowing them to amass personal fortunes. When new plants open it is frequently the case that a company union has already signed a contract with the boss before any workers are hired. Under the USMCA such contracts will be illegal, while workers will have the right to a secret ballot to elect truly independent union leaders. This is an attractive idea for many in the U.S. Congress—but these political leaders have insisted that the proposed sweeping change in collective bargaining contracts must be backed by enforcement. Mexico's chief negotiator for the USMCA, Jesús Seade, managed in April to push through the Mexican Senate the revisions in Mexico's labor laws to now enshrine free elections, secret ballots and majority approval of any collective bargaining agreement. Thus far, however, no details have been presented as to how enforcement of these new labor law provisions will be institutionalized. If Seade can present a reasonable set of enforceable new labor law amendments to the U.S. Congress, much of the hesitancy within the Congress for ratification of the USMCA will fall away.

The move to obliterate the "protection" contract racket is part of a larger package that will eliminate the tripartite labor conciliation councils (comprised of management, labor, and a government representative) which have historically been used to legally settle labor disputes in Mexico. Instead, the current plan is to institute a direct form of labor-management arbitration, eliminating the state's agency to mediate between capital and labor. Critics see this step as effectively increasing the power of capital over labor. The final step in the augmentation of Mexico's labor law is to require that employers conform to a weak version of the International Labour Organization's (ILO) labor standards. The ILO's "Declaration on Rights at Work," which would eliminate child labor and discrimination in the workplace, acknowledge "freedom of association," and impose occupational health and safety standards along with "acceptable conditions of work with respect to the minimum wage," are all steps that AMLO's government is anxious to make.

Recently, retired Congressman Sandy Levin and labor analyst Harely Shaiken traveled to San Luis Potosí—part of Mexico's north-south "Detroit Corridor" which begins at the border and runs almost to Mexico City. There, they noted the difference that independent unions will likely make by contrasting a Goodyear Tire plant where workers are paid about $1.50 per hour under a "protection" contract with the nearby Continental Tire plant where independent union workers made $6 per hour (with better benefits).

How the employer's confederation, Coparmex, will respond to this challenge remains to be seen. Their strategy will likely be to lure workers into not joining an independent union. Coparmex wants to checkmate the new labor law by deploying the resistance of their 36,000 affiliated members who employ nearly five million workers, accounting for an estimated 30% of the GDP. The employer's federation may be able to extract some advantages from the new labor structure if the drive for independent unions results in the atomization of workers' organizations. Presently every worker within a collective bargaining unit, regardless of status, faces the employer as one united force. Within the new structure it may be possible to divide workers along skill lines so that a given plant would operate under several contracts. It remains to be seen if the gains expected from the elimination of "protection" contracts will be partially lost as employers find other ways to check the power of workers through atomization or other subterfuges which would impact labor law.

## The "Right to Invest" Is the Right to Pollute and Plunder

It should be stressed that the USMC agreement will reduce the power of what is known as the Investor State Dispute Settlement (ISDS) provision of NAFTA. U.S. corporate interests viewed ISDS as the heart of NAFTA because it allowed them nearly free reign to invest in any area of Mexico's economy under its "right to invest" clause. At that time, only Mexico's nationally-owned oil and gas industry and its electrical production and distribution entities were off-limits. But that was swept away in 2014 when President Peña Nieto jammed through an energy-sector privatization program. Under his program, Mexico could no longer take any action to prevent foreign-owned energy companies from controlling oil and gas assets or buying up the electrical systems, regardless of their behavior in violating safety or ecological standards.

However, with the USMC agreement, the "right to invest" clause will be eliminated. Thus passage of the USMC agreement will enable Mexico to prevent U.S. and Canadian mining companies from buying up land and then engaging in environmentally damaging practices. But this much needed restoration of national sovereignty over foreign investors will not be in effect in the energy sector. As Forbes magazine noted in 2018: "Mexico is now one of the best areas for new energy investment in the entire world, with an unmatched hundreds of billions of dollars in oil, gas, and power opportunities up for grabs." For the nine U.S. energy companies that now have a presence in Mexico as a result of the 2014 Mexican privatization bill, the Trump Administration created a big loophole. These energy giants will essentially retain the "right to invest" clause and other measures designed to force Mexico to relinquish its national sovereignty. Thus, Forbes continued by noting that U.S. companies were "salivating" at Mexico's open door: "Ultimately, ISDS [now applying only to the energy sector] will help [the United States] ensure that Mexico doesn't descend into another Venezuela, which not long ago nationalized many U.S. and U.S.-allied energy assets and awarded project stakes to Russian and Chinese companies."

## The Mexican Auto Sector—NAFTA's Greatest Conquest

The USMC agreement will significantly restructure the economic bloc that the United States formed in the early 1990s. At that point in time, many of the emerging forms of an intensified international rivalry based in new technologies of industrial organization were only hazily understood by key negotiators. Under NAFTA, the internationalization of capital reached new heights, allowing for the cheap and fast movement of components and parts across vast distances. Nowhere has this "shrinking of space effect" been more apparent than in the global auto industry. When NAFTA was implemented, its greatest accomplishment was to massively shift important portions of the U.S. auto sector to Mexico. No other aspect of manufacturing came remotely close to the preeminence of the auto sector: In 2017 Mexico built 3.6 million automobiles, exporting 3.2 million, 83% of which went to the United States. Net exports (exports minus vehicles and parts imported) at $60.1 billion in 2017 made the auto sector the largest earner of foreign exchange, and in 2018 employment in the auto sector reached a record 840,000 workers. Even with their low wages, auto assembly workers were considered well paid compared to the rest. But the largest portion of auto-sector workers labored in Mexico's vast and overwhelmingly foreign-owned auto parts industry where they were paid a pittance for low-skill assembly activities.

During the time that NAFTA was in effect, production networks, in general, shifted rapidly, prioritizing intercontinental flows of intrafirm components and parts. For example, worldwide auto parts exchanges (imports, exports, reimports, and re-exports) from 2000 to 2012 more than doubled to reach a level of approximately $3.5 trillion. The production process has become increasingly fragmented, with vertical integration disintegrating as outsourcing rose. One of the core activities embedded in these newly emerged processes of internationalization is labor arbitrage—setting up diverse activities designed to maximize access to cheap labor. This has been a key structural feature of the revolution in the geographic siting of production locations, creating complex global value chains and supplier/subcontractor networks.

## Local Content and "America First"

All of these recent changes have conditioned the USMC agreement in terms of what are known as the "rules of origin" which determine the share of auto content produced within the North American bloc. Under the 1994 accord, 62.5% of production was to take place in the North American region—now, under the USMC agreement it will be 75%. At least 40% of all production will require a minimum-wage payment of $16 per hour. The agreement may impose a requirement that 70% of aluminum, steel, and glass—the three primary inputs into auto production—will have to come from the region. The importance of the new rules of origin will be enhanced by tariffs and barriers hindering imports from Europe and Asia. The U.S. nationalist objectives are driving the USMC agreement as part of a much broader strategic industrial and trade policy intended to subordinate its international rivals.

Twenty-five years ago Mexico was the low-wage playground for the largest U.S. auto companies: Mexico forfeited its aspirations for national development and became a mere maquiladora supplier for an array of manufacturers. Yet, particularly as a result of the dramatic downturn in 2008-2009, industrial capital from Japan, Germany, and Korea has poured through Mexico's backdoor over the last 10 years, and China now threatens to invest in Mexico, too. Mexico's national territory is now used by U.S. rivals who freely export their production into the United States under the NAFTA schema. Indeed, by 2017 U.S. firms owned only a bit more than one-third of the installed capacity (i.e., the value of existing auto plants) in Mexico's sizeable auto sector. Before the 2008-2009 crisis Mexico was the locus for 10 auto assembly plants, half of which were owned by the Big Three—General Motors, Ford, and Chrysler. Since then, eight new assembly plants have been built, only two of which are U.S.-owned; and only seven of the 18 auto assembly plants in Mexico by the end of 2019 will be U.S.-owned.

A particular, and defining, aspect of the process of displacing U.S. dominance in the auto industry has been the ability of rivals to thrive by supplying auto parts and components produced outside of the NAFTA region. The formulation that guided NAFTA—that U.S.-based firms (and some Canadian-based firms) would export auto parts, components, and modular assemblies that would then be inserted into automobiles in assembly plants in Mexico where labor costs were low and then imported back to the United States and Canada—has gone awry. There has been an explosive growth in imported auto parts and components arriving from outside of North America in recent years. Compared to 1994, there has been a twenty-fold increase in non-North American auto imports, with an increase of 46% since 2008.

In 2017 approximately 35% of Mexico's steel imports came from Japan and Korea and a more modest amount from Germany. In the same year Mexico imported $5.9 billion of aluminum, with data regarding suppliers incomplete. In 2017 Mexico was the world's ninth-largest importer of aluminum and the 12th-largest importer of steel. Thus, as a complement to a new strategy designed to reassert U.S. dominance in all stages of the auto industry, and to pressure Mexico to remove its welcome mat at its backdoor to Asia and Europe, the U.S. imposed large tariffs on steel and aluminum imported from Mexico in 2018.

The USMCA's requirement that 40% of the content of all autos made in the North American bloc be made by workers making at least $16 per hour means that almost one-half of the car will have to be made in either the United States or Canada. This legislation is particularly aimed at Hyundai, KIA, Volkswagen, Mazda, and Toyota. These companies frequently assemble in Mexico with less than 10% of a vehicle's value being comprised of parts, components, and labor originating in the United States. Most of these firms obtain their auto parts from their country of origin—Korea, Japan, or Germany.

Still, the largest share of Mexico's auto parts industry is owned by U.S. giants such as Delphi. This company has plants throughout Mexico—it is one of the country's largest employers, operating with 50,000 extremely low-paid workers. The 40% rule for "high wage" $16 per hour work (45% for pickup trucks) can be fulfilled by increasing the imported "core parts" components of the vehicles assembled in Mexico. For example, U.S.-based plants can produce and then export to Mexico more motors, transmissions, and chassis. In addition, 10% of the value of autos imported into the United States from Mexico can be from U.S.-sited research and development.

Within the new structure taking form in North America, Mexico's subordinated and dependent stature will not change; Mexicans will remain mired in the most labor intensive and poorest-paid activities of the auto sector. At least, this is the case and the intention under the provisions that the U.S. government has negotiated and seeks to pursue in 2019 for the final passage of the USMC agreement.

Already facing a sinking national economy and threats of debilitating capital flight from Mexico's oligarchs, the progressive new president, López Orbrador, will have only six short years to re-channel deeply embedded social patterns and entrenched institutional structures that have encased NAFTA thus far. Whether his efforts will extend to remolding the giant Mexican auto sector, or whether his untested cadres have the capacity and will to do so, remains to be seen. ❏

*Sources*: Banco de México "Evolución Reciente de las Exportaciones Automotrices de México": (banxico.org.mx); Mary Burfisher, F. Lambert, and T. Matheson, "NAFTA to USMCA: What is Gained?," IMF Working Paper, WP/19/73, March, 2019; "Meet the New NAFTA," Center for Automotive Research, October 16, 2018 (cargroup.org); Clement, Jude, "NAFTA 2.0: ISDS Supports U.S. Oil, Natural Gas, and Electricity Companies," Forbes, April 29, 2018 (forbes.com); Stephanie Dhue and Kayla Tausche, "GOP begins grassroots campaign to sell Trump's trade deal with Mexico and Canada to skeptical voters and lawmakers," CNBC, March 26, 2019 (cnbc. com); "Van por diálogo empresarios de EU y gobierno mexicano" April 10, 2019 El Universal (el-mexicano.com); Susana González G., "Cumbre de alto nivel entre líderes y empresarios de EU y México," La Jornada, April 10, 2019 (jornada.com.mx); Sander Levin and Harley Shaiken, "A North American Road to the Middle Class," The Hill, September 28, 2018 (thehill.com) National Highway Traffic Safety Administration, American Automobile Labeling Act Reports, 2017 (nhtsa. gov); "Plantas de automóviles en México," El País, 2017 (elpais.com); Arturo Páramo, "Plan

Nacional de Desarrollo pondrá fin a neoliberalismo," Excelsior, March15, 2019 (excelsior.com. mx); "¿México será beneficiado por USMCA?" Cuestione, October 1, 2018 (cuestione.com); Trade Works for America, February 10, 2019, "Trade Works for America Coalition Announces Former Senator Heidi Heitkamp and Phil Cox as Bipartisan Co-Chairs" (tradeworksforamerica.com); Juan Carlos Cruz Vargas, "La IP será la "piedra angular" para el crecimiento económico, adelanta Alfonso Romo," Proceso, July 9, 2018 (proceso.com.mx); Napoleón Gómez Urrutia, "Surge el nuevo sindicalismo mexicano," La Jornada, April 11, 2019 (jornada.com.mx); U.S. Chamber of Commerce, U.S.-Mexico Economic Council (USMXECO) CEO Dialogue (uschamber.com); U.S. International Trade Commission, "U.S.-Mexico-Canada Trade Agreement: Likely Impact on the U.S. Economy and on Specific Industry Sectors," April 18, 2019 (usitc.gov); U.S. Trade Representative, "Estimated Impact of the United States-Mexico-Canada Agreement on the U.S. Automotive Sector," April 18, 2019 (ustr.gov); USMCA Coalition, February 26, 2019 "What is the USMCA?" (usmcacoaliton.org); Susana González G., May 14, 2019 "Alerta Imef por fuga de capitales ante incertidumbre" La Jornada (jornada.com.mx).

Article 6.4

# THE EUROPEAN UNION AND THE EUROZONE

## BY THE *DOLLARS & SENSE* COLLECTIVE
January/February 2001, last revised December 2016

The European Union forms the world's largest single market—larger than the United States or even the three NAFTA countries together. From its beginnings in 1951 as the six-member European Coal and Steel Community, the association has grown both geographically (now including 28 countries) and especially in its degree of unity. All national border controls on goods, capital, and people were abolished between member countries in 1993. And 17 of the European Union's members now share a common currency (the euro), collectively forming the "eurozone."

## The EU and the "Social Charter": Promises Unkept

At first glance, open trade within the European Union seemed to pose less of a threat for wages and labor standards than NAFTA or the WTO. Even the poorer member countries, such as Spain, Portugal, and Greece, were fairly wealthy and had strong unions and decent labor protections. Moreover, most EU countries, including top economic powers like France, Germany, Italy, and the United Kingdom, had strong parties (whether "socialist," social democratic, or labor) with roots in the working-class movement. This relationship had grown increasingly distant over time; still, from the perspective of labor, the European Union represented a kind of best-case scenario for freeing trade. The results are, nonetheless, cautionary.

The main thrust of the European Union, like other trade organizations, has been trade and investment. Labor standards were never fully integrated into the core agenda of the EU. In 1989, 11 of the then-12 E.U. countries signed the "Charter of the Fundamental Social Rights of Workers," more widely known as the "Social Charter." (Only the United Kingdom refused to sign.) Though the "Social Charter" did not have any binding mechanism—it is described in public communications as "a political instrument containing 'moral obligations'"—many hoped it would provide the basis for "upward harmonization," that is, pressure on European countries with weaker labor protections to lift their standards to match those of member nations with stronger regulations. The years since the adoption of the "Social Charter" have seen countless meetings, official studies, and exhortations but few appreciable results.

Since trade openness was never directly linked to social and labor standards and the "Social Charter" never mandated concrete actions from corporations, European business leaders have kept "Social Europe" from gaining any momentum simply by ignoring it. Although European anti-discrimination rules have forced countries like Britain to adopt the same retirement age for men and women, and regional funds are dispersed each year to bring up the general living standards of the poorest nations, the social dimension of the European Union has never been more than an appendage for buying off opposition. As a result, business moved production, investment, and employment in Europe toward countries with lower standards, such as Ireland and Portugal.

The European Union also exemplifies how regional trading blocs indirectly break down trade regulations with countries outside the bloc. Many Europeans may have hoped that the European Union would insulate Europe from competition with countries that lacked social, labor, and environmental standards. While the European Union has a common external tariff, each member can maintain its own non-tariff trade barriers. E.U. rules requiring openness between member countries, however, made it easy to circumvent any E.U. country's national trade restrictions. Up until 1993, member states used to be able to block indirect imports through health and safety codes or border controls, but with the harmonization of these rules across the EU, governments can no longer do so. Since then, companies have simply imported non-E.U. goods into the European Union countries with the most lax trade rules, and then freely transported the goods into the countries with higher standards. (NAFTA similarly makes it possible to circumvent U.S. barriers against the importation of steel from China by sending it indirectly through Mexico.)

European Union members that wished to uphold trade barriers against countries with inadequate social, labor, and environmental protections ended up becoming less important trading hubs in the world economy. This led E.U. countries to unilaterally abolish restrictions and trade monitoring against non-E.U. nations. The logic of trade openness seems to be against labor and the environment even when the governments of a trading bloc individually wish to be more protective.

## The Eurozone: Caught in a Bind

The process of European economic integration culminated with the establishment of a common currency (the euro) between 1999 and 2002. The creation of the euro seemed to cap the rise of Europe, over many years, from the devastation of the Second World War. Step by step, Western Europe had rebuilt vibrant economies. The largest "core" economy, Germany, had become a global manufacturing power. Even some countries with historically lower incomes, like Ireland, Italy, and Spain, had converged toward the affluence of the core countries. The euro promised to be a major new world currency, ultimately with hundreds of millions of users in one of the world's richest and seemingly most stable regions. Some commentators viewed the euro as a potential rival to the dollar as a key currency in world trade, and as a "reserve" currency (in which individuals, companies, and national banks would hold financial wealth).

Of the 28 European Union member countries, only 19 have adopted the euro as their currency (joined the "eurozone"). One of the most important E.U. economies, the United Kingdom, for example, retained its own national currency (the pound). The countries that did adopt the euro, on the other hand, retired their national currencies. There is no German deutschmark, French franc, or Italian lira anymore. These currencies, and the former national currencies of other eurozone countries, stopped circulating in 2001 or 2002, depending on the country. Bank balances held in these currencies were converted to euros. People holding old bills and coins were also able to exchange them for euros.

The adoption of the euro meant a major change in the control over monetary policy for the eurozone countries. Countries that have their own national currencies generally have a central bank (or "monetary authority") responsible for policies affecting the country's overall money supply and interest rates. In the United States, for example, the Federal Reserve (or "the Fed") is the monetary authority. For eurozone countries, monetary policy is made not by a national central bank, but by the European Central Bank (ECB). ECB policy is made by 25-member "governing council," including the six members of the bank's executive board and the directors of each of the 19 member countries' central banks. The six executive-board members, meanwhile, come from various eurozone countries.

While all countries that have adopted the euro are represented on the governing council, Germany has a much greater influence on European monetary policy than other countries. Germany's is the largest economy in the eurozone. (France's economy is just over two-thirds the size of Germanys; Italy's, just over half; Spain's, just over one-third; the Netherlands', less than one-fourth.) German policymakers, meanwhile, have historically made very low inflation rates their main priority (to the point of being seen as "inflation-phobic"). Even during the current crisis, as economist Paul Krugman puts it, "what we're seeing is an ECB catering to German desires for low inflation, very much at the expense of making the problems of peripheral economies much less tractable."

For countries, like Germany, that were hit less hard by the global Great Recession, the "tight money" policy did not prevent a fairly quick return to normal levels of unemployment. For the harder-hit countries, however, the results have been disastrous. These countries are mired in a deep economic crisis, in heavy debt, and unable to adopt a traditional "expansionary" monetary policy on their own (since the eurozone monetary policy is set by the ECB). For them, a looser monetary policy could stimulate demand, production, and employment, even without causing much of an increase in inflation. In Europe today, however, there are vast unused resources—including millions of unemployed workers—so more demand could stimulate the production of more goods, and need not result in rising inflation.

Somewhat higher inflation, moreover, could actually help stimulate the harder-hit European economies. Moderate inflation can stimulate demand, since it gives people an incentive to spend now rather than wait and spend later. It also reduces the real burdens of debt. Countries like Greece and Spain are drowning in debt, both public and private. These debts are generally specified in nominal terms—as a particular number of euros. As the price level increases, however, it reduces the real value of a nominal amount of money. Debts can be paid back in euros that are worth less than when the debt was incurred. As real debt burdens decrease, people feel less anxious about their finances, and may begin to spend more freely. Inflation also redistributes income from creditors, who tend to be wealthier and to save more of their incomes, to debtors, who tend to be less wealth and spend most of theirs. This, too, helps boost demand.

## The Crisis of the European Union

The current crisis has led many commentators to speculate that heavily indebted countries, like Greece or Spain, might decide to abandon the euro and leave the European Union. (Greece has appeared the most likely candidate to go that route. A possible Greek exit from the euro and the European Union is widely referred to as "Grexit." This need not mean that they would repudiate (refuse to pay) their public debt altogether. They could, instead, convert their euro debts to their new national currencies. The resoration of monetary-policy sovereignty would give them more freedom to pursue an expansionary policy. Increasing the money supply could lower interest rates, stimulate spending, and boost economic growth and employment. To the extent that monetary expansion resulted in somewhat higher inflation, it would also reduce the real debt burden.

So far, neither Greece, nor Spain, nor any other hard-hit country has moved to exit the European Union. The only country that has, ironically, is the United Kingdom, which is not even a member of the eurozone, and so is not subject to the loss of monetary-policy sovereignty that makes such a move, arguably at least, a serious coniseration in eurozone countries. Rather, the vote in the July 2016 referendum, which narrowly went in favor of "Brexit," appears to have been heavily influenced by anti-immigrant sentiment.

The current crisis, some economists argue, shows how the euro project was misguided from the start. Paul Krugman, for example, argues that the common currency was mainly driven by a political (not economic) aim—the peaceful unification of a region that had been torn apart by two world wars. It did not make much sense economically, giiven the real possibility for divergent needs of different national economies. Today, it remains a real possibility that the eurozone, or even the European Union itself, could come apart again. ❑

*Sources:* Paul Krugman, "European Inflation Targets," *New York Times* blog, January 18, 2011 (krugman.blogs.nytimes.com); European Central Bank, Decision-making, Governing Council (www.ecb.int/); European Central Bank, Decision-making, Executive Board (www.ecb.int/); Federal Statistical Office (Statistisches Bundesamt Deutschland), Federal Republic of Germany, Short-term indicators, Unemployment, Consumer Price Index (www.destatis.de); Paul Krugman, "Can Europe Be Saved?" *New York Times*, January 12, 2011 (nytimes.com).

*Article 6.5*

# TRUMP'S WITHDRAWAL FROM THE WORLD HEALTH ORGANIZATION

*A cover-up for his abject failure on Covid-19.*

**BY PRABIR PURKAYASTHA**
*July 2020, Independent Media Institute*

**M**icrobes do not recognize borders. We are all safe only when everybody is safe. In a pandemic, to attack the only body we have for global cooperation endangers everyone. That is why the U.S. withdrawal from the World Health Organization (WHO) is dangerous not only for the United States, but for all of the world.

President Donald Trump's decision to withdraw from the WHO is a continuation of his administration's commitment to wielding a wrecking ball to the international framework of treaties and organizations. Whether it is arms control, climate change, trade, or the WHO, the United States sees these agreements and institutions as fetters on its hegemonic powers to shape the world. Trump may express this pathology in its most ugly form, but the disease runs far deeper.

Trump's excuse for withdrawing from the WHO is that it did not do its job well on the Covid-19 pandemic and was soft on China. Condemning Trump's move, Devi Sridhar, professor of global public health at the University of Edinburgh and adviser to the Scottish government, tweeted, "Donald Trump's withdrawal of U.S. from the WHO ignores the key role the agency plays in outbreak prevention and response. Not only for Covid, but also for polio, malaria, TB, plague, yellow fever, cholera, Zika virus, and neglected tropical diseases." She also pointed out that it is because of such international agreements that the WHO received information from China on the novel pathogen on December 30, 2019 and declared the "highest alarm bell the world has"—a Public Health Emergency of International Concern—on January 30, 2020.

Trump is trying to pass the buck to the WHO for his administration's abject failure to prepare the United States for the Covid-19 pandemic. The U.S. Centers for Disease Control and Prevention (CDC) could not even prepare a proper test kit for two months for detecting SARS-CoV-2, the virus that causes the Covid-19 disease. China, Germany, and South Korea, to name a few, all had working test kits well before the CDC. One of these, Berlin's Charité hospital test kit, has been supplied by the WHO to more than 120 countries. The WHO had delivered this test kit to 57 countries well before the CDC—with an annual budget almost three times the WHO's (the CDC's annual budget is about $6.8 billion against the WHO's two-year budget for 2020–2021 of about $4.8 billion)—could get its test kits to work.

The United States has a bipartisan unity on its being the sole global hegemon. Its wars of invasion—from Korea to Vietnam, and Afghanistan to Iraq—have had bipartisan support. Its right wing, which in any other part of the world would be regarded as the loony right, believes that it can impose its will on the world through unilateral action: using military force and economic sanctions. The other side, the more globalist right believes that this hegemony can be exercised more easily with a combination of using the global institutions from within and unilateral action outside.

What does the WHO do, and what are the risks to the world of a U.S. pullout? Almost all countries have reposed their faith in the WHO as the only international instrument we have in fighting pandemics and infectious diseases. So, the U.S. action will inflict some financial damage to the WHO, but it is not a threat to its existence or mandate.

The WHO has an annual budget of about $2.2–$2.4 billion (its two-year budget for 2018–19 is $4.4 billion, and its two-year budget for 2020-21, as mentioned above, is $4.8 billion). According to the WHO, about 80% of its budget is funded by "voluntary contributions" made by member countries as well as organizations including philanthropic foundations and the private sector. The remaining 20% is covered by what are called "assessed contributions" of countries. The assessed contribution of the United States is about $120 million for 2020. Based on the Congressional Research Service's figures for U.S. voluntary contributions to the WHO from 2012–2018 (data is not available for 2019–2020), it is my estimate that the U.S. voluntary contribution to the WHO for 2020 is about $320 million, and that, along with its assessed contribution of $120 million, is about 20% of the WHO's current $2.2–$2.4 billion annual budget.

Because the assessed contributions are too low to fund the WHO on their own, voluntary contributions from countries and private funders have become the major component of its budget. Consequently, the WHO has become progressively more dependent on private interest groups and country interests that then dominate its agenda. After the United States and the United Kingdom, the Bill and Melinda Gates Foundation is the third biggest contributor to the WHO's total budget.

Compared to its mandate of health for all, and fighting disease and epidemics across the world, it is a measly budget. Just put the WHO budget numbers in perspective—as I mentioned above, the U.S. CDC's annual budget is roughly three times bigger than that of the WHO. The WHO also has no powers over sovereign countries and has to work with governments.

Even with these constraints, the WHO has had remarkable success in eradicating smallpox, bringing down the number of polio infections from the scourge they once were to today's small numbers, and interventions in other infectious diseases. Controlling the Ebola epidemic required multi-country and multi-agency cooperation that would not have been possible without the WHO's intervention (albeit its efforts had some critics). It is the only agency with technical competence, drawn from different regions, that can coordinate the efforts of different countries and their agencies.

Sure, we can criticize the WHO for its mistakes, initially on not advising the wearing of masks and not emphasizing the role of airborne fine droplets, or aerosols, in closed spaces. However, it raised the flag of pandemic early, it came out with clear recommendations on testing and tracking, and its multidisciplinary team worked with China to control the epidemic there, figuring out information essential to combat the virus and sharing it with the world.

A WHO report released on February 24, 2020 based on its collaboration with China made other countries aware that controlling the spread of Covid-19 required a more stringent protocol that is more like that of SARS than the flu. As a result, policy changes were made in countries like New Zealand. Countries who had experienced the 2003 SARS outbreak, such as Vietnam and South Korea, were already following the SARS protocol of using masks, extensive testing, and isolating those who were infected. Vietnam, in spite of a shared border with China, has controlled the epidemic completely and has not reported a single Covid-19 death.

Why is the WHO's coordinating role so important? Unlike human populations, microbes, as stated earlier, have no borders. They travel not only locally through water and air, but also, in an interconnected world like ours, via passengers traveling by air, water, or land. They infect animals and birds, both domesticated and in the wild. That is why quarantining the infected and isolating countries from others is only a short-term measure. The only long-term way to fight pandemics is either to eradicate the virus completely or to confine it to small pockets of outbreaks, through the use of vaccines and other public health measures. This battle cannot be won by one country. That is why gutting the WHO, the only competent public health instrument of global cooperation we have, is a road to disaster.

While there have been many warnings that a new pandemic was inevitable, the flu virus was thought to be the major threat. Its ability to mutate rapidly, using reservoirs of domesticated animals—chickens and pigs—and migratory birds, has been recognized as a long-term pandemic threat. The memory of the 1918 influenza epidemic lent credit to the seriousness of the flu threat.

The WHO has created a global network and infrastructure that can monitor flu outbreaks all over the world. Its Global Influenza Surveillance and Response System (GISRS), functioning for more than 65 years, identifies "novel influenza viruses and other respiratory pathogens" and provides vital information for the upcoming season's likely flu strains and vaccine composition recommendations. The GISRS is the only global platform that allows countries to share virus strains so that they can receive vaccines through the WHO's programs at concessional rates, and not at the prohibitively expensive market rates for the poorer countries.

Which countries benefit from such a virus sharing platform? The bulk of influenza vaccines are used in the United States and western Europe. The United States uses more flu vaccine than any other country. Meanwhile, nearly 50% of the global population—Africa, West Asia, South Asia, and Southeastern Asia—uses only 5% of the world's flu vaccines, even though the bulk of flu samples come from these countries.

Walking out of the WHO leaves at risk not only the global flu program, but also our ability to fight a new influenza pandemic that can rival the one in 1918. At that time, it killed an estimated 50–100 million people (15–20 million of those casualties were in British India alone). Since the world's population was about one-fourth of our current numbers, this would mean casualties of 200–400 million by today's count, even without factoring in the effects of modern travel's ability to speed up the spread of contagion.

No matter where a disease begins, stopping the spread at the source before it becomes a pandemic also protects the populations of other countries. Why, then, would the United States pull out when it is the net beneficiary of the WHO's disease monitoring and prevention program?

The right wing opposes public health policies in favor of individual-centric, privatized health care, with Big Pharma mopping up huge profits from life-saving medicines. This remains the case now, even though a pandemic can only be success-fully fought at the global level. Public health yields immeasurable profits for society, but not for private hospitals or Big Pharma.

The WHO, with its warts and all, still stands for global cooperation and foster-ing public health policies, and is the only instrument we have for global cooperation. It is hated by the right wing precisely for these reasons. The right-wing friends of Trump—Jair Bolsonaro, Boris Johnson, and Narendra Modi—do not criticize the United States for quitting the WHO, even though their countries need the WHO as much as the rest of the world. The attitude that every person must be for themselves, and every country for itself, is a part of their worldview as well. ❑

*Sources*: Prabir Purkayastha, "American Exceptionalism May Be Pushing the World into its Most Dangerous Period Ever," Independent Media Institute, June 2, 2020 (independentmediainstitute. org); Renée Graham, "The perfect storm: Fauci's truth vs. Trump's lies," *Boston Globe*, July 14, 2020 (bostonglobe.com); Jon Cohen, "The United States badly bungled coronavirus testing—but things may soon improve," *Science*, February 28, 2020 (sciencemag.org); Charité and the DZIF, "Researchers develop first diagnostic test for novel coronavirus in China," January 16, 2020 (charite.de); World Health Organization, WHO COVID-19 Preparedness and Response Progress Report - 1 February to 30 June 2020, August 3, 2020 (who.int); Lawrence Gostin, "Two Legal Experts Explain Why The U.S. Should Not Pull Funding From The WHO Amid COVID-19 Pandemic," *Forbes*, April 13, 2020 (forbes.com); Christopher Kelly and Stuart Laycock, *America Invades: The Controversial Story of How We've Invaded or Been Militarily Involved with Almost Every Country on Earth* (Book Publishers Network, 2014); Elaine Ruth Fletcher and Svet Lustig Vijay, "WHA Concludes With Call For Strong WHO And Equitable Access To COVID-19 Treatments – But US Assault Casts Shadow Over Future," Health Policy Watch, May 19, 2020 (healthpolicy-watch.news); World Health Organization, Programme Budget, 2020-2021 (who.int); World Health Organization, "How WHO is Funded," (who.int); World Health Organization, "Assessed contributions payable by Member States and Associate Members 2020-2021," (who.int); Erica Werner, "Congressional Democrats allege Trump's move to defund World Health Organization is illegal," *Washington Post*, April 15, 2020 (washingtonpost.com); Congressional Research Service, "U.S. Funding to the World Health Organization (WHO)," April 30, 2020 (crsreports.congress. gov); Gargeya, "AC/VC: The Shock of WHO Funding," People's Health Movement, July 7, 2018 (phmovement.org); World Health Organization, "Ebola then and now: Eight lessons from

West Africa that were applied in the Democratic Republic of the Congo," April 10, 2020 (who.int); Vera Scott, Sarah Crawford-Browne, and David Sanders, "Critiquing the response to the Ebola epidemic through a Primary Health Care Approach," BMC Public Health, May 17, 2016 (bmcpublichealth.com); World Health Organization, Report of the WHO-China Joint Mission on Coronavirus Disease 2019 (COVID-19), February 24, 2020 (who.int); AnaMaldonado, Manolo de los Santos, Subin Dennis, and Vijay Prashad, *Coronashock and Capitalism*, Tricontinental: Institute for Social Research, July 2020 (thetricontinental.org); Christina Potter, "Zero Covid-19 Deaths in Vietnam," Outbreak Observatory, July 9, 2020 (outbreakobservatory.org); Our World in Data, "Emerging COVID-19 success story: Vietnam's commitment to containment," June 30, 2020 (ourworldindata.org); World Health Organization, "Global Influenza Surveillance and Response System (GISRS)," (who.int); Arnold S. Monto, "Reflections on The Global Influenza Surveillance and Response System (GISRS) at 65 Years: An Expanding Framework for Influenza Detection, Prevention, and Control," *Influenza and Other Respiratory Viruses*, February 19, 2018; World Health Organization, "Pandemic Influenza Preparedness (PIP) Framework," (who.int); Surabhi Pandey, Snehal Manjrekar, and Onkar Sumant, "Influenza Vaccine Market by Vaccine Type Global Opportunity Analysis and Industry Forecast, 2019–2026," Allied Market Research, October 2019 (alliedmarketresearch.com); Helen Branswell, "U.S. withdrawal from WHO threatens to leave it 'flying blind' on flu vaccines," Stat News, June 29, 2020 (statnews.com); Chuck Dinerstein, "Influenza Vaccination Is Global, But Not The Same," American Council on Science and Health, October 26, 2018 (acsh.org); Michael T. Osterholm and Mark Olshaker, "Chronicle of a Pandemic Foretold," *Foreign Affairs*, July/August 2020 (foreignaffairs.com); Vanessa Baird, "Only Internationalism Can Beat COVID-19," New Internationalist, April 6, 2020 (newint.org); Ronald G. Shafer, "The World Health Organization—under attack by Trump—was targeted by conservatives in 1948, too," *Washington Post*, April 19, 2020 (washingtonpost.com).

# Chapter 7

# LABOR IN THE GLOBAL ECONOMY

*Article 7.1*

## THE GLOBALIZATION CLOCK

**BY THOMAS PALLEY**
*May/June 2006; revised November 2018*

Over the past forty years real wages have stagnated in developed economies, and there has also been a massive increase in income and wealth inequality. Those developments are substantially attributable to the neoliberal economic policy paradigm which has dominated policymaking. Globalization is a critical element of that paradigm, and it has been a major contributing factor to wage stagnation and increased inequality.

The neoliberal policy era did not happen in a vacuum. Instead, it needs to be explained by political economy, which shows how particular economic interests triumphed in capturing political power and the world of economic ideas (i.e. economic theory), and how those ideas and policies were accepted by society. The Globalization Clock provides a metaphor for understanding that political process as it relates to globalization. It helps explain why globalization has been so politically difficult to turn back despite its injurious effects. A key reason is globalization's adverse impact on political solidarity, with globalization aggravating the pre-existing decline in solidarity caused by the rise of the consumer society.

Political economy has historically been constructed around the divide between capital and labor, with firms and workers at odds over the division of the economic pie. Within this construct, labor is usually represented as a monolithic interest, yet the reality is that labor has always suffered from internal divisions—by race, by occupational status, and along many other fault lines. Neoliberal globalization has in many ways sharpened these divisions, which helps to explain why corporations have been winning and workers losing.

One of these fault lines divides workers from themselves: since workers are also consumers, they face a divide between the desire for higher wages and the desire for lower prices. Historically, this identity split has been exploited to divide union from nonunion workers, with anti-labor advocates accusing union workers of causing higher prices. Today, globalization is amplifying the divide between people's interests as workers and their interests as consumers through its promise of ever-lower prices.

Consider the debate over Walmart's low-road labor policies. While Walmart's low wages and skimpy benefits have recently faced scrutiny, even some liberal commentators argue that Walmart is actually good for low-wage workers because they gain more as consumers from its "low, low prices" than they lose as workers from its low wages. But this static, snapshot analysis fails to capture the full impact of globalization, past and future.

Globalization affects the economy unevenly, hitting some sectors first and others later. The process can be understood in terms of the hands of a clock. At one o'clock is the apparel sector; at two o'clock, the textile sector; at three, the steel sector; at six, the auto sector. Workers in the apparel sector are the first to have their jobs shifted to lower-wage venues; at the same time, though, all other workers get price reductions. Next, the process picks off textile sector workers at two o'clock. Meanwhile, workers from three o'clock onward get price cuts, as do the apparel workers at one o'clock. Each time the hands of the clock move, the workers taking the hit are isolated. In this fashion, globalization moves around the clock, with labor perennially divided.

Manufacturing was first to experience this process, but technological innovations associated with the Internet are putting service and knowledge workers in the firing line as well. Online business models are making even retail workers vulnerable—consider Amazon.com, for example, which has opened a customer support center and two technology development centers in India. Public-sector wages are also in play, at least indirectly, since falling wages mean falling tax revenues. The problem is that each time the hands on the globalization clock move forward, workers are divided: the majority is made slightly better off while the few are made much worse off.

Globalization also alters the historical divisions within capital, creating a new split between bigger internationalized firms and smaller firms that remain nationally centered. This division has been brought into sharp focus with the debate over the trade deficit and the overvalued dollar. In previous decades, manufacturing as a whole opposed running trade deficits and maintaining an overvalued dollar because of the adverse impact of increased imports. The one major business sector with a different view was retailing, which benefited from cheap imports.

However, the spread of multinational production and outsourcing has divided manufacturing in wealthy countries into two camps. In one camp are larger multinational corporations that have gone global and benefit from cheap imports; in the other are smaller businesses that remain nationally centered in terms of sales, production and input sourcing. Multinational corporations tend to support an overvalued dollar since this makes imports produced in their foreign factories cheaper. Conversely, domestic manufacturers are hurt by an overvalued dollar, which advantages import competition.

This division opens the possibility of a new alliance between labor and those manufacturers and businesses that remain nationally based—potentially a potent one, since there are approximately 7 million enterprises with sales of less than $10 million in the United States, versus only 200,000 with sales greater than $10 million. However, such an alliance will always be unstable as the inherent labor-capital conflict over income distribution can always reassert itself. Indeed, this pattern is already evident in the internal politics of the National Association of Manufacturers (NAM), whose members have been significantly divided regarding the overvalued dollar. As one way to address this division, the group is promoting a domestic "competitiveness" agenda aimed at weakening regulation, reducing corporate legal liability, and lowering employee benefit costs—an agenda designed to appeal to both camps, but at the expense of workers.

Solidarity has always been key to political and economic advance by working families, and it is key to mastering the politics of globalization. Developing a coherent story about the economics of neoliberal globalization around which working families can coalesce is a key ingredient for solidarity. So, too, is understanding how globalization divides labor. These narratives and analyses can help counter deep cultural proclivities to individualism, as well as other historic divides such as racism. However, as if this were not difficult enough, globalization creates additional challenges. National political solutions that worked in the past are not adequate to the task of controlling international competition. That means the solidarity bar is further raised, calling for international solidarity that supports new forms of international economic regulation. ❑

*Article 7.2*

# GLOBALIZATION AND THE END OF THE LABOR ARISTOCRACY

## BY JAYATI GHOSH
*March/April 2017*

Twenty-first century imperialism has changed its form. In the 19th century and the first half of the 20th century, it was explicitly related to colonial control; in the second half of the 20th century it relied on a combination of geopolitical and economic control deriving from the clear dominance of the United States as the global hegemon and leader of the capitalist world (dealing with the potential threat from the Communist world). It now relies more and more on an international legal and regulatory architecture—fortified by various multilateral and bilateral agreements—to establish the power of capital over labor. This has involved a "grand bargain," no less potent for being implicit, between different segments of capital. Capitalist firms in the developing world gained some market access (typically intermediated by multinational capital) and, in return, large capital in highly developed countries got much greater protection and monopoly power, through tighter enforcement of intellectual property rights and greater investment protections.

These measures dramatically increased the bargaining power of capital relative to labor, globally and in every country. In the high-income countries, this eliminated the "labor aristocracy" first theorised by the German Marxist theorist Karl Kautsky in the early 20th century. The concept of the labor aristocracy derived from the idea that the developed capitalist countries, or the "core" of global capitalism, could extract superprofits from impoverished workers in the less developed "periphery." These surpluses could be used to reward workers in the core, relative to those in the periphery, and thereby achieve greater social and political stability in the core countries. This enabled northern capitalism to look like a win-win economic system for capital and labor (in the United States, labor relations between the late 1940s and the 1970s, for example, were widely termed a "capital-labor accord"). Today, the increased bargaining power of capital and the elimination of the labor aristocracy has delegitimized the capitalist system in the rich countries of the global North.

Increasing inequality, the decline in workers' incomes, the decline or absence of social protections, the rise of material insecurity, and a growing alienation from government have come to characterise societies in both developed and developing worlds. These sources of grievance have found political expression in a series of unexpected electoral outcomes (including the "Brexit" vote in the UK and the election of Trump in the United States). The decline of the labor aristocracy—really, its near collapse—has massive implications, as it undermines the social contract that made global capitalism so successful in the previous era. It was the very foundation of political stability and social cohesion within advanced capitalist countries, which is now breaking down, and will continue to break down without a drastic restructuring of the social and economic order. The political response to this decline has been expressed primarily in the rise of right-wing, xenophobic, sectarian, and reactionary political tendencies.

## 21st Century Imperialism

The early 21st century has been a weird time for imperialism. On the one hand, the phase of "hyper-imperialism"—with the United States as the sole capitalist superpower, free to use almost the entire world as its happy hunting ground—is over. Instead, the United States looks significantly weaker both economically and politically, and there is less willingness on the part of other countries (including former and current allies, as well as those that may eventually become rival powers) to accept its writ unconditionally. On the other hand, the imperial overreach that was so evident in the Gulf Wars and sundry other interventions, in the Middle East and around the world, continues despite the decreasing returns from such interventions. This continued through the Obama presidency, and it is still an open question whether the Trump presidency will lead to a dramatic reduction of this overreach ("isolationism") or merely a change in its direction.

The latter point is important, because there is little domestic political appetite in the United States for such imperial adventures, due to the high costs in terms of both government spending and the loss of lives of U.S. soldiers. The slogans that recently resonated with the U.S. electorate, such as that of "making America great again" were in that sense somewhat self-contradictory—looking towards an imagined past in which the American Dream could be fulfilled relatively easily (at least for some), without recognising that this was predicated upon the country's global hegemony and far-flung empire.

All this does not mean that there have been no changes in global economic and political power: there have been and will continue to be significant and even transformative changes. However, changes in the relative positions of different countries on the economic and geopolitical ladder do not mean that the basic imperialistic tendencies that drive the global system have disappeared—indeed, they may even become more intense as the struggle for economic territory becomes more acute.

This is particularly evident in the global spread of multinational corporations and their new methods of functioning, particularly with the geographic disintegration of production. Technological changes—advances in shipping and container technology that dramatically reduced transport times and costs, as well as the information technology revolution that enabled the breakdown of production into specific tasks that could be geographically separated—have been critical to this process. Together, they made possible the emergence of global value chains, which are typically dominated by large multinational corporations, but involve networks of both competing and cooperating firms. The giant corporations are not necessarily in direct control of all operations. Indeed, the ability to transfer direct control over production—as well as the associated risks—to lower ends of the value chain is an important element in increasing their profitability. This adds a greater intensity to the exploitation that can be unleashed by such global firms, because they are less dependent upon workers and resources in any one location, can use competition between suppliers to push down their prices and conditions of production, and are less burdened by national regulations that might reduce their market power.

This transformation has therefore given rise to what has been called the "Smiling Curve" of exchange values and profits. Value added and profits are concentrated in the pre-production (such as product design) and post-production (marketing and branding) phases of a value chain. These now provide immense economic rents to the global corporations that dominate them, due to the intellectual property monopolies these corporations enjoy. The case of Apple phones is now well known:

---

### Poorer Than Our Parents?

A recent report from the McKinsey Global Institute, "Poorer than Their Parents? Flat or falling incomes in advanced economies" (July 2016) shows how the past decade has brought significantly worse economic outcomes for many people in the developed world.

### Falling Incomes.

In 25 advanced economies, 65-70% of households (540-580 million people) "were in segments of the income distribution whose real incomes were flat or had fallen" between 2005 and 2014. By contrast, between 1993 and 2005, "less than 2 percent, or fewer than ten million people, experienced this phenomenon." In Italy, a whopping 97% of the population had stagnant or declining market incomes between 2005 and 2014. The equivalent figures were 81% for the United States and 70% for the United Kingdom. The worst affected were "young people with low educational attainment and women, single mothers in particular." Today's younger generation in the advanced countries is "literally at risk of ending up poorer than their parents," and in any case already faces much more insecure working conditions.

### Shifting Income Shares

The McKinsey report noted that "from 1970 to 2014, with the exception of a spike during the 1973–74 oil crisis, the average wage share fell by 5 percentage points in the six countries studied in depth" (United States, United Kingdom, France, Italy, the Netherlands and Sweden); in the "most extreme case, the United Kingdom, by 13 percentage points." These declines occurred "despite rising productivity, suggesting a disconnect between productivity and incomes." Productivity gains were either grabbed by employers or passed on in the form of lower prices to maintain competitiveness.

Declining wage shares are widely seen as results of globalization and technological changes, but state policies and institutional relations in the labor market matter. According to the McKinsey report. "Swedish labor policies such as contracts that protect both wage rates and hours worked" resulted in ordinary workers receiving a larger share of income. Countries that have encouraged the growth of part-time and temporary contracts experienced bigger declines in wage shares. According to E.U. data, more than the actual producers in China (both companies and workers) earn only about one-tenth of the final price of the good; the rest is taken by Apple for product design, marketing, and distribution. The producers of coffee beans across the developing world earn a tiny percentage of the price of coffee, in contrast to the high profits of a multinational chain like Starbucks. Small farmers and laborers growing cocoa beans earn next to nothing, compared to the leading sellers of chocolate, all of which are Northern companies. The economic rents associated with the pre- and post-production phases have been growing in recent years. Meanwhile, the production phase, from which workers and small producers mainly derive their incomes, is exposed to cutthroat competition between different production sites across the world, thanks to trade and investment liberalization. Therefore, incomes generated in this stage of the value chain are kept low.

The overall result is twofold. First, this has resulted in an increase in the supply of the "global" labor force (workers and small producers who are directly engaged in production of goods and services). Second, the power of corporations to capture

---

40% of E.U. workers between 15 and 25 years have insecure and low-paying contracts. The proportion is more than half for the 18 countries in the eurozone, 58% in France, and 65% in Spain.

The other side of the coin is the rising profit shares in many of these rich countries. In the United States, for example, "after-tax profits of U.S. firms measured as a share of the national income even exceeded the 10.1% level last reached in 1929."

### Policy Matters

Government tax and transfer policies can change the final disposable income of households. Across the 25 countries studied in the McKinsey report, only 20-25% of the population experienced flat or falling disposable incomes. In the United States, government taxes and transfers turned a "decline in market incomes for 81% of all income segments … into an increase in disposable income for nearly all households." Government policies to intervene in labor markets also make a difference. In Sweden, the government "intervened to preserve jobs, market incomes fell or were flat for only 20%, while disposable income advanced for almost everyone." In most of the countries examined in the study, government policies were not sufficient to prevent stagnant or declining incomes for a significant proportion of the population.

### Effects on Attitudes

The deteriorating material reality is reflected in popular perceptions. A 2015 survey of British, French, and U.S. citizens confirmed this, as approximately 40% "felt that their economic positions had deteriorated." The people who felt worse-off, and those who did not expect the situation to improve for the next generation, "expressed negative opinions about trade and immigration." More than half of this group agreed with the statement, "The influx of foreign goods and services is leading to domestic job losses." They were twice as likely as other respondents to agree with the statement, "Legal immigrants are ruining the culture and cohesiveness in our society." The survey also found that "those who were not advancing and not hopeful about the future" were, in France, more likely to support political parties such as the far-right Front National and, in Britain, to support Brexit.

*Source*: McKinsey Global Institute, "Poorer than Their Parents?" July 2016 (mckinsey.com).

rents—from control of knowledge, from oligopolistic/monopolistic market structures, or from the power of finance capital over state policy—has greatly increased. Overall, this has meant a dramatic increase in the bargaining power of capital relative to labor, which in turn has resulted in declining wage shares (as a percentage of national income) in both developed and developing countries.

## Implications for Workers

These processes imply worsening material conditions, for most workers, in both the periphery and the core. Imperialism has generally weakened the capacity for autonomous development in the global South, and worsened economic conditions for workers and small producers there, so that is not altogether surprising. The growth of employment and wages in China is as a break from that pattern and an example of some benefits of global integration, at least for a subset of working people in the developing world. The beneficiaries, however, remain a minority of the workers in the global South. In other countries generally seen as "success stories" of globalization, like India, the economic realities for most people are much bleaker.

The more obvious—and potent—change that has resulted from this phase of global imperialism has been the decline of the labor aristocracy in the North. The opening of trade, and with it a global supply of labor, meant that imperialist-country capital was no longer as interested in maintaining a social contract with workers in the "home" country. Instead, it could use its greater bargaining power to push for ever-greater shares of national income everywhere it operated. This was further intensified by the greater power of mobile finance capital, which was also able to increase its share of income as well. In the advanced economies at the core of global capitalism, this process (which began in the United States in the 1990s) was greatly intensified during the global boom of the 2000s, when median workers' wages stagnated and even declined in the global North, even as per capita incomes soared. The increase in incomes, therefore, was captured by stockholders, corporate executives, financial rentiers, etc.

The political fallout of this has now become glaringly evident. Increasing inequality, stagnant real incomes of working people, and the increasing material fragility of daily life have all contributed to a deep dissatisfaction among ordinary people in the rich countries. While even the poor among them are still far better off than the vast majority of people in the developing world, their own perceptions are quite different, and they increasingly see themselves as the victims of globalization. Decades of neoliberal economic policies have hollowed out communities in depressed areas and eliminated any attractive employment opportunities for youth. Ironically, in the United States this favored the political rise of Donald Trump, who is himself emblematic of the plutocracy.

Similar tendencies are also clearly evident in Europe. Rising anti-European Union sentiment has been wrongly attributed only to policies allowing in more migrants. The hostile response to immigration is part of a broader dissatisfaction related to the design and operation of the European Union. For years now, it has been clear that the European Union has failed as an economic project. This stems from the very design of the economic integration—flawed, for example, in the enforcement of monetary integration without banking union or a fiscal federation that would have helped deal with imbalances between E.U. countries—as well as from the particular neoliberal economic policies that it has forced its members to pursue.

This has been especially evident in the adoption of austerity policies across the member countries, remarkably even among those that do not have large current-account or fiscal deficits. As a result, growth in the European Union has been sclerotic at best since 2004, and even the so-called "recovery" after 2012 has been barely noticeable. Even this lackluster performance has been highly differentiated, with Germany emerging as the clear winner from the formation of the Eurozone. Even large economies like France, Italy, and Spain experienced deteriorating per capita incomes relative to Germany from 2009 onwards. This, combined with fears of German domination, probably added to the resentment of the European Union that is now being expressed in both right-wing and left-wing movements across Europe. The European Union's misguided emphasis on neoliberal policies and fiscal austerity packages has also contributed to the persistence of high rates of unemployment, which are higher than they were more than a decade ago. The "new normal" therefore shows little improvement from the period just after the Great Recession—the capitalist world economy may no longer be teetering on the edge of a cliff, but that is because it has instead sunk into a mire.

It is sad but not entirely surprising that the globalization of the workforce has not created a greater sense of international solidarity, but rather undermined it. Quite obviously, progressive solutions cannot be found within the existing dominant economic paradigm. But reversions to past ideals of socialism may not be all that effective either. Rather, this new situation requires new and more relevant economic models of socialism to be developed, if they are to capture the popular imagination. Such models must transcend the traditional socialist paradigm's emphasis on centralized government control over an undifferentiated mass of workers. They must incorporate more explicit emphasis on the rights and concerns of women, ethnic minorities, tribal communities, and other marginalised groups, as well as recognition of ecological constraints and the social necessity to respect nature. The fundamental premises of the socialist project, however, remain as valid as ever: The unequal, exploitative and oppressive nature of capitalism; the capacity of human beings to change society and thereby alter their own futures; and the necessity of collective organisation to do so. ❑

*This is an excerpted version of an article that appeared in the March/April 2017 issue of* Dollars & Sense. *Portions of that article appeared in the author's earlier article, "The Creation of the New Imperialism: The Institutional Architecture,"* Monthly Review, *July 2015.*

*Article 7.3*

# TRANSNATIONAL CAPITAL AND TRANSNATIONAL LABOR

## AN INTERVIEW WITH WILLIAM K. TABB
*November/December 2017*

**W**illiam K. Tabb is an economist and author of The Restructuring of Capitalism in Our Time *(2012),* Economic Governance in the Age of Globalization *(2004), and* The Amoral Elephant: Globalization and the Struggle for Social Justice in the Twenty-First Century *(2001). He spoke with* Dollars & Sense *in July 2017 on the global economic crisis, its causes and consequences; the transnational capitalist class and neoliberal globalization; and the prospects for resistance and alternatives to capitalism now and in the future. —Eds.*

**Dollars & Sense**: If we look at a world map showing GDP growth rates in 2009 or 2010, during the Great Recession, we see most of the high-income countries of North America, Europe, and East Asia with negative growth rates. Meanwhile, we see some of South America, much of Africa, and most of South Asia and East Asia still with positive economic growth. Why would the wealthiest and most powerful countries be at the epicenter of a global economic crisis?

**William Tabb:** The crisis was triggered in the financial sector, and while that didn't cause the problem, it brought the economy down. The financial crisis itself was created by the over-indebtedness in the richer countries and the extent of leverage, that is of borrowing, mostly by the private-sector, actually, and the slow rate of growth in their economies. They dealt with the slow rate of growth in the economy by offering people the chance to borrow more money. And they did. As they borrowed more and more, they reached the point that they couldn't pay it back, especially the mortgages and, within that, the subprime mortgage in the United States. But that same property crash happened in a number of other advanced countries. The other thing that was behind the borrowing was the stagnation of income for working classes across the advanced capitalist world. Slowing growth in the real economy and rapid growth in the financial economy came from increased unequal distribution of income, where the 1%—in Occupy Wall Street's terms—accrued more and more of the surplus created. They put it into finance because there was no point in producing more goods and services, investing in the real economy, because most people didn't have the money because of the stagnation of incomes. So you had the slowing down leading to the financialization.

The other piece of that was the globalization of the economy, in which industry or deindustrialization had killed so many of the good and many unionized jobs, which added to the stagnation pressures.

**D&S:** Just to follow up on that, do you think it's useful to talk about a possibility where—even if the crisis detonated in the higher-income countries—they might have offloaded more of the fallout onto other countries? People talk about Germany "exporting unemployment" to other countries, but these were mostly countries in the European periphery. Is it possible to imagine the high-income countries doing something similar on a global scale?

**WT:** To begin with the German case which you raise: It's an important one, because what the Germans succeeded in doing was holding down the wages in their own country, so that they could continue to export. The rest of Europe became less competitive, with the euro, since they were all tied to the same currency. The German economy grew basically by exploiting their neighbors in Europe. As far as the developing countries are concerned: many were commodity producers, and with the downturn, commodity prices fell and they were damaged heavily through that.

I also wanted to go back to the way that finance hurt Latin America and Asia in earlier crises, where the same form of borrowing was interrupted by the United States' monetary policy. The countries that had borrowed first in the Latin American debt crisis of the 1980s and then in the Asian crisis of the '90s, suddenly had to pay back debt that they couldn't pay back because of the suddenness of the change.

In the current period, or the period since 2007–2008 with the downturn, something similar happened, in which the developing countries did suffer the consequences of the slowdown in the core. The extent to which this was the higher-income countries "putting it on them" rather than merely co-suffering—it's a harder one for me to answer.

**D&S:** You mentioned the Latin American debt crisis, which served as the lance point, in many countries, for the imposition of "neoliberal" economic policies. The United States government was certainly in the forefront of spreading this "free market" or "neoliberal" economic policy paradigm to other parts of the world, in Latin America and elsewhere, and giant U.S. corporations have certainly been major beneficiaries. Is the hegemonic position of the United States in the capitalist world economy dependent on the continuation of this paradigm?

**WT:** It certainly is important to transnational capital, and especially to U.S.-based transnational capital. But one of the things to think about is that the nationality of capital has become more internationalized. For many major U.S. corporations, or major German or French corporations, the stock is owned much more widely, so that their headquarters may still be in the country of origin but capital has become more internationalized in terms of ownership and control. So, yes, for American corporations it is very important, but it is important for all transnational capital.

What neoliberalism does is force the countries of Latin America or other developing countries to hold their own wages down in order to be competitive in the global marketplace. Capital is mobile, and transnational capital will buy from the lowest cost sources, given that their supply chains can alter where production is taking place. It gives them bargaining power for lower taxes in the countries of the Third World, lower wages for the workers in those countries, and incentives to in fact locate there. So a great deal of the profitability of transnational capital comes from this greater bargaining power over both the workers of the world and the countries of the world, especially the less powerful countries that are more dependent on transnational capital.

**D&S:** How far do theories of a "transnational capitalist class" and "transnational capitalist state" get us in understanding the restructuring of the capitalist world economy in the late 20th century? Do those ideas help us explain the transition from the clashing colonial empires of a century ago (each seeking to carve out exclusive access for their own capitalist companies) to today's global regime maintaining global access (to markets, natural resources, labor, etc.) for transnational capital?

**WT:** I had earlier been skeptical of the theory, because all of the actions of local capitalist classes—in terms of protecting their interests—were strong going into the 1980s and the 1990s. But we did see a major change, a change that actually originated earlier, as national development strategies gave way—with elites, instead of

---

### The Evolution of Imperialism

A century ago, it was clear that the division of labor was the Global South producing raw materials and the "core" countries of the world system producing industrial goods. The peripheral countries produced raw materials which were sold at low prices because of the lower cost of reproducing labor power in those countries as well as the military stronghold the colonial power had, and their ability to appropriate land and labor from the peoples of the Global South. That was first called "colonialism," later "imperialism." Some of these countries got their independence—became formally independent—but the economic relationship continued, and the countries of the core continued to exploit them basically in the same manner.

You did have a period of national development, of autocentric development, at the end of World War II. This was a strategy where national elites, pushed by progressive movements in these countries, tried to pursue a different form of development. Even groups like OPEC [the Organization of the Petroleum Exporting Countries] trying to raise the price of oil by coming together. The Bandung Conference of 1954 of progressive Third World leaders—called the "Third" World between the Soviet system and the Western capitalist system—trying to negotiate a better deal for their countries.

Neoliberalism basically undid that. So we move from the earlier period, of 100 years ago, of straight, exploitative, military, violent control, to informal control. When the colonial powers left a particular country, they tried to leave in place leaders who had been educated in the colonial country, chosen by the foreign ministries of the colonial powers, to be cooperative in a period when the former colony had become formally independent. That was challenged by some of the important leaders in the postwar period—Nehru in India, Sukarno in Indonesia, and others—who tried to negotiate in a very meaningful sense for the Global South. They were succeeded, unfortunately, by leaders who were more in favor of the later development of transnational control. —WT

trying to follow autonomous development and trying to protect themselves from foreign capital, becoming instead junior partners foreign capital and giving up the national independence and autonomous development.

When that happened, they became junior partners for transnational capital and to a much greater extent were integrated into the global capitalist class. This was a significant change from the era of national Keynesianism of the postwar period into global neoliberalism, where transnational capital is able not only to penetrate these countries, but the elites of these countries see their interests in working as part of a global capitalist class. I think that the theory, as it has been developed, is now much more convincing and the evidence for it is much greater.

*D&S:* How do you see the prospects for a new anti-capitalist politics, meaning a politics that aims at the replacement of the capitalist system with a new form of economic organization on a world scale? Does the globalization of capital undermine the viability of the "working class" as a driving force of social change, or could it foster (as one of its contradictions) a truly "transnational working class" that could be an agent of a global economic transformation?

**WT:** One of the things Karl Marx saw in the 1840s, when he and Frederick Engels were writing the *Communist Manifesto*, was that capitalism was a world system (which was pretty impressive insight back then) and that the global working class had nothing to lose and much to gain by uniting against capital. The idea that this might happen was dismissed by many people, but Marx just keeps coming back. In the current period, as global capital gets more and more control, it becomes more and more clear what is really going on. So in the United States, we have a situation where a little over half of young people are anti-capitalist and prefer socialism. This is a major change. The other change, speaking for the moment about the United States, is that surveys are showing that people identify not as middle class (because they are being pushed out of the middle class and people who are coming into the economy have not been given a chance for a middle-class standard of living) but as working class.

The rise of the right is the same thing as we saw in the 1930s: When the left becomes stronger—the progressive movement, the workers movement becomes stronger—it's only a violent, racist, xenophobic, Trump-like administration that can try to contain what in our country would be the base of the Democratic Party, the trade union movement, young people, Black Lives Matter, the fight for the $15 an hour minimum wage. These movements are getting stronger, and organizing at the local level is important. We're seeing the same trends, not only in the other advanced countries—in England especially, with [Jeremy] Corbyn—but in the countries that have been hardest hit by the crisis. We're seeing strong left-wing movements in Greece and Spain. Latin America has become more complex, as the left-wing governments that came in had trouble delivering on what they wished to deliver, given that they were part of a global system. They were unable on their own, even though they were able to improve conditions, to fundamentally challenge capitalism.

I think the idea that capitalism will be challenged—it will be challenged in the advanced countries and perhaps in China, where the number of strikes and the extent of unrest is really quite substantial, although the Communist Party power remains very strong. As the Chinese economy slows down—and their financial system, the overextension of debt, their banks getting in trouble—I would not rule out a serious change there as well. It is true, in the short run, that neoliberalism and transnational capital have restructured the economy, but it is not a sustainable model. The model cannot produce growth that is ecologically sensible in this period, which becomes much more of a challenge and people around the world are much more aware of that. So I am actually encouraged that—maybe not tomorrow—but that we're moving into an era where class analysis becomes more important, Where resistance to capitalism, which ten, 20, or 30 years ago would've been considered beyond the conversation, now becomes part of the conversation. ❑

*Article 7.4*

# ESSENTIAL—AND EXPENDABLE—MEXICAN LABOR

*On both sides of the border, Mexican workers are now essential—to U.S. corporations.*

## BY MATEO CROSSA AND JAMES M. CYPHER

*July/August 2020*

Lear Corporation—one of the world's largest auto parts manufacturers—rose to position 148 on *Fortune* magazine's famous list of the 500 largest firms in 2018. It operates with roughly 148,000 workers spread across 261 locations. Its largest presence is in Mexico, where approximately 40,000 low-paid workers make seats and labor-intensive electronic wiring systems to be used, primarily, by the U.S. auto giants in auto-assembly plants on both sides of the border. The largest share of these workers slog away in three huge Lear plants located in the notoriously dangerous border town of Ciudad Juárez in Mexico.

On April 10, 2020 a worker named Rigoberto Tafoya Maqueda died from Covid-19, which had swept in from the north. He had been diagnosed in Lear's clinic with a mild allergy and was forced to continue working without a face mask, gloves, or hand sanitizer. A short time later, he went to the government's Social Security hospital, on foot, where he died. Four days later, according to Lear, 13 more workers at the plant had died—but the workers' labor union claimed that the actual number of work-related deaths from the pandemic was 30. Lear claimed it was not responsible in the least, while offering hollow condolences to surviving family members.

As of late May, no investigation of the workplace had been conducted and no legal charges of negligence had been raised against Lear or any of the other 320 *maquiladoras*—also known as *maquilas*, or more recently, by outraged workers, as "*maKILLadoras*"—that employ approximately 230,000 in Juárez where workers have been sickened. By early May, 104 of these workers had perished, by early June the estimated number of worker deaths was above 200. In all of Mexico, this city, with the largest concentration of low-wage assembly plants, had the highest incidence of pandemic deaths—a mortality rate 2.5 times the national average.

Tijuana is the city with the second largest number of *maquilas* in Mexico. There, one in four "formal" sector workers (workers with registered jobs and certain rights to health care) work as low-wage laborers producing components for automobiles and many other industries. Tijuana is located in the state of Baja California in Mexico, where the highest number of pandemic deaths—519—had been recorded as of May 15. Of those deceased, 432 were *maquila* workers. By June 4, Tijuana had the highest number of Covid-19 deaths, 671, of any city in Mexico.

## U.S. Business, U.S. State Department Demand: The *Maquilas* Must Open

Ciudad Juárez and Tijuana are tangible symbols of the imposed power structures under which transnational corporations operate throughout the Global South, most particularly in Mexico. In these two border cities, 1,000 miles apart, we find nearly one-fifth of the *maquila* workforce—500,000 out of a total of 2.6 million workers. Here, in response to corporations' treatment of workers during the pandemic, the scene has included bitter strikes, social outrage, and numerous well-attended protests all aimed at imposing plant closures and paid leave. The plant owners have refused to assume any responsibility whatsoever for their negligence, insisting that the work must go on. Instead, they have pressured local and federal governmental agencies to ensure that, in spite of an unsanitary environment, no new safety and health regulations of the workplace will be imposed. After reopening in late May, the plants have taken some measures to reduce health risks among the workers, including the use of masks and plastic dividers at workstations and in company lunchrooms.

At the same time, plants have increased the pace of production exponentially. Even with the measures taken, there have continued to be outbreaks of Covid-19 at the assembly plants. Indeed, the long-powerful U.S. National Association of Manufacturers (NAM) has used every opportunity to ensure that no sustained period of plant closures be implemented—including sending an unprecedented letter to Mexico's president on April 22, signed by 327 corporate titans who enjoy the lucrative benefits of sweating Mexican workers. Signatories included the heads of 3M Corporation ($32 billion in sales in 2019), Arcelor/Mittal USA ($15 billion in sales 2019), and Caterpillar ($54 billion in sales 2019). Using a lot of imagination, and no small amount of chutzpah, these captains of industry demanded that President Andrés Manuel López Obrador (or AMLO, as he is known)—who had declared at the start of his presidency that the neoliberal era that had defined Mexico's economy since 1986 was over—declare that Mexican autoworkers were engaged in an "essential activity." The letter demanded that the president assure that "all interruptions in the North American manufacturing supply chain would be minimized in these critical moments." AMLO responded immediately by stating that Mexico and the United States would come to an agreement and that "there were exceptional questions" to resolve with the United States.

Has there ever been an occasion when a president of a sovereign nation has been told that its populace—beset by a vicious pandemic—would have to march into poisoned plants in order to maintain the profit margins of foreign-owned corporations?

If that was not enough, Christopher Landau, the U.S. ambassador to Mexico, gave himself a pat on the back in late April by declaring via Twitter, "I'm doing all I can to save supply chains between Mexico, the United States, and Canada." Immediately joining the fray, the employers' and manufacturers' "peak business organizations"—long the real rulers of Mexico—began to lobby and orchestrate political pressure to guarantee that *maquila* output would not be interrupted. The large owners associations included the *Consejo Coordinador Empresarial* (CCE), which is comprised of the largest Mexican firms, and the arch-conservative Mexican Employers Association (COPARMEX), which was formed in 1929 by the anti-union oligarchy based in industrial Monterrey, echoed the arguments presented by the NAM. Also joining in was the Association of the Mexican Auto Industry (which was founded in 1951 by Chrysler, Ford, General Motors, Nissan, and Volkswagen, and lists *no* Mexican-owned companies as members).

## A National Security Issue?

At this point, an unexpected actor entered the scene: The Undersecretary of Defense of the United States, Ellen Lord, declared to reporters in late April, "I think one of the key things we have found out are some international dependencies…" adding that "Mexico right now is somewhat problematic for us." In her remarks, Lord said nothing about the Mexican workers who toil in the *maquilas* becoming ill or dying. (*Maquilas* are now located throughout the country, not just along the U.S.-Mexican border.) She also added the "national security" argument to her framing of the pandemic's impact on U.S.-Mexico supply chains: "these companies are especially important for our U.S. airframe production." And, indeed, over the past 20 years the United States has outsourced a modest amount of aerospace production: in Mexico this consists of labor-intensive components that are used by the U.S. civilian aviation firms, along with some Pentagon military contractors, and are typically manufactured in *maquilas*. One example of this minor sideline of *maquila* manufacturing—and the conditions that workers face at these factories—is a Honeywell plant in Juárez where, on April 22, workers engaged in a three-day wildcat strike after learning that Covid-19 had spread into the plant, killing at least one worker.

One protesting worker summarized the situation:

> They do not want to give us [sick] days, we are worried because of the pandemic, management does not listen to us, they only tell us [to keep working] and they will give us a bonus of $18-$31.50 [dollars per week] but they will not respond to our demands, we have been on strike three days but the truth is that they are paying no attention to us.

## Inaugurating the USMCA

The U.S. pressure game got quick results: on May 12 the Mexican government declared that the aerospace *maquilas* (which, as of 2020, had only 57,000 direct employees) and the very large auto parts and auto assembly industry—which employs nearly 960,000 workers and is a mainstay of the "export-at-all-costs" neoliberal model—were "essential" industries. With this decree, the alarm bells ceased in the United States. Further, the Mexican government set June 1, 2020 as the date to return to full operation in the auto industry, which ensured that the beginning of the NAFTA-II agreement (officially the United States-Mexico-Canada Agreement, or the USMCA) was still on track for July 1, 2020. President Donald Trump will undoubtedly use the official launch of the USMCA to maximum effect as he hones his electoral strategy. AMLO supports this new agreement to "help stop the fall of the economy" and promote new foreign investments.

The list of transnational firms that are already in production—or will shortly resume—where Covid-19 has spread is a long one, and includes such companies as: Lear Corporation, Honeywell, Syncreon Borderland, Foxconn, Plantronics, Leoni, Rockwell, Mahle, Electrocomponentes de México, Electrolux, Hubbell, Commscope, Toro Company, Ethicon, Cordis, Syncreon, Flex, Keytronic, Optron, TPI, and APTIV. In April, shutdowns affected approximately 60% of all *maquiladora* workers in Juárez—a situation that was probably representative for the entire industry—suggesting that as many as 3,000 of the 5,162 *maquiladora* firms operating in April temporarily closed. The companies that are reopening are doing so without regard for the deaths of hundreds of their plant workers (some registered, some not). These firms have been the most enthusiastic advocates of restarting production as they have sought to drown out the resistance of their workers. On May 10, the *maquila* association (Index) reported that 55% of the *maquilas* were in operation. On May 19, as a great number of plants reopened, *maquila* workers in Jauréz and Matamoros marched to demand the closure of many plants, including those operated by Foxconn in Santa Teresa (where there were six Covid-19-related deaths, according to the workers), Electrocomponentes de México (10 deaths), Lear (30 deaths), Electrolux (seven deaths), Toro (two deaths), and Regal (13 deaths). The workers asserted that none of these operations—which make a range of products, from snow removal equipment to home appliances—were essential and that none of them had met the sanitation requirements as mandated two months earlier. In Juárez, 66 *maquilas* that make neither auto parts nor aviation parts (i.e., those never categorized as "essential") have remained in operation throughout the health crisis.

All across the borderland, from Tijuana (with an estimated 1,000 *maquilas*) through Mexicali in Baja California to Nogales, Sonora (with 70% of *maquilas* in operation on May 18), and on to Juárez, Chihuahua, and then to Ciudad Acuña, Cohauila (where 23,000 workers returned to their plants on May 20) and to the other end of the border in Matamoros, Tamaulipas (where the hospitals were full of dying workers), these states, and 269 municipal governments, had capitulated to the pressure from the United States to reopen. Meanwhile, the Mexican federal government refused to impose its own hygienic measures.

## NAFTA: Myth of Development, Reality of Deindustrialization

The destructive impact of the pandemic on Mexico reveals further the direct consequences of 26 years of neoliberalism under NAFTA, which exacerbated inequality and largely destroyed the nation's public health system, while imposing a new regime of food precarity as once nationally produced grains sold at controlled prices are now imported. This shift away from producing staple foods in Mexico has resulted in the displacement of millions of peasant cultivators—many of whom eventually migrated to the United States to work in the dirtiest, hardest, most unstable, and unrewarded jobs available.

What's more, despite the increased prosperity that NAFTA promised, throughout the NAFTA era average workers' wages—measured in terms of their purchasing power of basic goods—have generally declined. Over the past nearly three decades, exports have surged (especially in auto and auto parts manufacturing), and Mexico has been forced to de-industrialize as the domestic market has drowned in a sea of cheap imports. As a result, the industrial share of the GDP fell from 36.2% in 1993 (the last year before NAFTA took effect) to only 29.6% in 2017 as manufacturing ceased to be the driving force of the economy. In the period from 2003 to 2016, national content (with value originating in Mexico) across Mexico's broad manufacturing export sector averaged only 41%, while 59% of the value of manufacturing exports does not originate in Mexico. Using cheap labor to process imported inputs into goods that are largely exported to the United States now defines Mexico's ever-plodding economy. A large portion of the millions of manufacturing sector jobs that were lost in the United States after 1993 were transferred to Mexico where an enormous army of impoverished wage workers crowded into the *maquiladora* firms—which, as mentioned, now directly employ 2.6 million throughout Mexico.

As was the case in 1992–1993, when the business and political elites of Mexico opened the road to NAFTA—portraying the agreement as a much-needed lever to promote development—these same forces are now eagerly awaiting the USMCA. This delusionary enthusiasm found its way into an essay written by AMLO and published by the office of the president on May 16, 2020:

> To be the neighbor of the most powerful economy in the world under the current circumstances of global recession will help us to drive forward our productive activities and create new jobs. It is a fact that the agreement will attract more foreign investment to our industrial export sector.

But the rage of the *maquila* workers has further unmasked this myth of economic development, despite the fact that, after some attention received in April, the media has largely ceased coverage of labor strife on the border. On the first of May, International Workers Day, the streets of Ciudad Juárez woke up to graffiti proclaiming "STOP MAKILLAS." In this manner a diverse collective of workers began a campaign to raise awareness about perilous workplace conditions—announcing that "*el virus es la maKILLa*" (the virus is the *ma*KILL*a*) and that "*la makilla te aniquila*" (the *ma*KILL*a* will annihilate you)—and to demand new protections centered on *Salud, Trabajo y Dignidad* (Health, Work, and Dignity). Through these protests, they were able to communicate to the nation the completely arbitrary and unaccountable manner in which the transnational firms were operating along the border and throughout the country. The current policy is for these firms to force workers into the plants (lest they literally starve) on the pretext that they are involved in "essential" activities. Firms expect workers to continue doing their jobs without sanitary protections, given that distancing in these factories is impossible. Indignant workers have drawn attention to those who have been summarily fired, without justification as required by the labor law, when they resisted being forced into the deadly plants. These workers were then denied their indemnification for losing their jobs. (The labor law requires that employers pay workers fired without cause three months of salary plus 20 days of pay for every year of service, and a number of other smaller payments.)

"STOP MAKILLAS!" was also the cry heard on May 12, when the Mexican government declared that *maquila* workers in the aerospace and auto industries were "essential" (essential to the United States) and had to be forced to work, regardless of the utter absence of health and safety protections for workers. The workers responded by demanding they be put on leave at full pay (as well as that all necessary sanitary measures be taken).

But workers' concerns and their demands are clearly unimportant to the U.S. government and hundreds of U.S. companies operating in Mexico. U.S. Ambassador Landau was blunt in his advocacy of reopening in his widely circulated statement:

> We have to protect [people's] health without destroying the economy. It's not impossible. … I'm here to look for win-win solutions. On both sides of the border, investment = employment = prosperity.

And so, only four weeks after shutting their doors, the *maquilas* were open without any clear information as to which, if any, measures had been taken to protect the returning workers. Most workers were forced back onto the shop floor (although some large export firms delayed until June 1). The agencies of the Mexican government (at all levels) and the company-controlled unions had fallen over backwards to ensure that the profits would soon again be flowing, primarily to the United States. In the border state of Chihuahua, for example, 93% of the 122 "essential" workplaces inspected were approved for operation by June 1. However, two weeks later, additional plant inspections resulted in the closure of 44 out of 208 *maquiladoras* for lack of compliance with sanitation requirements.

## Drafted to Serve: Mexican Workers under the Defense Production Act

In March, the nationwide cries for more medical equipment evoked calls from Washington, D.C. to essentially conscript medical supply firms under the Defense Production Act. This Act was implemented in 1950 to force and enable the private sector to prioritize production and delivery of strategic supplies in a time of national emergency. The president then demurred, while stating that such a policy would amount to "nationalizing our businesses," then suggested that applying the act would be similar to steps taken in Venezuela under President Hugo Chávez (1999–2013).

According to President Trump, running out of crucial medical supplies during an unprecedented pandemic was not a sufficient reason to invoke the production authority of the state—failing market forces all along the medical supply chain could not be tampered with lest the United States slip into Venezuelan-style economic paralysis.

On the other hand, as the pandemic predictably arrived at the nation's cramped and fetid slaughterhouses, discomforting the Big Four meatpackers (JBS, with $39 billion in sales in 2017; Tyson, with $38 billion in sales; Cargill, the largest privately-owned firm in the United States, with $20 billion in sales; and Smithfield, with $15 billion in sales) and disrupting shoppers, these meatpacking behemoths did nothing. At their plants, the meatpackers could not be bothered to protect workers; and the spike of Covid-19 cases among meatpacking employees led to a slowdown in the slaughtering of animals, which led to shortages of meat. The president quickly swung 180° to apply the Act in late April. This mobilized a "critical infrastructure," especially the Big Four's infrastructure that very comfortably controls approximately 80% of the beef industry. (The top four in pork slaughterers controlled 64% of the market in 2011, while the top four in poultry producers controlled 56% of the market in 2019.) Unlike meeting the demand for medical supplies during a pandemic, slaughtering animals was, apparently, too "critical" to be left to the "free" market.

In 2017 the United States exported 13% of the cattle slaughtered, along with 27% of pigs, and 17% of chickens to other countries. While the Defense Production Act's powers could control foreign markets (exports and/or imports), U.S. slaughterhouses were left free to sell to the highest bidder.

In effect, U.S. slaughterhouse workers and all others involved in the meatpacking supply chain had been drafted to ensure that the flow of profits for the Big Four continued. Implementing the Act meant that workers could no longer receive unemployment benefits. They were now "free to choose" between zero income and near-zero job prospects outside the meatpacking plants or work in one of the three most impacted job sectors (the other two being nursing homes, which mass deaths from Covid-19 have turned into veritable death camps, and prisons and jails, where infections have run rampant).

## There's No Business Like Agribusiness

Right behind the arms-contracting corporations and aerospace firms that swarm the Pentagon stands the mollycoddled U.S. agribusiness interests. Just as the Pentagon was long ago "captured" by the arms contractors who weave in and out of top positions in the Department of Defense in order to return to the contracting firms through Washington's "revolving door," so, too, do the corporate chieftains of agribusiness rotate through the Department of Agriculture and the many other federal and state agencies that work hard to ensure that profits stay high in the agricultural sector.

In this sector government assistance at the local, state, and federal level has long been readily forthcoming to control the labor force and manage the surges in demand for seasonal tasks. Meatpacking, of course, can be undertaken without too much regard to the seasons. It is therefore rightly considered a manufacturing process that long ago adopted "continuous" production processes—often on a 24-hour basis. Like the seasonal-crop farm labor force, slaughterhouses long ago found that the best labor force is an immigrant labor force, documented or not. And, predictably enough, nearly 50% of this labor force consists of "Hispanics." Since nearly two-thirds of all Hispanics (according to the U.S. Census) are Mexican-born, we find that the use of the Defense Production Act to keep the slaughterhouses open is part of the larger process now taking place in both Mexico and the United States to force poor Mexicans to risk pandemic death, or long-term decrepitude, in order to make vehicles and auto parts for the U.S. populace and to ensure that its meat-centric diet is maintained. Embodied Mexican labor—workers who were expelled from Mexico during the long night of neoliberalism (1986–2018)—is the key component of the meatpacking supply chain in the United States. *Disembodied* Mexican labor is the key labor-intensive input of the U.S. auto/auto parts supply chain, as we have explained above.

## Werner Sombart's "Free Lunch"

Famously, in *Why Is There No Socialism in the United States?*, Werner Sombart claimed (in 1906) that U.S. workers, unlike their counterparts in Europe, were loyal to "the promised land of capitalism" because it provided them with "reefs of roast beef." Indeed, before Prohibition (1920–1933) a typical saloon in the United States provided an overflowing sideboard "free lunch" for the "thirsty" patrons—roast beef being a mainstay. Sated, workers could then proceed to "bring home the bacon."

So, what would happen if "reefs" of roast beef disappeared from the food system, along with that defining metric, bacon? We have seen that exhausted health care workers have been made to wait for protective equipment until the "free market" got good and ready to sell them such equipment at whatever prices the market will bear. But could the general populace be made to wait for meat at prohibitive prices? Oh, no.

In a society where well-being has largely been defined by the ability to consume, it has long been taken as a given that meat, or any other food item, would be immediately available in any quantity desired, provided that the buyer had sufficient funds. When that turned out to not be the case, the Defense Production Act was immediately deployed to force an overwhelmingly immigrant labor force to make an ugly decision—go to the front and hope to dodge the pandemic's bullets or face deportation, hunger, or both. Suddenly, from the long valleys of California to the largely Midwest slaughterhouses, Mexican workers who had risked arrest and deportation to get to the United States were carrying letters or cards showing that they were "essential." The farmworkers were, as usual, forced to face a daily diet of poisonous pesticides and the risk of infection from the deadly pandemic. But slaughterhouse workers must spend their work shift in tight quarters, in a closed structure among hundreds of workers, usually with circulating air that will bring all possible viral pathogens right to them.

# The Pandemic Behind the Pandemic: Neoliberalism

Behind the pandemic of 2020, which has left Latinos with nearly a six times higher infection rate than the average Iowan, lies a deeper pandemic which has spread despair across the United States for four decades. This pandemic—known well outside the United States as neoliberalism—transformed the once heavily unionized labor force in the meatpacking industry into low-wage, disposable drudges. Wages that were 15% above the national manufacturing average in the 1970s had, by the 1990s, fallen 20% below the median. Once subject to industry-wide bargaining agreements, plant unions now bargain weakly: in 2019 only 19% of the 292,000 meat processing workers were union members. In the 1980s and 1990s slaughterhouses were mostly shifted to "right-to-work" rural states to break the legacy of the large-city unions. These states allow workers a "free ride"—they can have the benefits of a union contract without paying dues—and this feature makes it almost impossible to maintain a union shop. Doubling up, employers began recruiting immigrants, particularly from Mexico. Today, the labor force has a turnover rate ranging from 60–100%, and the meatpackers union has been largely silent as the pandemic has spread.

Just prior to the decision to impose a military-style command system in the slaughterhouses, the Big Four dominating the supply chain (and the many small operations), facing massive pandemic outbreaks, demanded that the federal government impose labor rules that would exempt them from any workplace liability for death or illness arising from the pandemic. Corporations are maneuvering to use the Defense Production Act as a "liability shield" in order to stave off an expected wave of lawsuits alleging workplace negligence—such a wave would raise their liability insurance rates. Under the new arrangement, proven "negligence" may not trigger a court award—workers would have to prove "gross negligence, recklessness, or willful misconduct." Operating under the Defense Production Act, the meatpacking plants have become the spearhead of big U.S. capital—if they can weaken workers' rights to a demand a safe workplace, such new legal arrangements will be used by all sectors to weaken labor safety standards and drive down their operating costs.

Meanwhile, across the Midwest, the South, and the Rockies, where most plants are located, right-wing governors are working hand-in-glove with the meat barons, county health departments, and the Occupational Safety and Health Administration to hide any and all information with regard to infection rates and deaths from the pandemic. Only days after Trump invoked the Defense Production Act, data releases on the pandemic's spread at the slaughterhouses all but ceased. Still, county-wide data showed that in Finney County, Kan., home to a Tyson slaughterhouse, the infection rate on May 25, 2020 was one in every 26 people. This is nearly eight times the very high national average. The same results, as recorded by the *New York Times* map "Coronavirus in the United States," could be found over and over again: Cargill's plant in Ford County, Kan. produced an infection rate of one in every 21 people and Tyson's giant plant in Dakota City—operating with 4,300 workers—left nearby Woodbury County, Iowa with an infection rate of one in 39.

In Mexico and the United States, millions of "essential" Mexican workers—essential to the profits of U.S. super-corporations—are pressed to toil on: they must ensure that the U.S. populace face an even larger oversupply of motor vehicles and whatever "reefs of roast beef" remain after the lucrative export market has been supplied. ❑

*Sources*: De la Redacción, "Industriales de EU piden a México reabrir fábricas" *La Jornada*, April 23, (journada.com.mx); Manuel Fuentes, "Maquiladoras, a laborar por órdenes del Norte," *La Silla Rota*, May 20, 2020 (lasillarota.com); Joe Gould, "COVID closed Mexican factories that supply US defense industry. The Pentagon wants them opened" *Defense News*, April 21, 2020 (defensenews. com); Paola Gamboa, "Un bono de 700 pesos no vale más que mi vida" *El Heraldo de Juárez*, April 20 2020 (elheralddeJuárez.com.mx); Patricia Mayorga, "Indiferencia gubernamental y empresarial expone a obreros de maquilas al COVID-19," *La Verdad*, June 19, 2020 (laverdadJuárez.com); "Iztapalapa y Tijuana, cerca de los 700 muertos por COVID-19; ¿qué municipios registran más contagios?," *Medio Tiempo*, June 6, 2020 (mediotiemp.com); "Piden cerrar maquiladoras en frontera mexicana por la pandemia de COVID" *INFOBE: México* , May 19, 2020 (infobae.com); Marco Antonio López, "Empleados acusan que los obligan a trabajar pese a muertes por COVID en maquiladoras de Chihuahua" *Animal Político,* May 18, 2020 (animalpolitico.com); René Villareal, "Comercio exterior y el desarrollo de capacidades" *Comercio Exterior*, Oct.-Dec. 2018; Andrés Manual López Obrador, "The New Political Economy in the time of the Corona Virus," Office of the President, May 16, 2020 (lopezobrador.org.mx); Alberto Morales, "AMLO comparte ensayo la nueva política económica en los tiempos del coronavirus" *El Universal*, May 16, 2020 (eluniversal.com.mx); Shawn Fremstad, Hye Jin Rho and Hayley Brown, "Meatpacking Workers are a Diverse Group," Center for Economic Policy Research, April 29, 2020 (cepr.net); Roger Horowitz, "The decline of unionism in America's meatpacking industry," *Social Policy* (32: 3, 2002); Union Stats, 2019 "Union Membership by Occupation: Standard Occupational Classification 7810—Butchers and Meat Processors," 2019 (unionstats.com); Michael Corkery, David Yaffe-Bellany and Drek Kravitz, "Meat Workers Left in the Dark Under Pressure" *New York Times*, May 25, 2020 (nytimes.com); "Coronavirus Map: Tracking the Global Outbreak" *New York Times*, May 25, 2020 (nytimes.com).

# Chapter 8

# MIGRATION

*Article 8.1*

## WALLED OFF FROM REALITY

*Trump's claims about immigration economics are without merit.*

**BY JOHN MILLER**
*November/December 2015*

> Mexico's leaders have been taking advantage of the United States by using illegal immigration to export the crime and poverty in their own country. The costs for the United States have been extraordinary: U.S. taxpayers have been asked to pick up hundreds of billions in healthcare costs, housing costs, education costs, welfare costs, etc. ... The influx of foreign workers holds down salaries, keeps unemployment high, and makes it difficult for poor and working class Americans—including immigrants themselves and their children—to earn a middle class wage.
>
> — "Immigration Reform That Will Make America Great Again," Donald Trump campaign website

Donald Trump's immigration plan has accomplished something many thought was impossible. He has gotten mainstream and progressive economists to agree about something: his claims about the economics of immigration have "no basis in social science research," as economist Benjamin Powell of Texas Tech's Free Market Institute put it. That describes most every economic claim Trump's website makes about immigration: that it has destroyed the middle class, held down wages, and drained hundreds of billions from government coffers. Such claims are hardly unique to Trump, among presidential candidates. Even Bernie Sanders has said that immigration drives down wages (though he does not support repressive nativist policies like those proposed by Trump and other GOP candidates).

Beyond that, even attempting to implement Trump's nativist proposals, from building a permanent border wall to the mass deportation of undocumented immigrants, would cost hundreds of billions of dollars directly, and forfeit the possibility of adding trillions of dollars to the U.S. and global economies by liberalizing current immigration policies. That's not counting the human suffering that Trump's proposals would inflict.

## No Drag on the Economy

Even the most prominent economist among immigration critics, Harvard's George Borjas, recognizes that immigration has had a large positive effect on the U.S. economy. By his calculations, immigrant workers (documented and undocumented) add $1.6 trillion to the U.S. economy each year, or 11% of Gross Domestic Product (GDP). The great bulk of that additional income (97.8% according to Borjas) goes to immigrant workers. But that still leaves what he calls an "immigrant surplus" of $35 billion a year, which goes to non-immigrants, including workers, employers, and other users of services provided by immigrants.

Others have emphasized the disproportionate impact that immigrants have had on innovation in the U.S. economy. A study for the Kauffman Foundation found that, in 2006, foreign nationals residing in the United States were named as inventors or co-inventors in over 25% of all U.S. patent applications. Around the same time, another study found that immigrants were the founders of over half of all Silicon Valley startups and almost one-third of Boston startups.

## Immigrants Didn't Do It

U.S. workers have undoubtedly fallen on hard times. The reasons are manifold: slow economic growth; pro-rich, anti-worker, anti-poor policies; the decline of unions; "free-trade" globalization; and so on. But immigration isn't one of those reasons, especially when it comes to "the middle class." Not only has immigration benefitted the U.S. economy, but economists find no evidence that immigration causes a widespread decrease in the wages of U.S.-born workers.

Estimates vary, but the best economic studies point to the same conclusion: over the long run, immigration has not caused the wages of the average U.S. born worker to fall. Immigration critic Borjas calculated that, from 1990 to 2010, immigrant labor pushed down the wages of (pre-existing) U.S. workers by 3.2% in the short run. But even he conceded that over the long run, wages of native-born and earlier immigrant workers recovered to their previous level. Other economists find immigration to have a positive long-run effect on wages. Gianmarco Ottaviano and Giovanni Peri found that, from 1990 to 2006, immigration reduced wages of native-born workers in the short run (one to two years) by 0.7%, while over the long run (ten years) immigration into the United States boosted wages 0.6%.

Neither Ottaviano and Peri's nor even Borjas's estimates of the wage effects of immigration are consistent with Trump's claim that immigration is destroying the middle class. But what happens when we look at the wages of native-born workers by level of education? The Ottaviano-Peri study shows, in the long run, immigration is associated with an increase in wages across all education levels. Borjas's study reports that immigration has negative effects on the wages of native-born college graduates and especially on workers with less than a high-school education (those at the "bottom" of the labor market, mostly in low-wage jobs), even in the long run. But again concedes a positive effect for the 60% of U.S. workers with either a high school degree or some college (but no degree).

These results are probably a headscratcher for anyone who has taken introductory economics. After all doesn't increasing the supply of labor, through immigration, drive down its price (the going wage)? Well, no.

Immigrant workers do add to the supply of labor. But the economic effects of immigration do not stop there. Immigrants largely spend their wages within the U.S. economy. Businesses produce more—and hire more workers—to meet the increased demand. The cost savings from hiring cheaper immigrant labor also frees up businesses to expand production and hire more workers overall. Both those effects increase the demand for labor, offsetting the effects of added labor supply.

Economist David Card concludes that, taking into account these demand-side effects, "the overall impacts on native wages are small—far smaller than the effects of other factors like new technology, institutional changes, and recessionary macro conditions that have cumulatively led to several decades of slow wage growth for most U.S. workers."

## Complements or Substitutes?

The effect of immigration on native-born workers with less than a high-school education remains a matter of dispute. Borjas insists that the costs of immigration are visited disproportionately upon those with the least education (and, to a lesser extent, those with the most education). He estimates, in a couple of different studies, that over the long run the wages of native-born high school dropouts fell 3-5% due to immigration.

But these estimates rely on the assumption that immigrant and native-born workers are substitutes for each other, and therefore compete for the same jobs. But, in fact, their skills differ in important ways. The first is their command of English. The Immigrant Policy Institute found that approximately one-half of the 41 million immigrants ages five and older speak English less than "very well." In addition, immigrant workers often have culture-specific skills— from cooking to opera singing to soccer playing, to cite examples given by Ottaviano and Peri—that differ from those of native-born workers.

When Ottaviano and Peri accounted for the imperfect substitutability between immigrants and natives, the negative of effect of immigration on native high school dropouts disappeared, and their wages were shown to rise by 0.3% over the long run.

## Giving More Than They Get

Nor is there a credible case that undocumented immigrants are draining the public coffers by consuming more public services than they pay for. Immigrants migrate to jobs, not to welfare, and are disproportionately of working age. They are not major beneficiaries of the most generous U.S. welfare-state programs—Social Security and Medicare, which serve the elderly, not the young or the poor. And undocumented immigrants are already ineligible for most government benefits. (Even documented immigrants are ineligible for many federal programs, at least for some years after their arrival.)

On top of that, immigrants, both documented and undocumented, do pay taxes. They pay sales taxes, payroll taxes, and often income taxes. And they pay far more in taxes than they receive in benefits. That puts Trump's outrage over $4.2 billion in "free tax credits ... paid to illegal immigrants" in a different light. In 2009, the federal government did in fact pay $4.2 billion in child tax credits to low-income tax filers using an Individual Taxpayer Identification Number (ITIN), the vast majority of them undocumented immigrants. But that same year, those ITIN filers paid an estimated $12 billion into a Social Security system from which they are not eligible to collect any benefits.

## Trillions Left on the Sidewalk

Before the 1882 Chinese Exclusion Act, the United States allowed completely free immigration into our country. Immigration from elsewhere remained unrestricted until the eve of World War I. And immigrants flooded into the country and contributed mightily to its economic development.

Liberalizing immigration policies, unlike Trump's proposed border wall or mass deportations, could once again benefit the U.S. economy. Economists Angel Aguiar and Terrie Walmsley found that deporting all undocumented Mexican immigrants from the United States would reduce U.S. GDP by about $150 billion, while granting legal status to unskilled, undocumented Mexican workers (without additional effective border enforcement) would raise it by nearly that amount. And the potential gain for the global economy from liberalizing immigration policies is far greater. In fact so large that economist Michael Clemens likens liberalizing immigration to picking up "trillion-dollar bills on the sidewalk."

Such policies would also specifically improve conditions for workers, immigrant and native, in the United States. Immigrant workers, especially the estimated eleven million undocumented immigrants, tend to have less bargaining power than native-born workers. A policy granting undocumented immigrants legal status would make it easier for them to insist on their rights at work, and to organize and form unions. That's why the AFL-CIO and unions like UNITE HERE and SEIU now favor it.

For those who remain concerned about the effects of immigration on U.S. born low-wage workers, there are obvious policies that would improve the lot of all low-wage workers: Boosting the minimum wage, making it easier for workers to organize unions, and making the welfare state more generous and inclusive, so people don't have to accept whatever lousy job they can find. These are the policies that are called for, not keeping immigrants out. ❑

*Sources:* George Borjas, "Immigration and the American Worker: A Review of the Academic Literature," Center for Immigration Studies, April 2013; Vivek Wadhwa, Foreign-Born Entrepreneurs: An Underestimated American Resource," Kauffman Foundation, Nov. 24, 2008; Michael A. Clemens, "Economics and Emigration: Trillion-Dollars Bills on the Sidewalk?" *Journal of Economic Perspectives*, Summer 2011; Gianmarco Ottaviano and Giovanni Peri, "Rethinking the Effects of Immigration on Wages," National Bureau of Economic Research, August 2006; Gianmarco Ottaviano and Giovanni Peri, "Immigration and National Wages: Clarifying the Theory and Empirics," National Bureau of Economic Research, August 2008; Gianmarco Ottaviano and Giovanni Peri, "Rethinking the Effect of Immigration on Wages," *Journal of the European Economic Association*, February 2012; George Borjas and Lawrence Katz, "The Evolution of the Mexican-Born Workforce n the United States," in George Borjas, ed., *Mexican Immigration to the United States,* 2007; Benjamin Powell, "Why Trump's Wrong on Immigration," Independent Institute, Sept. 15, 2015; Angel Aguiar and Terrie Walmsley, "The Importance of Timing in the U.S. Response to Illegal Immigrants: A Recursive Dynamic Approach," Global Trade Analysis Project, Working Paper No. 75, 2013; David Card, "Comment: The Elusive Search For Negative Wage Impacts of Immigration," *Journal of the European and Economic Association*, February 2012; Glenn Kessler, "Trump's Immigration plan include many claims that lack context," *Washington Post*, Aug. 20, 2015; Linda Qiu, "Trump's says illegal immigrants get $4.2B in tax credits but doesn't count their taxes paid," PolitiFact, Aug. 18, 2015; Michael Greenstone and Adam Looney, "What Immigration Means for U.S. Employment and Wages," Brookings on Job Numbers, May 4, 2012; Jie Zong and Jeanne Batalova, "Frequently Requested Statistics on Immigrants and Immigration in the United States," Migration Policy Institute, Feb. 26, 2015.

*Article 8.2*

# "MIGRATION IS A FORM OF FIGHTING BACK"
*Looking at the Root Causes of Migration*

## BY DAVID BACON
*September/October 2018*

For eight years at the West County Detention Center in Richmond, Calif., monthly vigils were organized by faith communities and immigrant rights organizations to support those inside. These protests ,and the testimony of detainees' families, were so powerful that the county sheriff in July announced he was canceling the contract he signed long ago with the federal government to house the prisoners.

While that was a victory, it did not lead to freedom for most of them, however, who were transferred to other detention centers. Instead, it has forced us to examine deeper questions. In those vigils we heard the living experiences of people who have had no alternative to leaving their homes and countries to escape violence, war, and poverty, who now find themselves imprisoned in the detention center. We have to ask, who is responsible? Where did the violence and poverty come from that forced people to leave home, to cross the border with Mexico, and then to be picked up and incarcerated here?

Whatever the immediate circumstances, there is one main cause for the misery that has led migrants to the United States: the actions of the government of this country, and the wealthy elites that the government has defended.

## Taking Responsibility

I went to Guatemala several times over the last two decades with my friend Sergio Sosa. Sergio was brought up in the church. As a young man he was on his way to becoming a priest. Then he became a *combatiente* (a participant in the social struggle and war in Guatemala from the late '70s to the early '90s), but he remained a friend of Bishop Bobadilla in Huehuetenango, a disciple of Archbishop Romero in El Salvador (who was assassinated at the beginning of El Salvador's insurrection and war of the same period). One evening Bobadilla, Sergio, and I spent a long time talking with about the civil war of the 1980s, and the fact that the massacres of tens of thousands of indigenous inhabitants of the mountains above Huehuetenango were carried out with guns that came from the United States, by soldiers whose officers had gone to the School of the Americas in Georgia.

Yet in all the talk I felt no anger from the bishop toward me as someone from the United States. "Why not?" I asked. "Because we know you have as little control over your government as we do over ours, probably less," Bishop Bobadilla answered. "But you're interested in us. You want to hear about what happened, you know it was wrong, and you want to take some responsibility for it."

Today when I read about the women and children from Guatemala in detention, when we hear their voices and see their photographs, I think about what Bobadilla said.

It sounds so unbelievably hopeful—this idea that as people here in this country we want to take responsibility, and recognize the history of all that's happened between us and the people of Central America.

How did these children come to be here? And what does taking responsibility mean? It's not enough to believe that all children should be valued and cared for with the greatest tenderness and love. We need to know why they're here, in such an obviously dangerous and painful situation, enduring separation from their families and the adults in their lives.

You don't hear much discussion of responsibility or acknowledgement of history in the discourse of our national leaders. And it's not just the racist slurs of Trump.

To Sergio, migration is not just a journey from one point to another. Migration is a form of resistance to empire. "People from Europe and the U.S. crossed borders to come to us, and took over our land and economy," he points out. "Now it's our turn to cross borders. Migration is a form of fighting back."

## U.S.-Sponsored Wars

Migration from Central America has been happening for very long time, but modern migration began with the wars. Refugees fled El Salvador and Guatemala because of massacres. Sergio says, "Our army was trained at the School of the Americas, and they would come back afterwards and kill our own people. The United States used its power, and we buried the dead."

This means we have had separated families for at least 35 years. When families settled in U.S. cities, many lived in the MacArthur Park neighborhood in downtown Los Angeles. In the 1990s this neighborhood was the focus of the Ramparts scandal, which exposed massive corruption in the Community Resources Against Street Hoodlums (or C*R*A*S*H) anti-gang unit of the Los Angeles Police Department.

In the name of combating gang activity among young immigrants from Central America, cops dished out unprovoked shootings and beatings, planted false evidence, framed suspects, stole and dealt narcotics themselves, robbed banks, lied in court, and covered up evidence of their crimes. It was one of the most extensive cases of police misconduct in U.S. history. The young people they targeted were imprisoned and then deported. The names of their gangs in Central America refer to Los Angeles streets.

Some 129,726 people convicted of crimes were deported to Central America from 2000 to 2010. With the deportations, the two most prominent Los Angeles gangs—the Mara Salvatrucha 13 and the Barrio 18—quickly became the two largest transnational gangs. In El Salvador, Guatemala, and Honduras, U.S. law enforcement assistance pressured local police to adopt a mano dura or hardline approach to gang members. Many young people deported from the United States were incarcerated almost as soon as they arrived. Prisons became schools for gang recruitment.

U.S. funding for law enforcement and the military still flows, two decades after the wars ended, through the Central America Regional Security Initiative (CARSI). Marine Corps General John Kelly, when he was commander of the U.S. Southern Command, said that migration was a national security threat, calling it a "crime-terror convergence." Today he's Trump's chief of staff in the White House.

## Imposing Economics

During and after the war, the United States imposed an economic model on Central American countries based on producing for export, in "export processing zones" where companies could operate without complying with normal taxes, environmental regulations, and labor standards. San Pedro Sula in Honduras, called a "murder capital" by the *New York Times*, is not just a city of gangs. It's a factory town.

One of San Pedro Sula's working women, Claudia Molina, described the conditions there: "Our work day is from 7:30 AM to 8:30 PM," Molina told me, "sometimes until 10:30, from Monday to Friday. On Saturday we start at 7:30 AM. We get an hour for lunch, and work until 6:30 PM. We take a half hour again to eat, and then we work from 7 PM until midnight. We take another half hour rest, and then go until 6 on Sunday morning. Working like this I earned 270 lempiras per week [about $30 at the time]." When Molina and her coworkers tried to organize a union, 600 women were fired.

Over 95% of the women in the Honduran plants are younger than 30, and half younger than 20. To keep women from getting pregnant and leaving the factory to have children, USAID funded contraceptive distribution posts staffed by nurses in EPZ factories, including Osh Kosh B'Gosh. You can make the clothes for U.S. babies, but don't have any of your own.

And kids themselves are workers. Girls between 10 and 14 make up 16% of the women in the factories.

The U.S. government promoted policies providing low-cost labor to U.S. corporations, promoting economic development that tied the economies of Central American countries to U.S. corporate investment.

By the end of the 1990s, the number of Salvadorans in the United States had reached two million. And U.S. taxes didn't just pay for war and maquiladoras; they funded an even larger strategy of encouraging foreign investment through privatizing state utilities, services, and assets, and of negotiating "free-trade" agreements with Mexico (the North American Free Trade Agreement—NAFTA) and with Central American countries (the Central American Free Trade Agreement—CAFTA).

## Policy as Leverage

The United States used immigration as a lever to force governments to go along. In 2004 Deputy Secretary of State for Latin America Otto Reich threatened to cut remittances if people voted for the left-wing Farabundo Martí National Liberation Front (FMLN) in El Salvador. After the FMLN lost, CAFTA was signed and implemented in 2005 by the government that Reich supported.

In Honduras, the congress had to ratify CAFTA in a secret meeting at midnight, when no opposition parties were present. Then, in 2009 a tiny wealthy elite overthrew

Honduran President Manuel Zelaya because he raised the country's minimum wage, gave subsidies to small farmers, cut interest rates, and instituted free education.

Raising living standards would have given people a future at home. Nevertheless, after a weak protest, the Obama administration gave de facto approval to the coup regime that followed. If social and political change had taken place in Honduras, we would see far fewer Hondurans trying to come to the United States.

Many of the children and families coming from Central America to the United States today are therefore coming to reunite with their families, who were divided by war and earlier migration. They are responding to the threat of violence caused by criminalization and deportations. They are looking for economic survival in countries tied to the neoliberal economic model.

These are the real causes. There is no lax enforcement, and the claim that kids are coming because they think they'll be allowed to stay is a myth. Around 400,000 people are still deported every year, and 350,000 people spend some time in an immigrant detention center. The Border Patrol has 20,000 agents, and the United States spends more on immigration enforcement than the FBI and DEA budgets combined.

The migration of Central Americans, including children, has been used by Tea Party and Border Patrol to push to expand that budget, to build more private detention centers, to increase funding for CARSI and the military, and to kill the DACA program (Deferred Action for Childhood Arrivals, the Obama-era order that allowed young people brought to the United States without documents as children to stay). The hysteria played a big part in electing President Trump, with chants at his rallies of "Build the Wall!"

But children will keep coming so long as we don't take responsibility for dealing with causes of migration. Knowing where the violence and poverty are coming from, and who benefits from this system, is one step toward ending it. But we also have to know what we want in its place. What is our alternative to the detention centers, and the imprisonment of the people inside? To the hundreds of people who still die on the border every year?

## What's the Alternative?

We have had alternative proposals for many years. One set of alternatives was called the Dignity Campaign. The American Friends Service Committee had another. They all had certain commonsense ideas in common:

- An end to mass detention and deportations, and the closing of the detention centers.

- An end to the militarization of the border.

- An end to the idea that working without papers should be a crime.

These proposals also tried to deal with the root causes by calling for:

- An end to the trade agreements and economic reforms that force people into poverty and make migration the only means to survive.

- An end to military intervention, to military aid to right-wing governments, and to U.S. support for the repression of the movements fighting for change.

The migration of Central Americans has benefited our labor and social justice movements. One big example was Justice for Janitors in Los Angeles, where Central American janitors defied the police and were beaten up in Century City, but finally won a contract.

It is a powerful combination—workers on the bottom with not much to lose in minimum wage jobs, and politically sophisticated organizers hardened in a war zone.

That should inspire progressive movements in the United States to look at immigration in a different way. Simply being an immigrant may not bend a person politically to the left. But many immigrants bring organizing skills and working-class political consciousness with them, depending on where they come from, and their previous experiences.

## The Right to Stay Home

Mixtec professor Gaspar Rivera Salgado says, "The right to stay home, to not migrate, has to mean more than the right to be poor, or the right to go hungry. Choosing whether to stay home or leave only has meaning if each choice can provide a meaningful future, in which we are all respected as human beings."

That right can't be achieved in Central America alone. The policies pursued by our government, whether through war and military aid, or through trade agreements and pressure to keep wages low, all produce migration. When we look at the families in detention centers today, we have the responsibility to give them a world in which the choice to leave Guatemala or El Salvador or Honduras is truly voluntary—where they have a future with dignity if they choose to stay. The ability to stay home is as important as the ability and right to migrate.

If you think this is just a dream, remember that a decade after Emmett Till was lynched in Mississippi, the U.S. Congress passed the Civil Rights Act. That same year, 1965, Congress put the family preference immigration system into law, the only pro-immigrant legislation we've had for a hundred years.

That was no gift. A civil rights movement made Congress pass that law. When that law was passed we had no private immigrant detention centers. There were no walls on our border with Mexico, and no one died crossing it, like the hundreds who now perish in the desert every year. There is nothing permanent or unchangeable about these institutions of oppression. We have changed our world before, and our movements here can do that again. ❑

*Article 8.3*

# EUROPE'S REFUGEE "CRISIS"

**BY JAYATI GHOSH**
*September 2015; Frontline*

If you read or watched or listened only to the mainstream media in the North, you could be forgiven for believing that the current influx of refugees into countries of Europe is not just an important concern, but actually even the single biggest crisis in that continent. You might also think that the flow of desperate refugees escaping from terrible conditions is mainly confined to that region, and that their numbers are so large that the societies will be simply unable to cope, because of the hugely increased burden on basic infrastructure and facilities in those countries.

Every day, television screens show images of people pouring into towns and cities, crowding up border crossings or landing at sea (if they are lucky) and filling up transport hubs in certain European countries. International and national newspapers carry stories of some compassion, along with greater instances of more xenophobic responses of local populations. Government leaders (particularly in eastern and central Europe) are shown declaring that their country cannot possibly take in so many people, many of whom may not even be "real" refugees but simply economic migrants. Borders are being reinforced and aggressively policed; walls and barbed wire fences are being put up; desperate groups of travellers are even being shot at in the attempt to prevent further influx.

Yet this tragic phenomenon that is receiving so much global publicity is but a small trickle in the huge flow of people displaced globally by wars and conflicts in the areas where they live. According to UNHCR [the United Nations Refugee Agency], in 2014 alone, nearly 14 million people were forcibly displaced due to civil war or other violence. Most of these moved within their own country—11 million people, who are internal refugees losing everything, and often retaining only the most uncertain of citizenship rights precisely because of the internal conflicts.

The three million who were cross-border refugees added to the estimated global total of 60 million displaced people, 19.5 million cross-border refugees and 1.95 million asylum seekers in 2014. Obviously in 2015 the numbers have gone up further, and the conflicts in many countries of origin have only intensified. But most of these displaced people—86% of them, in fact—are hosted by developing countries. The Least Developed Countries, with some of the lowest per capita incomes in the world and very poor conditions of infrastructure available to their own previously resident populations, were home to a quarter of the world's refugees in 2014.

Last year, Turkey became the country with the largest number of refugees, at 1.59 million. It was followed by Pakistan (1.51 million), Lebanon (1.15 million), Iran (982,000), Ethiopia (659,500), and Jordan (654,100). In terms of population, Jordan was the most affected, with one refugee for every three local residents, followed by Lebanon with one refugee to every four Lebanese. Some of the poorest countries in the world, like Chad and South Sudan, provide refuge to large numbers of displaced people who are significant in number in relation to the local population.

Put these huge numbers in the context of the much smaller number of people trying to enter Europe (still in their thousands), and there is really no comparison in terms of burden on the host society. This is especially so as all the countries of Europe (including those that see themselves as poorer and economically struggling at present) are far better off not only in terms of per capita income but also in terms of provision of basic amenities and services for the people.

Coping with large numbers of refugees is obviously much more difficult for poor countries. In areas that are already drought-prone, water-starved, and with large hungry populations, consider the burden of ensuring water and food access to many newly displaced people. Where medical facilities are already very inadequate, imagine trying to provide even minimal medical services to refugees who are probably in even greater dire need. In societies where even all the local children are not in school, think of what adding large numbers of refugee children who probably do not share the language and also are likely to be traumatised and so may require therapy, will entail in terms of public costs.

The material implications of having larger numbers of refugees are clearly being felt in many of these countries, whether in terms of increased rationing of electricity and water, a greater burden on health services, or pressure on other infrastructure. Yet we do not hear of these countries closing their borders on people who are desperately fleeing to save their lives, nor is it the case that right-wing tendencies in these societies have gained huge public support by attacking these helpless migrants. It is also significant that somehow the huge and growing numbers of refugees across the developing world are never treated as crisis situations by the global media.

So it is worth asking why the European response (and the U.S. attempt to look away from the issues as having no direct relevance to themselves) has been, in the main, so very churlish and self-obsessed. The most relevant question, of course, is of how the establishment in both the United States and Europe has been able to deny any responsibility for the current movement of displaced persons across borders—and how complicit the mainstream media has been in this process.

At the end of 2014, according to the UNHCR, more than half (53%) of all refugees worldwide came from just three countries: the Syrian Arab Republic (3.88 million), Afghanistan (2.59 million), and Somalia (1.11 million). Since the start of the current year, the number from Syria has increased greatly, and just the number of asylum seekers from Syria in the developed countries has more than doubled in the first six months of 2015 compared to the same period last year. Large numbers of refugees have also come from Iraq and Libya, all countries now devastated by internal conflicts arising from the clumsy western imperialist attempts to force political change in these countries through the use of external force.

Not for nothing have many observers like James Paul and Vijay Prashad described these unhappy people as "regime change refugees," fleeing countries that are now in the throes of dreadful civil wars driven by very extremist forces, including those that are particularly oppressive to women. Yet the overt accountability of the governments of countries that went to war and thereby created these huge instabilities is certainly not acknowledged by themselves, and rarely alluded to in the media coverage of all this. It is true that this is somewhere in the back of many minds: in recent weeks an official of one of the least welcoming East European countries is reported to have asked "Why should we provide homes for these refugees when we didn't invade their countries?" Yet the essential culpability and therefore responsibility of those who did invade those countries is not pointed to when the issue of dealing with the refugees comes up. And so the leaders in the United States and the UK, for example, can simply look the other way since the migrants are not washing up against their own shores.

The petty selfishness of western leaders—and, unfortunately, far too many in their societies—has thus been most thoroughly exposed. The horrific conditions and direct threats to life and security in the countries that people are fleeing; the extremely dangerous and life-threatening journeys that must be made (almost daily confirmed by the appalling accounts of deaths in transit); the knowledge of the highly precarious existence in largely unwelcoming countries of destination—all of these suggest that such migrants are truly desperate and deserve the greatest compassion. Yet this most basic human empathy has been sadly lacking for the most part.

Indeed, Germany has been praised for its relatively generous response. Yet this too has been more churlish in recent weeks, and it pales into insignificance compared to the much greater generosity of countries that are far less materially equipped to handle such inflows, such as Jordan, Lebanon, and Pakistan. Asylum seekers do not have an easy time anywhere, but the richer countries have without question been meaner, more oppressive, and more restrictive in their dealings with them.

So then the question must be: why such a difference in social and public response? It is hard to think that this is largely because of racial or cultural differences alone, because the refugees do not come from homogenous societies, nor do they necessarily enter similar ones in other developing countries. One possible explanation could still be a cultural one, though: the deep penetration of the ideology of neoliberalism, which celebrates individualism and generates a Darwinian sense of competition and struggle for survival, in which one's own success ultimately depends on someone else's failure. It is worth noting that even in Europe, the formerly socialist countries that have become the most eager adherents to "free market" principles have also turned to becoming the most aggressively right-wing, even fascist, in their approach to less fortunate outsiders.

It is as if all principles of social solidarity were thrown out along with any vestiges of economic socialism. Countries that have in addition been exposed to a long period of public austerity that has undermined living standards of the masses seem to be even more prone to such resentful swings. Sadly, the celebration of the market seems to have done more than generate patterns of unequal growth and reduced respect for human rights: it also seems to have undermined the basic principles of solidarity and ethical behaviour without which human societies will find it hard to function. ❑

Article 8.4

# THE RISE OF MIGRANT WORKER MILITANCY

**IMMANUEL NESS**
*September/October 2006*

Testifying before the Senate immigration hearings in early July, Mayor Michael Bloomberg affirmed that undocumented immigrants have become indispensable to the economy of New York City: "Although they broke the law by illegally crossing our borders or overstaying their visas, and our businesses broke the law by employing them, our city's economy would be a shell of itself had they not, and it would collapse if they were deported. The same holds true for the nation." Bloomberg's comment outraged right-wing pundits, but how much more outraged would they be if they knew that immigrant workers, beyond being economically indispensable, are beginning to transform the U.S. labor movement with a bold new militancy?

After years of working in obscurity in the unregulated economy, migrant workers in New York City catapulted themselves to the forefront of labor activism beginning in late 1999 through three separate organizing drives among low-wage workers. Immigrants initiated all three drives: Mexican immigrants organized and struck for improved wages and working conditions at greengroceries; Francophone African delivery workers struck for unpaid wages and respect from labor contractors for leading supermarket chains; and South Asians organized for improved conditions and a union in the for-hire car service industry. (In New York, "car services" are taxis that cannot be hailed on the street, only arranged by phone.) These organizing efforts have persisted, and are part of a growing militancy among migrant workers in New York City and across the United States.

Why would seemingly invisible workers rise up to contest power in their workplaces? Why are vulnerable migrant workers currently more likely to organize than are U.S.-born workers? To answer these questions, we have to look at immigrants' distinct position in the political economy of a globalized New York City and at their specific economic and social niches, ones in which exploitation and isolation nurture class consciousness and militancy.

## Labor Migration and Industrial Restructuring

New immigrant workers in the United States, many here illegally, stand at the crossroads of two overwhelming trends. On one hand, industrial restructuring and capital mobility have eroded traditional industries and remade the U.S. political economy in the last 30 years in ways that have led many companies to create millions of low-wage jobs and to seek vulnerable workers to fill them. On the other hand, at the behest of international financial institutions like the International Monetary Fund, and to meet the requirements of free-trade agreements such as NAFTA, governments throughout the global South have adopted neoliberal policies that have restructured their economies, resulting in the displacement of urban workers and rural farmers alike. Many have no choice but to migrate north.

A century ago the United States likewise experienced a large influx of immigrants, many of whom worked in factories for their entire lives. There they formed social networks across ethnic lines and developed a class consciousness that spurred the organizing of unions; they made up the generation of workers whose efforts began with the fight for the eight-hour day around the turn of the last century and culminated in the great organizing victories of the 1930s and 1940s across the entire spectrum of mining and manufacturing industries.

Today's immigrants face an entirely different political-economic landscape. Unlike most of their European counterparts a century ago, immigration restrictions mean that many newcomers to the United States are now here illegally. Workers from Latin America frequently migrate illegally without proper documentation; those from Africa, Asia, and Europe commonly arrive with business, worker, student, or tourist visas, then overstay them.

The urban areas where many immigrants arrive have undergone a 30-year decline in manufacturing jobs. The growing pool of service jobs which have come in their stead tend to be dispersed in small firms throughout the city. The proliferation of geographically dispersed subcontractors who compete on the basis of low wages encourages a process of informalization—a term referring to a redistribution of work from regulated sectors of the economy to new unregulated sectors of the underground or informal economy. As a result, wages and working conditions have fallen, often below government-established norms.

Although informal work is typically associated with the developing world—or Global South—observers are increasingly recognizing the link between the regulated and unregulated sectors in advanced industrial regions. More and more the regulated sector depends on unregulated economic activity through subcontracting and outsourcing of work to firms employing low-wage immigrant labor. Major corporations employ or subcontract to businesses employing migrant workers in what were once established sectors of the economy with decent wages and working conditions.

Informalization requires government regulatory agencies to look the other way. For decades federal and state regulatory bodies have ignored violations of laws governing wages, hours, and workplace safety, leading to illegally low wages and declining workplace health and safety practices. The process of informalization is furthered by the reduction or elimination of protections such as disability insurance, Social Security, health care coverage, unemployment insurance, and workers compensation.

By the 1990s, substandard jobs employing almost exclusively migrant workers had become crucial to key sectors of the national economy. Today, immigrants have gained a major presence as bricklayers, demolition workers, and hazardous waste workers on construction and building rehab sites; as cooks, dishwashers, and busboys in restaurants; and as taxi drivers, domestic workers, and delivery people.

Employers frequently treat these workers as self-employed. They typically have no union protection and little or no job security. With government enforcement shrinking, they lack the protection of minimum-wage laws and they have been excluded from Social Security and unemployment insurance.

These workers are increasingly victimized by employers who force them to accept 19th-century working conditions and sub-minimum wages. Today, New York City, Los Angeles, Miami, Houston, and Boston form a nexus of international labor migration, with constantly churning labor markets. As long as there is a demand for cheap labor, immigrants will continue to enter the United States in large numbers. Like water, capital always flows to the lowest level, a state of symmetry where wages are cheapest.

In turn, the availability of a reserve army of immigrant labor provides an enormous incentive for larger corporations to create and use subcontracting firms. Without this workforce, employers in the regulated economy would have more incentive to invest in labor-saving technology, increase the capital-labor ratio, and seek accommodation with unions.

New unauthorized immigrants residing and working in the United States are ideal workers in the new informalized sectors: Their undocumented legal status makes them more tractable since they constantly fear deportation. Undocumented immigrants are less likely to know about, or demand adherence to, established labor standards, and even low U.S. wages represent an improvement over earnings in their home countries.

## Forging Migrant Labor Solidarity

The perception that new immigrants undermine U.S.-born workers by undercutting prevailing wage and work standards cannot be entirely dismissed. The entry of a large number of immigrants into the underground economy unquestionably reduces the labor market leverage of U.S.-born workers. But the story is more complicated. In spite of their vulnerability, migrant workers have demonstrated a willingness and a capacity to organize for improvements in their wages and working conditions; they arguably are responding to tough conditions on the job with greater militancy than U.S.-born workers.

New York City has been the site of a number of instances of immigrant worker organizing. In 1998, Mexicans working in greengroceries embarked on a citywide organizing campaign to improve their conditions of work. Most of the 20,000 greengrocery workers were paid below $3.00 an hour, working on average 72 hours a week. Some did not make enough to pay their living expenses, no less send remittances back home to Mexico. Following a relentless and coordinated four-year organizing campaign among the workers, employers agreed to raise wages above the minimum and improve working conditions. Moreover, the campaign led state Attorney General Eliot Spitzer to establish a Greengrocer Code of Conduct and to strengthen enforcement of labor regulations.

In another display of immigrant worker militancy, beginning in 1999 Francophone African supermarket delivery workers in New York City fought for and won equality with other workers in the same stores. The workers were responsible for bagging groceries and delivering them to affluent customers in Manhattan and throughout the city. As contractors, the delivery workers were paid no wage, instead relying on the goodwill of customers in affluent neighborhoods to pay tips for each delivery.

The workers were employed in supermarkets and drug stores where some others had a union. Without union support themselves, delivery workers staged a significant strike and insurrection that made consumers aware of their appalling conditions of work. In late October, workers went on strike and marched from supermarket to supermarket, demanding living wages and dignity on the job. At the start of their campaign, wages averaged less than $70 a week. In the months following the strike the workers all won recognition from the stores through the United Food and Commercial Workers that had earlier neglected to include them in negotiations with management. The National Employee Law Project, a national worker advocacy organization, filed landmark lawsuits against the supermarkets and delivery companies and won backwage settlements as the courts deemed them to be workers—not independent contractors in business for themselves.

Immigrant workers have organized countless other campaigns, in New York and across the country. How do new immigrants, with weak ties to organized labor and the state, manage to assert their interests? The explanation lies in the character of immigrant work and social life; the constraints immigrant workers face paradoxically encourage them to draw on shared experiences to create solidarity at work and in their communities.

The typical migrant worker can expect to work twelve-hour days, seven days a week. When arriving home, immigrant workers frequently share the same apartments, buildings, and neighborhoods. These employment ghettos typify immigrant communities across the nation. Workers cook for one another, share stories about their oppressively long and hard days, commiserate about their ill treatment at work, and then go to sleep only to start anew the next day.

Migrant women, surrounded by a world of exploitation, typically suffer even more abuse than their male counterparts, suffering from low wages, long hours, and dangerous conditions. Patterns of gender stratification found in the general labor market are even more apparent among migrant women workers. Most jobs in the nonunion economy, such as construction and driving, are stereotypically considered "men's work." Women predominate in the garment industry, as domestic and child care workers, in laundries, hotels, restaurants, and ever more in sex work. A striking example of migrant women's perilous work environment is the massive recruitment of migrant women to clean up the hazardous materials in the rubble left by the collapse of the World Trade Center without proper safety training.

Isolated in their jobs and communities, immigrant workers have few social ties to unions, community groups, and public officials, and few resources to call upon to assist them in transforming their workplaces. Because new immigrants have few social networks outside the workplace, the ties they develop on the job are especially solid and meaningful—and are nurtured every day. The workers' very isolation and status as outsiders, and their concentration into industrial niches by employers who hire on the basis of ethnicity, tend to strengthen old social ties, build new ones, and deepen class solidarity.

Immigrant social networks contribute to workplace militancy. Conversely, activism at work can stimulate new social networks that can expand workers' power. It is through relationships developed on the job and in the community that shared social identities and mutual resentment of the boss evolves into class consciousness and class solidarity: migrant workers begin to form informal organizations, meet with coworkers to respond to poor working conditions, and take action on the shop floor in defiance of employer abuse.

Typically, few workplace hierarchies exist among immigrants, since few reach supervisory positions. As a result, immigrant workers suffer poor treatment equally at the hands of employers. A gathering sense of collective exploitation usually transforms individualistic activities into shared ones. In rare cases where there are immigrant foremen and crew leaders, they may recognize this solidarity and side with the workers rather than with management. One former manager employed for a fast-food sandwich chain in New York City said: "We are hired only to divide the workers but I was really trying to help the workers get better pay and shorter hours."

Migrant workers bring social identities from their home countries, and those identities are shaped through socialization and work in this country. In cities and towns across the United States, segmentation of migrant workers from specific countries reinforces ethnic, national, and religious identities and helps to form other identities that may stimulate solidarity. Before arriving in the United States, Mexican immigrant workers often see themselves as peasants but not initially as "people of color," while Francophone Africans see themselves as Malian or Senegalese ethnics but not necessarily "black." Life and work in New York can encourage them to adopt new identifications, including a new class consciousness that can spur organizing and militancy.

Once triggered, organizing can go from workplace to workplace like wildfire. When workers realize that they can fight and prevail, this creates a sense of invincibility that stimulates militant action that would otherwise be avoided at all costs. This demonstration effect is vitally important, as was the case in the strikes among garment workers and coal miners in the history of the U.S. labor movement.

## "Solidarity Forever" vs. "Take This Job and Shove It"

The militancy of many migrant workers contrasts sharply with the passivity of many U.S.-born workers facing the same low wages and poor working conditions. Why do most workers at chain stores and restaurants like Walmart and McDonalds—most of whom were born in the United States—appear so complacent, while new immigrants are often so militant?

Migrants are not inherently more militant or less passive. Instead, the real workplace conditions of migrant workers seem to produce greater militancy on the job. First, collective social isolation engenders strong ties among migrants in low-wage jobs where organizing is frequently the only way to improve conditions. Because migrants work in jobs that are more amenable to organizing, they are highly represented among newly unionized workers. Strong social ties in the workplace drive migrants to form their own embryonic organizations at work and in their communities that are ripe for union representation. Organizing among migrant workers gains the attention of labor unions, which then see a chance to recruit new members and may provide resources to help immigrant workers mobilize at work and join the union.

Employers also play a major role. Firms employing U.S. workers tend to be larger and are often much harder to organize than the small businesses where immigrants work. In 2003, the Merriam-Webster dictionary added the new word McJob, defined as "a low-paying job that requires little skill and provides little opportunity for advancement." The widely accepted coinage reflects the relentless 30-year economic restructuring creating low-end jobs in the retail sector.

Organizing against Home Depot, McDonalds, Taco Bell, or Walmart is completely different from organizing against smaller employers. Walmart uses many of the same tactics against workers that immigrants contend with: failure to pay overtime, stealing time (intentionally paying workers for fewer hours than actually worked), no health care, part-time work, high turnover, and gender division of labor. The difference is that Walmart has far more resources to oppose unionization than do the smaller employers who are frequently subcontractors to larger firms. But Walmart's opposition to labor unions is so forceful that workers choose to leave rather than stay and fight it out. Relentless labor turnover mitigates against the formation of working class consciousness and militancy.

The expanding non-immigrant low-end service sector tends to produce unskilled part-time jobs that do not train workers in skills that keep them in the same sector of the labor market. Because jobs at the low end of the economy require little training, workers frequently move from one industry to the next. One day a U.S.-born worker may work as a sales clerk for Target, the next day as a waiter at Olive Garden. Because they are not stuck in identity-defined niches, U.S. workers change their world by quitting and finding a job elsewhere, giving them less reason to organize and unionize.

The fact that U.S.-born workers have an exit strategy and migrant workers do not is a significant and important difference. Immigrant workers are more prone to take action to change their working conditions because they have far fewer options than U.S.-born workers. Workers employed by companies like Walmart are unable to change their conditions, since they have little power and will be summarily fired for any form of dissent. If workers violate the terms of Walmart's or McDonalds' employee manual by, say, arriving late, and then are summarily fired, no one is likely to fend for them, as is usually the case among many migrant workers. While migrant workers engage in direct action against their employers to obtain higher wages and respect on the job, U.S. workers do not develop the same dense connections in labor market niches that forge solidarity. Employers firing new immigrants may risk demonstrations, picket lines, or even strikes.

Immigrant workers are pushed into low-wage labor market niches as day laborers, food handlers, delivery workers, and nannies; these niches are difficult if not impossible to escape. Yet immigrant workers relegated to dead-end jobs in the lowest echelons of the labor market in food, delivery, and car service work show a greater eagerness to fight it out to improve their wages and conditions than do U.S. workers who can move on to another dead-end job.

## The Role of Unions

Today's labor movement is in serious trouble; membership is spiraling downward as employers demand union-free workplaces. Unionized manufacturing and service workers are losing their jobs to low-wage operations abroad. Unions and, more importantly, the U.S. working class, are in dire straits and must find a means to triumph over the neoliberal dogma that dominates the capitalist system.

As organizing campaigns in New York City show, migrant workers are indispensable to the revitalization of the labor movement. As employers turn to migrant labor to fill low-wage jobs, unions must encourage and support organizing drives that emerge from the oppressive conditions of work. As the 1930s workers' movement demonstrates, if conditions improve for immigrants, all workers will prosper. To gain traction, unions must recognize that capital is pitting migrant workers against native-born laborers to lower wages and improve profitability. Although unions have had some success organizing immigrants, most are circling the wagons, disinterested in building a more inclusive mass labor movement. The first step is for unions to go beyond rhetoric and form a broad and inclusive coalition embracing migrant workers. ❑

# Chapter 9

# DEVELOPMENT AND "UNDERDEVELOPMENT"

*Article 9.1*

## NEOLIBERALISM AS NEOCOLONIALISM

**BY JAYATI GHOSH**
*May/June 2020*

The damaging effects of neoliberalism—and the terrible legacy it leaves behind even for governments trying to change their countries' economic directions— are by now well known: growing domestic wealth and income inequalities, the erosion of regulations on capital, the elimination of protections for workers, the increased instability of economic life (with periodic business-cycle crises), the obsession with fiscal austerity policies that dismantle the welfare state and deprive citizens of their economic rights, and ever-deepening and spreading financialization. All of these features of neoliberalism are now generally accepted, even by some of its defenders. Now the Covid-19 pandemic is bringing home the fact that neoliberalism is posing a massive danger to public health and, therefore, to the very survival of societies.

One feature that is less remarked upon—and often even less noticed—is the role that neoliberal policies have played globally, in reinforcing contemporary imperialism. This has occurred through the way neoliberalism operates in developing countries, including in so-called "emerging markets." This tendency of neoliberalism is often disguised by the recent "rise" of some Southern powers, most of all China, and the perception that these changes make earlier notions of imperialism outdated. Yet in many ways, current global economic structures impose constraints upon developing countries that are so severe that they are actually quite similar to the constraints that are characteristic of the period of direct colonial control. Neoliberalism has created a revamped form of neocolonialism.

## Financialization and Neocolonialism

The first and most obvious route through which neoliberalism imposes a new colonial-like control is through financial liberalization and the associated financialization of much of economic life. Financialization has been marked not just in advanced economies but in many developing countries as well. Financial deregulation has undermined the diversity of financial structures, suited to the particular national context and to the advancement of economic development objectives, created in the newly independent developing countries in the mid-20$^{th}$ century. Developing countries—even those at relatively low levels of economic development and diversification—were told, instead, that financial liberalization was essential for them to attract external capital that, in turn, was supposedly essential to finance economic development. Indeed, the International Monetary Fund (IMF) and the World Bank have actively pushed financial liberalization on developing countries, regardless of their specific contexts and degree of development, and particularly in the wake of balance-of-payments crises that revealed their external vulnerability.

There are, of course, several other ways in which the new global architecture of trade, investment, and finance has reduced the policy autonomy of developing countries and undermined their prospects for productive diversification and sustainable economic expansion. For example, intellectual property rights and the monopoly privileges they confer on multinational companies—mostly based in the global North—have been significant, by sharply reducing the possibilities of emulation that formed the basis of almost all successful industrialization from the 19$^{th}$ century onwards, in currently rich countries like Germany, the United States, Japan, and so on. Trade liberalization and export obsession empowered extractive industries (like mining, petroleum, forestry, etc.) and forced a shift back to primary product exports in many developing countries, thereby stalling and in some cases even reversing their attempts at economic diversification and structural transformation. But in this piece, I will focus specifically on financial liberalization and its effects.

Policymakers across the developing world, and especially those in finance ministries, internalized the view that financial liberalization was necessary to improve the functioning of the financial sector. This was supposed to be the key to increased profitability and competitiveness. It was supposed to make financial intermediation—the linkage between savers and borrowers—more effective. It was also the supposed key to attracting international capital and thereby increasing the resources that were available for domestic investment. These ideas were usually supported by the media, which caters to the elite in most developing countries. Their constant reiteration ensured that such measures had wide support among both elites and the middle class, who often have the most political voice in these countries.

As a result, many key features of existing financial structures and policies in developing economies were eliminated. Developing-country governments had directed credit to specific key industries. Without such policies no country has successfully industrialized. They had created financial institutions to serve specific development purposes, such as development banks and other institutions to finance long-term investment. They had imposed domestic regulations that prevented financial fraud and the siphoning off of savings for private gain rather than social purpose. They had imposed controls on cross-border capital flows to reduce vulnerability to global economic conditions. They had established controls on foreign ownership of financial assets, preventing the external takeover of key resources. It is worth noting that the one major economic success story of recent decades—the People's Republic of China—did not embark on financial liberalization policies. Even now the Chinese state retains significant control over domestic financial institutions and cross-border movements of capital.

The effects of financial liberalization across the developing world are, sadly, now only too obvious. Globally, there are three major consequences: First, the international financial system has been transformed in ways that substantially increase systemic risk, and make the system more crisis-prone. Within the financial world, there is a complex web of entanglement, with all firms mutually exposed to different kinds of risks, but each individual firm exposed in differing degrees to particular financial entities. It is difficult to judge the actual risk exposure of individual financial institutions. This makes a mockery of prudential regulation, such as "capital adequacy" ratios, which have supposedly become stricter over time, since it is difficult to actually define or measure the extent of capital when risk weights can be changed and assets themselves are loosely defined. The process of financial consolidation has substantially increased the risks associated with the system.

Second, for developing countries, there were further dangers associated with exposure to new kinds of risk. Financial liberalization creates a propensity to financial crisis, both external and internal. Such crises can have a deflationary impact on real economic activity and reduce access to funds for small-scale producers, both urban and rural. This in turn has major social effects in terms of loss of employment and the decline of standards of living for most citizens. Financial liberalization also reduces developing countries' domestic policy autonomy. With increased exposure to global financial markets, and completely unbridled international capital flows, it is no longer possible for a country to control the amount of capital inflow or outflow. Both movements can create undesirable consequences. If, for example, international investors suddenly flood a country with foreign portfolio investments, it can cause the national currency to appreciate. Unless the capital inflows are simply (and wastefully) stored up in the form of accumulated foreign exchange reserves, they are necessarily associated with current account deficits. This occurs because, as the exchange rate appreciates, exports become more expensive, and imports become cheaper, making domestic production less competitive, and shifting production away from traded goods (imports and exports) to non-traded activities (including finance and real estate). Over time, this can also derail the project of industrialization, especially when dynamic economies of scale are involved so that lower production reduces opportunities of learning by doing and production synergies. Financial liberalization has therefore created a new problem which is analogous to what economists dubbed "Dutch disease," (so called because of the experience of the Netherlands with the sudden discovery of North Sea oil that increased oil exports and rendered other forms of domestic production less competitive) with capital inflows causing an appreciation of the real exchange rate that, in turn, causes changes in the real economy.

Third, an even more powerful impact of financial liberalization is that it forces governments to adopt deflationary fiscal policies to appease financial interests. To begin with, the need to attract internationally mobile capital means that there are limits to taxation, especially on capital. Typically, trade liberalization has already reduced the indirect tax revenues (as from tariffs) of states undertaking financial liberalization. With financial liberalization creating pressures to limit other taxes, the overall tax-to-GDP ratio often deteriorates. This imposes limits on government spending, since finance capital is generally opposed to large fiscal deficits. Financial liberalization, therefore, reduces both the possibilities for countercyclical macroeconomic policies—where the state increases spending to boost demand during an economic downturn—and the developmental or growth-oriented activities of the state.

## Finance and Development

Financial liberalization can dismantle the very financial structures that are crucial for economic growth and development. While the relationship between financial structure, financial growth, and overall economic development is complex, the basic issue of financing for development is how to mobilize or create real resources. In the classical development literature of the mid-20th century, finance in the sense of money or financial securities came into play only when looking at the ability of the state to tax away a part of the surplus to finance its development expenditures, given the obstacles to deficit-financed spending. By and large, the financial sector was seen as adjusting to the requirements of the real economy.

In this brave new world of today, when the financial sector is increasingly left unregulated or minimally regulated, market signals determine the allocation of investible resources. It was earlier believed that this is both desirable and more

---

### *Small Producers Under Financial Liberalization*

In the developing world, financial liberalization has especially negative effects on employment-intensive sectors such as agriculture. For small-scale producers, the transaction costs of borrowing tend to be high, the risks are many, and collateral is not easy to come by. The agrarian crisis in most parts of the developing world is at least partly, often substantially, related to the decline in peasant farmers' access to institutional finance, which is the direct result of financial liberalization. Reductions in state-directed credit toward peasant farmers and other small producers have contributed to rising costs of credit, greater difficulty accessing necessary working capital for cultivation and other activities, and the reduced economic viability of cultivation.

All of these effects have added directly to rural distress. In India, for example, the deep crisis of the cultivating community has been associated with farmer suicides, mass outmigrations from rural areas, and even deaths from starvation. There is strong evidence that, in different parts of rural India, these and other forms of distress have been related to the decline of institutional credit, which has forced farmers to turn to private moneylenders and involved them once more in interlinked transactions to their substantial detriment.

efficient, but both actual historical experience and analyses since then have underlined that the most successful development experiences have emerged from "getting prices wrong," that is, moving away from market signals. Financial deregulation means that available savings are allocated by financial intermediaries to the sectors that are most profitable. In other words, private benefits, rather than overall social benefits, determine the allocation of savings and investment. Credit is directed to non-priority and import-intensive but more profitable sectors. Investible funds are concentrated in the hands of a few large players. Savings are directed to already well-developed centers of economic activity. The socially desirable role of financial intermediation therefore becomes muted.

Financial liberalization also has a negative impact on any medium-term strategy of ensuring growth in particular sectors through directed credit, which had been the basis for the industrialization process through much of the 20th century. In a large number of developing countries in the past, the financial structure was developed with economic development objectives in mind. Financial structures were created to deal with the difficulties associated with late industrial entry.

By the 20th century, minimum capital requirements for entry in most sectors were high because technology for factory production had evolved in a capital-intensive direction since the Industrial Revolution. Competition from more established producers meant that firms had to concentrate on production for a protected domestic market or be supported with finance to survive long periods of low capacity utilization (during which they could find themselves a foothold in world markets). Not surprisingly, therefore, most late industrializing countries created strongly regulated and even predominantly state-controlled financial institutions aimed at mobilizing savings and using the allocation of credit to influence the size and structure of investment. They did this through directed credit policies and differential interest rates, and the provision of investment support to the nascent industrial class in the form of equity, credit, and low interest rates.

By dismantling these structures, financial liberalization destroys important policy instruments that historically evolved in late industrializers. This reduces their ability to ensure economic growth through the diversification of production, given the difficulties generated by international inequality (and especially by the fact that other countries have already industrialized). Financial liberalization is therefore likely to have depressing effects on growth for other reasons than just deflationary bias. It keeps countries stuck in their positions in the global value-added ladder, or may even cause regression and downward movement, much as direct colonial control did in an earlier age.

All of this is even more significant because the process of financial liberalization across the globe has not generated greater net flows of capital into the developing world, as was expected by its proponents. Rather, for the past several years, the net flows have gone in the reverse direction. Even the "emerging markets," which have been substantial recipients of capital inflows, have not experienced increases in overall investment rates, and have built up their external reserves instead. This is only partly because of precautionary measures to guard against possible financial crises; it also indicates prior excess of savings over investment resulting from the deflationary macroeconomic stance.

The workings of international financial markets have actually contributed to international concentration. Developing countries, particularly those in Asia, hold their reserves in U.S. Treasury bills and other safe securities. This contributes to the U.S. economy's absorption of more than two-thirds of the world's savings over the past two decades. At the same time, developing countries are losing out from holding their reserves, these very-low-yielding "safe" assets, while capital inflows into these same countries generally reap much higher rates of interest. This undesirable form of financial intermediation is in fact a direct result of the financial liberalization measures which have simultaneously created deflationary impulses and increased financial fragility across the developing world.

## Financialization and Political Control

Other aspects of global financial markets—for example the very unequal and unjust treatment of the sovereign debt of developing countries, which typically ensures the assets of North-based creditors while forcing citizens in poor countries to bear the costs of adjustment and repayment—also contribute to the several ways in which the period of neoliberal globalization has worsened the relative position of such countries and hampered the development project. Without the more obvious political control evident under colonialism, neoliberalism has enabled the flourishing of colonial-style economic relations between countries.

These tendencies have become more apparent—and indeed intensified—in the current Covid-19 pandemic that is sweeping across the globe. While some core advanced countries are currently adversely hit by the spread of the virus, the economic fallout in the developing world has already been far more disastrous, even in countries that have not yet been very badly hit by the contagion. Sharp reversals of capital flows, collapses in export and tourism revenues, currency depreciations, and resulting problems of debt servicing have created a perfect storm for developing countries, many of whom are also imposing severe containment measures like lockdowns that are destroying domestic economic activity. Already, capital movements have indicated a global "flight to safety" to U.S. Treasury Bills, which enable the U.S. government to institute a massive stimulus program of government spending and even larger interventions of bond purchases by the U.S. Federal Reserve. Such strategies are simply not available to other countries, particularly developing countries that will face massive external headwinds even as they struggle to cope with the potential havoc created by large-scale infection and the economic consequences of lockdowns.

If anything, current tendencies therefore reaffirm the basic point made in this article: While current structures of imperialist political control are not as explicit and obvious as those of direct colonial control, they nevertheless still function to enforce global inequality, the global division of labor, and imperialist exploitation of the resources and labor of the "periphery." ❑

*Sources*: Alice Amsden, *Asia's Next Giant* (Oxford University Press, 1989); Erik Reinert, *How Rich Countries Got Rich and Why Poor Countries Stay Poor* (Anthem Press, 2007); United Nations Conference on Trade and Development (UNCTAD), *Trade and Development Report* (2016).

*Article 9.2*

# MEASURING ECONOMIC DEVELOPMENT
*The "Human Development" Approach*

**BY ALEJANDRO REUSS**
*April 2012*

Some development economists have proposed abandoning per capita GDP, the dominant single-number measure of economic development, in favor of the "human development" approach—which focuses less on changes in average income and more on widespread access to basic goods.

Advocates of this approach to the measurement of development, notably Nobel Prize-winning economist Amartya Sen, aim to focus attention directly on the *ends* (goals) of economic development. Higher incomes, Sen notes, are *means* people use to get the things that they want. The human development approach shifts the focus away from the means and toward ends like a long life, good health, freedom from hunger, the opportunity to get an education, and the ability to take part in community and civic life. Sen has argued that these basic "capabilities" or "freedoms"—the kinds of things almost everyone wants no matter what their goals in life may be— are the highest development priorities and should, therefore, be the primary focus of our development measures.

If a rising average income guaranteed that everyone, or almost everyone, in a society would be better able to reach these goals, we might as well use average income (GDP per capita) to measure development. Increases in GDP per capita, however, do not always deliver longer life, better health, more education, or other basic capabilities to most people In particular, if these income increases go primarily to those who are already better-off (and already enjoy a long life-expectancy, good health, access to education, and so on), they probably will not have much effect on people's access to basic capabilities.

Sen and others have shown that, in "developing" countries, increased average income by itself is not associated with higher life expectancy or better health. In countries where average income was increasing, but public spending on food security, health care, education, and similar programs did not increase along with it, they have found, the increase in average income did not appear to improve access to basic capabilities. If spending on these "public supports" increased, on the other hand, access to basic capabilities tended to improve, whether average income was increasing or not. Sen emphasizes two main lessons based on these observations: 1) A country cannot count on economic growth alone to improve access to basic capabilities. Increased average income appears to deliver "human development" largely by *increasing the wealth a society has available for public supports*, and not in other ways. 2) A country does not have to prioritize economic growth—*does not have to "wait" until it grows richer*—to make basic capabilities like long life, good health, and a decent education available to all.

# The Human Development Index (HDI)

The "human development" approach has led to a series of annual reports from the United Nations Development Programme (UNDP) ranking countries according to a "human development index" (HDI). The HDI includes measures of three things: 1) health, measured by average life expectancy, 2) education, measured by average years of schooling and expected years of schooling, and 3) income, measured by GDP per capita. The three categories are then combined, each counting equally, into a single index. The HDI has become the most influential alternative to GDP per capita as a single-number development measure.

Looking at the HDI rankings, many of the results are not surprising. The HDI top 20 is dominated by very high-income countries, including thirteen Western European countries, four "offshoots" of Great Britain (Australia, Canada, New Zealand, and the United States), and two high-income East Asian countries (Japan and South Korea). Most of the next 20 or so are Western or Eastern European, plus a few small oil-rich states in the Middle East. The next 50 or so include most of Latin America and the Caribbean, much of the Middle East, and a good deal of Eastern Europe (including Russia and several former Soviet republics). The next 50 or so are a mix of Latin American, Middle Eastern, South and Southeast Asian, and African countries. The world's poorest continent, Africa, accounts for almost all of the last 30, including the bottom 24.

## TABLE 1: HDI RANKS COMPARED TO INCOME-PER-CAPITA RANKS (2010)

| Highest HDI ranks compared to income per capita ranks (difference in parentheses)* | Lowest HDI ranks compared to income per capita ranks (difference in parentheses) |
|---|---|
| New Zealand (+30) | Equatorial Guinea (-78) |
| Georgia (+26) | Angola (-47) |
| Tonga (+23) | Kuwait (-42) |
| Tajikistan (+22) | Botswana (-38) |
| Madagascar (+22_ | South Africa (-37) |
| Togo (+22) | Qatar (-36) |
| Fiji (+22) | Brunei (-30) |
| Ireland (+20 | Gabon (-29) |
| Iceland (+20) | United Arab Emirates (-28) |
| Ukraine (+20) | Turkey (-26) |

* The numbers in parentheses represent a country's GDP-per-capita rank minus its HDI rank. Remember that in a ranking system, a "higher" (better) rank is indicated by a lower number. If a country is ranked, say, 50th in GDP per capita and 20th in HDI, its number would be 50 – 20 = +30. The positive number indicates that the country had a "higher" HDI rank than GDP per capita rank. If a country is ranked, say, 10th in GDP per capita and 35th in HDI, its number would be 10 – 35 = -25. The negative number indicates that the country had a "lower" HDI rank than GDP per capita rank.

Source: United Nations Development Programme, Indices, Getting and using data, 2010 Report—Table 1: Human Development Index and its components (hdr.undp.org/en/statistics/data/).

It is not surprising that higher GDP per capita is associated with a higher HDI score. After all, GDP per capita counts for one third of the HDI score itself. The relationship between the two, however, is not perfect. Some countries have a higher HDI rank than GDP per capita rank. These countries are "over-performing," getting more human development from their incomes, compared to other countries. Meanwhile, some countries have a lower HDI rank than GDP per capita rank. These countries are "under-performing," not getting as much human development from their incomes, compared to other countries. The list of top "over-performing" countries includes three very high-income countries that had still higher HDI ranks (Iceland, Ireland, and New Zealand), three former Soviet republics (Georgia, Tajikistan, and Ukraine), two small South Pacific island nations (Fiji, Togo), and two African countries (Madagascar, Tonga). The list of top "under-performing" countries includes four small oil-rich countries (Brunei, Kuwait, Qatar, and United Arab Emirates) and five African countries (Angola, Botswana, Equatorial Guinea, Gabon, and South Africa).

The UNDP also calculates an inequality-adjusted HDI. Note that, for all the measures included in the HDI, there is inequality within countries. The inequality-adjusted HDI is calculated so that, the greater the inequality for any measure included in the HDI (for health, education, or income), the lower the country's score. Since all countries have some inequality, the inequality-adjusted HDI for any country is always lower than the regular HDI. However, the scores for countries with greater inequality drop more than for those with less inequality. That pushes some countries up in the rankings, when inequality is penalized, and others down. Among the thirteen countries moving up the

## TABLE 1: INEQUALITY-ADJUSTED HDI RANKS COMPARED TO UNDADJUSTED HDI RANKS (2010)

| Highest inequality-adjusted HDI ranks compared to undadjusted HDI ranks (difference in parentheses) | Lowest inequality-adjusted HDI ranks compared to undadjusted HDI ranks (difference in parentheses) |
| --- | --- |
| Uzbekistan (+17) | Peru (-26) |
| Mongolia (+21) | Panama (-20) |
| Moldova (+16) | Colomcia (-18) |
| Kyrgistan (+15) | South Korea (-18) |
| Maldives (+14) | Bolivia (-17) |
| Ukraine (+14) | Belize (-16) |
| Philippines (+11) | Brazil (-15) |
| Sri Lanka (+11) | Namibia (-15) |
| Tanzania, Viet Nam, Indonesia, Jamaica, Belarus (+9) | El Salvador (-14) |
| | Turkmenistan (-12) |

*Source:* United Nations Development Programme, 2010 Report, Table 3: Inequality-adjusted Human Development Index (hdr.undp.org/en/media/HDR_2010_EN_Table3_reprint.pdf).

most, five are former Soviet republics. Among the ten moving down the most, seven are Latin American countries. The United States narrowly misses the list of those moving down the most, with its rank dropping by nine places when inequality is taken into account.

## GDP Per Capita and HDI

The relationship between income per capita and the HDI is shown in the "scatterplot" graph below. (Instead of GDP per capita, the graph uses a closely related measure called Gross National Income (GNI) per capita.) Each point represents a country, with its income per capita represented on the horizontal scale and its HDI score represented on the vertical scale. The further to the right a point is, the higher the country's per capita income. The higher up a point is, the higher the country's HDI score. As we can see, the cloud of points forms a curve, rising up as income per capita increases from a very low level, and then flattening out. This means that a change in GDP per capita from a very low level to a moderate level of around $8000 per year is associated with large gains in human development. Above that, we see, the curve flattens out dramatically. A change in income per capita from this moderate level to a high level of around $25,000 is associated with smaller gains in human development. Further increases in income per capita are associated with little or no gain in human development.

This relationship suggests two major conclusions, both related to greater economic equality.

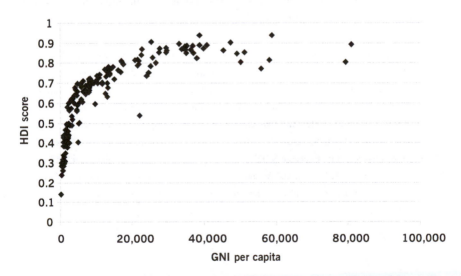

RELATIONSHIP BETWEEN HDI AND INCOME PER CAPITA (2010)

*Source:* United Nations Development Programme, Indices, 2010 Report - Table 1 Human Development Index and its components (hdr.undp.org/en/statistics/data/).

First, achieving greater equality in incomes between countries, including by redistributing income from high-income countries to low-income countries, could result in increased human development. Over the highest per capita income range, from about $25,000 on up, increases in income are not associated with higher human development. Decreases in income above this threshold, by the same token, need not mean lower human development. On the other hand, over the lowest income range, below $8000, increases in income are associated with dramatic gains in HDI (largely due to increased public supports). Therefore, the redistribution of incomes from high-income countries to low-income countries could increase human development in the latter a great deal, while not diminishing human development in the former by very much (if at all)—resulting in a net gain in human development.

Second, high-income countries might make greater gains in HDI, as their incomes continued to increase, if a larger share of income went to low-income people or to public supports. Part of the reason that the relationship between per capita income and HDI flattens out at high income levels may be that there are inherent limits to variables like life expectancy (perhaps 90-100 years) or educational attainment (perhaps 20 years). These "saturation" levels, however, have clearly not been reached by all individuals, even in very high-income countries. In the United States, as of 2008, the infant mortality rate for African-Americans was more than double that for whites. The life expectancy at birth for white females was more than three years greater than that of African-American females; for white males, more than five years greater than for African-American males. As of 2010, over 40% of individuals over 25 years old have no education above high school. Over 60% have no degree from a two- or four-year college. It is little wonder that higher income would not bring about greatly increased human development, considering that, over the last 30 years, many public supports have faced sustained attack and most income growth has gone to people already at the top. ❑

*Sources:* Amartya Sen, *Development as Freedom* (New York: Oxford University Press, 1999); United Nations Development Programme, Indices, Getting and using data, *2010 Human Development Report*, Table 1 Human Development Index and its components (hdr.undp.org/en/ statistics/data/); United Nations Development Programme, *2010 Human Development Report*, Table 3: Inequality-adjusted Human Development Index (hdr.undp.org/en/media/HDR_2010_ EN_Table3_reprint.pdf); U.S. Census Bureau, *The 2012 Statistical Abstract*, Births, Deaths, Marriages, & Divorces: Life Expectancy, Table 107. Expectation of Life and Expected Deaths by Race, Sex, and Age: 2008; Educational Attainment, Population 25 Years and Over, U.S. Census Bureau, Selected Social Characteristics in the United States, *2010 American Community Survey*, 1-Year Estimates.

*Article 9.3*

# FAMINE MYTHS
*Five Misunderstandings Related to the 2011 Hunger Crisis in the Horn of Africa*

## BY WILLIAM G. MOSELEY
*March/April 2012*

The 2011 famine in the horn of Africa was one of the worst in recent decades in terms of loss of life and human suffering. While the UN has yet to release an official death toll, the British government estimates that between 50,000 and 100,000 people died, most of them children, between April and September of 2011. While Kenya, Ethiopia, and Djibouti were all badly affected, the famine hit hardest in certain (mainly southern) areas of Somalia. This was the worst humanitarian disaster to strike the country since 1991-1992, with roughly a third of the Somali population displaced for some period of time.

Despite the scholarly and policy community's tremendous advances in understanding famine over the past 40 years, and increasingly sophisticated famine early-warning systems, much of this knowledge and information was seemingly ignored or forgotten in 2011. While the famine had been forecasted nearly nine months in advance, the global community failed to prepare for, and react in a timely manner to, this event. The famine was officially declared in early July of 2011 by the United Nations and recently (February 3, 2012) stated to be officially over. Despite the official end of the famine, 31% of the population (or 2.3 million people) in southern Somalia remains in crisis. Across the region, 9.5 million people continue to need assistance. Millions of Somalis remain in refugee camps in Ethiopia and Kenya.

The famine reached its height in the period from July to September, 2011, with approximately 13 million people at risk of starvation. While this was a regional problem, it was was most acute in southern Somalia because aid to this region was much delayed. Figure 1 provides a picture of food insecurity in the region in the November-December 2011 period (a few months after the peak of the crisis).

The 2011 famine received relatively little attention in the U.S. media and much of the coverage that did occur was biased, ahistorical, or perpetuated long-held misunderstandings about the nature and causes of famine. This article addresses "famine myths"—five key misunderstandings related to the famine in the Horn of Africa.

## Myth #1: Drought was the cause of the famine.

While drought certainly contributed to the crisis in the Horn of Africa, there were more fundamental causes at play. Drought is not a new environmental condition for much of Africa, but a recurring one. The Horn of Africa has long experienced erratic rainfall. While climate change may be exacerbating rainfall variability, traditional livelihoods in the region are adapted to deal with situations where rainfall is not dependable.

The dominant livelihood in the Horn of Africa has long been herding, which is well adapted to the semi-arid conditions of the region. Herders traditionally ranged widely across the landscape in search of better pasture, focusing on different areas depending on meteorological conditions.

The approach worked because, unlike fenced in pastures in America, it was incredibly flexible and well adapted to variable rainfall conditions. As farming expanded, including large-scale commercial farms in some instances, the routes of herders became more concentrated, more vulnerable to drought, and more detrimental to the landscape.

Agricultural livelihoods also evolved in problematic ways. In anticipation of poor rainfall years, farming households and communities historically stored surplus crop production in granaries. Sadly this traditional strategy for mitigating the risk of drought was undermined from the colonial period moving forward as households were

## FIGURE 1: FOOD INSECURITY IN THE HORN OF AFRICA REGION, NOVEMBER-DECEMBER 2011.

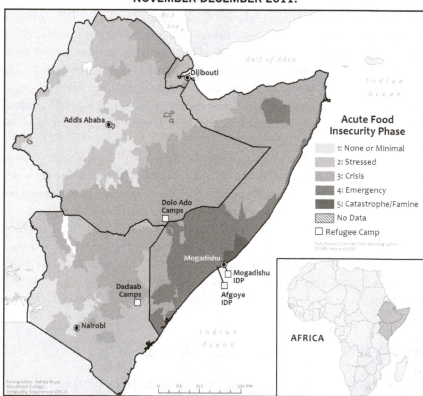

Based on data and assessment by FEWS-Net (a USAID-sponsored program).

Cartography by Ashley Nepp, Macalester College.

encouraged (if not coerced by taxation) to grow cash crops for the market and store less excess grain for bad years. This increasing market orientation was also encouraged by development banks, such as the World Bank, International Monetary Fund, and African Development Bank.

The moral of the story is that famine is not a natural consequence of drought (just as death from exposure is not the inherent result of a cold winter), but it is the structure of human society which often determines who is affected and to what degree.

## Myth #2: Overpopulation was the cause of the famine.

With nearly 13 million people at risk of starvation last fall in a region whose population doubled in the previous 24 years, one might assume that these two factors were causally related in the Horn of Africa. Ever since the British political economist Thomas Malthus wrote "An Essay on the Principle of Population" in 1798, we have been concerned that human population growth will outstrip available food supply. While the crisis in Somalia, Ethiopia and Kenya appeared to be perfect proof of the Malthusian scenario, we must be careful not to make overly simplistic assumptions.

For starters, the semi-arid zones in the Horn of Africa are relatively lightly populated compared to other regions of the world. For example, the population density of Somalia is about 13 persons per sq. kilometer, whereas that of the U.S. state of Oklahoma is 21.1. The western half of Oklahoma is also semi-arid, suffered from a serious drought in 2011, and was the poster child for the 1930s Dust Bowl. Furthermore, if we take into account

### Land Grabs in Africa

Long term leases of African land for export-oriented food production, or "land grabs," have been on the rise in the past decade. Rather than simply buying food and commodity crops from African farmers, foreign entities increasingly take control of ownership and management of farms on African soil. This trend stems from at least two factors. First, increasingly high global food prices are a problem for many Asian and Middle Eastern countries that depend on food imports. As such, foreign governments and sovereign wealth funds may engage in long-term leases of African land in order to supply their own populations with affordable food. Secondly, high global food prices are also seen as an opportunity for some Western investors who lease African land to produce crops and commodities for profitable global markets.

In the Horn of Africa, Ethiopia (which has historically been one of the world's largest recipients of humanitarian food aid) has made a series of long-term land leases to foreign entities. The World Bank estimates that at least 35 million hectares of land have been leased to 36 different countries, including China, Pakistan, India and Saudi Arabia. Supporters of these leases argue that they provide employment to local people and disseminate modern agricultural approaches. Critics counter that these leases undermine food sovereignty, or people's ability to feed themselves via environmentally sustainable technologies that they control.

differing levels of consumption, with the average American consuming any times more than the average Somali does in a normal year, then Oklahoma's population density of 21.1 persons per sq. kilometer equates to that of 591 Somalis.

Despite the fact that Oklahoma's per capita impact on the landscape is over 45 times that of Somalia (when accounting for population density and consumption levels), we don't talk about overpopulation in Oklahoma. This is because, in spite of the drought and the collapse of agriculture, there was no famine in Oklahoma. In contrast, the presence of famine in the Horn of Africa led many to assume that too many people was a key part of the problem.

Why is it that many assume that population growth is the driver of famine? For starters, perhaps we assume that reducing the birthrate, and thereby reducing the number of mouths to feed, is one of the easiest ways to prevent hunger. This is actually a difficult calculation for most families in rural Africa. It's true that many families desire access to modern contraceptives, and filling this unmet need is important. However, for many others, children are crucial sources of farm labor or important wage earners who help sustain the family. Children also act as the old-age social security system for their parents. For these families, having fewer children is not an easy decision. Families in this region will have fewer children when it makes economic sense to do so. As we have seen over time and throughout the world, the average family size shrinks when economies develop and expectations for offspring change.

Second, many tend to focus on the additional resources required to nourish each new person, and often forget the productive capacity of these individuals. Throughout Africa, some of the most productive farmland is in those regions with the highest population densities. In Machakos, Kenya, for example, agricultural production and environmental conservation improved as population densities increased. Furthermore, we have seen agricultural production collapse in some areas where population declined (often due to outmigration) because there was insufficient labor to maintain intensive agricultural production.

Third, we must not forget that much of the region's agricultural production is not consumed locally. From the colonial era moving forward, farmers and herders have been encouraged to become more commercially oriented, producing crops and livestock for the market rather than home consumption. This might have been a reasonable strategy if the prices for exports from the Horn of Africa were high (which they rarely have been) and the cost of food imports low. Also, large land leases (or "land grabs") to foreign governments and corporations in Ethiopia (and to a lesser extent in Kenya and Somalia) have further exacerbated this problem. These farms, designed solely for export production, effectively subsidize the food security of other regions of the world (most notably the Middle East and Asia) at the expense of populations in the Horn of Africa. These trends are consistent with the Amartya Sen's insight that, throughout history, most famines are not the result of an absolute lack of food or production, but rather a situation where the hungry do not have access to the food being produced.

## Myth #3: Increasing food production through advanced techniques will resolve food insecurity over the long run.

As Sub-Saharan Africa has grappled with high food prices in some regions and famine in others, many experts argue that increasing food production through a program of hybrid seeds and chemical inputs (a so-called "New Green Revolution") is the way to go.

While outsiders benefit from this New Green Revolution strategy (by selling inputs or purchasing surplus crops), it is not clear if the same is true for small farmers and poor households in Sub-Saharan Africa. For most food insecure households on the continent, there are at least two problems with this strategy. First, such an approach to farming is energy intensive because most fertilizers and pesticides are petroleum based. Inducing poor farmers to adopt energy-intensive farming methods is short sighted, if not unethical, if experts know that global energy prices are likely to rise. Second, irrespective of energy prices, the New Green Revolution approach requires farmers to purchase seeds and inputs, which means that it will be inaccessible to the poorest of the poor, i.e., those who are the most likely to suffer from periods of hunger. In order to improve access, or "entitlements," to use Amartya Sen's language, we need low cost approaches that are accessible to poor farmers.

If not the New Green Revolution approach, then what? Many forms of bio-intensive agriculture are, in fact, highly productive and much more efficient than those of industrial agriculture. For example, crops grown in intelligent combinations allow one plant to fix nitrogen for another rather than relying solely on increasingly expensive, fossil fuel-based inorganic fertilizers for these plant nutrients. Mixed cropping strategies are also less vulnerable to insect damage and require little to no pesticide use for a reasonable harvest. These techniques have existed for centuries in the African context and could be greatly enhanced by supporting collaboration among local people, African research institutes, and foreign scientists.

## Myth #4: U.S. foreign policy in the Horn of Africa was unrelated to the crisis.

Many Americans assume that U.S. foreign policy bears no blame for the food crisis in the Horn and, more specifically, Somalia. This is simply untrue. The weakness of the Somali state was and is related to U.S. policy, which interfered in Somali affairs based on Cold War politics (the case in the 1970s and 80s) or the War on Terror (the case in the 2000s).

During the Cold War, Somalia was a pawn in a U.S.-Soviet chess match in the geopolitically significant Horn of Africa region. In 1974, the U.S. ally Emperor Haile Selassie of Ethiopia was deposed in a revolution. He was eventually replaced by Mengistu Haile Mariam, a socialist. In response, the leader of Ethiopia's bitter rival Somalia, Siad Barre, switched from being pro-Soviet to pro-Western. Somalia was the only country in Africa to switch Cold War allegiances under the same government. The U.S. supported Siad Barre until 1989 (shortly before his demise in 1991). By doing this, the United States played a key role in supporting a long-running dictator and undermined democratic governance.

More recently, the Union of Islamic Courts (UIC) came to power in 2006. The UIC defeated the warlords, restored peace to Mogadishu for the first time in 15 years, and brought most of southern Somalia under its orbit. The United States and its Ethiopian ally claimed that these Islamists were terrorists and a threat to the region. In contrast, the vast majority of Somalis supported the UIC and pleaded with the international community to engage them peacefully. Unfortunately, this peace did not last. The U.S.-supported Ethiopian invasion of Somalia begun in December 2006 and displaced more than a million people and killed close to 15,000 civilians. Those displaced then became a part of last summer and fall's famine victims.

The power vacuum created by the displacement of the more moderate UIC also led to the rise of its more radical military wing, al-Shabaab. Al-Shabaab emerged to engage the Transitional Federal Government (TFG), which was put in place by the international community and composed of the most moderate elements of the UIC (which were more favorable to the United States). The TFG was weak, corrupt, and ineffective, controlling little more than the capital Mogadishu, if that. A low-grade civil war emerged between these two groups in southern Somalia. Indeed, as we repeatedly heard in the media last year, it was al-Shabaab that restricted access to southern Somalia for several months leading up to the crisis and greatly exacerbated the situation in this sub-region. Unfortunately, the history of factors which gave rise to al-Shabaab was never adequately explained to the U.S. public. Until July 2011, the U.S. government forbade American charities from operating in areas controlled by al-Shabaab—which delayed relief efforts in these areas.

## Myth #5: An austere response may be best in the long run.

Efforts to raise funds to address the famine in the Horn of Africa were well below those for previous (and recent) humanitarian crises. Why was this? Part of it likely had to do with the economic malaise in the U.S. and Europe. Many Americans suggested that we could not afford to help in this crisis because we had to pay off our own debt. This stinginess may, in part, be related to a general misunderstanding about how much of the U.S. budget goes to foreign assistance. Many Americans assume we spend over 25% of our budget on such assistance when it is actually less than 1%.

Furthermore, contemporary public discourse in America has become more inward-looking and isolationist than in the past. As a result, many Americans have difficulty relating to people beyond their borders. Sadly, it is now much easier to separate ourselves from them, to discount our common humanity, and to essentially suppose that it's okay if they starve. This last point brings us back to Thomas Malthus, who was writing against the poor laws in England in the late 18th century. The poor laws were somewhat analogous to contemporary welfare programs and Malthus argued (rather problematically) that they encouraged the poor to have more children. His essential argument was that starvation is acceptable because it is a natural check to over-population. In other words, support for the poor will only exacerbate the situation. We see this in the way that some conservative commentators reacted to last year's famine.

The reality was that a delayed response to the famine only made the situation worse. Of course, the worst-case scenario is death, but short of death, many households were forced to sell off all of their assets (cattle, farming implements, etc.) in order to survive. This sets up a very difficult recovery scenario because livelihoods are so severely compromised. We know from best practices among famine researchers and relief agencies in that you not only to detect a potential famine early, but to intervene before livelihoods are devastated. This means that households will recover more quickly and be more resilient in the face of future perturbations.

## Preventing Famines

While the official famine in the horn of Africa region is over, 9.5 million people continue to need assistance and millions of Somalis remain in refugee camps in Ethiopia and Kenya. While this region of the world will always be drought prone, it needn't be famine prone. The solution lies in rebuilding the Somali state and fostering more robust rural livelihoods in Somalia, western Ethiopia and northern Kenya. The former will likely mean giving the Somali people the space they need to rebuild their own democratic institutions (and not making them needless pawns in the War on Terror). The latter will entail a new approach to agriculture that emphasizes food sovereignty, or locally appropriate food production technologies that are accessible to the poorest of the poor, as well as systems of grain storage at the local level that anticipate bad rainfall years. Finally, the international community should discourage wealthy, yet food-insufficient, countries from preying on poorer countries in Sub Saharan African countries through the practice of land grabs. ❑

*Sources:* Alex de Waal, *Famine That Kills: Darfur, Sudan*, Oxford University Press, 2005; William G. Moseley, "Why They're Starving: The man-made roots of famine in the Horn of Africa," *The Washington Post*. July 29, 2011; William G. Moseley and B. Ikubolajeh Logan, "Food Security," in B. Wisner, C. Toulmin and R. Chitiga (eds)., *Toward a New Map of Africa*, Earthscan Publications, 2005; Abdi I. Samatar, "Genocidal Politics and the Somali Famine," Aljazeera English, July 30, 2011; Amartya Sen, *Poverty and Famines*, Oxford/Clarendon, 1981; Michael Watts and Hans Bohle, "The space of vulnerability: the causal structure of hunger and famine," *Progress in Human Geography*, 1993.

*Article 9.4*

# LAND REFORM
*A Precondition for Sustainable Economic Development*

**BY JAWIED NAWABI**
*May/June 2015*

> *It is in the agricultural sector that the battle for long-term economic development will be won or lost. —Gunnar Myrdal, economist and Nobel laureate*

The phrase "land reform" often conjures up memories, for those leaning right, of frightening extreme-left ideologies. On the progressive left, meanwhile, land reform is often treated as a passé topic.

With the advent of rising inequality, climate change, weak government institutions, failed states, terrorism, corruption, and a whole slew of other socio-economic problems—sown or exacerbated by three decades of neoliberal policies in the "developing world" (Global South)—it is high time we revisit the issue of land reform. We need to bring it back to the center of the discussion on sustainable economic development. Land reform is not political extremism; rather, it is a critical policy mechanism for the world to address issues of poverty, hunger, urban slums, and good governance.

What is "land reform"? It is usually defined as the redistribution of large landholdings to smaller ones. Land is transferred from large landlords to those who have been working the land as tenants (such as sharecroppers) or paid agricultural workers, as well as dispossessed underemployed or unemployed urban workers who migrated from rural areas looking for employment and wound up living in urban slums. That is one model of land reform. Another model is redistribution in the form of rural communes or cooperative or collective farms. A combination of the two models is also possible.

## Reemergence of Land Reform Movements

Despite the attempts by international institutions (like the IMF and World Bank) and oligarchic political elites in the global South to suppress land reform policies, there have been growing social movements pushing for land reform in the last two decades. Neoliberal "free trade" policies have exposed small farmers to devastating global competition (especially from giant mechanized industrial farms in the global North), leaving hundreds of millions of them dispossessed, and have forced them into the reserve army of impoverished unemployed or underemployed living in urban slums. From Brazil and Mexico to the Philippines and Zimbabwe, social movements for a more just and fair distribution of wealth—particularly land—are confronting these devastating consequences of neoliberalism.

Social protest has led even elite institutions such as the World Bank to acknowledge the issue. The Bank's World Development Report 2008: Agriculture for

Development, at least rhetorically put agriculture and the productivity of small farmers "at the heart of a global agenda to reduce poverty."

## Agriculture as a Technical Problem?

The central tendency of mainstream economic development theory since the 1940s and 1950s has been to view agriculture as a mere stepping stone towards industrialization. Economist Arthur W. Lewis' "dualist" model was particularly influential in casting agricultural labor in developing countries as redundant—with a "surplus" of workers adding little or nothing to agricultural production. This surplus labor force, Lewis argued, should be moved out of the agricultural sector—this would supposedly not reduce output—and into the industrial, which he viewed as the key sector of the economy.

Besides moving inefficient peasants out of the rural sector, mainstream development economists proposed to boost agricultural yields by consolidating small farms into large ones—supposedly to take advantages of economies of scale. Thus, instead of reducing land concentration, this would increase it, essentially accomplishing a reverse land reform. Such an industrial model of agriculture would use expensive capital equipment (imported from the global North), petroleum-based fertilizers, herbicides, and pesticides. Today's version of the model increasingly pushes the adoption of genetically modified seeds controlled by corporations like Monsanto.

During the 1960s and 1970s, this frame of thought led many international institutions (such as the World Bank, Asian Development Bank, etc.) and governments in the global South to embrace the "Green Revolution." The Green Revolution was essentially a plan to use "science and technology" to increase crop production in developing countries. The use of fertilizers, pesticides, and high-yield crop varieties was supposed to boost agricultural productivity, reduce rural poverty, solve problems of hunger and malnutrition, and thus avoid peasant movements and rural political instability. This was, as economists James M. Cypher and James L. Dietz put it, a "strategy wherein it was hoped that seed technologies could be substituted for missing land reform and for more radical 'red revolutions' of the socialist variety threatening to sweep across the globe at the time."

Viewing agricultural productivity as a purely technical problem, advocates of the Green Revolution did not aim to transform the structure of land inequality and landlord power. To take the case of India, the Green Revolution boosted

### Land Reform and Colonization

If we broaden the concept of land reform, the whole process of colonial settlement in North America, Central and South America, Australia, and New Zealand was one big land reform, appropriating the lands of indigenous peoples and distributing it to the European settlers. So land reform can be understood as a much more common experience of the "developed" world than it is usually thought of in the economic literature.

agricultural yields, making the country technically self-sufficient in food production. However, the changes primarily benefited medium and large-sized landowners who used capital-intensive technologies, high-yielding mono-crop seeds, and large inputs of fertilizers and pesticides. "Rural inequity worsened because of the growing prosperity of the large and medium farmers and the unchanged position of the landless and small farmers," concludes Indian scholar Siddharth Dube. "And because large farms use more capital and less labour per unit of produce than small farms, rural employment grew much less than it would have if land reform had taken place and the increase in production come from smaller farms."

## The Economic and Socio-Political Cases for Land Reform

There are two broad arguments for the importance of land reform. The first is based on the widely observed inverse relationship between farm size and output per unit of land area: smaller farms produce more per acre of land than larger farms. Smaller land holdings are more productive and ecologically sustainable for a number of reasons:

1) Higher labor intensity. Small farmers use more labor per unit of land, which helps generate more output and more employment per unit.
2) Higher multiple cropping. They grow more crops per year on a given piece of land.
3) Higher intensity of cultivation. Small farmers leave a lower proportion of land fallow or uncultivated. In addition, they cultivate crops that are higher value-added per unit of land.
4) Lower negative environmental impacts. Small farms use fertilizers, pesticides, and other agrochemicals more sparingly than large farms. This reduces negative impacts of harmful chemicals on workers and neighbors. Small farmers, overall, have a greater incentive to employ environmentally sustainable techniques than large industrial ones.

While the economic case for land reform can be construed as a narrow technical

---

### Good Governance

The "good-governance functions" of the state are policies beneficial to the large majority of the population. Good-governance states exercise control over a certain territory, depend on a broad part of their population for revenue, and in turn provide the population with a wide range of public goods: the rule of law, transportation infrastructure (paved roads, extensive and affordable public transportation, etc.), public utilities (electricity, clean water, sewage systems), human services (health, education systems), and job security or at least temporary unemployment insurance.

argument on how best to boost agricultural productivity—which land-reform opponents could argue is unnecessary due to the advent of the Green Revolution—the socio-political argument is aimed against this kind of narrow technical thinking. The importance of a land reform is in changing the hierarchical structure of agrarian class relations while increasing productivity. The idea is to break the power of landlords, who keep peasants as a captive labor force in rural areas and act as a conservative political force at the local and national levels of the state.

The central mechanism by which landlords wield their power is through patron-client networks that give them control over local and regional government institutions. Landlords keep the poor majority dependent on them for jobs and access to land, while also using them as a captive power base for local elections (in countries where there are elections, such as India and Brazil). This way, they can block the development of state programs providing public goods—like public roads, clinics, schools, water systems, etc.—for everyone. Instead, they perpetuate a more narrowly targeted development relying on private goods—fertilizer, pesticides, expensive high-yield seeds, privately controlled water wells, loans that put peasants in ever-deeper debt, etc. They provide, also, a form of private insurance system for those clients who exhibit proper loyalty, in contrast to social support systems available to all—which would reduce the peasants' vulnerability and the landlord's power. The consequence is that the state's good-governance capacities are distorted and corrupted, favoring the narrow interests of the landlords and the political elite that is connected to them (often by kinship).

Transformative socio-political land reform for developing countries is aimed at diminishing wealth inequalities in the initial stages of development and breaking the grip on power of the upper-class elite (including not only landlords but also big industrial, financial, and commercial capitalists generally allied with them). This democratization of society would make it possible to orient the state towards long-term national development policies which can create more conducive socioeconomic and sociopolitical conditions serving the population as a whole, and not just the elite.

The socioeconomic conditions would include a more egalitarian class structure in the rural sector, greater incentives for farmers to increase their productivity due to owning the land they work, greater farmer incomes allowing the farmers to send their children to school, better nutrition due to higher caloric intake, and greater small-farmer purchasing power leading to greater demand for the products of labor-intensive manufacturing. The sociopolitical democratization would mean the breaking of landlord power, political stabilization resulting from the inclusion of the peasant masses in the political system, and democratization of decision making now liberated from landlord capture of local and national state bureaucracies.

## Land Reform Is Not Enough

There have been many more failed land reforms than successful ones. Reforms have failed mainly because they have not been thorough enough in breaking the power of the landed elite, and in extending the role of the government in an inclusive development process. Across Latin America—in Mexico, Bolivia, Brazil, Chile, and Peru—land reforms have had partial success, but for the most part have not dislodged rural elites and their industrial counterparts from political dominance. This has contributed to an image of land reform, even among the progressive left, as a tried and failed policy. There are also examples of half-successful land reforms in South and East Asia—in India, the Philippines, Indonesia, and Thailand—where peasants did reap some benefits like reliable ownership titles, which allowed them to borrow on better terms, boosted crop yields, and reduced malnutrition, though without fundamentally altering the class structure.

On the other hand, successful land reforms were thorough, extensive, and swift. Key examples in the twentieth century include Japan, Taiwan, South Korea, and China. Land in the first three countries was distributed as family-sized farms. (China initially had a collectivized land reform.) Looking at the Japanese and South Korean cases: In Japan in 1945, 45% of the peasants were landless tenants. By 1955, only 9% were tenants and even they benefited from much-strengthened protective laws. In pre-reform South Korea in 1944, the top 3% of landholders owned about 64% of the land, with an average holding of 26 hectares. By 1956, the top 6% owned just 18% of the land, with an average of about 2.6 hectares. Meanwhile, 51% of family farmers owned about 65% of the land, with an average holding of 1.1 hectares.

Nowhere in Latin America or Africa, nor elsewhere in Asia (except Kerala, India), did land reforms come so close to such equalization and radical reshaping of traditional social structures. The East Asian land reforms succeeded in bringing about the long-term national development policies by creating more conducive socioeconomic and sociopolitical conditions—breaking the existing power structure, allowing for the emergence of developmentally oriented states (as opposed to neoliberal models that saw state promotion of economic development as anachronistic and "inefficient"). Successful land reforms require follow up—supportive policies investing in rural infrastructure development (irrigation, electricity, roads, health clinics, schools), plus providing services such as clear and legitimate land records, micro-credit at reasonable rates of interest, and training for farmers in the newest skills for sustainable farming. Japan, Taiwan, South Korea, and arguably even China's development paths serve as examples of transformative land reforms in the last fifty years. What these countries achieved was remarkable growth with equity. ❑

*Sources:* Irma Adelman, "Income Distribution, Economic Development and Land Reform," *American Behavioral Scientist*, Vol. 23, No. 3 (pgs. 437-456), Jan/Feb 1980; Miguel A. Altieri, "No: Poor Farmers Won't Reap The Benefits," *Foreign Policy*, Summer 2000; James K. Boyce, Peter Rosset, Elizabeth A. Stanton, "Land Reform and Sustainable Development," Working Paper Series No. 98, Political Economy Research Institute, University of Massachusetts-Amherst, 2005; Sarah Blaskey and Jessee Chapman, "Palm Oil Oppression," *Dollars & Sense*, May/June 2013; Celia A. Dugger, "World Bank Report Puts Agriculture at Core of Antipoverty Effort," *New York Times*, Oct. 20, 2007; H. Ronald Chilcote, *Power and The Ruling Classes in Northeast Brazil: Juazeiro and Petrolina in Transition*, Cambridge University Press, 1990;

Michael Courville and Raj Patel, "The Resurgence of Agrarian Reform in the Twenty-First Century," In Peter Rosset, Raj Patel, and Michael Courville, eds., *Promised Land: Competing Visions Agrarian Reform*, Food First Book, 2006; James M. Cypher and James L. Dietz, *The Process of Economic Development* (3rd ed., Routledge, 2009; Siddarth Dube, *In the Land of Poverty: Memoirs of an Indian Family: 1947-1997*, Zed Books, 1998; Mike Davis, P*lanet of Slums*, Verso, 2007; Peter Dorner, *Land Reforms and Economic Development*, Penguin Books, 1972; Peter Evans, *Embedded Autonomy: States and Industrial Transformation*, Princeton University Press, 1995; Penelope Francks, with Johanna Boestel and Choo Hyop Kim, *Agriculture and Economic Development in East Asia: From Growth to Protectionism in Japan, Korea and Taiwan*, Routledge, 1999; Jayati Ghosh, "Equality, Sustainability, Solidarity," *Dollars & Sense*, Jan/Feb 2015; Keith Griffin, Azizur Rahman Khan, and Amy Ickowitz (GKI), "Poverty and Distribution of Land," *Journal of Agrarian Change*, July 2002; Jonathan M. Harris, *Environmental and Natural Resource Economics: A Contemporary Approach*, Houghton Mifflin Company, 2002; Frances Hagopian, "Traditional Politics Against State Transformation in Brazil," In Joel S. Migdal, Atul Kohli and Vivienne Shue, eds., *State Power and Social Forces: Domination and Transformation in the Third World*, Cambridge University Press, 1994; Yoong-Deok Jeon and Young-Yong Kim, "Land Reform, Income Redistribution, and Agricultural Production in Korea," *Economic Development and Cultural Change*, Vol. 48, No. 2, January 2000; Cristobal Kay, "Why East Asia Overtook Latin America: Agrarian Reform, Industrialization and Development," *Third World Quarterly*, Vol. 23, No. 6, December 2002; John Lie, *Han Unbound: The Political Economy of South Korea*, Stanford University Press, 1998; Moyo Sam and Paris Yeros, eds., *Reclaiming the Land: The Resurgence of Rural Movements in Africa, Asia and Latin America*, Zed Books, 2005; Raj Patel, *Stuffed and Starved: The Hidden Battle for World's Food System*, 2nd ed, Melville House, 2012; James Putzel, "Land Reforms in Asia: Lessons From the Past for the 21st Century," Working Paper Series No. 00-04, London School of Economics Development Studies Institute, 2000; Debraj Ray, *Development Economics*, Princeton University Press, 1998; Peter M. Rosset, "Fixing Our Global Food System: Food Sovereignty and Redistributive Land Reform," In *Agriculture and Food in Crisis: Conflict, Resistance, and Renewal*, Monthly Review Press, 2010; Peter M. Rosset, "The Multiple Functions and Benefits of Small Farm Agriculture," Policy Brief No. 4, The Institute For Food and Development Policy, Oakland, California, 1999; Vandana Shiva, *Soil Not Oil: Environmental Justice in an Age of Climate Crisis*, South End Press, 2008; Rehman Sobhan, *Agrarian Reform and Social Transformation: Preconditions for Development*, Zed Books, 1993; Lance Taylor, Santosh Mehrotra, and Enrique Delamonica, "The Links between Economic Growth, Poverty Reduction, and Social Development: Theory and Policy," In Santosh Mehrotra and Richard Jolly, *Development with a Human Face: Experiences in Social Achievement and Economic Growth*, Oxford University Press, 2000; Michael P. Todaro, *Economic Development*, 7th ed., Addison-Wesley, 2000; Jong-Sung You, "Inequality and Corruption: The Role of Land Reform in Korea, Taiwan, and the Philippines," Presented at the Annual Conference of the Association for Asian Studies, Atlanta, April 2008; Jong-Sung You, "Embedded Autonomy or Crony Capitalism? Explaining Corruption in South Korea, Relative to Taiwan and the Philippines, Focusing on the Role of Land Reform and Industrial Policy," Annual Meeting of the American Political Science Association, Washington, D.C., Sept. 1-4, 2005; Tim Wegenast, "The Legacy of Landlords: Educational Distribution and Development in a Comparative Perspective," *Zeitschrift für Vergleichende Politikwissenschaft*, Volume 3, Issue 1, April 2009; Maurice Zeitlin and Richard Earl Ratcliff, *Landlords and Capitalists: The Dominant Class of Chile*, Princeton University Press, 1988.

*Article 9.5*

# CAPITAL FLIGHT FROM AFRICA
*What Is to Be Done?*

## BY JAMES K. BOYCE
*November 2015*

I am old enough to remember when the subject of illicit financial flows was not discussed in polite company. The topic was relegated to the shadows of official discourse. It is gratifying to see this important issue moving squarely onto the agenda of the international community.

The terms "capital flight" and "illicit financial flows" sometimes are used interchangeably, but they are distinct concepts. Capital flight is usually defined as unrecorded capital outflows and measured as the missing residual in the balance of payments, after corrections for underreported external borrowing and trade misinvoicing. All capital flight is illicit, but not all illicit financial flows are capital flight. Capital flight is illicit by virtue of illegal acquisition, illegal transfer, illegal holding abroad, or some combination of the three.

Illicitly acquired capital is money obtained through embezzlement, bribes, extortion, tax evasion, or criminal activities. Wealth acquired by these means is often transferred abroad clandestinely in an effort to evade legal scrutiny as to its origins.

Illicitly transferred funds are outflows not reported to government authorities. Mechanisms include smuggling of bank notes, clandestine wire transfers, and falsification of trade invoices.

Illicitly held funds are assets whose earnings are not declared as income to national authorities of the owner's country. The concealment of foreign holdings may be motivated by the desire to evade prosecution for illicit acquisition of the funds, or may be for taxation evasion, or both.

The broader universe of illicit financial flows includes not only capital flight but also payments for smuggled imports, transactions connected with illicit trade in narcotics and other contraband, outflows of illicitly acquired funds that were domestically laundered before flowing overseas through recorded channels, and transfer pricing by the corporate sector. These, too, are illicit, but they are not the same as capital flight.

## Capital Flight and External Debt

Countries often experience external borrowing and capital flight simultaneously. At first glance this may seem anomalous. Why would we observe large capital flows in both directions at once? External borrowing implies that both lenders and borrowers expect attractive investment returns. Yet capital outflows appear to signal higher returns elsewhere. In practice, the two phenomena may not only co-exist but also be causally linked. External borrowing can lead to capital flight, and capital flight can lead to external borrowing. Understanding these linkages is important for the formulation of appropriate policy responses.

In debt-fueled capital flight, external borrowing finances private wealth accumulation outside the borrowing country. On the borrower side, the government contracts loans in the name of the public. Officials and other politically connected individuals then siphon part or all of the money into their own pockets—via kickbacks, padded procurements contracts, and diversion of funds—and stash part or all of the proceeds abroad for safekeeping. On the lender side, loan officers are rewarded for simply "moving the money," creating myopic incentives to turn a blind eye to these risks.

In flight-fueled external borrowing, flight capital finances external loans. A private individual illicitly parks funds abroad and then "borrows" them back. A key motive for such round tripping is concealment of the origins of the funds. The borrower reaps further illicit gains if, as often happens, liability for repaying the loan ultimately passes to the government by virtue of public guarantees in the event of default. Such transactions are attractive to bankers because they generate fees and commissions on both sides.

Econometric analysis indicates that for each new dollar of external borrowing by African countries, as much as 60 cents exits Africa as capital flight in the same year. The tight year-to-year correlation between external borrowing and capital flight suggests that debt management is important in addressing the problem of capital flight. Of course, not all flight capital originates in external borrowing. Statistical analysis shows that natural resource extraction, for example, is also strongly correlated with capital flight.

## Stolen asset recovery

Let me now turn to policy responses, starting with efforts to recover and repatriate stolen assets. Some success has been scored on this front. For example, $700 million held in Swiss bank accounts by Nigeria's former military ruler Sani Abacha and his family has been recovered and repatriated. To be sure, the amounts recovered are modest compared to the total magnitude of capital flight, but they are not inconsequential. An added benefit of such recoveries is their demonstration effect, which may help to deter future capital flight.

Over the past two decades the international community has begun building institutional infrastructure to assist in stolen asset recovery. The United Nations Convention against Corruption includes articles on asset recovery and mutual legal assistance. The Stolen Asset Recovery Initiative, launched in 2007 by the United Nations Office on Drugs and Crime and the World Bank, provides technical assistance in tracing stolen wealth, asset seizure and confiscation, and enlisting international cooperation. Many countries have established Financial Intelligence Units to investigate transactions related to criminal activity, and anti-money laundering legislation requires banks and other financial institutions to file reports on suspicious transactions.

A key feature of this emerging international architecture is that when investigators identify substantial foreign holdings of politically exposed persons and others

## U.S. Banks and the Dirty Money Empire

*Every instance of capital flight must involve parties abroad, to receive the funds. In 2001, au-*
*thor James Petras (in a longer article excerpted here) detailed the culpability of leading U.S.*
*banks in facilitating hundersds of billions in capital flight. As he put it, "The money launder-*
*ing business ... is carried out by the United States' most important banks. The bank officials*
*involved in money laundering have backing from the highest levels of the banking institutions.*
*These are not isolated offenses perpetrated by loose cannons." —Eds.*

Washington and the mass media have portrayed the United States as being in the forefront of
the struggle against narcotics trafficking, drug-money laundering, and political corruption. The
image is of clean white hands fighting dirty money from the Third World (or the ex-Communist
countries). The truth is exactly the opposite. U.S. banks have developed an elaborate set of policies for transferring illicit funds to the United States and "laundering" those funds by investing
them in legitimate businesses or U.S. government bonds. The U.S. Congress has held numerous hearings, provided detailed exposés of the illicit practices of the banks, passed several anti-
laundering laws, and called for stiffer enforcement by public regulators and private bankers.
Yet the biggest banks continue their practices and the sums of dirty money grow exponentially.
The $500 billion of criminal and dirty money flowing annually into and through the major U.S.
banks far exceeds the net revenues of all the information technology companies in the United
States. These yearly inflows surpass the net profits repatriated from abroad by the major U.S.
oil producers, military industries, and airplane manufacturers combined. Neither the banks nor
the government have the will or the interest to put an end to practices that provide such high
profits and help maintain U.S. economic supremacy internationally. ...

Hundreds of billions of dollars have been transferred, through the private-banking and corre-
spondent-banking systems, from Africa, Asia, Latin America, and Eastern Europe to the biggest
banks in the United States and Europe. In all these regions, liberalization and privatization of
the economy have opened up lucrative opportunities for corruption and the easy movement of
booty overseas. Authoritarian governments and close ties to Washington, meanwhile, have ensured impunity for most of the guilty parties. Russia alone has seen over $200 billion illegally
transferred out of the country in the course of the 1990s. The massive flows of capital out of
these regions—really the pillaging of these countries' wealth through the international banking
system—is a major factor in their economic instability and mass impoverishment. The resulting
economic crises, in turn, have made these countries more vulnerable to the prescriptions of the
International Monetary Fund and the World Bank, including liberalized banking and financial
systems that lead to further capital flight. — James Petras

**Sources:** "Private Banking and Money Laundering: A Case Study of Opportunities and Vulnerabilities,"
Permanent Subcommittee on Investigations of the Committee on Governmental Affairs, United States
Senate, One Hundred Sixth Congress, November 9-10, 2000; "Report on Correspondent Banking:
A Gateway to Money Laundering," Minority Staff of the U.S. Senate Permanent Subcommittee on
Investigations, February 2001.

suspected of criminal activity, asset holders can be required to prove that the wealth was acquired legitimately. Pending the outcome of the legal proceedings, the assets can be restrained or seized.

## Selective Debt Repudiation

Debts that fuel capital flight can be considered "odious" under international law. Selective repudiation of odious debt—which is distinct from across-the-board default—can prevent the diversion of scarce public resources into debt service payments on loans from which the public derived no benefit. Repudiation of odious debts also would change the incentive structure for creditors, encouraging due diligence and helping to improve the quality of future lending.

Odious debts are liabilities contracted by governments without the consent of the people, from which the people did not benefit, in circumstances where creditors knew or should have known these conditions to hold. They include funds stolen by corrupt individuals and money used to maintain the power of authoritarian regimes. Determining which loans served bona fide development purposes and which are odious is a challenging task. Systematic audits can help to establish which debts are legitimate and which offer objective grounds for repudiation. Where there is evidence of systematic misuse of borrowed funds, the burden of proof can be placed upon creditors to demonstrate that their loans were used for legitimate purposes, much as the burden of proof can be placed upon politically exposed persons to prove the legitimacy of foreign assets held in their names.

In this arena, there is scope for innovations in international governance. An impartial body for arbitration of odious debt disputes is sorely needed. A United Nations commission chaired by Nobel laureate Joseph Stiglitz called in 2009 for the creation of an international bankruptcy court that could consider, "where appropriate, partial debt cancellation." The IMF has noted that such a body could be charged with adjudicating claims of odious debts. The creation of such a forum could do much to curb debt-fueled capital flight and flight-fueled external borrowing.

## Regulatory Reforms in International Banking

Further efforts are also needed to increase transparency in international banking. Most flight capital is domiciled in what are commonly referred to as offshore financial centres. The most important of these are not tropical islands, but rather New York, London, and other international banking centers. Improved transparency requires strengthening the enforcement of existing banking regulations and closing loopholes arising from the inadequate harmonization of banking regulations across countries.

An important piece in efforts to improve financial transparency is cross-country exchange of information on investment income, including interest, dividends, and capital gains. This necessitates information on beneficial ownership so that the recipients cannot conceal their identities behind shell companies and trusts. Banks and other financial institutions, including brokers and insurance companies, should be required to report this information to their governments, who can then share the information with the governments of income recipients.

Recent years have seen some progress on this front. In 2009, the exchange of information upon request became the international standard, monitored by the Global Forum on Exchange of Information and Transparency for Tax Purposes. This gave tax authorities access to information on offshore investment income, although it put the onus on them to identify specific individuals or firms in order to request this information. In 2013, the G20 Finance Ministers and Central Bank Governors endorsed the automatic exchange of information—rather than exchange upon request—as the new international standard. Bilateral agreements are now laying the foundation for multilateral cooperation to implement this policy.

## Conclusion

Capital flight occurs for a variety of reasons. Two important motives are the desire to conceal funds that have been illicitly acquired and the desire to evade taxation. Individuals who engage in capital flight are aided and abetted in illicit transfers of funds by officers in banks and other financial institutions who are in a position to profit from these transactions as long as they are not detected and subjected to penalties. Foreign borrowing and extractive resource revenues are important correlates of capital flight, suggesting that these are significant sources for the illicit acquisition of private wealth.

Growing recognition of these problems is spurring international efforts to mitigate the consequences of past capital flight and to reduce its recurrence in future years. These include efforts to recover stolen assets, relieve external debt burdens, and promote transparency and due diligence in international banking. The creation of an impartial body to adjudicate cases of odious debts would further strengthen this international architecture. If well designed and implemented, these initiatives will help to curtail malfeasance, improve incentive structures, and contribute to a more efficient and equitable international financial architecture. ❑

*Sources:* J-P. Brun, et al., *Asset Recovery Handbook: A Guide for Practitioners*, Stolen Asset Recovery Initiative, World Bank and United Nations Office on Drugs and Crime, 2011; J. King, *The Doctrine of Odious Debt in International Law*, 2015; International Monetary Fund, *Sovereign Debt Restructuring—Recent Developments and Implications for the Fund's Legal and Policy Framework*, 2013; L. Ndikumana, J.K. Boyce, and A.S. Ndiaye, "Capital Flight from Africa: Measurement and Drivers," in I. Ajayi and L. Ndikumana (eds.), *Capital Flight from Africa: Causes, Effects and Policy Issues*, 2015; Organization for Economic Cooperation and Development, *Action Plan on Base Erosion and Profit Shifting*, 2013; N. Shaxson, *Treasure Islands: Tax Havens and the Men Who Stole the World*, 2011; United Nations, *Recommendations of the Commission of Experts of the President of the United Nations General Assembly on Reforms of the International Monetary and Financial System*, 2009.

# Chapter 10

# THE STATE, GLOBALIZATION, AND DEVELOPMENT

*Article 10.1*

## WHAT EVER HAPPENED TO DEVELOPMENT?

**BY JAWIED NAWABI**
*January/February 2018*

## Introduction

Since World War II, if we count the number of countries which can been be considered to have moved from being "Third World" (or "developing") countries to being developed countries, how many countries make the list? By my count it would be five: South Korea, Taiwan, Singapore, Hong Kong, and Qatar. China is on its way and certain regions of China are already fit to be termed "developed." In Africa, out of the 54 countries, we cannot confidently tally any to have attained developed status (South Africa is termed an "Emerging Market Economy"). Latin America has had several more decades since independence to build an industrial base. (Most of Latin America, not including the Caribbean, nominally gained independence between the 1820s and 1880s, 80-150 years before most of Africa, the Caribbean (outside of Haiti), and most of Asia.) However, the region's industry has not reached globally competitive levels compared to the Asian "Tigers." Latin America and the Caribbean's share of world income grew from about 5.8% in 1985 to about 7.2% in 2010. Meanwhile, East Asia and Pacific's (excluding Japan) grew from 4.1% in 1985 to 11.6% in 2010.

An increasing share of total world income has been going to the developing part of the world. In 1995, about 17.5% of world income went to 83% of the world population (developing countries); by 2010, the figure had increased to about 30.3% (mostly because of East Asia). But that means that about 70% of the income still went to the richest 17% of the world population (the developed world) down from about 83%. This distribution is still starkly uneven: About 3

### What Is the "Third World"?

The term "Third World" refers to a wide array of countries which have wide living standard differences today but that share a common colonial historical background. They are predominately countries of Asia, Africa, and Latin America/Caribbean that have gained formal political independence since World War II and that were part of a non-alignment movement during the Cold War. The non-alignment movement originated with the intention to chart a third path of political and economic development for the newly independent countries, different from either the U.S. model of capitalism or the Soviet model of communism. (Since they were not part of the "Western World" or the "Eastern World" in the previous "two world" division of the globe, the term "Third World" was coined.) In that spirit, they struggled to protect their political sovereignty and formulate approaches to development which would not be dominated by the leading powers. Today, these same countries (about 125 of them) are struggling against the onslaught of neoliberalism. Thus, "Third World" is not just a geographic designation of countries of the Global South nor an economic category but rather a conceptual project of newly independent countries who have struggled to develop their own economic and political systems without being dominated by the big colonial/neocolonial powers.

billion people, out of a world population of 7 billion, live on less than $2.50 a day, and about half of them (1.5 billion) live on less than $1.25, experiencing what international development agencies call "extreme poverty." Out of those living in extreme poverty, 800-900 million (depending how we count) experience hunger or what the UN terms chronic undernourishment. Out of these hundreds of millions of hungry people, one million children die yearly from malnourishment. So why have so few countries—out of about 120 newly independent countries that have emerged since WWII—achieved successful development?

## The Optimism of Decolonization and Hope of Development

This question poses a challenge to mainstream economics, which has theorized that less-developed countries enjoy certain "advantages of backwardness" (like being able to copy technologies already developed elsewhere). If they simply have high rates of saving and investment in physical capital, within one to two generations they should be able to reach income parity with the developed world. So why haven't they?

After World War II, with the struggles of de-colonization movements, the concept of "growth and development" for Third World countries became an ideological battle ground. The industrialized capitalist countries, engaged in postwar reconstruction, experienced an economic boom that is today considered "the golden era of capitalism." Meanwhile, the Third World countries that had gained political independence remained mired in poverty and destitution. And because of the fear for the spread of the socialist system, the governments of the advanced capitalist West constantly pushed Third World governments, even to the point of using covert and overt physical force, to adopt to the laws of the "free" market and "free" trade. The capitalist market system, they assured the Third World leaders, would surely move their countries out of poverty and towards prosperity and progress.

What had to happen, according to probably the most influential and famous modernist theorist, Walt Whitman Rostow, was for so-called backward countries to emulate Western ways. Rostow believed that development was a linear path through five stages along which all countries travel. The five stages were traditional society, the preconditions for take-off, the take-off, the drive to maturity, and the age of high mass-consumption. Of course, the West had traveled these paths and reached the ultimate destination, which is the mature capitalist economic system and high-mass consumption. All that had to happen now was for the West to share its technology, capital, educational systems, form of governments, and most especially their value system, with those traditional countries. Then the latter, too, would be able to achieve the preconditions that would propel them into economic takeoff. This assumes the "advantage" of the newly independent countries of not having to reinvent the wheel of how to develop.

Keynesian policies—especially government management of total demand, with the aim of maintaining economic growth and high employment—were used in the West to help reconstruct their economies after World War II. So the core Western international institutions and mainstream economics field, between the 1950s and 1960s, tolerated or even encouraged a more central role for the state in the economic development for the newly independent countries. However, the modernist theories and the mainstream economic theories did not have a sophisticated understanding of the legacies of colonialism and their role in the Third World countries' impoverished economies and lack of proper developmental institutions. Their equations assumed all states to be the same (just like the dominant model of economic growth assumed that all countries had access to the same level of technology). Thus, they did not differentiate between the newly independent countries and the developed Western states in terms of state effectiveness.

Unfortunately, colonialism had forcefully incorporated the Third World countries as subordinate economies, solely producing primary (raw materials) commodities for advanced capitalist markets. The diversity, scope, and technological sophistication of local industry was suppressed. In the years following independence, these asymmetric trade relations resulted in further disadvantages for Third World countries, in the form of deteriorating "terms of trade" of their primary commodities for the manufactured goods of the developed economies. Raul Prebisch and Hans Singer's empirical studies showed how the prices of the Third World countries' primary products steadily declined relative to those of the manufactured products they purchased from the advanced developed countries—a pattern that continued from the 1950s to the late 1990s. As economist Louis Putterman put it:

> It takes more and more cocoa, rubber, coffee, tea, bananas, tin or copper to buy an automobile, a truck or a piece of heavy equipment. When an index of the prices of non-fuel primary commodities is divided by an index of the unit value of manufactured goods constructed so their ratio is 100 in 1960, this ratio is found to have fallen from 131 in 1900, and it continues falling to reach 67 in 1986.

By the early 1970s it had become clear that this was leading the developing countries into balance of payments problems: They were importing much more than exporting, which left little capital for investing into the advancement of their economies, kept them dependent on manufactured parts and goods from the developed world, and resulted in a major debt crisis. Data from the World Bank show the continuing falling prices of non-fuel commodities up to 1999.

On the political level, most of the new independent countries—mostly in Africa and Asia, some in Latin America—lacked state institutions which were linked to and dependent on the population for the majority of their revenues. Instead, these countries were saddled with colonial state institutions which were designed by the colonizing powers to extract resources through despotic power. The term "despotic power," as used by sociologist Michael Mann, means having coercive power over society. In states with "despotic power" policing and military capabilities are emphasized, but administrative capacity for complex projects (like building rural roads, electrical power grids, public housing and transportation, public education, etc.) remains limited. Postcolonial states, with only very rare exceptions, did not have built-in professionalized bureaucracies which were accountable to the masses of the people. The postcolonial state was not open to the influence of civil society institutions—like labor unions that advocate for safer work conditions, rural farmers who want local rural roads, or a legal system independent from the coercive powers of the state. Since the postcolonial states were forcefully grafted onto indigenous societies, the governing elites were not challenged to build what Mann terms infrastructural power—power through society instead of over society.

The states which emerged from the post-World War II independence struggles exhibited the characteristics of either predatory or intermediate states. Governing elites were mainly from the landed class, part of the oligarchy which controlled the resources of the country. Alternately, if there emerged a political elite ideologically committed to the country's national development, it was not able to gain sufficient autonomy from the oligarchy to direct an independent course for the country's economy on behalf of the majority of its population. Instead, the states that emerged were dependent upon international sources for financial and military support and not sufficiently embedded with their own populations.

# Neoliberalism: Shift from State-Led to Market-Led Development and Declining Growth Rates

By the 1970s, the economies of the Third World had not shown significant results in converging towards the economies of the developed countries. Meanwhile, inside the United States and other developed economies, there was a counter-reaction to Keynesian policies, which business and government elites blamed for slow growth and high inflation (known as "stagflation"). This created the intellectual and political climate for a backlash against the role of the state in the economy. The argument was that "government is too big," stifling private entrepreneurship and investment—thus, there was a need to privatize state services and deregulate private industries. The state was viewed as creating opportunities for corruption and distorting the market's efficient allocation of resources. This was the start of so-called "free market" (or "neoliberal") policies, which were pushed on the Third World by international financial institutions like the World Bank and International Monetary Fund. Starting in the 1970s, they started placing policy conditions on loans and other forms of assistance for developing countries much more explicitly than previous decades.

Preventing states from intervening in the economy and unleashing the disciplining pressures of market competition, the argument went, would make the developing countries' economies perform more efficiently and productively. According to neoliberal theory (or the "Washington Consensus") the behavior of individuals in the market, due to self-interested motivations, was also capable of explaining public official malfeasance. As economist Ha-Joon Chang described the Washington Consensus in his article "The Economic Theory of the Developmental State":

> Its contention was that the universally valid assumption of self-seeking motives by individuals should also be applied to politics as well as to economics and that it is therefore wrong to believe that the objective of the state, which is ultimately determined by certain individuals, will be commensurate with what is good for society. On this premise, various models of neo-liberal political economy characterized the state as an organization controlled by interest group, politicians or bureaucrats who utilize it for their own self-interest, producing socially undesirable outcomes. The possibility that at least some state may be run and influenced by groups whose objectives are not mere self-enrichment or personal aggrandizement but less personal things such as welfare statism or economic modernization was not even seriously contemplated on the grounds of the alleged self-seeking motives behind all human actions.

For the neoliberals, the solution was to deregulate private industries and privatize industries owned by Third World governments. Both government regulation and government ownership, it was believed, allowed officials to enrich themselves—demanding kick-backs and engaging in other "rent-seeking" behavior. Privatization would force these inefficient and subsidized industries to become disciplined, to adopt reforms and boost efficiency or else be punished by the competitive pressures of the market system. Competition would determine whether any particular industry or firm would swim or sink, depending on whether the proper reforms were made or not, and hence, indirectly benefit society with cheaper and higher-quality goods and services, and higher tax revenues.

The problem with the neoliberal theory of the state is that it does not distinguish between the various types of states that have existed in the capitalist world. Clearly, during the 1970s, the states of the developed world could not be considered to be as corrupt or inept as the newly independent states of the Third World. The characteristics of the minimalist state is assumed in neoliberal theory as if it is an automatic evolution of state institutions in all nation-states, however it is in these very basic bureaucratic functions that many developing nations have a critical shortage. It would have made sense to help the latter states become more institutionally effective, to build their infrastructural power so that they could perform at least the minimal state functions that neoliberalism delegated to the state. Instead, the World Bank/IMF complex, with their neoliberal policies, further weakened the already institutionally limited developmental aspects of these states, while helping to strengthen some of their policing powers. The developing countries were nudged, cajoled, even strong-armed to abandon the state-led model of development and adopt the market-led development model.

Listing the various roles of the state and the state's degree of involvement in the economy, moving from the most basic functions to the most extensive interventions:

1. Legal protection of private property, contract enforcement, and regulation
2. Defense of the state's sovereignty and territorial integrity (essentially policing the workers and the population at large)
3. Provision of public goods and services (schools, infrastructure, health, clean water, sanitation, rural and urban services)
4. Counter-cyclical policies (monetary and fiscal) due to the instability of the market system
5. Welfare services: unemployment, retirement, poverty programs
6. Coordination of development projects (indicative planning thru public-private cooperation)

The neoliberal advice to governments was and is to basically focus on functions 1-2, while delegating functions 3-6 as much as possible to a private sector exposed to the disciplinary pressures of competitive markets. The prediction was that private firms would do a much better job than the state in providing affordable private schools, clean water, health clinics, infrastructure like roads and bridges (with tolls), and private financial services for everyone from small farmers in the villages to large firms in the cities.

One would assume that, if the World Bank/IMF complex was advising the developing countries to downsize the state role in the economy, the total government expenditure (federal, state, and local) as the share of the economy would shrink in the advanced capitalist economies as well. In fact, as political economist, Atilio Boron argues, the developed countries do not practice what they preach to the developing world. Between 1970 and 1995, Boron shows, the core capitalist countries' average government expenditures grew from about 35% to 49%) Furthermore, in the 1990s "the proportion of public employees over the total population was 7.2% in the United States, 8.3% in Germany, 8.5% in England, 9.7% in France." Comparatively, in Latin America, public employees represented 3.5% of the population in Brazil and 2.8% in Chile and Argentina. Despite these numbers, Boron observes, the "pundits at the World Bank or the IMF have successfully insisted that Latin American states are 'too big' and should be downsized."

Even when we look at the financial press, we don't find much evidence that the economies with the least state involvement are the best performing economies for businesses to invest in. On the contrary, Forbes magazine, today one of the foremost publications in defense of the "free market" and "free enterprise," in 2016 ranked Sweden number one on its list of the top countries in which to do business. If we scroll down the same list, the top ten countries include Denmark, Holland, Finland, Norway, Ireland, England, and Canada. On average, their states account for 30-45% of GDP. Ironically, the very countries that are bastions of so-called welfare states (derogatorily called "nanny states") are considered by the pro-capitalist press to be the best places for business investors.

In almost all developing countries (Latin American and Caribbean, Africa, Middle East, South East Asia) the state contribution to GDP is much lower. For example, Mexico's is about 15% and Chile's is a little more than 20%. They are examples of the developing countries which arguably have insufficient government involvement as a percentage of their economies GDPs. Furthermore, these states rely overwhelmingly on indirect taxation like sales taxes and value added taxes (VAT), so their tax structures tend to be regressive (the poor and middle-class pay more). In contrast, the developed countries tend to rely on income and property taxes (direct taxes), and so have more progressive taxation (the higher income classes pay more), .

While neoliberalism was able to push the developing world away from state-led development toward more market-oriented policies, these latter policies have not shown positive results either. Economists Mark Weisbrot and Rebecca Ray have surveyed the scorecard on development between 1960 and 2010: The developing countries had higher growth rates during the years of government-led development, from 1960 to 1980, averaging about 2.5% per year, compared to 1.1% between 1980 and 2000—the high years of neoliberal policy. Latin America's average annual real GDP per capita growth rate in the era of "too big" government, 1960-1980, was 3.3%; during the height of the neoliberal era, 1980-2000, just 0.3%.

## Bringing Back the State in Economic Development

During the 1980s, while the majority of the developing world (and even the developed world) was experiencing declining growth rates, the East Asian countries were experiencing high growth. The institutions of the World Bank/IMF complex attempted to credit the East Asian economies' high growth rates to their adoptions of market policies.

Scholars such as Chalmers Johnson, Alice Amsden, Robert Wade, Peter Evans, and others (together, I term them the Role of the State in Economic Development, or RSED, school) critically responded to the neoliberal assumptions of efficient markets and government malfeasance as too simplistic and without sufficient historical depth. They were able to empirically establish that state intervention in rapidly industrializing countries of East Asia was, "characterized by market-reinforcing behavior, understood in the sense of supporting profitability for private investors .... The state versus market mind-set thus is simply not very helpful for understanding how the interaction of states and markets has served to produce a range of economic outcomes." So, instead of blanket generalizations—whether they come from the left, which views the state as nothing more than the executive committee of the bourgeoisie, or from the right, which argues that state intervention necessarily hinders economic growth and development—the real question is what kind of administrative structure do states need in order to enable growth and development within a market economy?

To the RSED school, this question required detailed study of each state. Why did some states perform as developmental states—guiding their economies to high living standards—while other states became predatory and impoverished their people? The fundamental characteristics of a developmental state are a determined elite which seeks their country's rapid development; relative autonomy of the state from powerful landed and industrial elites; a rational bureaucracy which is competent, powerful, and insulated from political swings; a somewhat authoritarian character which ensures that competing interests are subordinated to states' developmental goals of industrialization; and the capacity to manage effectively the economic sector through a broad range of policies. (The most important economic policies include tariffs, financial credit controls, technological promotion, human capital training, and competency in selecting which market signals to deliberately distort. Yes, states can promote development by deliberately altering market signals and incentives, for example, by using subsidies to help infant-industries become competitive in the international market. The developmental state, in short, is the highest authority committed to economic development through growth, productivity, and competitiveness.

The relationship between the state and market need not be a zero-sum relationship, but rather can be one of synergy. The argument of the RSED school was that market society could not be what it is without the role of the state. The active role of the state has been clear at least as far back as economic historian Karl Polanyi's masterpiece, *The Great Transformation: The Political and Economic Origins of Our Time* (1944). In the words of economist and Noble laureate Joseph Stilitz, Polanyi's analysis "exposes the myth of the free market: there never was a truly free, self-regulating market system. In their transformations, the governments of today's industrialized countries took an active role, not only in protecting their industries through tariffs, but also in promoting new technologies."

Theories of development have two axes around which they revolve: state-led development versus market-led development. Economic theories can be distinguished conceptually by the centrality of the state's role in "governing the market." Some theories envision a limited and passive role for the state because they view the market as an efficient mechanism for allocating resources to meet society's developmental needs. Government intervention, in this view, distorts prices and throws the market system into disequilibrium. In contrast, developmental economists like Ragnar Nurske, Paul Rosentein-Rodan, Albert Hirschman, Gunnar Myrdal, and Arthur Lewis—whose influence within academia and international institutions was at its height from the 1940s to late 1960s—viewed the state the one institution that could lead the "big-push" out of the poverty traps that ensnared the Third World. Unfortunately, by the 1970s, neoliberal/neoclassical economists rejected the theories of state-led development economists and excluded them from the policy calculations of the World Bank/IMF complex as well as the United Nations Development Program (UNDP). After about twenty years of neoliberal dominance in academia and international institutions (from 1980 to 2000), the RSED school and their state-led theories of development made a comeback. They undermined the intellectual hegemony of the neoliberal paradigm, demonstrating in their own original works the administrative and regulatory importance of the developmental state. They showed that economic development requires a state that is effective in managing the monetary system, protecting private property laws, setting taxes, funding public goods such as infrastructure and education, coordinating between industries, and promoting long-term investment—that is, in all six functions of the state listed above.

## Return to the 1950s Spirit of Development

If we are serious about solving the problem of development, we must bring back mass development projects through the developmental state. In the last 30 or 40 years, parallel to the downsizing of the states in the Third World, there has been a shift towards micro-oriented development projects. Such projects give non-government organizations (NGOs) and other charity aid organizations a central role, supported by the international institutions as well as mainstream economic theory. We have to make the case to returning international institutions to developmental policies—to what political scientist Eric Helleiner calls the "Forgotten Legacy of Bretton Woods"— infant industry tariffs protections, commodity price stabilization, international debt restructuring, short-term capital movement restrictions, and long-term development lending. In the spirit of the 1950s and 1960s, we must bring back the socially transforming aims of development policy—which include building the institutional capacity of states to collect taxes on a progressive basis, redistributing wealth through policies like radical land reforms, etc. Last but not least, the Third World needs to revive the planning and execution of their own regionally based and environmentally sustainable industrial policies. For these projects to be realized we need to build the developmental capacity of the Third World states. ❑

**Sources**: Nina Bandelj and Elizabeth Sowers, *Economy and State: A Sociological Perspective* (Polity Press, 2010); Nancy Birdsall, Augusto De La Torre, and Rachel Menezes, *Fair Growth: Economic Policies for Latin America's Poor and Middle-Income Majority* (Center for Global Development and Inter-American Dialogue, 2008); A. Atilio Boron, "Latin American Thinking on the State and Development: From Statelessness to Statelessness," in Sam Moyo and Paris Yeros (eds), *Reclaiming the Nation: The Return of the National Question in Africa, Asia and Latin America* (Pluto Press, 2011); Fred Block, "The Roles of the State in the Economy," in Neil J. Smelser and Richard Swedberg ; Ana Corbacho, Vicente Fretes Cibils, and Eduardo Lora (eds.), *More Than Revenue: Taxation as a Developmental Tool* (Palgrave Macmillan, 2013); Ha-Joon Chang, "The Economic Theory of the Developmental State," in Meredith Woo-Cumings (ed.), *The Developmental State* (Cornell University Press, 1999); James Cypher, *The Process of Economic Development* (Routledge, 2014); Robert Chernomas and Ian Hudson, *Economics in the Twenty-First Century: A Critical Perspective* (University of Toronto Press, 2016); Peter Evans, *Embedded Autonomy: States & Industrial Transformation* (Princeton University Press, 1995); Stephan Haggard, *Pathways From the Periphery: The Politics of Growth in the Newly Industrializing Countries* (Cornell University Press, 1990); Eric Helleiner, "International Policy Coordination for Development: The Forgotten Legacy of Bretton Woods" United Nations Conference on Trade and Development (UNCTAD Discussion Papers, No. 221), May 2015; Chalmers Johnson, *MITI and The Japanese Miracle: The Growth of Industrial Policy, 1925-1975* (Stanford University Press, 1982); Atul Kohli, *State-Directed Development: Political Power and Industrialization in the Global Periphery* (Cambridge University Press, 2004); Jonathan Krieckahaus, *Dictating Development: How Europe Shaped the Global Periphery* (University of Pittsburgh Press, 2006); Matthew Lange and Dietrich Rueschemeyer, "States and Development," in Lange, Matthew and Dietrich Rueschemeyer, *States and Development: Historical Antecedents of Stagnation and Advance* (Palgrave, Macmillan, 2005); Adrian Leftwich, *States of Development: On the Primacy of Politics in Development* (Polity Press, 2000); Michael Mann, *The Sources of Social Power: The Rise of Classes and Nation States, 1760-1914* (Vol.2) (Cambridge University Press, 1993); S.V.R. Nasr, "European Colonialism and The Emergence of Modern Muslim States," in John L. Esposito (ed.), *The Oxford History of Islam* (Oxford University Press, 1999); Ziya Onis, "The Logic of the Developmental State," *Comparative Politics*, Vol. 24, No. 1 (pp. 109-126), Oct. 1991; James Petras, "Imperialism and NGOs in Latin America," *Monthly Review*, Vol. 49, Issue 7, December 1997; Prashant Prakash, "Property Taxes Across G20 Countries: Can India Get It Right?" Oxfam India Working Papers, January 2013; Vijay Prashad, *The Darker Nations: A People's History of the Third World* (New Press, 2007); Louis Putterman, *Dollars and Change: Economics in Context* (Yale University Press, 2001); Revenue Statistics 2016: Tax Revenue Trends in OECD (oecd.org); Joseph Stiglitz, "Foreword," in Karl Polanyi, *The Great Transformation: The Political and Economic Origins of Our Time* (Beacon Press, 2001); Bob Sutcliffe, *100 Ways of Seeing an Unequal World* (Zed Books, 2001); David Waldner, *State Building and Late Development* (Cornell University Press, 1999); Mark Weisbrot and Rebecca Ray, "The Scorecard on Development, 1960-2010: Closing the Gap?" United Nations Department of Economic and Social Affairs (UN DESA Working Paper No. 106). June 2011

*Article 10.2*

# LATIN AMERICA NEEDS AN EFFICIENT DEVELOPMENTALIST STATE

## AN INTERVIEW WITH MATIAS VERNENGO
*October 2017,* El Economista *(Buenos Aires)*

**M**atias Vernengo is an economist and co-editor of Why Latin American Nations Fail: Development Strategies in the 21ˢᵗ Century. *This interview originally appeared in* El Economista *(Buenos Aires). It was translated from Spanish by* Dollars & Sense.

*El Economista:* To begin with, what make you decide to write the book? Why did you choose this point in time and what need did you mean to fill?

**Matias Vernengo:** The failure of the so-called Washington Consensus and the political reaction that made possible the election of leftist government in the region—now more than a decade ago—created the possibility for a new development strategy. Nonetheless, the global crisis that began with the end of the housing bubble in the United States and the European crisis made it clear what were the limits of these national, popular experiments in the region. The exhaustion on the commodity cycle, in particular, proves that the old problems of output specialization in the region are difficult to overcome. The book is a response to that, in the context of the resurgence of "new institutionalist" ideas about the role of institutions and the risk of a new Washington Consensus.

*EE:* To be sure, it's natural to want to improve, at the individual level and at the collective level, and to aspire to raise people's quality of life. In short, to develop. But, is this possible in Latin America and, if so, to what extent?

**MV:** I'm not proposing to "throw in the towel," like we say in Argentina. Still, we could ask: Isn't this road really difficult, and hasn't it been trod by only a few in the last few decades? In other words, what can the region realistically aspire to? We don't expect to become the next global superpower. Nor do we expect to reinvent the wheel. But it is possible to eliminate the worst problems of underdevelopment. For example, basic things, like food security, are relatively easy to solve. A combination of import substitution, export promotion, with the necessary industrial policies and domestic demand stimulation, which require redistributive policies, would make it possible to sustain reasonable growth rates and to avoid external constraints that normally put a brake on growth in "peripheral" countries. I don't know if it's possible to break what neoclassical economists call the "middle-income trap" because, in the end, only two or three countries have been able to do that, outside of the high-income "core" countries.

*EE:* One of the topics that the book covers is the role of institutions, and the authors engage critically with the institutionalist vision. What's the problem with Latin American institutions, which have been made in the image of those in other western countries, which have a substantially higher per capita GDP.

**MV:** It's not a matter of copying institutions. It's not by having an independent central bank, for example, that you bring inflation down. The central problem, in institutional terms, is the absence of an efficient developmentalist state. The old "structuralists" would tell you that it's the inability to create institutions that generate technological progress. Something like recreating a national Silicon Valley. Without a doubt, that's part of the problem. But there are also financial problems. The institutional problems of demand management, in my view, are not generally well understood. The management of external debt, of the persistent problem in managing the current account, are at the center of the limits on development. The institutions that peripheral countries need are not necessarily the same as those of developed countries. At least not the one of the present day. Institutional innovations, like the BRICs [Brazil, Russia, India, and China] Development Bank, for example, are relevant in this connection.

*EE:* The comparison of Latin America with the emerging economies of Asia is another "mirror" that appears repeatedly in the book. Is it possible to learn and copy something from them or, like some say, is that an unrealistic road for Latin America., given the societal differences between the two regions?

**MV:** In reality, this has been a permanent comparison in discussions about development. In particular, because after the 1980s debt crisis, Asian countries kept growing while Latin America basically stagnated. I think the simplistic lesson that they did well because they had lower exchange rates, and this allowed them to export more, is a gross oversimplification. We have to understand not only the institutions that allowed industrialization in Asia, related to the developmentalist state, but also the reorganization of global supply chains, which worked to the advantage of the expansion of manufacturing there.

*EE:* Finally, I'd like for you to suggest some ideas for policymakers in the region, especially in these "leaner" times compared to the first decade of the 2000s. Besides clear rules and orderly macroeconomic conditions, what are the prerequisites for development? What should they do in this challenging and competitive 21$^{st}$ century?

**MV:** It depends what you mean by orderly macroeconomic conditions. Look, the Industrial Revolution was accomplished in a period during which the English economy accumulated a public debt of more than 260% of GDP. That is, they had a big macroeconomic disequilibrium. More, it was a period of high inflation, which gave rise to the so-called "Bullionist Debate" and the beginnings of monetary theory. On the other hand, it's not easy to say what should be done. There's no magic formula. But going back to promoting national industrial development, which will make it possible to enter into global supply changes, producing higher value-added goods, and minimizing the need for external borrowing, those are courses of action that would lower the likelihood of external-debt crises. That would be a good start. ❑

*Article 10.3*

# THE ZIGS AND ZAGS OF NEOLIBERALISM IN LATIN AMERICA

## BY JAMES M. CYPHER
*November/December 2019*

On September 11, 1973, Latin America's most established democracy was overthrown in a military coup rooted in years of oligarchy-led destabilization policies and practices. As Chile's highly unequal social structure was challenged by an elected government, landowners and their allies—particularly the regal Edwards family, which controlled the commanding ideological heights through their newspaper and media empire—plotted and urged the U.S. government, then under the tutelage of Secretary of State Henry Kissinger, to join the fray.

What followed next was the immediate implementation by the "Chicago Boys"—former grad students of University of Chicago economist Milton Friedman—of a uniquely extreme version of laissez-faire economics. In Latin America *laissez-faire* ideas had long been known as "liberalism," and thus, under the military dictatorship of General Augusto Pinochet, the hyper laissez-faire doctrines and practices of the Chicago Boys involved much more than a return to established practices; they constituted a revolution against all humane restraints that limited the power of owners of capital (domestic and foreign) and their representatives. Always a slippery term, "neoliberalism" was coined in the late 1930s in Europe, but was then generally forgotten for decades. It only gained currency after Chile's new "markets know best" neoliberal socioeconomic structures spread to Uruguay after a military coup in 1973 (forcing wages down by 50% between 1973 and 1984) and then Argentina (with its "dirty war" against the left) in 1976. Latin Americans were distraught by this turn toward unbridled market power, the suppression of labor, and an array of policies that enabled national economic conglomerates and international financiers to "discipline" nation states. The threat of capital flight enforced the dominance of the new order, a dystopia Latin Americans labeled "neoliberalism."

To follow the ideas of Milton Friedman, a charismatic monetary crank who nurtured generations of Latin American economics graduate students, it was necessary to cast aside a legitimating vision of competitive market capitalism operating under governmental restraints, with modest social protections for the vulnerable. Friedman and his Latin American students promoted an anti-popular project earlier propounded by Austrian economists, especially Ludwig von Mises and Frederick von Hayek, who were nostalgic for the aristocratic privileges of neo-feudalism and deeply alarmed by the spread of the so-called "welfare state" from the 1930s onward. What Pinochet's minions imposed was not an updating of "free market" economic liberalism but rather a law-of-the-jungle, see-no-evil set of policies that abandoned civil liberties, overthrew unions and labor laws, and handed the keys to the kingdom to capital—particularly to finance capital (then headed by the Edwards family), land barons, and transnational mining companies.

Quickly, versions of Chile's model were, as noted, implemented in several nearby nations. By 1988, Mexico, under pressure from the International Monetary Fund (IMF) and an oligarchy that sensed its opportunity, installed a right-wing president who overturned decades of state-guided economic policies to follow the anti-labor restructuring format of the Chicago Boys. Still, some countries, particularly Brazil until 2019, resisted sweeping implementation of the neoliberal schema.

Of course, the Chicago School charlatans failed to conjure their promised economic revival and wages stagnated, or fell, while poverty and migration soared and the distribution of wealth became even more unequal throughout the "lost decade" of the 1980s and the following lost half-decade. (The 1980s and early 1990s were so designated due to near-zero economic growth.) But, as they did so, they "failed forward," as Jamie Peck explained in his illuminating book, *Constructions of Neoliberal Reason* (2013). That is, always unencumbered by its past policies and failed practices, neoliberalism fluidly transforms itself via a mutating process intended to preserve neoliberal rule. Thus, for example, in addition to decreeing the end of labor's organized economic power in the face of widespread unemployment, forced migration, and collapsed wages, second-stage neoliberalism promoted conditional cash transfers to sidelined workers willing to retrain and adapt to "flexible," precarious labor conditions.

Meanwhile, new technologies in mining and other extractive activities were quietly being implemented by the late 1990s—well-timed for the China boom which would float commodity prices, and most Latin American economies, steadily upward between 2002 and 2012 (or somewhat beyond in the case of oil and gas).

Exhausted by the disastrous deceptions of the Chicago Boys while finding respite when exports such as soy surged, Latin American citizens voted in left governments early in the 21st century: most noted was the popular revolt against IMF rule and neoliberal failure in Argentina that culminated in 2003 with a moderate-left government. But here and elsewhere the far-right successfully undermined a progressive shift that had begun in 2000 in Chile. There, after 10 years of progressive governments, the far-right oligarchs elected billionaire Sebastián Piñera, and then reelected him in 2017. By 2015 a devotee of Ayn Rand's "anarcho-capitalism," Mauricio Macri, had also taken power in Argentina.

In late 2018 the two largest nations in Latin America—Brazil and Mexico—moved in opposite directions, with Mexico's new president declaring the end of neoliberalism while Brazil's burning Amazon became another textbook expression of Friedman's possessive individualism—"free," unregulated land-grabbers were left unhindered to clear land to implement ecology-destroying agribusiness operations.

The conclusion is that, since 1973 (excepting the complex case of Venezuela), Latin America has shifted into and out of and then sometimes back into mutating neoliberal economic structures. While in power, left governments have been conditioned by prior neoliberal reforms that they have been unable to shake.

Neoliberalism has thrived, died, and been resurrected in a dizzying sequence that defies linear interpretation.

Thus, in October 2019, once solidly left Ecuador was in the throes of civil revolt over an IMF austerity program orchestrated and imposed by its recently established right-wing government. Days later, Chile erupted in revulsion from nearly a half-century of neoliberal policies. The past 45 years had left the vast majority of citizens constantly anxious, due to precarious employment (nearly 30% of the labor force was trapped in temporary employment), a future retirement income bordering on poverty (with a median monthly income of $290), and declining wages. One half of all full-time private-sector workers received an income below that necessary to keep a family of four out of poverty. As a resource-dependent economy, with nearly 50% of all exports being copper, privately owned copper mines paid no federal taxes whatsoever in 2016, as commodity prices remained low and copper production fell by nearly 40% from 2013 levels. But such hard-times exemptions did not apply to workers who continued to pay the 19% value-added tax on almost everything, as well as income taxes and other levies. Overall, even when commodity prices are high, through their general avoidance of many federal taxes and their artful use of consciously designed loopholes and their ability to keep wages down, the rich have raised a new structure of towering income and wealth disparity: the top 1% annually absconds with nearly 35% of the national income (when all capital income, such as retained profits paid to owners' shares, has been included in the calculation).

The social revolts against neoliberalism in Chile and Ecuador, along with the electoral defeat of Macri's disastrous neoliberal government in Argentina, are but the latest examples of Latin America's zigzagging trajectories. To these unsettled situations one must now add the latest zig, the coup in November against Bolivia's first indigenous-led government. The hacendado power elite—a hereditary caste of large "hacienda" landholders, now spearheaded by far-right soybean plantation magnates—and their transnational corporate allies seized the moment just as Bolivia's long booming economy settled into stagnation, with natural gas, which had sometimes been nearly 50% of all exports, suffering further collapse (by this September, the price for natural gas was a mere 12% of the September 2005 rate).

Meanwhile, almost simultaneous with the attempt to reinstitute neoliberalism in Bolivia, former Brazilian President Lula da Silva walked out of jail as false charges of corruption evaporated. Once again at center stage, his Workers' Party has gathered force to bedevil neoliberalism's latest Latin American incarnation—President Jair Bolsonaro—otherwise known as the "Trump of the Amazon." To these manifestations of civil unrest one must now add the discord in Colombia. Newfound protest of this all-out neoliberal regime has led to general strikes in November, forcing government concessions, including exempting the poorest 20% from the onerous value-added tax.

Taking a step back from all of these dizzying events, we should remember that the structural power of the small, vastly powerful economic elite in Chile has repeatedly thwarted the best attempts of elected progressive governments since 2000. The smug land-owning, extractive, and financial national elites—in Argentina, Bolivia, Chile, Ecuador, and elsewhere—now have no intention whatsoever to accommodate social change that would impinge, even marginally, on their freedom to maintain a resource-exporting economic model that has multiplied their wealth and power as the majority has (mostly) languished. Of course, history marches on; but, too frequently, it has marched in a circle, or a downward spiral, in Latin America. ❑

*Sources*: Tomás Bril-Mascarenhas and Aldo Madariaga, "Business Power and the Minimal State: The Defeat of Industrial Policy in Chile," *The Journal of Development Studies*, December 2017; Alejandro Chafuen, "The New Brazil: Philosophical Divisions Should Not Hinder Bolsonaro's Free Society Agenda," *Forbes*, February 19, 2019 (forbes.com); James Cypher, "Shifting Developmental Paradigms in Latin America: Is Neoliberalism History?" in Esteban Pérez and Matías Vernengo eds., *Ideas, Policies and Economic Development in the Americas* (Routledge, 2007); James Cypher, "Is Chile a Neoliberal Success?" *Dollars & Sense*, September/October 2004; Gonzalo Durán and Marco Kremerman, *Los Verdaderos Sueldos de Chile*, La Fundación SOL, August, 2019 (fundacionsol.cl); Lisa Duggan, "Ayn Rand and the Cruel Heart of Neoliberalism," *Dissent*, May 20, 2019 (dissentmagazine.org); Organisation for Economic Co-operation and Development, *Chile, Visión General*, February 2018 (oecd.org); Jaime Peck, *Constructions of Neoliberal Reason* (Oxford University Press, 2012); Programa de las Naciones Unidas para el Desarrollo (PNUD), *Desiguales. Orígenes, cambios y desafíos de la brecha social en Chile*, 2017; Mark Weisbrot and Andrés Arauz, "'Headwinds to Growth': The IMF Program in Ecuador," Center for Economic and Policy Research, July 2019 (cepr.net).

*Article 10.4*

# NEOLIBERALISM UNCHAINED
*Jair Bolsonaro and the Rise of the Extreme Right in Brazil*

## BY JAMES M. CYPHER
*January/February 2019*

The year of 2019 marks a consolidation of the steady slither into extreme right-wing rule in Brazil, as long-time congressman Jair Bolsonaro assumed the presidency on January 1. This slide into the vortex of far right la-la land began when the less-than-charismatic, but steady and solidly left, President Dilma Rousseff, of the Workers' Party (Partido dos Trabalhadores, or PT) was impeached in a slow-motion coup in 2016, supported by not a shred of evidence. She had led the giant nation of 209 million after Luiz Inácio "Lula" da Silva, also of the PT, completed two highly successful presidential terms in 2011. When Rousseff was ousted in 2016, the economy was undergoing its worst recession in decades. The economy shrank by 7% in 2015 and 2016. By the end of 2018, per capita income was no more than it was in 2013, thanks in part to austerity programs deployed by the conservative power bloc that toppled Rousseff.

Both Lula and Rousseff were "neo-developmentalist" leaders who attempted to realign Brazil's society through programs of income redistribution and industrial policies designed to address deindustrialization (see James M. Cypher, "Brazil's 'Big Push,'" D&S, March/April 2013). For a while there were good indications that Lula and the Workers' Party leaders had initiated a successful program of realignment. The administration was lauded worldwide for its "Zero Hunger" program which sought to address extreme poverty both in highly visible large urban areas and in Brazil's vast poverty encrusted outback, particularly the heavily Afro-Brazilian Northeast. An array of programs brought the poverty level down from 60 million in 2004 to 26.6 million in 2014. Still, Brazil's coddled 1%, the oligarchs, walked away with 27.8% of the national income in 2015—the highest level of wealth concentration of any nation.

## There's No Business Like Agribusiness

Had the Workers' Party been content with some commendable programs of redistribution, Brazil's powerful right wing—long led by giant and agile agribusiness corporations whose smothering weight in the congress is ever-present through its rural caucus (or Bancada Ruralista)—might have quietly sulked. After all, the Workers' Party was unwilling, for the most part, to help the relatively powerful landless movement (or Movimento Sim Terra) as it variously sought to occupy "unused" agricultural land, or, occasionally, promote buyouts of these lands.

The Ruralistas were quite profitably occupied throughout most of the years when the Workers' Party was in power (2003–2016) as they became the main beneficiaries of the commodity boom that began hesitantly in Latin America as the 21st century began. Indeed, by 2018 Brazil passed the United States as the world's number-one soybean producer, as agribusiness continues its massive shift into Brazil's central-west frontier and beyond. In Brazil's vast "Soylandia"—with some 55 million hectares cultivated in 2014—massive use of chemical-based cultivation has taken an environmental toll, while income distribution has skewed ever-more heavily toward the agrarian oligarchy. But soy was only the most visible aspect of the commodity boom; cotton production soared, while meat production jumped as did citrus output. The Workers' Party devoted a respectable amount of the public-sector budget to the expansion of ports, roads, and the rail system—but China's seemingly insatiable need for these commodities meant that the transportation system was perpetually clogged—until, of course, the inevitable occurred. The commodity boom ended, in general, in 2012, with the oil and gas industry able to escape its own bust until roughly 2014. Commodity booms always end in bouts of overproduction, the hangover effect lasting for years or decades—after which Latin American nations dutifully forget their long-cursed past and crank up commodity production, with mining often being a leading component, as it was from roughly 2000 to 2012.

While I was working as a researcher in Brazil for stints in 2010 and 2011, and most recently in 2016, well-regarded economists expressed their doubts to me regarding this (well-documented) view of boom-and-bust commodity cycles. "This time is different," I was informed again and again, for one big reason: China. They seemed, particularly to other Brazilians, to have a point. After all, China's economic trajectory was without precedent, particularly after its entry into the World Trade Organization in 2001, which gave its export sector carte blanche to ramp up production of an array of consumer goods exported everywhere, but particularly to the United States. In went the commodities and out went the transformed, manufactured, products—thanks to what appeared until recently to be an unending supply of cheap, but responsive, labor. According to many Brazilian economists, policymakers, and business people, China was on a long, steep, and smooth upward path. For a long time to come—went the conventional wisdom—China's need for commodities would not abate. In fact, Brazil, they claimed, was well situated to produce just those commodities that were destined to enjoy what economists term "a high-income elasticity of demand." Translated, this means that as the standard of living rises, dietary consumption shifts to preferable goods (or luxury goods). Beef and related items crowd out basic foods. High-end food consumption—just the items that Brazil could endlessly provide—would rise more than proportionately as China moved ever upward. So, why not enjoy the ride, and worry about the rest, if need be, decades down the road? Furthermore, it was argued—to some degree with good reason—Brazil was not "just" a commodity producer. Agribusiness was different—it was mechanized, it was scientifically advanced, it was innovative in finding new (non-traditional) products such as citrus and wine, and it yielded cross-benefits in terms of promoting manufacturing inputs (agricultural machinery) and technological spin-offs.

One dark component of this rosy picture had to do not with the future when the Brazilian agribusiness export machine crashed if China slowed down, as it has, but with the simple fact that China accepted ever-rising Brazilian commodities on the condition that Brazil did the same with manufactured products. Brazil was, and is, caught in a downward spiral of deindustrialization, although debate has raged for over a decade as to its extent and consequences.

The Workers' Party under Lula's dynamic leadership pushed for an industrial policy that would not only stop the slide into deindustrialization but would push Brazil up the technological ladder into high value-added, complex, and advanced industrial production. The project was one of state-led development—it echoed and built upon a once dominant school of thought known as Latin American Structuralism. The structuralists—most notably in Brazil those who followed the creative ideas of economist Celso Furtado (1920–2004)—were increasingly influential in guiding national development policy until the military coup of 1964. Furtado advocated social development—industrialization not based on social exclusion, but rather on attending to the necessities of poor workers, impoverished farmers, and all marginalized people.

## Coups in Brazil: Past and Present

Bolsonaro often lauds the military for its accomplishments from 1964 until the return of civilian rule in 1985. Economic growth was generally strong—until it was not, leading to the lasting contempt that the average Brazilian holds for that shattering period. The military leaders were developmentalists. They exercised great latitude in their pursuit of state-led development. They abhorred the "let the market work its magic" approach advocated by Milton Friedman and his Chicago Boys when they took power in Chile after the coup of 1973. Developmentalists they were, but not in the least were they concerned with social developmentalism as advocated by Furtado and the Workers' Party which followed his guidance, sometimes more in spirit than in fact, from 2004 to 2016. The military's lasting legacy was the reconsolidation of the oligarchy: most particularly the power of landowners who greatly benefited from various programs to "develop" the vast Amazon region.

It is worth recalling that the United States was extensively involved in the coup and in deep alliance with the oligarchs: at its core the disputed policies were those that challenged the autonomy of U.S. corporations to set the terms in Brazil. The government had the temerity to propose that the amount of repatriated corporate profits flowing back into the United States be capped. Even worse, perhaps, was the Furtado-inspired policy of land reform in the lower Amazon region—a dagger point right to the heart of the Bancada Ruralista. And the more oily aspect of the coup had to do with the effrontery of the government's intentions to buyout a sizeable number of oil refineries (overwhelmingly owned by U.S.-based corporations), turning them over to be run by the state-owned oil company Petrobras.

Within weeks after the coup U.S. foreign direct investment—which had dropped to a trickle as social development gained momentum—soared. The U.S. government immediately responded with largesse—$650 million in aid funds plus arranging for $450 million in needed loans. The military was off and running—it had friends in high places, not least Nelson Rockefeller. In their book Thy Will be Done, Gerard Colby and Charlotte Dennett document the deep linkages between the Bancada Ruralista and the Standard Oil scion as Rockefeller set up a vast chain of Brazilian companies to transform its subsistence agricultural practices to agribusiness in 1948—just after a controversial, but largely progressive, government was forced out in 1945 by the long-embedded oligarchy.

A crypto-coup in 1945, a coup in 1964, and yet another in 2016: so it has long gone in Brazil—any shift to a progressive stance seems to get a run for a while and then down comes the curtain. Here is what Le Monde Diplomatique noted in September 2018:

> The Bancada Ruralista has amassed the power to overthrow or maintain presidents. Both the impeachment of President Dilma Rousseff in 2016, as well as the preservation of President Michel Temer, on two occasions in 2017, were the result of the votes cast by the Parliamentary Front for Agriculture and Livestock [known as the FPA, the formal title of the Bancada Rural]. In 2016, in the House of Deputies, 182 (50%) of the 367 votes for impeachment were from this Front. In August of the next year, the first round of votes to initiate the same process against Temer, the tendency was inverted: 134 (51%) of the 263 votes against [impeachment]—in favor of preserving the president in the face of charges of corruption—were cast by members of the FPA.

The author goes on to further document the power of the Bancada Ruralista to dominate the legislative process, bend the executive branch to its will, influence the judiciary, and operate as the principal force in turning back environmental and human rights legislation. The agrarian oligarchs and their representatives in Congress were the leading edge of the right-wing juggernaut, but they were ably abetted by 1) the money-bags magnates of the highly concentrated private financial sector, who wielded their autonomous power over monetary policy throughout the years of Workers' Party rule (in 2018 the top four banks controlled 73% of the assets and issued 80% of the loans); 2) a large portion of industrialists able to amass quick wealth through monopoly power; 3) most evangelicals—over 20% of the population—who espouse a rightist ideology; 4) a sizeable middle class intent on assuring their personal security; and 5) a small number of giant media conglomerates that dominate the press and television and radio news, run by highly politicized members of the oligarchy who were determined to break the political hegemony of the Workers' Party. (Just nine family-owned corporate media groups control the lion's share of all media outlets—led by the Marinho family's Grupo Globo empire, now owned by three billionaire brothers, followed by the Bandeirantes group.)

## Neoliberalism Takes Hold

While many Brazilian economists, policymakers, and business people were willing to gamble that somehow—against all of Latin America's long history—it would be viable to passively jump on the China bandwagon and export the gigantic agri-business surplus, on the theory that "this time is different," the government of Lula generally advocated for a structuralist transformation wherein Brazil would broaden and deepen its industrial base primarily in order to develop its internal market. Pushing exports made sense in this approach—but only as a means of creating a quick surplus that could be plowed back into developing the national industrial base. Thus, the popular progressive government that took power in 2004 envisaged a series of government programs that would put Brazil on a sustainable path to social development. The linchpin of the strategy was to lead the reindustrialization process via the combined powers of the vast state development bank BNDES and the rapidly growing capacities of Petrobras, the national oil company. Serendipity seemed to provide the way forward—Petrobras began to move into the big leagues of oil production due to unexpected and large deep-water oil fields. Petrobras had the technological capacity to assemble and control much of the production process—including the tricky business of developing the offshore production and producing the giant perforation/production platforms that one could see taking shape on a vast bay just outside beautiful Rio de Janeiro. Petrobras sought to harness the vast sums proffered by BNDES to operate the vertical and horizontal linkages between the oil industry and many other sectors including shipbuilding, refining, chemicals, metal fabricating, and machine tools.

Into the mix, predictably, the end of the commodity boom arrived—for most commodities (as mentioned) around 2012 and for oil and gas by 2014. Lula had passed the baton to President Rousseff in 2011. She lacked Lula's charisma, his sense of political timing, his oratorical powers, his willingness to face his many challengers, his popular base, and the commodity boom that allowed him to go in two directions at once—let the agriculture sector have its way and vigorously promote social development. By 2012, with Rousseff in power for a little over a year, Brazil's export boom began to stall. Worse, China's growth slowed: by 2012 it was half what it had been in 2007, and its growth was relatively slow throughout 2018. Rousseff was faced with mounting economic problems—economic growth fell from nearly 8% in 2010 to 0% in 2014 and -4% in 2015, the budget deficit jumped from roughly 2% in 2012 to nearly 10% in 2015, and her political rating fell off the charts with nearly 75% of Brazilians giving her a "terrible" rating, all while evidence of sizeable corruption emerged within Petrobras.

Rousseff's successor, President Michel Temer, was clearly a way for Brazil to mark time. As Bolsonaro takes power, he will turn economic policy over to a genuine Chicago Boy, Paulo Guedes, an economist with the full backing of the business oligarchs. Guedes is slated to run not only the finance ministry but also the ministries of trade, planning, and the secretariat for public investment. Guedes claims he has a mandate to privatize the public sector, meaning in particular that Petrobras will be gutted, with the U.S. oil transnationals likely to carve out their sizeable share. The public-sector pension program, which is extremely generous, will be pared back as far as possible, and Guedes claims he will change Brazil's economic model—meaning that neoliberalism will be on the agenda. Neoliberalism, as practiced throughout Latin America from the 1980s in accordance with the dictates of the Washington Consensus, never caught on in Brazil. It is worth mentioning again that the military dictatorship was run by developmentalists who held state-led development (but not social development) in high regard. The Washington Consensus lauded the "magic" of the market and pushed for unrestrained globalization (giving transnational corporations access to all niches of the national economy). In contrast, the military promoted state-run national corporations such as Embraer—a policy that promoted some autonomous technological advancement, including in aeronautics.

Where Guedes stands ideologically—where Brazil will be forced to go under Bolsonaro—is where the Free Brazil Movement exists. This organization has received grants from the U.S.-based Atlas Network, a below-the-radar right-wing entity. Free Brazil emerged in 2014 and was known to be behind libertarian demonstrations that led to the toppling of the Rousseff presidency. Guedes is also linked to the recently formed Millennium Institute, which has received funding from Atlas, with Bloomberg News listing him as a founder.

Even worse, perhaps, will be the absolute free hand given to the Bancada Ruralista, which will take the lead in despoiling the vast tracts of land still untouched, or somewhat regulated, in the Amazon region. Any and all forms of extraction will be the order of the day as the lumber, water, oil, minerals, and biodiversity are plundered as fast as possible. That, at least, is what Bolsonaro has stated will be his policy. It brings to mind, now with a vengeance as never before, the old cliché once again: "Brazil is the land of tomorrow, and always will be." ❑

*Sources*: Rodolfo Borges, "Brazil Has the Highest Concentration of Income in the World Among the Richest 1%," El País, Dec. 14, 2017 (brasil.elpais.com); Ana Campoy, "Dilma Rousseff's Demise in Five Charts," Quartz, August 31, 2016 (qz.com); Luís Castilho, "Agro is Lobby: The Ruralist Group in the Congress," Le Monde Diplomatique Brasil, Sept. 4, 2018 (diplomatique. org.br); Gerard Colby and Charlotte Dennett, Thy Will Be Done: The Conquest of the Amazon : Nelson Rockefeller and Evangelism in the Age of Oil, Harper Collins, 1996; Lee Fang, "Sphere of Influence: How American Libertarians are Remaking Latin American Politics," The Intercept, August 9, 2017 (theintercept.com); Rachel Gamarski, Simone Iglesias, and Jackie Gu, "Bolsonaro's Men in Brazil: A Look at His Inner Circle," Bloomberg News, Oct. 26, 2018 (bloomberg.com); Instituto Millenium (institutomillenium.org.br); "Generals, 'Chicago Boy' Loom Large in Brazil's Next Government," teleSUR, Oct. 29, 2018 (tlesurenglish.net).

*Article 10.5*

# LEAKY GOVERNANCE
*The Politics and Economics of gasoline theft in Mexico.*

## BY FRANCISCO J. ALDAPE
*September/October 2019*

This past January, a gasoline pipeline explosion in the town of Tlahuelilpan in Mexico's Hidalgo state made headlines across the globe when the blast killed more than 130 people, one of the highest death tolls yet that has been caused by fuel theft. The illegal tapping of gasoline pipelines has been on the rise in Mexico since the start of the millennium—the number of reported illegal tappings increased from 213 in 2006 to 12,581 in 2018, and tappings increased 528% between 2012 and 2017.

The upward trend of crude oil prices at the beginning of this decade made the theft of fuel a very lucrative business for local gangs and cartels, and they were able to provide gasoline at lower prices to impoverished consumers through selling it on the black market, according to a 2018 study by Citizens' Observatory, a think tank in Mexico. In 2018, illegal taps siphoned around 56,000 barrels of fuel a day—totaling $3 billion in profits (even though the total amount of stolen hydrocarbon fuel represents a small percentage of the country's total oil production).

Mexico is the world's 11th biggest oil producer, and the 10,560-mile-long network of pipes that are used to transport the fuel stretch across mostly rural sections of the country. The majority of the pipes are just a few feet underground, making it easy to access and puncture fuel lines. Once a fuel line is punctured, the fuel can then be accessed by attaching a valve or a hose. However, fuel theft, known as huachicoleo, has also become increasingly dangerous. Local cartels and gangs routinely perform illegal drilling on pipelines and use violence to assert control over their illegally accessed supply. Yet attempts to puncture gas lines often result in massive leaks, leading people in rural communities to gather around pipelines to collect the free fuel. In fact, before the explosion that took place last January, there were videos showing a small military contingent trying to prevent more than 500 men, women, and children carrying red jerrycans, buckets, and whatever else they could find from gathering the leaking fuel, but without much success.

Elected on a platform of rooting out corruption, Andrés Manuel López Obrador, who became president last December, has pledged to take decisive action to regulate the provision of gasoline. Soon after his swearing-in, President López Obrador temporarily shut down several of the nation's main pipelines, deployed more than 5,000 soldiers and marines to patrol the pipelines, and used tank trucks guarded by military vehicles to distribute gasoline and diesel. He also asked all Mexican citizens to help with the problem of fuel theft by not using or selling stolen fuel. In particular, he requested that members of the most affected communities call the police to report illegal activities, and he encouraged the heads of families to prohibit their children from becoming involved in the thefts. While this strategy—particularly the decision to shut down several pipelines—initially resulted in fuel shortages for several days and created long lines at gas stations in the capital and some central states, it seems to have reduced the number of thefts considerably. Three months after the plan to end fuel theft was introduced by the new government, gasoline theft dropped from 81,000 barrels a day in November 2018 to 4,000 barrels a day in April 2019—a reduction of 95%—according to Octavio Romero Oropeza, the CEO of Petróleos Mexicanos (PEMEX), the state-owned oil company. Moreover, President López Obrador's strategy has allowed PEMEX to increase their profits by $600 million, and Romero Oropeza is confident that PEMEX can now regulate an adequate supply of fuel to meet the total national demand.

The substantial increase in the number of illegal taps of gas pipelines in Mexico—as well as the López Obrador administration's successful intervention in curbing the thefts—highlight the crucial role that government plays in determining how markets work. (This is an especially challenging task given that an ideal market, which would be equitable and function smoothly, does not exist, least of all in Mexico.) Fuel theft in Mexico is just one of many examples of how a breakdown in government controls can cause markets to go off the rails: the 2008 financial crisis amply demonstrated that financial markets do not serve social ends when set loose from oversight; workers are at a greater risk when labor markets are ill-governed; and consumers are at a greater risk when consumer protection laws are not enforced.

Using the situation in Mexico as a jumping-off point, we can examine the importance of government regulation on how oil markets function. We can also use the fuel theft example to explore why some essential goods, such as fuel, are distributed through the market, whereas others, like air, are (typically) treated as a common good. What can this episode tell us about the dynamics between oil markets and government regulation? And how do President López Obrador's policies fit with growing international demands to diminish reliance on fossil fuels in light of the ecological risks posed by climate change?

## Markets Need Governance

For markets to be governed toward socially positive ends, the governance needs to be carried out by those with democratic legitimacy who have an interest in using their position to carry out public-spirited purposes. But governance is easily corrupted, and taking on corruption is a tall order. More than half a century of government corruption and crony capitalism laid the groundwork for the rapid increase in the number of fuel thefts in Mexico. In the absence of legitimately and competently administered democratic governance, an unstable sort of governance asserted through violence—that is, organized crime—stepped into the void. In keeping with the rampant government corruption that has cropped up across many sectors, some government officials and PEMEX employees have been accused of collaborating with criminal organizations, contributing to the rise in the number of fuel thefts in recent years. In light of these problems, the strategy adopted by President López Obrador—the country's first progressive president in more than 70 years—to restore some type of governance of the oil industry involves reorganizing PEMEX and carrying out a moral campaign aimed at establishing PEMEX's legitimacy by combating corruption within the company and maintaining control of the country's energy resources, which are considered vital to fostering economic development.

Even the most libertarian economists recognize the need for governments to enforce contracts, and would applaud the suppression of theft. However, President López Obrador has also used policy to determine who can get access to fuel at what prices, a choice that most mainstream economists would argue against. Economic orthodoxy holds that markets are already sufficiently self-regulated in the sense that the unencumbered interaction between buyers and sellers will tend to produce an equilibrium (and ideal) price. At a theoretical level, the equilibrium price is considered to clear the demand and supply of goods, which usually implies that at this price buyers and sellers are satisfied with their transaction. But as we shall see, in the real world outside of economics textbooks, our social goals require more hands-on governance.

## Public vs. Private Goods

Indeed, a significant part of governance consists of figuring out what is treated as private property that can be traded on the market in the first place. Some goods and services are made available to everyone free of charge. These are known as "public goods." Typical examples of public goods include water fountains in public parks, public roads, public schools, or public sanitation. Why then, does PEMEX sell their product, rather than provide it free of charge to all who need it, the way that, for example, public school education is supplied? Selling gas effectively imposes a significant burden on individuals who may lack the necessary means to access this essential good. Despite a general decrease in petroleum prices around the world in the last couple of years, gasoline prices in Mexico have averaged 20.51 Mexican pesos a liter for regular gasoline, which is equivalent to $3.95 a gallon in the United States, according to GlobalPetrolPrices.com (a website that tracks prices at gas stations). Faced with these prices, many of the poor families in Mexico that do not have enough purchasing power to cover the cost of their daily needs are forced to seek alternatives, such as consuming stolen gasoline, which, in turn, reinforces the rise of illicit activities performed by the huachicoleros (gas thieves).

So treating gas as a private good is problematic, but treating it as a public good would raise other concerns. Mexico does rely on fossil fuels, but the question of how to ensure adequate access for all to this (currently) essential good should be a short-term question. A better question is this: In what ways can the government, along with business and social organizations, help to reduce or eliminate the entrenched dependence on oil and gasoline around the world? Given the extensive historical reliance of many capitalist countries on fossil fuels to promote economic development, developing economies like Mexico could continue relying on these resources to catch up with more advanced countries. However, this is a dangerous approach, as less-developed countries may suffer more from ecological disasters. According to a recent U.N. report, titled "Poverty & Death: Disaster Mortality 1996–2015," approximately 90% of natural disaster deaths take place in low- and middle-income countries. We need emissions reductions in the wealthiest economies and emissions avoidance in developing economies. In the case of Mexico, the centrality of its oil industry and the policies pursued by President López Obrador to encourage the construction of a new oil refinery may, in the long-run, represent a serious detriment to his overall goal of a more prosperous Mexico.

Despite the environmental concerns and the potential barriers to access imposed by selling gas as a private good, PEMEX revenues can be, and at times have been, an important source of funding for other government activities that improve the lives of the most vulnerable. Though President López Obrador does not propose that gas be distributed as a public good, he does propose that the sale of gas should once again be used as a source of revenues for public, pro-poor programs.

## Governments Can Choose Social Goals for the Market

PEMEX has managed the production and distribution of gasoline since 1938 when President Lázaro Cárdenas declared the nationalization of all petroleum reserves, including those used by foreign oil companies in Mexico. Since then, the production of oil has provided a significant source of government revenues, and it accounted for approximately 32% of total government revenues in 2017. In general, the profitability of the oil industry has closely followed the erratic movements of international crude oil prices, in particular during the late 2000s when the price of oil rose to over $140 per barrel. However, in more recent years, the country has been faced with a severe decline in domestic oil and gas production, and in 2014 the government implemented a series of reforms that privatized sections of the energy sector in an attempt to boost production with greater private investment. For a variety of reasons, which include the mismanagement of both PEMEX and the industry as a whole, there has been a steady decline in Mexican crude oil production over the last decade, which intensified after 2014. PEMEX was unable to benefit from the surge in oil prices at the beginning of this decade because the company lacked responsible leadership and adequate financial resources. President López Obrador fiercely opposed attempts at privatization before his presidency; it will be interesting to see whether such a push for privatization will be halted or at least restricted under his leadership.

Above all, President López Obrador and his administration aim to reorganize and rehabilitate PEMEX so that the company can start producing more oil and once again become profitable without charging prohibitively high prices. (For more, see James M. Cypher and Mateo Crossa's "Dancing on Quicksand: A Retrospective on NAFTA on the Eve of Its Replacement," D&S, March/April 2019.) One reason for the current rise in fuel prices is the increasing use of automobiles, and the resulting increase in the need for fuel. Despite this increased demand, no new refineries have been built since the 1970s, which means that Mexico relies on imported gasoline from the United States. Fuel that is imported from the United States goes through many firms, all of which try to push up the price in order to increase their bottom line. Corruption has also added unnecessary costs that are then reflected in the price at the pump. In this respect, one of the most important policies of the new administration includes a project to build a new oil refinery in the southern state of Tabasco, which aims to provide greater employment opportunities in the region (100,000 jobs according to PEMEX) and help the country become closer to achieving energy independence. Thus, in addition to combating corruption in PEMEX and other political institutions, President López Obrador anticipates that through greater economic self-sufficiency and much greater political democratization, it may be possible to reorient the economy around the objective of helping the poorest members of society instead of only serving the interests of Mexico's oligarchs and transnational capital. He vows that everyone will have a representative voice in his government, but also highlights that they will give "preference to the most impoverished and vulnerable," affirming when he took the oath of office that "for the good of all, the poor come first." This principle applies to oil industry policies as much as any other sector.

Nevertheless, the new ecological challenges presented by climate change cast a significant cloud over any plans to use oil revenue for pro-poor development. Historically, petroleum was central in Mexico's political and economic development. In keeping with this history, President López Obrador seems to be putting all of his cards on the expected success of a resurgence in oil production and an increase in the global price of crude oil to promote the country's economic development. Still, recent downward trends in the price of crude oil and the difficulties of creating new oil refineries can work against these expectations. By contrast, other developed countries are implementing taxes on fossil fuels (or at least trying to, as in France, though without much success—see Aarth Saraph, "Understanding France's Gilets Jaunes," Article 10.6) and advocating for greater investments on renewable energies. So far President López Obrador has deflected criticisms for not including more "green" alternatives and for his seemingly unbounded optimism in fossil fuels to provide the necessary economic base for a stronger economy.

## What Gasoline Theft Teaches Us

The recent Mexican experience with gas pipelines, and the fossil fuel sector more broadly, reveals the importance of balancing public and private interests within an adequate regulatory framework. The escalation of fuel theft in Mexico and related accidents in many states have largely been a result of the lack of effective governance. The López Obrador administration understands that the government needs to provide a better regulatory framework to create more stable conditions in the distribution of gasoline, and has taken steps to do so.

However, the significant rise in gasoline prices across the nation—which has coincided with the privatization of sections of the energy industry—along with the push to reduce the use of fossil fuels in response to the climate change crisis, present several difficulties for the new administration. President López Obrador is working on the assumption that improving the administration of PEMEX and encouraging good social values (e.g., honesty) among its personnel and the broader citizenship will result in stronger governance of the oil industry. Whether or not these efforts will be enough remains to be seen. Furthermore, better governance of the oil industry can at best be a stopgap measure. To deal effectively with the new problems created by the ongoing climate crisis, it is essential to try to phase out fossil fuels, which also means challenging the vested interests of big oil companies and finding a different source of revenue for the Mexican government. Although President López Obrador's policies may be detrimental to the environment in the long term, this pragmatic approach remains the most promising option for achieving economic gains (such as increased employment opportunities and reduced gasoline costs) given the limited options available to his government in the present situation. This does not mean that Mexico should not do more to promote more environmentally friendly policies. Still, the tension between phasing out fossil fuels and adopting more renewable resources, which is faced by Mexico and other developing countries, requires a stronger commitment by more developed countries, such as the United States, to implement a set of policies to limit the overall emission of greenhouse gases and achieve a just transition to renewable energies. ❑

*Sources*: Matthew Bremner, "A Gas Heist Gone Wrong, an Explosion, and 137 Deaths in Mexico," Bloomberg Businessweek, June 26, 2019 (bloomberg.com); PEMEX, "Annual Reports (2006– 2018)" (pemex.com); Citizens' Observatory, "The theft of oil in pipelines: An enemy of the environment," November 2018 (igavim.org); CIA, "The World Factbook: Country Comparison, Crude Oil Production" (cia.gov); PEMEX Press Release, "Theft of fuel in Mexico decreases 95 percent and increases crude oil production," April 23, 2019 (pemex.com); Kirk Semple, "Mexico Declares Victory Over Fuel Thieves. But Is It Lasting?," *New York Times*, May 5, 2019 (nytimes.com); OECD, "Mexico's effort to phase out and rationalize its fossil-fuel subsidies," Nov. 15, 2017 (oecd.org);  U.S. Department of Commerce's International Trade Administration, "Mexico Country Commercial Guide," Oct. 12, 2018 (export.gov); Michael Hudson, "Global Warming and U.S. National Security Diplomacy," Socialist Economist, August 30, 2019 (socialisteconomist.com); Robert Brelsford, "PEMEX to proceed with Dos Bocas refinery project," Oil & Gas Journal, May 10, 2019 (ogj.com); Centre for Research on the Epidemiology of Disasters, "Poverty & Death: Disaster Mortality 1996–2015," U.N. Office for Disaster Risk Reduction, October 12, 2016 (cred.be).

*Article 10.6*

# THE RETURN OF CAPITAL CONTROLS

## BY ARMAĞAN GEZICI
*January/February 2013, Updated November 2019*

In the wake of the global financial crisis, low interest rates and slow growth in advanced economies have led to a massive influx of capital into so-called emerging markets, where interest rates and growth have been higher. International investors, seeking higher returns, have moved their funds away from advanced economies into emerging-market securities like stocks, bonds, and mutual funds. The governments of many developing countries, as a result, have become increasingly concerned about the effects of these capital inflows—including stronger currencies, asset-price bubbles, and even inflation. In March 2012, Brazil's President Dilma Rousseff accused developed nations of unleashing a "monetary tsunami," which is undermining the competitiveness of emerging economies like her own. These concerns have motivated many countries to introduce measures to cope with cross-border capital flows.

Starting in late 2009, for example, Brazil began to implement "capital controls"—including a tax on capital inflows and other measures—to keep its currency (the real) from growing stronger against the dollar. Several Asian countries, including South Korea, Taiwan, and Thailand, have also implemented controls of various kinds on capital inflows. Over the last decade, even some European economies hit by crises (including Iceland, Cyprus, and Greece) have enforced restrictions on capital flows. Suddenly, it appears, capital controls are back.

## What Ever Happened to Capital Controls?

The debate about controls on international capital flows goes back to the World War II era. During the Bretton Woods negotiations (1944) establishing the international monetary order for the postwar period, Britain's chief negotiator, John Maynard Keynes, and his U.S. counterpart, Harry Dexter White, agreed that a distinction should be made between "speculative" capital and "productive" capital. Both believed that speculative (or "hot money") capital flows should be subject to controls. Keynes went further, arguing that "control of capital movements, both inward and outward, should be a permanent feature of the postwar system." For much of the postwar period, controls such as restrictions on the types of assets banks could hold and limits on capital outflows (used even by the United States between 1963 and 1973) were, indeed, implemented by many capitalist countries. Beginning in the 1980s, however, international financial institutions like the International Monetary Fund (IMF), many Western governments, and private high finance began to oppose capital controls. The U. S. government and the IMF became staunch advocates of "capital-account liberalization" (that is, the deregulation of international capital flows) during this period.

The recent crisis resulted in widespread recognition, around the world, that deregulated financial activity can result in major economic disruptions. In most of the world's largest economies, possible measures to re-regulate finance on the national level came back on the political agenda. Cross-border finance, however, was largely left out of the discussion, as if it did not require any regulation. Conventional discussions of this issue have also involved a peculiar twist in terminology: financial regulations are typically called "regulations" when purely domestic, yet when they involve cross-border flows, they carry the more ominous-sounding label of "controls"—as if to emphasize the undesirable nature of these regulations from a free-market perspective.

## Why Capital Controls?

The essential problem with international capital flows is that they are "pro-cyclical"—that is, they amplify the patterns of the business cycle. Capital tends to flow in when economies are expanding, promoting "overheating" and inflation, and tends to flow out during downturns, exacerbating the decline in output and rise in unemployment. They also narrow the ability of governments to respond to cyclical economic problems. The economic literature on capital flows cites five fears that drive countries to adopt capital controls:

*Fear of appreciation*: Massive and rapid capital inflows may cause the country's currency to become stronger (increase in value relative to other currencies), making its exports more expensive and damaging its international competitiveness.

*Fear of "hot money"*: Short-term speculative capital inflows may cause financial instability and increase the fragility of the domestic financial system. The short-term nature of these flows leads to a "maturity mismatch" between domestic financial institutions' assets and liabilities. In effect, they have borrowed short-term while lending long-term. As the sudden reversal of hot money occurs at the whim of international investor sentiments, a domestic banking crisis is likely to follow.

*Fear of large inflows that can disrupt the financial system*, even if they are not all "hot money": Large inflows of foreign capital may feed asset bubbles, such as unsustainable increases in stock or real-estate prices or unsustainable booms in consumer credit.

*Fear of loss of monetary autonomy*: It is not possible for a country to achieve (simultaneously) full international capital mobility, monetary-policy autonomy, and exchange-rate stability. (This is known as the "trilemma" of international macroeconomics.) If a country does not control international capital flows, inflows can cause exchange-rate appreciation. The government can counteract this by increasing the money supply, but then its monetary policy is not independent. To avoid exchange-rate appreciation and sustain an independent monetary policy, a country should give up full capital mobility.

*Fear of capital flight*: In the event of a crisis, "herding" behavior by international investors may expose a country to the risk of sharp reversals in capital flows (with capital leaving just as quickly as it came).

## What Happened During the Crisis?

Between 2002 and 2007, there were massive flows of capital into emerging markets with high growth rates and relatively developed financial systems. This surge in capital inflows began shortly after the dot-com crisis in the United States as the Federal Reserve began to reduce interest rates and continued until the collapse of the U.S. investment house Lehman Brothers in September 2008. The ensuing downturn, which led global capital to flee to the "safety" of the U.S. market, lasted only a few years, yet wreaked havoc in emerging markets. (See figure.) While there was no comparable financial crisis in these economies, more than half of them experienced negative growth in 2009. Countries with already-large trade deficits were among the hardest hit, as they were highly dependent on capital inflows.

Between 2008 and 2011, however, the governments of the industrialized countries lowered interest rates in an attempt to stimulate production and employment. Capital again began to flow into emerging markets, attracted by higher interest rates and growth. The "carry trade" was a key mechanism that triggered these flows. In the carry trade, investors borrow money in one country at a low interest rate and invest it in another country at a higher rate. This strategy allows investors not only to exploit the differences in interest rates, but to also take advantage of exchange-rate movements. If the currency of the country with higher interest rates becomes stronger, over time, relative to the currency of the country with lower interest rates, investors stand to make even larger profits.

By late 2008, government policymakers in emerging economies had become alarmed about the problems these inflows could cause—currency appreciation, asset bubbles, inflation, and the sudden turn toward large outflows. From March 2009 to March 2010, Brazil saw the value of the real go up by 30% against the dollar, due at least in part to the carry trade. Under normal circumstances, the conventional macroeconomic tool to stem asset bubbles or inflation would have been an increase in interest rates. By increasing interest rates, monetary authorities would have curbed the appetite to borrow and reduced the amount of money available for spending in the economy. With less spending, the economy would slow down and inflation would decline. However, because of the carry trade, such a policy could actually fuel further inflows and therefore exacerbate these problems. For example, in 2009, interest rates were around 12% in Brazil and less than 1% in the United States; if Brazil had raised interest rates in an attempt to curb asset bubbles and inflation, it could actually have attracted even higher capital inflows.

The Brazilian government was the most vocal critic of these capital flows at the G-20's 2010 summit in Seoul. The Brazilian finance minister declared the surge

## PORTFOLIO CAPITAL FLOWS TO THREE DEVELOPING REGIONS

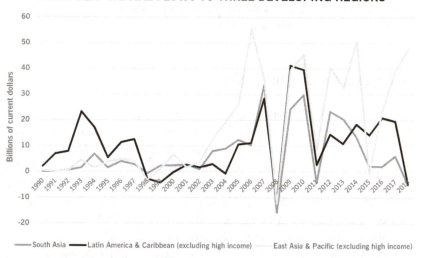

——South Asia ━━━Latin America & Caribbean (excluding high income)  ——East Asia & Pacific (excluding high income)

*Source:* World Bank, Data, Portfolio equity, net inflows (BoP, current US$), (data.worldbank.org)

in capital flows, the subsequent exchange-rate appreciations, and the various policy responses by emerging countries to be the beginning of a "currency war." In late 2009, the Brazilian government imposed a 2% tax on various forms of capital inflows. In October 2010, it twice increased the tax rate, first to 4% and then to 6%. In January 2011, Brazil introduced new reserve requirements on capital inflows to curb the appreciation of the real against the dollar.

In 2009, nations across Asia also began to deploy controls, having seen large appreciations of their currencies. Between the end of 2008 and early 2010, South Korea's currency (the won) appreciated by over 30% against the dollar. Starting in July 2010, South Korean banks faced new restrictions on their international currency holdings. The South Korean government also tried to steer investment away from speculation by permitting bank loans in foreign currencies only for the purchase of raw materials, for foreign direct investment, and for the repayment of debts. Meanwhile, in November 2009, the government of Taiwan banned foreign investment funds from investing in certificates of deposit with domestic banks, a move aimed at preventing foreign investors from betting on currency appreciation. At the end of 2010, it also placed restrictions on banks' holdings of foreign currencies. In 2010, Thailand introduced a 15% tax on interest income and capital gains earned by foreign investors. The same year, Indonesia placed limits on short-term external borrowing and introduced a one-month minimum holding period for foreign investors purchasing some types of government-issued securities.

The academic debate over the effectiveness of capital controls is still seen as inconclusive. A study by Kevin Gallagher of the Global Development and Environment Institute (GDAE) provides a preliminary assessment for the cases of Brazil, Taiwan, and South Korea. All three were trying to create a space for independent monetary policy and stem the appreciation of their currencies by placing restrictions on capital mobility.

Interest rates between the United States and each of these nations have become less correlated. (A strong correlation between interest rates may indicate that, when the U.S. Fed lowers interest rates, causing capital flows to these other countries, the latter are forced to respond with lower interest rates of their own to stem the appreciation of the currency. That is, they lack monetary independence.) So these findings suggest that the controls have, to some extent, allowed a more autonomous monetary policy.

In the cases of Brazil and Taiwan, there is some evidence that controls have been associated with a slower rate of currency appreciation. But in the case of South Korea, currency appreciation has continued and the rate of appreciation has actually increased since controls were initiated. This difference can be explained by the structural differences across these countries, as well as the different types of controls used. South Korea's strong export performance is an important factor putting upward pressure on the value of its currency. (Demand for a country's exports is one factor in determining the demand for its currency, since that country's companies usually require payment in the national currency.) Moreover, unlike Brazil and Taiwan, South Korean authorities did not use any of the "price-based controls" that would have automatically placed additional costs on international investors seeking to enter Korean markets. These differences in effectiveness can shed some light on what kinds of capital controls might work in different countries, given their unique conditions.

Regardless of the academic views on the effectiveness of controls adopted in the immediate wake of the global financial crisis, other countries have been experimenting with controls. For example, when the European Central Bank decided not to provide further liquidity assistance for Greek banks in 2015, the Greek government implemented controls on bank transfers from Greek banks to foreign banks, to avoid an uncontrolled bank run and the complete collapse of the Greek banking system. These measures proved helpful in preventing a crisis of the Greek banking system. As the economy moved toward relative stability, capital controls were completely eliminated by September 2019. In October 2019, with concerns over outflows of foreign currency, the central bank of Argentina announced restrictions on the amount of dollars individuals could buy. While the loss of value in the Argentinian peso against the U.S. dollar seems to have stopped for now, it is too early to judge their effectiveness and longevity, considering a new government will take the helm in December 2019.

## The IMF and Capital Controls

Not long after developing-country governments began implementing capital controls, official views about controls began to shift. It was a surprise to many to see the IMF advocating for the use of capital controls on outflows in Iceland as part of that country's post crisis stand-by agreement in 2008. Since 2010, the IMF has produced a series of official papers on capital-account liberalization, on capital inflows and outflows, and on the multilateral aspects of regulating international capital flows. In November 2012, it released a comprehensive "institutional view" on when and how nations should deploy capital-account regulations. The same institution that pushed for the global deregulation of cross-border finance in the 1990s now says that capital-account liberalization is more of a long-run goal, and is not for every country at all times. The IMF now accepts that capital controls—which it has renamed "capital-flow management measures"—are permissible for inflows, on a temporary basis, en route to liberalization; regulations on capital outflows, meanwhile, are permissible only during or just after financial crises.

While more flexible than its previous stances, the new IMF position still insists on the eventual deregulation of global financial flows and emphasizes that controls should only be temporary. Behind this insistence lies the institution's ideological commitment to free markets, as well as the influence of finance capital and Wall Street interests on the institution's decision making. As the experience of developing economies in the recent crisis bears out, rather than being treated as temporary measures, capital controls should be adopted as permanent tools that can be used counter-cyclically—to smooth out economic booms and busts. As described earlier, international capital flows are strongly pro-cyclical. By regulating inflows during a boom, a government can manage booms better, while avoiding exchange-rate problems or additional inflationary pressures. By restricting outflows during a downturn, it can mitigate capital flight, which has the potential of triggering financial crisis, and create some room for expansionary monetary policy.

The IMF guidelines, in addition, give scant attention to policy-design issues related to capital controls. A great deal of international experience shows that controls can lose their effectiveness over time, as foreign investors learn to evade regulation through the use of financial derivatives and other securities. Nations such as Brazil and South Korea have increasingly "fine-tuned" their regulations in an attempt to keep ahead of investors' ability to circumvent them.

The IMF also fails to acknowledge that capital flows should be regulated at "both ends." The industrialized nations are usually the source of international capital flows, but generally ignore the negative spillover effects on other countries. So far, the entire burden of regulation has fallen on the recipients of inflows, which are mostly developing countries.

## Where to Now?

As industrialized nations aim to recover from the crisis, they hope that credit and capital will stay "at home." Meanwhile, the developing world has little interest in having to receive capital inflows. This creates an obvious alignment of interests. Industrialized nations could adjust their tax codes and deploy other types of regulation to keep capital in their countries, as emerging markets deploy capital controls to reduce the level and change the composition of capital flows that may destabilize their economies.

One important obstacle to such coordination is the prohibition, in many trade and investment treaties, on the regulation of cross-border finance. Trade and investment agreements with the United States, such as the North American Free Trade Agreement (NAFTA) and the Dominican Republic-Central America Free Trade Agreement (CAFTA-DR), provide the least flexibility. Since the 2003 U.S.-Chile Free Trade Agreement, every U.S. trade or investment agreement has required the free flow of capital (in both directions) between the United States and its trading partners, without exception.

With the exception of speculators who profit from volatility in the markets, all nations and actors within them would benefit from the financial stability that an international system of financial regulation could help provide. After the opening of capital markets in developing economies, in varying degrees, we have seen extreme volatility of international capital flows. This volatility has been exacerbated by the monetary policies of advanced economies: over the past 30 years expansionary monetary policy in advanced economies has led to capital flows to emerging-market economies, while contractionary policies have produced the reversal of capital flows and, in turn, helped set off the crises of the 1980s and 1990s. The stability provided by an international system of capital controls would not only allow emerging economies to preserve their own growth and stability but also improve the effectiveness of policies in advanced economies.

Some financial interests, however, would have to bear the costs. Capital controls would either make financial transactions more costly, reducing profit margins, or not allow financial companies to take advantage of certain investment opportunities, again reducing potential profits to investors. These "losers" from a capital-controls regime are highly concentrated and very powerful politically. The "winners," in terms of the general public, are comparatively scattered and weaker politically. Despite the optimism that briefly emerged, especially in policy circles, about a future with more effective regulation of international capital flows, these political realities may be the biggest obstacles for 21st-century capital controls. ❑

*Sources:* Kevin Gallagher, "Regaining Control? Capital Controls and the Global Financial Crisis," Political Economy Research Institute, Working Paper 250, 2011; Stephany Griffith-Jones and Kevin P. Gallagher, "Curbing Hot Money Flows to Protect the Real Economy," *Economic and Political Weekly,* Jan. 15, 2011, Vol. XLVI, No 3; Ilene Grabel, "Not Your Grandfather's IMF: Global Crisis, Productive Incoherence, and Developmental Policy Space," Political Economy Research Institute, Working Paper 214, 2010; International Monetary Fund, The Liberalization And Management Of Capital Flows: An Institutional View, Washington, D.C., 2011.

Chapter 11

# THE POLITICAL ECONOMY OF EMPIRE

*Article 11.1*

## COLONIALISM, "UNDERDEVELOPMENT," AND THE INTERNATIONAL DIVISION OF LABOR
### BY ALEJANDRO REUSS
*November 2012*

The creation of large modern empires, in the last 500 years or so, linked together, for the first time, the economies of different continents into a "world economy." Colonial powers like Spain, Portugal, France, and Britain (also Belgium and the Netherlands) conquered territories and peoples in Africa, Asia, and the Americas, creating far-flung global empires. The horrors of colonialism included plunder, slavery, and genocide on an epic scale. The conquest of the Americas resulted in the greatest "demographic catastrophe" (sudden fall in population) in human history. Many indigenous people were killed by violence or the strains of forced labor, many more by the exotic diseases brought in by European colonists (against which the peoples of the Americas had no natural immunity). Europeans kidnapped and enslaved millions of Africans, many of whom died from the horrors of the "middle passage." Those who survived arrived in the Americas in chains, to be exploited on plantations and in mines.

People often think of colonialism as "ancient history." Unlike the United States and much of the rest of the Americas, however, most of the countries of Africa and Asia have gained independence only in recent decades. The Indian subcontinent was a British colony until the late 1940s, ultimately dividing into three independent countries (India, Pakistan, and Bangladesh) in two subsequent partitions. Much of southeast Asia, likewise, did not gain independence until the 1940s or 1950s. For most current African states, meanwhile, independence dates from the 1950s, 1960s, or 1970s.

## Colonialism and the International Division of Labor

When we speak of the division of labor within a society, we mean that different people specialize in different kinds of work. The international division of labor, in turn, involves different countries producing different kinds of goods. One country, for example, may be mostly agricultural; another, mostly industrial. Even among agricultural producers, one may produce mostly grains and another mostly fruits and vegetables. Among industrial countries, one may be a major producer of cars or planes, while another may produce clothing.

While the breakdown of total production, among different industries, is often pretty similar for different "developed" economies, it is likely to differ quite a bit between "developed" and "developing" economies. Sometimes, international trade in goods links together countries that produce similar types of goods. A great deal of world trade goes between different "developed" economies, many of which export the same kinds of goods to each other. However, international trade also links together economies that produce different kinds of goods. It is this second kind of linkage that we have in mind when we talk about the "international division of labor."

Colonialism created patterns in the international division of labor that have proved very difficult to escape. Colonial powers were not, by and large, interested in the development of conquered areas for its own sake. Often, the were interested simply in stripping a colony of all the wealth they could as fast as they could. The

---

### Changing Labels: "Underdeveloped" or "Developing"?

What are now termed "less-developed" or "developing" countries were, until recently, often described as "underdeveloped." The use of this term declined for a couple of reasons:

First, it came to be viewed as having pejorative connotations. That is, it took on very negative unspoken meanings, in particular the view that the people of "underdeveloped" countries were to blame for their own plight. It is now widely viewed as offensive to call a country "underdeveloped."

Second, political movements in many of these countries between the 1960s and 1980s took over and transformed the meaning of the word. Their countries, they argued, had not been born "underdeveloped," they had been "underdeveloped" by the colonial powers (or former colonial powers) that dominated the world economy. The shift away from the use of this term was, in part, a way for political and economic elites (both in "developed" and "developing" countries) to silence this argument.

original Spanish conquerors of the Americas, for example, were interested first and foremost in gold and silver. First they took all the gold and silver ornaments they could lay their hands on. Then they enslaved the indigenous people and forced them to labor in the mines, shipping vast quantities of gold and silver back to Europe. European empires also began to develop agricultural colonies. Colonies in tropical regions, especially, made it possible to produce goods—like sugar, coffee, and tobacco—which were highly prized and not widely available in Europe. In many places, slaves (in the Americas, mainly Africans) did the back-breaking plantation work. Sometimes, colonists simply took the lands of local people, leaving them with little choice but to work for meager wages on the plantations.

As some colonial powers began to industrialize, their colonies took on new significance. First, colonies became sources of materials for industry. Britain's textile industry, for example, began with woolen cloth, but gradually shifted toward cotton. Partly, the cotton came from its former colony, the United States, where it was grown primarily on slave plantations in the South. Increasingly, however, it came from colonies like Egypt and India. Second, colonies became "captive" markets for manufactured exports. Colonial powers restricted their colonies' trade with other countries, so one country's colony could not trade with another colonial power. (In effect, the imperial powers were practicing their own form of "protectionism," with barriers to trade surrounding the entire empire.) They sometimes even required that trade *between* their colonies go through the "mother" country, where customs duties (taxes) were collected for the imperial coffers.

Partly, colonial powers got the most out of their colonies by restricting the kinds of goods that could be produced there. Some economic historians argue that colonial restrictions, designed to keep India a captive market for the British textile industry, destroyed India's own textile industry. Others emphasize the cheapness of British-made cloth, made using modern water- or coal-powered machinery. Even if the latter is true, however, this does not mean colonialism was blameless. If India had been an independent country, it could have imposed tariffs, in order to protect its "infant" textile manufacturing. But economic policy for India was made in London, and those policies were designed to keep India open to British manufactures. In the end, instead of producing textiles itself, India became a producer of raw material for the British textile industry. This was a pattern that repeated itself across the colonial world, with industrial development stifled and the colonies pushed into "primary goods" production.

## Political Independence and Economic "Dependency"

Even after becoming politically independent, many former colonial countries seemed to remain trapped in the colonial-era international division of labor. They had not been able to develop manufacturing industries as colonies, and so they continued to import manufactured goods. To pay for these goods, they continued to export primary products. In many countries, the specialization in a single export good was so extreme that these became known as "monoculture" economies ("mono" = one). In some former colonies, important resources like land and mines remained under the control of foreign companies. In many cases, these were from the former colonial "mother" country. Sometimes, however, a rising new power replaced the old colonial power. After independence from Spain, for example, much of South America became part of Britain's "informal empire." Meanwhile, the United States supplanted Spain and other European colonial countries as the dominant power in Central America and the Caribbean, plus parts of South America.

Critics argued that this situation kept the former colonies poor and "dependent" on the rich industrial countries. (The subordination of the former colonies was so reminiscent of the old patterns of colonialism, that this was often labeled "neo-colonialism" or "imperialism.") The United States' relationship to smaller, poorer, and less powerful countries—especially in its "sphere of influence" of Latin America—exemplified many of the key patterns of post-independence neo-colonialism: Foreign companies extracted vast amounts of wealth, in the form of agricultural goods and minerals, while paying paltry wages to local workers. They employed skilled personnel from their home countries and used imported machinery, so their operations formed economic "enclaves" unconnected to the rest of the country's economy. Finally, they sent the profits back to their home countries, rather than reinvesting them locally, and so did little to spur broader economic development. Critics argued that this system was designed, in the words of Uruguayan author Eduardo Galeano, to bleed wealth out of these countries' "open veins."

Some economists pointed out some major economic disadvantages to specialization in "primary products," which are worth discussing in more detail.

First, economists associated with the United Nations Economic Commission for Latin America (known by its Spanish acronym, CEPAL) observed that the prices of primary products had tended to decline, over time, in relation to the prices of manufactured goods. The lower-income countries, therefore, had to sell larger and larger amounts of the goods they exported (more tons of sugar, coffee, copper, aluminum, or whatever) to afford the same amounts of the goods they imported (cars, televisions, or whatever).

Second, specialization in primary-product exports exposed low-income countries to wild fluctuations of world-market prices for these goods. The world-market price of a cash crop could be very high one year and very low the next. An especially bad year, or a few bad years in a row, might wipe out any savings farmers or farm workers might have from previous good years, and leave them destitute. Ironically, farmers might go hungry, even if the land was fertile and the weather had been good. For most cash crops, including fiber crops (like cotton) and specialized food crops (like coffee and sugar), the farmers could not survive by eating the harvest if world prices were too low. So a move towards cash crops could exacerbate poverty and food insecurity.

The governments of these countries might have found it difficult to challenge this state of affairs, even had they wanted to. Their economies, after all, were heavily dependent on exports to the dominant country (whose government could cut off access to its markets, should it be provoked). In many cases, however, local political elites have enjoyed close political and economic ties to the multinational companies, and little interest in changing anything. As long as they maintained "order," kept workers from organizing unions or demanding higher wages, and protected the multinational companies' investments, they could be sure to keep the favor of the dominant country's government and the multinational companies. In the cases where opposition movements did arise, calling for changes like the redistribution of land ownership or the nationalization of important resources, the dominant power could intervene militarily, if local elites were not up to the task of putting the rebels down.

## Changes in the International Division of Labor

For much of the twentieth century, a key dividing line among capitalist economies was between the "industrial" economies of the United States and Western Europe and the "non-industrial" economies of most of Latin America, Africa, and Asia. These two kinds of economies were linked: The high-income industrial economies imported agricultural products and minerals (or "primary products") from the low-income non-industrial economies, and exported manufactured goods (or "secondary products") in return.

In more recent decades, the international division of labor has changed in important ways. First, many formerly "non-industrial" economies have developed substantial manufacturing sectors, often by deliberately promoting manufacturing development through government policies like protective trade barriers, low-interest loans, etc. In some cases, what had been "less developed" economies, such as Japan and South Korea, have become major global industrial producers. Second, foreign investment has created a growing "export platform" manufacturing sector in some countries. Large corporations have increasingly engaged in "offshoring"—locating production facilities outside the countries where they are headquartered and have their traditional base of operations, and exporting the output back to the "home" market or to other countries.

In high-income countries, even as manufacturing employment has declined as a percentage of total employment, other sectors have grown. Over the last few decades, employment in "services" has accounted for an increasing proportion of total employment in high-income countries. When people think of services, they often think of low-wage employment in fast-food restaurants or big-box stores. Services, however, also include education, health care, finance, and other industries which can involve high-skill, and sometimes highly paid, work. All of these services can be "exported"—performed for people who reside in and earn their incomes in other countries—either because they can be done remotely (like most financial services, and some health care and education) or because the recipients travel to the place where providers are located (like students from abroad studying at U.S. universities).

Often, people think the relative decline in manufacturing employment in high-income countries is due only to offshoring—to companies "moving" manufacturing jobs from one country to another. To a great extent, however, the increasing mechanization of production (the substitution of machines for labor) was already driving this process decades before offshoring became a significant factor. As assembly-line employment has declined in high-income countries, fields like product engineering and design have accounted for an increasing proportion of the jobs in the manufacturing sector.

## The End of "Underdevelopment"?

Advocates of "globalization" have pointed to the growth of export-oriented manufacturing in some less developed countries as a positive sign. The countries experiencing the least development, they argue, are those that have remained marginal to the new global economy—especially because official corruption, political instability, or government hostility toward foreign investment have made them unattractive locations for offshore production. These countries, the globalization advocates argue, need *more* globalization, not less—and therefore should adopt "neoliberal" policies eliminating barriers to international trade and investment.

Critics of the current form of globalization, and of the "offshoring" approach to economic development, on the other hand, point to several less-than-shining realities.

First, it is not always true that the least-developed economies have been relatively untouched by the global economy. In many cases, multinational companies, usually with the connivance of local elites, have seized and extracted valuable resources such as minerals or petroleum, with near-total disregard for the effects on the local population. This process has led to the most extreme patterns of "enclave" development, where the only things developed are the means to get the wealth out of the ground and bound for world markets.

Second, countries aggressively embracing neoliberal economic policies have not always seen a dramatic increase in manufacturing employment. "Free trade agreements" have typically eliminated both barriers to trade and barriers to international investment. The elimination of trade barriers has opened up profitable new markets for multinational companies, while also being an essential ingredient of the offshore-production model. The imports that have flooded in to lower-income countries due to the elimination of tariffs and other barriers, however, have battered domestic industries. As a result, many countries have seen the increase in "offshore" or "export-platform" employment in manufacturing offset by the decimation of domestic manufacturing for the domestic market.

Third, when multinational companies "offshore" manufacturing to lower-income countries, they do not relocate all phases of the manufacturing process. Export-platform production typically involves relatively "low-skill" assembly and finishing work. Meanwhile, functions like engineering, design and styling, marketing, and management largely remain in the company's "home" country. (If you look on the back of an iPhone, for example, you will see that it says, "Designed by Apple in California. Assembled in China.") Countries whose governments simply throw their doors open to multinational corporations—without imposing, for example, "technology transfer" requirements that can help spur domestic technological development—may remain stuck in the assembly-and-finishing phase, much as "less-developed" countries in an earlier era were stuck as primary-product producers.

In the 1950s and 1960s, radical theorists of economic dependency emphasized that "underdevelopment" was not simply an *absence* of development. Indeed, even in that era, there was visible economic development in so-called underdeveloped countries, as there is today in what are now termed "developing" countries. Rather, they argued that we should think of underdevelopment as a *form* of development—of dependent, subordinated, exploited development. Capitalist development, they argued, produced both development (for countries in the wealthy "core") and underdevelopment (in the poorer "periphery"). While offshore production may bring a certain form of industrial development, and may be changing the international division of labor in some ways, it is also reproducing old patterns of subordination. ❑

*Article 11.2*

# DOES U.S. PROSPERITY *DEPEND* ON EXPLOITATION?

**BY ARTHUR MacEWAN**
*March/April 2019*

> Dear Dr. Dollar:
> *I regularly hear the claim that U.S. prosperity depends on exploiting poorer countries, but I have never once seen an actual argument for it. What is the support for this claim?*
> —Ryan Cooper, via Twitter

Let's start with the two congenital bloodstains on the cheek of U.S. economic development—slavery and the genocide/taking-of-lands of Native American peoples.

Certainly, the prosperity of the United States has depended to a substantial degree on the labor of slaves, based on stealing people from poor societies, disrupting the social order, and depleting the labor force of those societies. In the decade leading up to the Civil War, for example, the value of raw cotton exports accounted for over half of the value of all U.S. exports. Then there were the direct profits from the slave trade, which built the fortunes of several northern U.S. and European families. And the initial phase of U.S. industrialization, the cotton textile industry, was based on low-cost slave-produced cotton.

As to the economic role of lands taken from Native Americans, the value, though incalculable, was immense. Indeed, some historians have argued that a major pillar of U.S. economic success was the availability of "open land"—the so-called "frontier thesis." Not to mention that a large part of that "frontier" was the huge tract of land taken from Mexico after the Mexican-American War.

U.S. economic success—from slavery, "open land," and other aspects of exploiting people of low-income societies—meant different things for different groups. Clearly, for example, southern plantation owners, financiers of the slave trade, and owners of northern cotton mills reaped major gains. Yet, the economic growth that these activities generated seeped down to a broad spectrum of society, benefiting others less than elites, but benefiting many nonetheless—of course, not including the slaves themselves. Likewise, while large-scale ranchers and land speculators gained disproportionately from stealing the lands of Native Americans, many homesteaders also benefited from "opening" the West. The Native Americans themselves, like the slaves, did not share in the prosperity.

### U.S. Economic Interests and Military Action

*Excerpt from a speech delivered in 1933 by retired Major General Smedley Butler, USMC.*

"I spent 33 years and four months in active military service and during that period I spent most of my time as a high-class muscle man for Big Business, for Wall Street, and the bankers. In short, I was a racketeer, a gangster for capitalism. I helped make Mexico and especially Tampico safe for American oil interests in 1914. I helped make Haiti and Cuba a decent place for the National City Bank boys to collect revenues in. I helped in the raping of half a dozen Central American republics for the benefit of Wall Street. I helped purify Nicaragua for the International Banking House of Brown Brothers in 1902–1912. I brought light to the Dominican Republic for the American sugar interests in 1916. I helped make Honduras right for the American fruit companies in 1903. In China in 1927 I helped see to it that Standard Oil went on its way unmolested. Looking back on it, I might have given Al Capone a few hints. The best he could do was to operate his racket in three districts. I operated on three continents."

## Dependence on Government Support

As with slavery and the decimation of the Native American nations, economic activity beyond the current boundaries of the United States depended on government support, importantly including military support. This was especially evident in the "Gunboat Diplomacy" era in the early decades of the 20th century, when military action abroad was explicitly tied to economic interests, as was famously described and denounced by retired U.S. Marine Corps (USMC) Major General Smedley Butler (see box).

As Butler's statement makes clear, the activities being protected were often those of particular U.S. firms, not the prosperity of the U.S. economy in general. Indeed, in many cases, though the firms benefited, the military costs of the actions outweighed the direct benefits to the U.S. economy. Yet, by protecting the activities of particular firms, the U.S. government was protecting the access of U.S. firms to global markets and resources—that is, protecting the firms' ability to exploit the people and resources in many parts of the world. This access was driven by U.S. firms' search for profits and the firms' owners were the primary beneficiaries. Access, however, also provided low-cost goods—everything from bananas to oil—and markets for U.S. products to the benefit of the U.S. population generally.

At the outset of World War II in late 1939, working with the private, elite Council on Foreign Relations, the U.S. government began planning for the postwar era. According to Laurence H. Shoup and William Minter, in their 1977 book *Imperial Brain Trust*:

> The main issue for consideration [in this planning] was whether America could be self-sufficient and do without the markets and raw materials of the British Empire, Western hemisphere, and Asia. The Council thought that the answer was no and that, therefore, the United States had to enter the war and organize a new world order satisfactory to the United States.

For the United States, the outcome of the war was successful, of course, not only in its immediate military goal of defeating the Axis Powers, but also in establishing U.S. dominance and relatively unfettered access to the markets and raw materials of what the U.S. government referred to as the "Grand Area."

Among the concerns of the planners' efforts to secure the "Grand Area" was Southeast Asia. In one of their memoranda, they wrote, "the Philippine Islands, the Dutch East Indies, and British Malaya are prime sources of raw materials very important to the United States in peace and war; control of these lands by a potentially hostile power would greatly limit our freedom of action." Vietnam would later become the focal point of securing this area from a "hostile power."

## The Issue Is Access

The issue in all of this is not the value of some particular resource or raw material. The issue is always access—access that is unfettered by a hostile local government or by costly regulations designed to promote local economic expansion. Since early in the 20th century, access to oil has been a dominant factor in the foundation of U.S. prosperity, and access to oil has often meant the political-military dominance of lower-income countries. Access to oil, however, has not meant simply that the United States would be able to purchase the oil produced in other countries, but that U.S. oil companies would be able to play the central role in controlling that oil and reaping the associated profits. Whatever other motivations were involved in the U.S. invasion of Iraq and the more recent actions against Venezuela, oil was certainly a major factor.

The dominance by U.S. companies of the global oil industry certainly brought profits to the companies. Yet, as the economy became increasingly oil-dependent, oil was relatively inexpensive, providing a major element in the foundation of U.S. prosperity. And much of this oil came from low-income countries. The formation of the Organization of Petroleum Exporting Countries (OPEC) in 1960 did bring about some change, forcing up the price of oil.

## Varied Impacts: Countries or Classes?

However, the major oil companies have been able to maintain a great deal of power through sharing more with the elites of some of the oil-source countries. This "sharing" experience with oil, which is common in much of the relationships between U.S. firms and the low-income countries in which they operated, underscores the point that it is not quite accurate to say that *countries* are exploited by U.S. operations. Different social groups—different classes—in the countries are affected quite differently by these operations, some are thoroughly exploited while others benefit.

In the 21st century, the focus of U.S. economic connections to poor countries has shifted somewhat. Markets and raw materials remain important, but low-cost labor and lax (or lack of) environmental regulations have become important as well. All along, financial activity has played a role (see the Smedley Butler box). Access to low-cost labor and avoidance of environmental regulations have often been obtained indirectly, through reliance on local contractors supplying goods to U.S. firms (subcontracting). Walmart is a prime example, but many other firms have also been able to provide U.S. consumers with inexpensive items produced by low-wage labor.

It is true that many of the workers supplying goods to the United States have better jobs than they had had prior to engagement with the U.S. market. And, on a broader level, some countries have attained economic growth (though its benefits often go disproportionately to elites) from their connection to the U.S. economy. Nonetheless, U.S. prosperity at least in part depends on those workers receiving low wages, often working in unsafe or unclean environments, and denied basic rights.

Moreover, in examining the impact of U.S. firms' operations in low-income countries, a distinction needs to be made between the immediate and direct impact and the longer run and more general impact. The former may carry benefits, as the trade and investment created by these operations can generate some economic expansion and much-needed jobs in the low-income countries. Over the longer run, however, U.S. engagement tends to support unequal social structures and a weakening of an internal foundation for long run prosperity in these countries. Furthermore, the U.S. government, in its role as a supporter of U.S. firms' operations around the world, has often intervened to prevent social change that might have led to real improvements in the lives of people in low-income countries. (The list of interventions that Smedley Butler gives only begins to tell the story.)

## Pillars of Prosperity

In addition to the international economic relations between the United States and low-income countries, the United States also has extensive economic relations with high-income countries as well. Indeed, the majority of U.S. global trade and the majority of foreign investment by U.S. firms is with other high-income countries. This activity does not generally have the same exploitive characteristics as U.S. firms' penetration of low-income parts of the world. Both are pillars on which U.S. prosperity has depended.

There are other pillars as well. For example, the relatively high degree of education among the U.S. population and the skills that many immigrants brought with them to this country are also pillars of prosperity. But, surely, the exploitation of people in low-income countries has been an important pillar. ❑

**Sources:** Smedley D. Butler, *War is a Racket: The Antiwar Classic by America's Most Decorated Soldier* (Feral House, 2003); Walter Rodney, *How Europe Underdeveloped Africa* (Black Classic Press, 2011); Andre Gunder Frank, *The Development of Underdevelopment* (Monthly Review Press, 1966); Arthur MacEwan, "Capitalist Expansion, Ideology and Intervention," *Review of Radical Political Economics*, Vol. 4, No. 1, Winter 1972; John Miller, "After Horror, Apologetics: Sweatshop apologists cover for intransigent U.S. retail giants," *Dollars & Sense*, September/October 2013; Arthur MacEwan, "Is It Oil?" *Dollars & Sense,* May/June 2003; Arthur MacEwan, "Is It Oil?—The Issue Revisited," *Dollars & Sense,* March/April 2017.

*Article 11.3*

# PUERTO RICO'S COLONIAL ECONOMY

**BY ARTHUR MacEWAN**
*November/December 2015*

Dear Dr. Dollar:

It seems like Puerto Rico's economic and financial mess came out of nowhere. Until recently, there wasn't much about Puerto Rico in the press, but what there was seemed to portray things as fine, with a generous amount of funds going to the island from Washington. Sometimes, Puerto Rico was held up as a model for economic development. So where did the current mess come from?　　—*Janet Sands, Chicago, Ill.*

Puerto Rico is a colony of the United States. Colonial status, with some exceptions, is not a good basis for economic progress.

Recently, the details of the Puerto Rican economic mess, and especially the financial crisis, have become almost daily fodder for the U.S. press. Yet, the island's colonial status and the economic impact of that status, which lie at the foundation of the current debacle, have been largely ignored.

Puerto Rico, like other colonies, has been administered in the interests of the "mother country." For example, for many years, a provision of the U.S. tax code, Section 936, let U.S. firms operate on the island without incurring taxes on their Puerto Rican profits (as long as those profits were not moved back to the states). This program was portrayed as a job creator for Puerto Rico. Yet the principal beneficiaries were U.S. firms—especially pharmaceutical firms. When this tax provision was in full-force in the late 1980s and early 1990s, it cost the U.S. government on average more than $3.00 in lost tax revenue for each $1.00 in wages paid in Puerto Rico by the pharmaceuticals. (What's more, the pharmaceuticals, while they did produce in Puerto Rico, also located many of their patents with their Puerto Rican subsidiaries, thus avoiding taxes on the profits from these patents.)

Puerto Ricans are U.S. citizens, but residents of the island have no voting representatives in Congress and do not participate in presidential elections. The Puerto Rican government does have a good deal of autonomy, but is ultimately under U.S. law. And without voting representatives in Congress, Puerto Rico is unable to obtain equal status in federal programs or full inclusion in important legislation. A good example of the latter, which has become especially important in the ongoing financial crisis, is that U.S. law excludes the Puerto Rican government from declaring bankruptcy, an option available to U.S. states and their cities.

It is often asserted that the U.S. government provides "generous" benefits to Puerto Rico. Perhaps the largest federal payment to Puerto Ricans is Social Security. Yet Puerto Ricans on the island pay Social Security taxes just like residents of states and the District of Columbia. Likewise, Puerto Ricans pay Medicare taxes just like residents of the states, but, unlike residents of the states, their Medicare benefits are capped at a lower level. Among the important programs from which residents of Puerto Rico are excluded, a big one is the earned income tax credit (EITC). As a result, a two-parent, two-child family in Puerto Rico earning $25,000 a year ends up, after federal taxes and credits, with about $6,000 less income than a family in the states with the same earnings and family structure.

Opponents of extending the EITC to residents of Puerto Rico argue that they should not get the EITC because they are not liable for federal income taxes. Yet many EITC recipients in the states pay no federal income taxes simply because their incomes are so low (e.g., the family in the above example). Moreover, the EITC was established to offset the burden on low-income families of Social Security and Medicare taxes, which Puerto Rico residents do pay, and to reduce poverty, of which Puerto Ricans have more than their share.

If Puerto Rico gets "generous" benefits from Washington, several states are treated more generously. In particular, if states are ranked in terms of their "net receipts" per capita from the federal government—that is, funds received from the federal government minus federal taxes—in a typical year about one-third of the states rank above Puerto Rico (though the number varies somewhat in different years). In 2010, for example, West Virginia received $8,365 per capita more in federal expenditures than were paid from the state in federal taxes; Kentucky $7,812 more; Vermont $6,713 more; and Alaska and Hawaii topped the list with $11,123 per capita and $10,733 per capita more respectively from the federal government than they paid to the federal government. That year Puerto Rico received on net $4,697 per capita.

Beyond these particular disadvantages of colonial status, Puerto Rico suffers from a pervaisive condition of "dependency." In setting economic policy, the Puerto Rican government has continually looked beyond the island, to investments by U.S. firms and favors from Washington. As James Dietz has usefully summed up the situation in his 2003 book Puerto Rico: Negotiating Development and Change: "...Puerto Rico's strategy of development lacked a focus on the systematic support or fostering of local entrepreneurs and local sources of finance." As a consequence "the central role of domestic entrepreneurs, skilled workers and technological progress that underlies sustained economic progress" has been weaker in Puerto Rico than in sovereign nations where sustained economic progress has proceeded more rapidly. Moreover, government policy and decisions by investors tend to be short-sighted, failing to build the foundation for long-term economic progress. The poor condition of the public schools and the weak physical infrastructure are examples of the consequences.

All of these factors have retarded the Puerto Rican economy for decades. The island did experience a burst of economic activity in the post-World War II period, heavily dependent on low-wage labor, privileged access to the U.S. market, and federal and local tax breaks for U.S. firms. As wages rose and other parts of the world gained access to the U.S. market, the economy faltered. From the mid-1970s into the early 2000s, Puerto Rico lost economic ground compared to the states.

The severe recession that then emerged in 2006 and that Puerto Rico has suffered under for the past decade, only partially attenuated by heavy government borrowing on the bond market, was an outcome to be expected from the economy's long-term weakness and, in fact, was precipitated by that heavy government borrowing.

By 2006, the Puerto Rican public debt was 70% as large as GNP. (Now it is slightly more than 100%.) Under this debt pressure, in an effort to cut its expenditures, the government temporarily laid off without pay 100,000 workers (almost 10% of the total work force). Had the Puerto Rican economy not been so weak and had the U.S. economy not soon entered the Great Recession, perhaps the downturn from this layoff shock would have been brief. But the weak economy and then recession in the states undercut any basis for quick recovery. In 2009 and 2010, Puerto Rico did receive a share of the funds in the American Recovery and Reinvestment Act (ARRA), which attenuated but did not end the island's recession. The boost from the ARRA funds was too small and too short-lived.

Many commentators and Puerto Rican government officials try to explain the emergence of Puerto Rico's recession by the termination of the Section 936 tax breaks and call for a renewal of 936 provisions to aid the economy. However, for the firms, the tax breaks did not end, but were maintained under other tax code provisions, and there was virtually no decline of employment in 936 firms as the tax provision was being phased out between 1996 and 2006. After 2006, however, the employment provisions of Section 936, as weak as they were, did collapse. As a result, while exports of pharmaceuticals have grown apace in subsequent year, for example, employment in the industry has dropped sharply. Perhaps the termination of 936 contributed to the continuation of the downturn, through its impact on employment, but it was not the primary or major causal factor. Most important, a renewal of 936 provisions is not a solution to Puerto Rico's economic difficulties.

Controversy over Puerto Rico's status has been a dominating theme of the island's politics for decades. Various polls have shown a rough split between maintaining the current status and statehood, with the latter gaining an edge in the 2012 poll associated with the election. The polls show support for independence far behind.

The current colonial status, in addition to its negative economic impact, involves a fundamental violation of human rights and democracy. Puerto Ricans should be given a clear choice between independence and statehood; maintenance of the current colonial status (or a somewhat different colonial status that has some support) should be off the table. Beyond the interests of the Puerto Ricans, how can those of us in the states make a claim to democracy while we hold Puerto Rico as our colony? ❑

Article 11.4

# "TIED" FOREIGN AID

## BY ARTHUR MacEWAN
*January/February 2012*

Dear Dr. Dollar:

People complaining about the ungrateful world often talk about the "huge" U.S. foreign aid budget.In fact, isn't U.S. foreign aid relatively small compared to other countries?What's worse, I understand that a lot of economic aid comes with strings attached, requiring that goods and services purchased with the aid be purchased from firms in the aid-giving country.This channels much of the money back out of the recipient country.That sounds nuts!What's going on?          —*Katharine Rylaarsdam, Baltimore, Md.*

The U.S. government does provide a "huge" amount of development aid, far more than any of the other rich countries.In 2009, the United States provided $29.6 billion, in development aid—Japan was number two, at $16.4 billion.

But wait a minute.What appears huge may not be so huge. The graph below shows the amount of foreign development aid provided by ten high-income countries *and* that amount as a share of the countries' gross domestic products (GDP).Yes, the graph shows that the United States gives far more than any of these other countries.But the graph also shows the United States gives a small amount relative to its GDP.In 2009, U.S. foreign development aid was two-tenths of 1% of the country's GDP.Only Italy gave a lesser amount relative to its GDP.

### DEVELOPMENT AID, AMOUNT AND PERCENT OF GDP, 2009

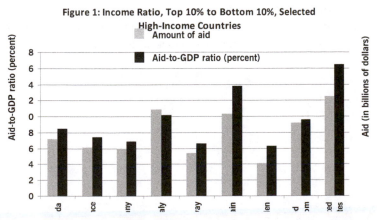

Figure 1: Income Ratio, Top 10% to Bottom 10%, Selected High-Income Countries

*Source:* OECD, Official Development Assistance by Donor (stats.oecd.org).

The world's rich countries have long committed to providing 0.7% of GDP to foreign development aid.In 2009, only Norway and Sweden met this goal. The U.S. government did not come close.

Moreover, a large share of U.S. foreign aid is "tied aid"; governments that receive the aid must spend the funds by buying goods and services from U.S. firms. Generally the recipient countries could get more goods and services if they could spend the money without this restriction.So the economic development impact of the aid is less than it appears. Also, whatever the "foreign aid" does for the recipient country, it is a way of channeling money to U.S. firms.

Not only must the recipient country pay more for the goods and services, but the "multiplier impact" is much less.That is, since the money goes to U.S. companies rather than local suppliers, fewer local jobs and salary payments are created; so less is re-spent in the local economy.A 2009 report on aid to Afghanistan by the Peace Dividend Trust notes: "By using Afghan goods and services to carry out development projects in Afghanistan, the international community has the opportunity to spend a development dollar twice. How? Local procurement creates jobs, increases incomes, generates revenue and develops the Afghan marketplace —all of which support economic recovery and stability."Yet most of the aid "for Afghanistan" went to foreign "experts," foreign construction firms, and foreign suppliers of goods.

The U.S. government ties much more of its aid than do most other donor countries.A report by the Organization for Economic Cooperation and Development (OECD) estimated that in the mid-2000s, 54.5% of U.S. aid was tied.Of the 22 donor countries listed in the report (including the United States), the average share of tied aid was only 28.4%.The report notes a "widespread movement to untying [aid], with the exception of the United States."

It is important to recognize that U.S. foreign aid is an instrument of U.S. foreign policy, and is thus highly concentrated in countries where the U.S. government has what it views as "strategic interests." For example, in 2008 almost 16% of U.S. development assistance went to Afghanistan and Iraq, while the top 20 recipient countries received over 50%.

So, yes, the U.S. government provides a "huge" amount of foreign development aid—or not so much.It depends on how you look at things. ❑

*Article 11.5*

# HAITI'S FAULT LINES
*Made in the U.S.A.*

## BY MARIE KENNEDY AND CHRIS TILLY
*March/April 2010*

The mainstream media got half the story right about Haiti. Reporters observed that Haiti's stark poverty intensified the devastation caused by the earthquake on January 12, 2010. True: hillside shantytowns, widespread concrete construction without rebar reinforcement, a grossly inadequate road network, and a healthcare system mainly designed to cater to the small elite all contributed mightily to death and destruction.

But what caused that poverty? U.S. readers and viewers might be forgiven for concluding that some inexplicable curse has handed Haiti corrupt and unstable governments, unproductive agriculture, and widespread illiteracy. Televangelist Pat Robertson simply took this line of "explanation" to its nutty, racist conclusion when he opined that Haitians were paying for a pact with the devil.

But the devil had little to do with Haiti's underdevelopment. Instead, the fingerprints of more mundane actors—France and later the United States—are all over the crime scene. After the slave rebellion of 1791, France wrought massive destruction in attempting to recapture its former colony, then extracted 150 million francs of reparations, only fully paid off in 1947. France's most poisonous legacy may have been the skin-color hierarchy that sparked fratricidal violence and still divides Haiti.

While France accepted Haiti's independence once the government started paying up, the United States, alarmed by the example of a slave republic, refused to recognize Haiti until 1862. That late-arriving recognition kicked off a continuing series of military and political interventions. The U.S. Marines occupied Haiti outright from 1915 to 1934, modernizing the infrastructure but also revising laws to allow foreign ownership, turning over the country's treasury to a New York bank, saddling Haiti with a $40-million debt to the United States, and reinforcing the status gap between mulattos and blacks. American governments backed the brutal, kleptocratic, two-generation Duvalier dictatorship from 1957-86. When populist priest Jean-Bertrand Aristide was elected president in 1990, the Bush I administration winked at the coup that ousted him a year later. Bill Clinton reversed course, ordering an invasion to restore Aristide, but used that intervention to impose the same free-trade "structural adjustment" Bush had sought. Bush II closed the circle by backing rebels who re-overthrew the re-elected Aristide in 2004. No wonder many Haitians are suspicious of the U.S. troops who poured in after the earthquake.

Though coups and invasions grab headlines, U.S. economic interventions have had equally far-reaching effects. U.S. goals for the last 30 years have been to open Haiti to American products, push Haiti's self-sufficient peasants off the land, and redirect the Haitian economy to plantation-grown luxury crops and export assembly, both underpinned by cheap labor. Though Haiti has yet to boost its export capacity, the first two goals have succeeded, shattering Haiti's former productive capacity. In the early 1980s, the U.S. Agency for International Development exterminated Haiti's hardy Creole pigs in the name of preventing a swine flu epidemic, then helpfully offered U.S. pigs that require expensive U.S.-produced feeds and medicines. Cheap American rice imports crippled the country's breadbasket, the Artibonite, so that Haiti, a rice exporter in the 1980s, now imports massive amounts. Former peasants flooded into Port-au-Prince, doubling the population over the last quarter century, building makeshift housing, and setting the stage for the current catastrophe.

In the wake of the disaster, U.S. aid continues to have two-edged effects. Each aid shipment that flies in U.S. rice and flour instead of buying and distributing local rice or cassava continues to undermine agriculture and deepen dependency. Precious trucks and airstrips are used to marshal U.S. troops against overblown "security threats," crowding out humanitarian assistance. The United States and other international donors show signs of once more using aid to leverage a free-trade agenda. If we seek to end Haiti's curse, the first step is to realize that one of the curse's main sources is … us. ❑

# Chapter 12

# NATURAL RESOURCES AND THE ENVIRONMENT

*Article 12.1*

## CAN WE AFFORD A STABLE CLIMATE?
*Worst-Case Risks vs. Least-Cost Solutions*

**BY FRANK ACKERMAN**
*March/April 2019*

The damages expected from climate change seem to get worse with each new study. Reports from the Intergovernmental Panel on Climate Change (IPCC) and the U.S. Global Change Research Program, and a multi-author review article in *Science*, all published in late 2018, are among the recent bearers of bad news. Even more signs of danger continue to arrive in a swarm of research articles, too numerous to list here. And most of these reports are now talking about not-so-long-term damages. Dramatic climate disruption and massive economic losses are coming in just a few decades, not centuries, if we continue along our present path of inaction.

It's almost enough to make you support an emergency program to reduce emissions and switch to a path of abrupt decarbonization: Something like the Green New Deal, the emerging proposal that would rapidly replace fossil fuels with massive investment in energy efficiency and clean energy, combined with high wages and standards, and fairness in the distribution of jobs and opportunities.

But wait: Isn't there something about economics we need to figure out first? Would drastic emission reductions pass a cost-benefit test? How do we know that the Green New Deal wouldn't require spending too much on climate policy?

In fact, a crash program to decarbonize the economy is obviously the right answer. There are just a few things you need to know about the economics of climate policy in order to confirm that Adam Smith and his intellectual heirs have not overturned common sense on this issue.

## Worst-Case Risks: Why We Need Insurance

For uncertain, extreme risks, policy should be based on the credible worst-case outcome, not the expected or most likely value. This is the way people think about insurance against disasters. The odds that your house won't burn down next year are better than 99%—but if you own a home, you probably have fire insurance anyway. Likewise, young parents have more than a 99% chance of surviving the coming year, but often buy life insurance to protect their children if the worst should occur.

Real uncertainty, of course, has nothing to do with the fake uncertainty of climate denial. In insurance terms, real uncertainty consists of not knowing when a house fire might occur; fake uncertainty is the (obviously wrong) claim that houses never catch fire. See my book *Worst-Case Economics* for a more detailed exploration of worst cases and (real) uncertainty, in both climate and finance.

For climate risks, worst cases are much too dreadful to ignore. What we know is that climate change could be very bad for us; but no one knows exactly how bad it will be or when it will arrive. How likely are we to reach tipping points into an irreversibly worse climate, and when will these tipping points occur? As the careful qualifications in the IPCC and other reports remind us, climate change could be very bad surprisingly soon, but almost no one is willing to put a precise number or date on the expected losses.

One group does rush in where scientists fear to tread, guessing about the precise magnitude and timing of future climate damages: economists engaged in cost-benefit analysis (CBA). Rarely used before the 1990s, CBA has become the default, "common sense" approach to policy evaluation, particularly in environmental policy. In CBA-world, you begin by measuring and monetizing the benefits and the costs of a policy—and then "buy" the policy if, and only if, the monetary value of the benefits exceeds the costs.

There are numerous problems with CBA, such as the need to (literally) make up monetary prices for priceless values of human life, health, and the natural environment. In practice, CBA often trivializes the value of life and nature. Climate policy raises yet another problem: CBA requires a single number, such as a most likely outcome, best guess, or weighted average, for every element of costs (e.g., future costs of clean energy) and benefits (e.g., monetary value of future damages avoided by clean energy expenditures). There is no simple way to incorporate a wide range of uncertainty about such values into CBA.

## Costs of Emission Reduction Are Dropping Fast

The insurance analogy is suggestive, but not a perfect fit for climate policy. There is no intergalactic insurance agency that can offer us a loaner planet to use while ours is towed back to the shop for repairs. Instead, we will have to "self-insure" against climate risks—the equivalent of spending money on fireproofing your house rather than relying on an insurance policy.

Climate self-insurance consists largely of reducing carbon emissions, in order to reduce future losses. (Adaptation, or expenditure to reduce vulnerability to climate damages, is also important but may not be effective beyond the early stages of warming. And some adaptation costs are required to cope with warming that can no longer be avoided—that is, they have become sunk costs, not present or future policy choices.) The one piece of unalloyed good news in climate policy today is the plummeting cost of clean energy. In the windiest and sunniest parts of the world (and the United States), new wind and solar power installations now produce electricity at costs equal to or lower than fossil fuel-burning plants.

A 2017 report from the International Renewable Energy Agency (IRENA) projects that this will soon be true worldwide: global average renewable energy costs will be within the range of fossil fuel-fired costs by 2020, with on-shore wind and solar photovoltaic panels at the low end of the range. Despite low costs for clean energy, many utilities will still propose to build fossil fuel plants, reflecting the inertia of traditional energy planning and the once-prudent wisdom of the cheap-fuel, pre-climate change era.

Super-low costs for renewables, which would have seemed like fantasies 10 years ago, are now driving the economics and the feasibility of plans for decarbonization. The Green New Deal may not be free, but it's not nearly as expensive today as it would have been just a little while ago.

Robert Pollin, an economist who has studied Green New Deal options, estimates that annual investment of about 1.5% of GDP would be needed. That's about $300 billion a year for the United States, and four times as much, $1.2 trillion a year, for the world economy. Those numbers may sound large, but so are the fossil fuel subsidies and investments that the Green New Deal would eliminate.

In a 2015 study, my colleagues and I calculated that 80% of U.S. greenhouse gas emissions could be eliminated by 2050, with no net increase in energy or transportation costs. Since that time, renewables have only gotten cheaper. (Our result does not necessarily contradict Pollin's estimate, since the last 20% of emissions will be the hardest and most expensive to eliminate.)

These projections of future costs are inevitably uncertain, because the future has not happened yet. The risks, however, do not appear dangerous or burdensome. So far, the surprises on the cost side have been unexpectedly rapid decreases in renewable energy prices. These are not the risks that require rethinking our approach to climate policy.

The disastrous worst-case risks are all on the benefits, or avoided climate damages, side of the ledger. The scientific uncertainties about climate change concern the timing and extent of damages. Therefore, the urgency of avoiding these damages, or conversely the cost of not avoiding them, is intrinsically uncertain, and could be disastrously large.

## Climate Damages: Uncertain but Ominous, or $51 per Ton?

It has become common, among economists, to estimate the "social cost of carbon" (SCC), defined as the monetary value of the present and future climate damages

per ton of carbon dioxide or equivalent. This is where the pick-a-number imperative of cost-benefit analysis introduces the greatest distortion: huge uncertainties in
damages should naturally translate into huge uncertainties in the SCC, not a single
point estimate.

According to scientists, climate damages are deeply uncertain, but could be
ominously large. Alternatively, according to the best-known economic calculation,
lifetime damages caused by emissions in 2020 will be worth $51 per metric ton of
carbon dioxide, in 2018 prices.

These two rival views can't both be right. In fact, the $51 estimate comes from
an awkward and oversimplified calculation; while it yields a better estimate than
zero, it still threatens to obscure the meaning of deep uncertainty about the true
value of climate damages.

The federal government's calculation of the SCC began under the Obama
administration, which assembled an Interagency Working Group to address the
question. In the Working Group's final (August 2016) revision of the numbers,
the most widely used variant of the SCC was $42 per metric ton of carbon dioxide
emitted in 2020, expressed in 2007 dollars—equivalent to $51 in 2018 dollars.
Numbers like this were used in Obama-era cost-benefit analyses of new regulations, placing a dollar value on the reduction in carbon emissions from, say,
vehicle fuel-efficiency standards.

To create these numbers, the Working Group averaged the results from three
well-known models. These do not provide more detailed or in-depth analysis
than other models. On the contrary, two of them stand out for being simpler
and easier to use than other models. They are, however, the most frequently cited
models in climate economics. They are famous for being famous, the Kardashians
of climate models.

The Dynamic Integrated Climate-Economy (DICE) model, developed by
William Nordhaus at Yale University, offers a skeletal simplicity: it represents
the dynamics of the world economy, the climate, and the interactions between
the two with only 19 equations. This (plus Nordhaus' free distribution of the
software) has made it by far the most widely used model, valuable for classroom
teaching, initial sketches of climate impacts, and researchers (at times including
myself) who lack the funding to acquire and use more complicated models. Yet
no one thinks that DICE represents the frontier of knowledge about the world
economy or the environment. DICE estimates aggregate global climate damages
as a quadratic function of temperature increases (i.e., damages as a percentage
of world output are assumed to depend on the square of temperature increases),
rising only gradually as the world warms.

The Policy Analysis of the Greenhouse Effect (PAGE) model, developed by
Chris Hope at Cambridge University, resembles DICE in its level of complexity, and has been used in many European analyses. It is the only one of the three
models to include any explicit treatment of uncertain climate risks, assuming the
threat of an abrupt, mid-size economic loss (beyond the "predictable" damages)

that becomes both more likely and more severe as temperatures rise. Perhaps for this reason, PAGE consistently produces the highest SCC estimates among the three models.

And, finally, the Framework for Uncertainty, Negotiation, and Distribution (FUND) model, developed by Richard Tol and David Anthoff, is more detailed than DICE or PAGE, with separate treatment of more than a dozen damage categories. Yet the development of these damages estimates has been idiosyncratic, in some cases (such as agriculture) relying on relatively optimistic research from 20 years ago rather than more troubling, recent findings on climate impacts. Even in later versions, after many small updates, FUND still estimates that many of its damage categories are too small to matter; in some FUND scenarios, the largest cost of warming is the increased expenditure on air conditioning.

Much has been written about what's wrong with relying on these three models. The definitive critique is the National Academy of Sciences study, which reviews the shortcomings of the three models in detail and suggests ways to build a better model for estimating the SCC. (Released just days before the Trump inauguration, the study was doomed to be ignored.)

## Embracing Uncertainty

Expected climate damages are uncertain over a wide range, including the possibility of disastrously large impacts. The SCC is a monetary valuation of expected damages per ton of carbon dioxide. Therefore, SCC values should be uncertain over a wide range, including the possibility of disastrously high values. Yet the Working Group's methodology all but obscures the role of uncertainty in climate science.

A broader review of climate economics yields results consistent with the expected pattern. Look beyond the three-model calculation, and the range of possible SCC values is extremely wide, including very high upper bounds. Many studies have adopted DICE or another model as a base, then demonstrated that minor, reasonable changes in assumptions lead to huge changes in the SCC.

To cite a few examples: A meta-analysis of SCC values found that, in order to reflect major climate risks, the SCC needs to be at least $125.

A study by Simon Dietz and Nicholas Stern found a range of optimal carbon prices (i.e., SCC values), depending on key climate uncertainties, ranging from $45 to $160 for emissions in 2025, and from $111 to $394 for emissions in 2055 (in 2018 dollars per ton of carbon dioxide).

In my own research, co-authored with Liz Stanton, we found that a few major uncertainties lead to an extremely wide range of possible SCC values, from $34 to $1,079 for emissions in 2010, and from $77 to $1,875 for 2050 emissions (again converted to 2018 dollars).

Martin Weitzman has written several articles emphasizing that the SCC depends heavily on the unknown shape of the damage function—that is, the details of the assumed relationship between rising temperatures and rising damages. His

"Dismal Theorem" article argues that the marginal value of reducing emissions—the SCC—is literally infinite, since catastrophes that would cause human extinction remain too plausible to ignore (although they are not the most likely outcomes).

Whether or not the SCC is infinite, many researchers have found that it is uncertain, with the broad range of plausible values including dangerously high estimates. This is the appropriate economic reflection of scientific uncertainty about the timing and extent of climate damages.

## The Low Price of Self-Insurance

As explained above, deep uncertainty about the magnitude and timing of risks stymies the use of cost-benefit analysis for climate policy. Rather, policy should be set in an insurance-like framework, focused on credible worst-case losses rather than most likely outcomes. Given the magnitude of the global problem, this means "self-insurance"—investing in measures that make worst cases less likely.

How much does climate "self-insurance"—greenhouse gas emission reduction—cost? Several early (2008 to 2010) studies of deep decarbonization, pushing the envelope of what was technically feasible at the time, came up with mid-century carbon prices of roughly $150 to $500 per ton of carbon dioxide abated. (Prices were reported in 2005 dollars; multiply by 1.29 to convert to 2018 dollars.) Since then, renewable energy has experienced rapid progress and declining prices, undoubtedly lowering the cost of a maximum feasible reduction scenario.

Even a decade ago, at $150 to $500 per ton, the cost of abatement was comparable to or lower than many of the worst-case estimates of the SCC, or climate damages per ton. In short, we already know, and have known for a while, that doing everything on the least-cost emission reduction path will cost less, per ton of carbon dioxide, than worst-case climate damages.

That's it: the end of the  economic story about evaluating climate policy. We don't need more exact, accurate SCC estimates; they will not be forthcoming in time to shape policy, due to the uncertainties involved. Since estimated worst-case damages are rising over time, while abatement costs (such as the costs of renewables) are falling, the balance is tipping farther and farther toward "do everything you can to reduce emissions, now." That was already the correct answer some years ago, and only becomes more correct over time. ❑

*Sources*: U.S. Global Change Research Project, *Fourth National Climate Assessment, Volume II: Impacts, Risks and Adaptation in the United States*, 2018; Intergovernmental Panel on Climate Change (IPCC), *Special Report: Global Warming of 1.5°C*, 2018; Philip Duffy et al., "Strengthened scientific support for the Endangerment Finding for atmospheric greenhouse gases," *Science*, Dec. 13, 2018; Frank Ackerman, *Worst-Case Economics: Extreme Events in Climate and Finance*, Anthem Press, 2017; Frank Ackerman and Lisa Heinzerling, *Priceless: On Knowing the Price of Everything and the Value of Nothing*, The New Press, 2004; Frank Ackerman, *Poisoned for Pennies: The Economics of Toxics and Precaution*,

Island Press, 2008; International Renewable Energy Agency, *Renewable Power Generation Costs in 2017: Key Findings and Executive Summary*, 2018; David Roberts, "The Green New Deal, explained," Vox, 2018 (vox.com); Robert Pollin, "De-Growth vs. a Green New Deal," *New Left Review*, July-August 2018 (newleftreview.org); Frank Ackerman et al., "The Clean Energy Future: Protecting the Climate, Creating Jobs, Saving Money," Synapse Energy Economics, 2015 (frankackerman.com); U.S. Environmental Protection Agency, "The Social Cost of Carbon," 2017 (epa.gov); Interagency Working Group, "Technical Support Document: Technical Update of the Social Cost of Carbon for Regulatory Impact Analysis Under Executive Order 12866," August 2016 (epa.gov); Frank Ackerman and Charles Munitz, "Climate damages in the FUND model: A disaggregated analysis," *Ecological Economics* 77, 2012; Frank Ackerman and Charles Munitz, "A critique of climate damage modeling: Carbon fertilization, adaptation, and the limits of FUND," *Energy Research & Social Science*, 2016; National Academies of Science, Engineering and Medicine, *Valuing Climate Damages: Updating Estimation of the Social Cost of Carbon Dioxide*, National Academies Press, 2017; J.C.J.M. van den Bergh and W.J.W. Botzen, "A lower bound to the social cost of $CO_2$ emissions," *Nature Climate Change*, 2014; Simon Dietz and Nicholas Stern, "Endogenous growth, convexity of damage and climate risk: How Nordhaus' framework supports deep cuts in carbon emissions," *The Economic Journal*, 2015; Frank Ackerman and Elizabeth A. Stanton, "Climate risks and carbon prices: Revising the social cost of carbon," Economics E-journal, 2012; Martin Weitzman, "On modeling and interpreting the economics of catastrophic climate change," *Review of Economics and Statistics*, 2009.

*Article 12.2*

# IS A RAPID GREEN-ENERGY SWITCH PROHIBITIVELY COSTLY?

## BY ARTHUR MacEWAN
*March/April 2020*

Dear Dr. Dollar:

Virtually everyone now recognizes the reality of climate change. However, there is still opposition to making a major, rapid switch to green energy, based on the argument that there are substantial limits to green technology and that these limits could only be overcome at a prohibitively high cost. Is there validity to this argument?

—*Chip Carey, North Hampton, N.H.*

A switch to green energy could be costly. But a failure to switch would be far more costly, perhaps even catastrophic. In fact, the damage that is occurring because of our use of fossil fuels is already imposing substantial costs, as witness, for example, the severe fires and hurricanes of recent years. Worse yet, global warming and its impacts will only become more extreme in the coming years because greenhouse gases (carbon dioxide, especially) remain in the atmosphere for many decades. Nonetheless, it is still possible to take actions that will not only improve the situation in the long run, but will have immediate positive impacts on health and general well-being. (See the sidebar on the "hidden costs" of energy production.)

The switch to green energy does face some substantial cost barriers. Although these barriers have been exaggerated by opponents, some will have substantial—but by no means prohibitive—costs. Also, the switch could negatively affect many people who work in fossil fuel industries. Failure to mitigate this social impact would greatly inhibit the move to green energy, as well as being ethically offensive. Yet, there are programs (beyond the scope of this article, but see the Green New Deal's "just transition" provisions) that could ensure that this group of people does not suffer the burden of energy transformation.

There are various forms of green energy, including hydropower and geothermal power. Here, however, I will focus on solar and wind power, which are potentially the most important.

## The Good News

It used to be argued that wind- and solar-powered generation of electricity was excessively expensive, a good deal more expensive than generation using fossil fuels. Leaving aside the fact that this cost comparison did not include the very high social costs of generation by fossil fuels—climate change and damage to people's health—the argument is no longer valid. (See the sidebar regarding the environmental costs of wind and solar energy generation.)

The best estimates indicate that between 2009 and 2019, the cost of producing electricity by solar photovoltaic cells (in large-scale facilities, not rooftops) fell 89%, and the cost of producing electricity by wind power fell 70%. In this same period, the cost of electricity generation by coal fell 2% and the cost of producing electricity by natural gas fell 32%. In 2019, the costs of generation by solar or by wind were about the same and far cheaper than generation from fossil fuels, just 36% of the cost of generation by coal and about 70% of the cost of generation by gas. The actual cost estimates are shown in Table 1. (These are estimates of unsubsidized costs and include capital costs; again, they do not include social and environmental costs, what economists call "externalities" or "spillover effects," which are, of course, much higher for fossil fuel generation than green energy generation.)

The cost reductions have come as the demand for green energy has grown and governments around the world have provided support for expansion. According to a November 2019 article in the *Financial Times*, the advance "has been driven by solar expansion in the EU [European Union], India, and Vietnam as well as growth in onshore wind in the EU, US, and China." Increases in production have allowed economies of scale to lower costs. Also, new manufacturing techniques and new materials in solar photovoltaic panels have contributed to the cost reductions, as have taller towers, longer blades, and improved control systems in wind power.

The data suggest that new electrical generation capacity would use wind or solar instead of coal or natural gas, as the profit-maximizing firms that dominate the market would want to minimize costs; and the much smaller number of publicly-owned utilities would also want to minimize costs. There is some move in the direction of

### $160 Billion and Counting

A 2009 report from the National Research Council (a part of the U.S. National Academy of Sciences and U.S. National Academy of Engineering) made estimates of many of the "hidden costs" of energy production and use—in particular, the damage to human health from air pollution—that are not reflected in market prices of fossil fuels. The report's estimate of these "hidden costs" was $120 billion in the United States in 2005—which would be about $160 billion in 2020 prices. The figure primarily reflected the health damages from air pollution associated with electricity generation and vehicle transportation.

The actual "hidden costs" are much higher, as the Research Council notes that its estimate did not include damages from climate change, harm to ecosystems, effects of some additional air pollutants (e.g., mercury), or risks to national security.

*Source*: The National Academies of Sciences, Engineering, and Medicine, "Report Examines Hidden Costs of Energy Production and Use," October 19, 2009 (nationalacademies.org).

**TABLE 1: ESTIMATES OF COST PER KILOWATT HOUR OF VARIOUS METHODS OF ELECTRICITY GENERATION, AND PERCENT DECLINE, 2009 AND 2019**

|  | 2009 | 2019 | Percent Decline |
|---|---|---|---|
| Solar photovoltaic | 38.9 cents | 4.0 cents | 89% |
| Wind | 13.5 cents | 4.1 cents | 70% |
| Coal | 11.1 cents | 10.9 cents | 2% |
| Gas | 8.3 cents | 5.6 cents | 32% |
| Gas Peaker | 27.5 cents | 17.5 cents | 37% |

*Note*: Social costs (i.e., externalities or spill-over effects) are not included.

*Source*: Lazard, "Lazard's Levelized Cost of Energy Analysis—Version 13.0," November 7, 2019 (lazard.com).

these green sources of energy. In the United States between 2008 and 2018, in generation by utility firms, wind and solar photovoltaic generation together rose sixfold while total generation increased by only 1% (as the increase of green generation was roughly offset by a decline in other forms of generation). Yet, in 2018, these two sources accounted for only 8% of utility scale-generation.

## The Bad News

There is a catch, however. The sun does not shine all the time and the wind does not blow all the time. If there were a way to store electricity when the natural

---

### Environmental Impacts of Wind and Solar

It seems there is no such thing as completely "clean" energy, in that even electricity generation by wind and solar has some negative impacts. The Union of Concerned Scientists (UCS) reports: "Despite its vast potential, there are a variety of environmental impacts associated with wind power generation … They include land use issues and challenges to wildlife and habitat." And: "The environmental impacts associated with solar power can include land use and habitat loss, water use, and the use of hazardous materials in manufacturing, though the types of impacts vary greatly depending on the scale of the system and the technology used—photovoltaic (PV) solar cells or concentrating solar thermal plants (CSP)."

However, the UCS prefaces these statements with, "Fossil fuels—coal, oil, and natural gas—do substantially more harm than renewable energy sources by most measures, including air and water pollution, damage to public health, wildlife and habitat loss, water use, land use, and global warming emissions." And, of course, by the measure of climate change.

The negative environmental impacts of green energy need to be recognized so they can be diminished as much as possible, but they provide no reason to inhibit the switch from fossil fuels to wind and solar.

*Source*: Union of Concerned Scientists, "Environmental Impacts of Renewable Energy Technologies," March 5, 2013 (ucsusa.org).

environment (sun and wind) isn't cooperating, the problem of weather intermittency could be mitigated. But at present there is no way to do this on a large scale. Still, the problem could be significantly reduced if the electricity could be transmitted from those places where the sun is shining and the wind is blowing. In particular, the best place in the United States to produce solar energy is in the Southwest, and the best place for wind power is on the Great Plains.

Both of these regions, however, are far from the country's population centers (with the exception of southern California). In our present electric energy grid, it would be highly costly to transmit electricity over long distances. The wires heat up and much of the energy is thus lost in long-distance transmission.

So within the confines of the existing grid, the sites of generation must be close to the sites of use. This generally means that, for example, along the East Coast, a major reliance on wind and solar would have to be substantially supplemented with fossil fuel generation or other sources of green energy (e.g., hydropower) when the sun isn't shining and when the wind isn't blowing.

And it gets worse. Currently, this supplementary role is often played by gas "peaker" generation—that is, generation of electricity at peak demand times. Gas peaker generation is quite costly, about four times as costly as solar or wind generation. (See Table 1.) Currently, where low-cost green energy generation has become a significant part of generation, the price to consumers has not dropped, in part because some electricity generation still comes from costly peaker plants. Generation by these plants is so expensive because it requires that an entire facility be constructed but only used intermittently—so the fixed costs are spread over a relatively limited amount of output.

Gas peakers might be replaced with some kind of green energy generation—hydro or geothermal, for example. But these sources are not available at all sites, and

---

### AC/DC

Electricity can be transmitted and used as either alternating current (AC) or direct current (DC). An alternating current reverses its direction many times per second. A direct current flows in only one direction. Most machinery, lights, and household equipment run on AC, while items that run on batteries (e.g., cell phones) run on DC. AC can be transformed to DC and vice versa.

In any transmission of electricity—AC or DC—heat is generated and thus some of the electricity is lost in transmission. The current (the flow of electricity) affects the extent of heat generation and thus the loss of electricity in transmission. However, sending electricity with high force—that is, high voltage—allows electricity to be sent at a lower current. Thus, there is less heat generated per unit of electricity, which is to say less loss of electrical power in transmission.

Engineers have been able to develop DC transmission lines that can handle very high voltages, higher than can be handled by AC transmission. Thus, DC at high voltage can be transmitted over long distances with less loss than AC. Transmission over long distances, which would be inefficient (i.e., large losses) with AC, is thus efficient with DC.

the construction of large-scale hydropower facilities has its own environmentally destructive aspects—and is unlikely to occur anywhere in the United States. While nuclear power is sometimes advocated as a green option, it has its own well-known safety concerns, and efforts to deal with those concerns have made the cost of nuclear generation almost as high as gas peaker generation.

## Solutions to the Problems?

One potential solution to some of these problems is rebuilding our energy grids (of which there are four for the United States and Canada) and connecting those grids more fully to one another. Currently, transmission within each grid is by alternating current (AC). Electricity can also be transmitted in the form of direct current (DC). DC can be economically transmitted over long distances. For example, on a DC-based grid, energy could be economically transmitted from the Southwest or the Great Plains to the East Coast. The DC could be transmitted at a much higher voltage without loss, as compared to AC. Thus the new system is called high-voltage direct-current transmission, or HVDC. In addition to replacing the existing long-distance transmission lines, DC transmission would require building converter stations at both ends of the lines, to convert generated AC to DC for transmission and then back to AC for use. (See sidebar, "AC/DC.")

Changing the long-distance transmission from AC to DC would be a large and costly undertaking. However, over time the project would pay for itself through the lower-cost provision of electrical energy. Indeed, research by the U.S. Department of Commerce's National Oceanic and Atmospheric Administration (NOAA) found that this could be "the cheapest way to cut emissions," and that the new grid could be established within 15 years. The Department of Energy says that the creation of the HVDC grid would cost only $80 billion, but it could run much higher. For example, Senator Bernie Sanders's presidential campaign advocates putting the new grid underground and estimates a cost of $500 billion. However, NOAA says that consumers would save almost $50 billion per year (to say nothing of the greatly reduced social costs of climate change and health impacts).

There are possible other means by which the limits of green energy could be overcome. For example, when there is extra capacity (lots of sun and wind), water can be pumped up to a high-level reservoir and then released when the bases of green energy go down (a windless night), thus generating electricity by hydropower; the use of this pumping-up process could be expanded. Also, while there are no effective means for storing large amounts of energy, technological advances, including battery systems, are being pursued and could ease, if not eliminate, the intermittency problem of solar and wind power.

## One of Many Steps

Great increases in reliance on green energy are both necessary and possible, and the sharp decline in the costs of solar and wind power are major steps in the right direction. The problems of green energy generation—in particular, the intermittency of supply and the details of HVDC—are still to be solved in practice, but solutions appear both technically and economically feasible, with HVDC transmission a likely basis for progress.

Of course, beyond the green generation of electricity, there are additional steps that are needed to combat climate change. One of those additional steps is connected to green electric energy—namely shifting the basis of our transportation system from oil and gas to electricity. Another is energy conservation, by, for example, extensive programs to improve building insulation. And there is an important role for carbon dioxide sequestration, which would remove large amounts of this main greenhouse gas from the atmosphere through increasing forestation and other means.

## A Basis for Optimism

The costs of establishing green energy as the basis of our lives are not prohibitive. The technology for much of the change is known, and the costs, while large, are not outlandish—especially compared to the costs of no action. It would have been better if we had started to adopt green technology 40 years ago when the major oil companies knew, but hid, that continuing to rely on fossil fuels would cause climate change. But there is still time to take action that could save us from the worst disasters.

There are technical problems that remain to be solved. The lack of sufficient electricity storage capacity is an example. Also, shifting to green energy is not just a matter of replacing existing fossil fuel generation with green sources; there is also the need to provide for major growth in electricity demand, as transportation and heating systems move to electricity. Yet, the progress that has been made in surmounting technical problems in recent years provides a basis for optimism.

Optimism, however, cannot be fully justified unless there is a very large increase in governments' support for the switch to green energy.

Unsolved technical problems and costs are real, but the main barrier to change is political. It is necessary to overcome the great political power of those forces that have an interest in maintaining our energy system as it is—the fossil fuel companies and the many companies, including the financial institutions, tied to the fossil fuel industry. Also, it is essential to ensure that the many people whose jobs are tied to fossil fuels do not bear the brunt of the transition to green energy; placing the burden on them would not only be unfair, but would lead them to resist the necessary changes. ❑

*Sources*: Herman K. Trabish, "Is a national high voltage transmission system the cheapest way to cut emissions?," UtilityDive, Feb. 19, 2016 (utilitydive.com); NOAA Research News, "Rapid, affordable energy transformation possible," Jan. 26, 2016 (research.noaa.gov); Alexander E. MacDonald et al., "Future cost-competitive electricity systems and their impact on U.S. CO2 emissions," Nature Climate Change, May 6, 2016 (doi.org); Brian Murray, "The Paradox of Declining Renewable Costs and Rising Electricity Prices," *Forbes*, June 17, 2019 (forbes.com); U.S. Energy Information Administration (eia. gov); Aleksandra Wisniewska, "Prices are down and capacity is up as solar and wind take hold," *Financial Times*, Nov. 7, 2019 (ft.com).

*Article 12.3*

# IS ECONOMIC GROWTH ENVIRONMENTALLY SUSTAINABLE?

**BY ARTHUR MacEWAN**
*January/February 2018*

Dear Dr. Dollar:

I keep hearing progressive economists talking about environmental sustainability, in particular in the context of the looming catastrophe of global climate change. But when it comes to macroeconomics, they seem to switch to talking "growth, growth, growth." Aren't the two contradictory?
—*Anonymous, Washington, D.C.*

The first law of ecology is that everything is related to everything else.
—Barry Commoner

As is the case with many questions, the answer is "yes and no."

Economic growth of the kind we have had for the last two hundred years—or longer—is in conflict with environmental sustainability. More growth has meant the use of more carbon-based fuels, so this growth has spewed more and more carbon dioxide into the atmosphere—and thus global warming. (Global warming is not the only environmental issue, but it is the danger that threatens the existence of human society as we know it. So let's focus on it here.)

Yet, the carbon intensity of economic growth is not something beyond social control. There are ways to grow—meeting human needs and desires—that greatly reduce, if not eliminate, the global warming impact. Most macroeconomic analyses, however, focus simply on growth without consideration of how this growth would affect the environment. There are two reasons for this error, one bad and one good.

The bad reason is that most economists take the basic arrangements of society for granted. They take the nature of technology as "given," and do not question either the technology itself or the social and political forces that maintain the existing path of technology.

The good reason is that we have more than one problem, and growth can provide positive social outcomes—reducing unemployment, general economic insecurity, and absolute poverty. None of this does any good if we are all soon washed away by rising tides, but it is a good reason that economic growth cannot be jettisoned out of hand.

## Some Context

The environmental impact of human activity can be understood in terms of three factors:

- how many of us there are on the planet (population),
- the amount of output of goods and services produced per person (affluence), and
- the amount of environmental impact per unit of output (technology).

Over time, in terms of environmental impact, all three components of this relationship have gotten worse: population has grown and grown, the world as a whole has become more affluent, and technology has become more carbon intensive (more negative impact per unit of output). To halt global warming, it is necessary to pay attention to each of these factors.

## What Can Change?

Population growth, at least in the long-run, can be reduced. Making contraception safe and widely available can help. Also, increased educational and employment opportunities for women tend to reduce fertility. But many people, especially in the agricultural sectors of low-income economies, choose to have several children. Children are their security, providing more hands to do a family's work and providing support for aging parents. Without greater affluence—hard to attain without economic growth—population will continue to grow. (That the most rapid population growth in the world is centered in African countries, which are among the least prosperous, illustrates the point.)

Curtailing economic growth as a means to contain environmental destruction has at least two main problems. First, unless it involves a massive, global redistribution of income and wealth, it condemns those at the bottom (countries and people) to their current economic level—both morally reprehensible and probably politically impossible. It is also probably politically impossible to overcome the obstacles to a massive redistribution. There are about 7.5 billion people in the world and total production is about $125 trillion, which means that average income is about $16,667. With no growth and redistribution getting everyone to this level, it would be necessary to reduce average income in the United States by over 70%, and in the Euro area and Japan by over 60%.

The second barrier to curtailing growth is that capitalism, which is pretty much the operating system of the whole world these days, is like a bicycle: If it stops, it (and the rider) falls over. The system depends on profits, and profits depend on either growth or redistributing income upward, and the latter has its limits. Getting rid of capitalism, running the world economy a different way, could have salutary results—though other social systems can do, and have done, substantial damage to the environment. Certainly, the political problems of getting rid of capitalism and insuring that its replacement would be environmentally friendly is a politically daunting tasks.

## The Technology Option

Dealing with global warming needs to involve inhibiting population growth and curtailing economic growth—which means at least sharply constraining capitalism. But that's not enough. There need to be dramatic changes in the technology. At the present time, the most promising energy production technologies are wind power and photovoltaics. Also, energy conservation has great potential for reducing the emissions of greenhouse gases.

The effectiveness of the technology option has been demonstrated in other countries. As Frank Ackerman points out in "Are Nuclear Plant Closures a Mistake?" (Article 5.3), renewable electricity generation expanded from 5% of total German power consumption in 1999 to over 30% in 2015. Over the same period, Ackerman concludes, "there has been no increase in [carbon] emisions from the electric sector ... [and] the reliability of the German electric system has continued to improve."

The problem, then, is not so much technical (i.e., developing ways to reduce emissions). The problem is political. Halting subsidies to the fossil fuel industries and providing support for environmentally friendly technological change would be good beginnings. Also, a great deal could be accomplished through encouragement of energy conservation programs. Further steps will require major limitations on firms' operations, limitations that prevent them from ignoring the health, safety, and, ultimately, the survival of the populations. A difficult task, of course, but we really have no choice. ❑

Article 12.4

# AUSTERITY-OBSESSED EUROPE COULD COMBAT CLIMATE CHANGE WITHOUT RAISING TAXES

## BY DEAN BAKER
September 2019, Truthout

In the United States, there has been much attention given to the various proposals for a Green New Deal. While there have been legitimate questions about paying for a large push to reduce greenhouse gas emissions, many accept the need for such measures for the survival of the planet.

However, there has been less attention paid to the failure of European countries to act in this area, in spite of the fact that a substantial program would be virtually costless for Europe. There has been far more attention paid to the politics around Brexit in the United Kingdom than to the important question of how Europe will address global warming.

Just to be clear, the European countries have been far better global citizens in this area than the United States. Their per-person emissions are roughly half as much as the United States. Furthermore, many European countries have already taken aggressive measures to promote clean energy and encourage conservation.

But in the battle to slow global warming, simply doing better than the United States is not good enough. The European Union can and must do more to reduce its greenhouse gas emissions.

This is where the continent's mindless push for austerity comes into the picture. European governments, led by Germany, have become obsessed with keeping deficits low and balancing budgets. Most have small deficits or even budget surpluses.

Germany exemplifies the European austerity obsession with a budget surplus that is close to 2.0% of GDP ($420 billion in the U.S. economy). To some extent, fiscal austerity is not a choice. The eurozone's rules require low budget deficits for the countries that use the euro, but even countries outside the eurozone have joined the austerity party. The United Kingdom has a budget deficit of less than 1.5% of GDP, Denmark less than 0.5% of GDP, and Sweden has a budget surplus of close to 0.5% of GDP.

There are certainly circumstances under which budget deficits can be too high, but these clearly do not apply to the countries in the European Union at present. Inflation has been persistently low and has been falling in recent months. The inflation rate for the eurozone countries has averaged just 1.0% over the last 12 months.

The story is even more dramatic if we look at interest rates. The classic problem of a large budget deficit is that it leads to high interest rates that crowd out investment. Not only are interest rates extraordinarily low across Europe, in many countries, investors have to pay governments to lend them money.

The interest rate on a 10-year government bond in France is -0.43%. In the Netherlands, it is -0.57%, and in Germany it is -0.71%. That means investors have to pay Germany 0.71% annually to lend the government money.

This is the context in which the concern for low budget deficits in these countries is utterly mindless. The financial markets are effectively begging these governments to borrow more money, but they refuse to do so.

The need to address global warming makes this refusal especially painful. The fact that interest rates and inflation are so low indicates that these governments are needlessly sacrificing growth and jobs. That story is bad enough, but the picture is much worse when we consider the pressing need to address global warming.

These governments could either pay directly to install solar and wind power, or provide large subsidies to businesses and homeowners. They could be subsidizing the switch to electric cars and making mass transit cheap or free, while they vastly ramp up capacity. They could also be providing large subsidies to countries in the global South to take the same measures, and to also save the rainforest in the Amazon.

The best part of this story is that they don't need to raise taxes to pay for this spending. There is considerable slack in these economies, which means that they can devote several hundred billion dollars annually to slow global warming without requiring additional taxes from their populations. It is possible that a really ambitious program, which might be needed, will require additional tax revenue, but for now, these countries are needlessly leaving money on the table while the planet burns.

It is common in policy circles to ridicule U.K. Prime Minister Boris Johnson for his seemingly mindless pursuit of Brexit. While Johnson surely deserves much ridicule, the proponents of austerity deserve a much larger dose. Keeping people out of work by failing to take more aggressive steps to address global warming is far more clownish than anything that Boris Johnson is doing with Brexit. ❑

*Article 12.5*

# WHY SOME LEADERS IN POORER COUNTIRES ARE CHAMPIONING THE ENVIRONMENT

## BY ROBIN BROAD AND JOHN CAVANAGH

*July 2015; Triple Crisis Blog*

We have heard surprise expressed that two religious leaders from poorer countries, Pope Francis from Argentina and Cardinal Turskon from Ghana, have emerged as leading voices for action on the environment with their compelling June 2015 encyclical. The surprise comes from the assumption that poorer countries invariably prioritize economic growth and financial revenues—not the environment—and that only when beyond a certain threshold of per capita income do they shift priorities and take action in favor of the environment. As many readers know, this theory that only richer people in richer countries care about the environment is what some call the Environmental Kuznets Curve or the post-materialist hypothesis.

Our research on decisive action to protect the environment in El Salvador and Costa Rica suggests that this stereotype is outdated and the theory wrong. We zeroed in on El Salvador and Costa Rica because both have halted potentially lucrative metallic mining within the last decade due to its negative environmental impact.

In our new article in the journal *World Development,* we ask "why did these two governments do this?" Our goal now is to share our answers to that question. We posit three conditions under which governments of poorer countries take action to protect the environment, at times sacrificing large-scale financial gain:

1) The first condition is related to civil society: Poorer people, whose natural resource base is threatened by mining, can move from individual awareness to concern, to become organized, and then to engage with other sectors of civil society in pressuring their government to implement policy changes. This involves a combination of poorer people who have lived in the area long enough to grasp the environmental damage, with other segments of domestic civil society providing additional support and voice. Organizing begins locally in the mining areas but moves to a national level, putting pressure on governments.

2) The second condition is related to domestic business elites: In our case studies, we find that segments of the domestic economic elite who have interests based in protecting natural resources are more powerful than the elite and corporate interests that benefit from exploiting minerals. The power of global corporations is not strong enough, or is not connected enough to local economic elites, to change this calculus. Thus, foreign mining firms that want to mine often move from the national level (where they have not been successful) into the global arena, where they sue the governments under investment agreements and investor-state dispute structures.

3) The third condition is related to governments: We find that individuals and agencies within democratic governments who are willing and able not only to respond to civil society, but also to understand the ecological realities of natural-resource exploitation, can play a central role. We also find that far-sighted political leaders or bureaucrats, regardless of their party's politics, who come into office with either an understanding of environmental issues or a willingness to listen to non-governmental experts, can also become catalysts.

In both Salvadoran and Costa Rican mining policy, all three of these conditions came into play and reinforced one another, leading to decisive government action to halt environmentally destructive mining. In both countries, there was strong local citizen opposition to mining that combined with other civil society actors to form powerful national movements against mining. In El Salvador, rural farmers and communities provided the initial spark, with the church playing a significant integral role. In Costa Rica, rural communities were crucial, but urban environmentalists played an important role, as did academics and the media.

In terms of the business sector: in both countries, local and national business interests collectively had more to lose than gain from industrial mining and its ensuing environmental damage. In El Salvador, the farming and tourism sectors need water that mining seemed likely to further contaminate. The economic elites connected to these sectors were more numerous and powerful than local businesses that would benefit from foreign mining companies gaining mining concessions. In Costa Rica, the many sectors that benefit from eco-tourism (and agriculture) are similarly more numerous and powerful than the relatively small mining sector.

As for government, in both countries, at different times, there were key individuals and sometimes whole agencies within government who spoke out or took action against mining.

Comparing the influence of the three conditions: The first two conditions, strong civil society and weak pro-mining domestic business elites, seem particularly important since the recent histories of both El Salvador and Costa Rica reveal much more variation within key government agencies during the period in question. In El Salvador, even a relatively corrupt and pro-foreign business administration such as Antonio Saca's (2004-2009) could take action against gold mining given the country's strong civil society and weak pro-mining national business elites in the context of the country's extreme environmental degradation. In this case, individuals in the Saca government did indeed make a difference. And, in Costa Rica, there is the two-year period of 2008-2010 when, even with strong civil society, weak pro-mining national business elites, and a democratic government, the administration of Óscar Arias (who one might have assumed to be more pro-environment than the Saca administration) gave permission for Canadian firm Infinito Gold to mine at a very controversial site. Yet, even in this instance, a strong civil society and an independent Supreme Court eventually overturned Arias's pro-mining policies and stopped Infinito's mining.

The key point is that these two governments halted environmentally destructive gold mining even though both are relatively poor, small countries which would, according to conventional theory, choose short-term economic gains over longer-term environmental concerns.

Based on this work, we were not at all surprised that it was two religious leaders from poorer countries who have emerged as among the most vocal voices for action on environment (including climate). ❑

*Sources:* Robin Broad, "The Poor and the Environment: Friends or foes?" *World Development,* 22(6), June 1994; Robin Broad, "Corporate Bias in the World Bank Group's International Centre for Settlement of Investment Disputes: A Case Study of a Global Mining Corporation Suing El Salvador," *University of Pennsylvania Journal of International Law* 36 (2015); Robin Broad and John Cavanagh, "El Salvador Gold: Toward a Mining Ban," in Thomas Princen, Jack P. Martin, and Pamela L. Manno, eds., *Ending the Fossil Fuel Era* (MIT Press, 2015).

*Article 12.6*

# FARMERS HALT A LAND-GRAB IN MOZAMBIQUE

**BY TIMOTHY A. WISE**
*October 2018, Food Tank*

On July 26, 2018, farmers in Xai-Xai, Mozambique, achieved a milestone. They met to formalize their new farmers' association, elect leaders, and prepare a petition to the local government for land. The association, christened Tsakane, which means "happy" in the local Changana language, was the culmination of six years of resistance to a Chinese land-grab that had sparked protest and outrage. The association now has a request pending for its own land.

With the Chinese rice plantation floundering, the Tsakane farmers offer a vivid demonstration that perhaps the best way to grow more food is to give poor food producers more land.

## The Rise and Fall of a Land-Grab

I first visited the vast rice fields of Xai-Xai, three hours up the coast from the capital city of Maputo, in 2017. Since 2008, Mozambique had been one of the leading targets of large-scale agricultural investment projects, widely denounced as land-grabs by critics. Community resistance had halted most such projects in Mozambique, including ProSAVANA, the controversial Brazil-Japan initiative, which was intended to be the largest land-grab in Africa.

This one had taken hold. The Wanbao Grain and Oil company had taken over a Chinese "friendship farm" in 2011 with a 50-year lease on a 50,000-acre concession from the Mozambique government as part of the Lower Limpopo Irrigation District (RBL for its Portuguese name). With Chinese state financing, the company contracted the farming to four Chinese agriculture groups, developing 17,000 acres into rice fields fed by rehabilitated colonial-era irrigation canals.

On paper, the Wanbao Africa Agriculture Development Limited (WAADL) promised what large-scale foreign investment in agriculture might offer to a poor, hungry, underdeveloped country like Mozambique. Here was desperately needed capital invested in underutilized fertile land, rebuilding productive infrastructure and bringing in modern agricultural practices. Wanbao was training local farmers in its modern farming methods and setting them up as contract farmers with a stake in the project. What's more, the project wasn't growing cash crops, it was growing food. And not for people back in China, as the land-grab stereotype suggested; it was growing rice for the Mozambican market.

Heavily promoted by Mozambique's president at the time, Armando Guebuza, the rice was marketed under his recommended brand name, "Bom Gusto," meaning Good Taste.

That wasn't the taste left in the mouths of women who had lost their land, then fought to get it back.

## No Consultation or Consent

The difference between a large-scale agricultural development project and a land-grab is consultation and consent, and this one had neither. Some 7,000 farmers had moved onto the irrigated lands along the Lower Limpopo River in the 1980s after a state farm ceased operations. Farmers there told us they were encouraged to do so by the local government. Many crossed a small bridge built for them by the government to farm rice, maize, and vegetables or to graze their cattle.

Mozambique's Land Law is one of the most progressive in Africa, recognizing the land rights of peasant farmers whether or not they can show formal title, as long as they have been farming the land for 10 years or more. That applies not only to community or village land, it applies to estate land for which the government holds the formal land title.

Once Wanbao got its land concession, it wasted no time ignoring the Land Law. The bulldozers were there by early 2012. Gizela Zunguze, Gender Coordinator from Justica Ambiental (JA), the Friends of the Earth affiliate in Mozambique, took us to meet some of the farmers affected by the project.

In the dusty courtyard under the shade of a mango tree in the neighborhood of Brutela, Meldina Matsimbe told us she and other farmers had gone down to their lowland fields in January 2012 to find tractors opening roads and irrigation ditches across their fields, planted in maize, cowpeas, and vegetables. "They plowed right through ripe maize," Matsimbe told us through a translator. Two other women from the village nodded. There had been no consultation with the community, no warning, and no environmental impact assessment, as required by Mozambican law.

With JA's support, the community protested to the company and the local government authorities. The bulldozers stopped, and government authorities returned most of the land—250 acres used by about 60 families in the community. But some 12 acres still had not been returned.

What did they eat that year after their crops had been destroyed?

"We had nothing to eat," Matsimbe said. "We had to ask our neighbors for food."

Angélica Moyane told us a similar story in the neighboring village of Kana Kana. One Sunday in July 2013, a tractor came in unannounced and plowed right through the community's fields, destroying her garlic, lettuce, maize, onions, and cabbage along with the ripe crops of some 500 other farmers. "We could not even identify our own farms after the Chinese came through," she said.

Zunguze said JA found Mama Angélica and other farmers camped outside a government office in Xai-Xai demanding answers. Wanbao withdrew its machines a few days later and farmers returned to their ravaged fields. As in Brutela, the company offered no compensation for the destroyed crops, so crucial to small-scale farmers who live from one harvest to the next.

Frustrated by Wanbao's repeated incursions, the communities organized a march past the Wanbao offices and through the town on May 20, 2014, to the state governor's office to present a formal petition demanding the return of their land with compensation. Zunguze said the protest was tense, with 400 angry community members marching toward the provincial offices behind a "No to Wanbao" banner. Placards, most hand-written, demanded an end to land-grabbing. "We demand respect for our rights," read one woman's simple plea. Police tried to halt the march, but after a three-hour standoff, the marchers proceeded to the governor's office where Mama Angélica presented the petition.

The farmers never got a formal response, but the company land-grabbing slowed. The farmers could certainly take pride in resisting this land-grab, but their hard lives were no easier now.

## Failure to Yield

For better or for worse, Wanbao seemed to be failing, like so many other large-scale agriculture projects in Africa. In 2013, just as the project was bringing more of its acreage into production, floods destroyed 12,500 of the company's 17,000 acres of rice. The Chinese government canceled a loan in 2015 after concluding that the flood risks were too high. Climate change added insult to injury when a 2016 drought slowed the recovery from the flooding.

In April 2017, the only rice being produced was by contract farmers and some Indians who were subcontracting land. Even the outgrower farmers were dropping out. Wanbao had trained 68 local farmers and had gotten the more successful of them producing on five to ten acres each. But the company ran the outgrower scheme as a commercial operation, charging for services like plowing. They provided credit but required a 50% up-front cash payment for inputs, which was difficult for many farmers to afford. Farmers were obligated to sell to the company, and Wanbao paid a fixed and low price for the farmers' rice, regardless of market prices.

Contract farmer Boavida Madonda of Chimbonhanine told us that Wanbao paid well below market prices, was unreliable in getting seeds and inputs to them on time, and even expected farmers to arrange their own transportation to get inputs to their farms.

"It really isn't worth it," he said. He told us he wouldn't care if the project failed. "It was better before. I was my own boss. We had enough to eat."

When I returned in October 2017, Wanbao still had not secured financing, though there were always rumors of new money. But the project seemed to be failing. That would be a victory of sorts for the communities, but a hollow one. What would the community have to show for another failed project?

Zunguze was quick and firm when I asked her what the farmers wanted: "Give all the land back to the communities."

## Let Farmers Grow Food

Lost in Wanbao's struggle to finance the project and the Mozambican government's continued commitment to it was an obvious question: Wouldn't the land feed more hungry Mozambicans if the company left and local farmers were organized to grow rice and other food crops?

I'd seen exactly that, in fact, in Marracuene, just two hours down the highway toward Maputo. There I saw 7,000 farmers, mostly women, organized into 19 cooperatives and using rehabilitated colonial-era irrigation to grow food and cash crops year-round. Those women-led coops, affiliated with the National Peasant Union of Mozambique (UNAC), were growing food while improving the land with the adoption of intercropping and other agro-ecological practices. (See earlier articles here and here.)

Instead of giving all the best land and infrastructure—particularly irrigation—to foreign investors who then displace local farmers, why not give the land to those farmers? Help them organize into marketing cooperatives, water use associations, and credit unions. With the formal recognition of the Tsakane Farmers' Association, the Xai-Xai farmers are planning to do just that. They hope to get collective land title to 750 acres of good land for their 300 members.

"If the associations are registered and the farmers have collective rights to some land, maybe the land-grabbing can stop," Zunguze told me. Association leaders planned to visit neighboring National Farmers Union cooperatives to learn how agro-ecology could help them grow more food for their families and communities. ❑

# Chapter 13

# RESISTANCE AND ALTERNATIVES

Article 13.1

## EQUALITY, SOLIDARITY, SUSTAINABILITY

### AN INTERVIEW WITH JAYATI GHOSH
January/February 2015

*Jayati Ghosh is a professor of economics at the Centre for Economic Studies and Planning, Jawaharlal Nehru University, in New Delhi, India. She is a member of the Executive Committee of International Development Economics Associates (IDEAs), a global network of economists devoted to developing "alternatives to the current mainstream economic paradigm as formulated by the neoliberal orthodoxy." In this wide-ranging interview, Professor Ghosh addresses major challenges of global economic development, environmental sustainability, and global solidarity: the transfiguration of the world capitalist economy today (along with the reproduction of structures like the division between the wealthy "core" and exploited "periphery"), the prospects for the transformation and revival of socialist movements, the difficulties and possibility of overcoming divisions within the working class at the national and global levels, and the way forward towards egalitarian and sustainable societies. —Eds.*

**D&S:** We are scarcely two decades removed from the supposed global triumph of capitalism, the death of socialism, and (maximum hubris) proclamations of the "end of history." And yet we're seeing a revival of socialist movements—what you have called the "emerging left in the emerging world." What are the key factors explaining this revival?

**JG:** I think it is now becoming more evident to most people across the world that global capitalism—especially in its current neoliberal manifestation—is not likely to deliver genuinely better material conditions, security, and justice. This is generally still a largely inchoate and diffuse sense of unhappiness with the state of things in many parts of the

331

world. It is true that in some regions, like Latin America, there is a more developed sense of how neoliberal policies pushed the advance of aggressive and extremely unequal capitalist forces.

This emerging left has many features that distinguish it from the earlier, more centralizing and in some ways less socially sensitive left that characterized the second half of the 20$^{th}$ century in particular. For example, there is some rejection of top-down models of party organization which often distorted the idea of the Leninist vanguard, and greater respect for a plurality of opinions, even as many of these movements are more actively engaged in processes of electoral democracy. The language of human rights is explicitly used in these political formations, which in turn demands the recognition of a greater variety of identities that go beyond the class identities that were the standard form of division. So the rights of women, of indigenous communities, of marginalized groups within society in general, are more explicitly recognized. A specific concern regarding human interaction with nature is also an important element, tempering the earlier somewhat simplistic celebration of technology and human ingenuity, which was seen as trumping the requirements and rights of nature.

It is interesting that these features are to be found in new social and political movements in many parts of the world. They are found not just in Latin America, where they also were associated with some amount of political transformation and shifts in economic strategies, but also among movements in countries as far apart as Thailand, Spain, and South Africa.

*D&S:* The same does not seem to be true to nearly the same extent in the so-called "core" countries of Western Europe or North America. Why is that? And if the current crisis can't spark a profound questioning of capitalism, and discussion of alternatives to it, what can?

**JG:** It seems to me that in the core capitalist countries the left in every shape or form has taken a long time to recover from the existential blows delivered by the collapse of "socialism" in the Soviet Union and Eastern Europe, and the very market-oriented moves of Communist regimes in East Asia, including China and Vietnam. Interestingly, this blow has affected even those leftists who had rejected these models as not reflecting true socialism at all.

The social and political ascendancy of capitalism, despite its major recent crises and continuing inability to deliver either inclusive growth or social justice, is largely because of this sense that the alternative proved to be so apparently unpleasant and so different from original expectation. So there is some questioning of capitalism, but no real belief in a viable socialist alternative. This may be why the anger and resistance to the effects of the way capitalism functions is now finding expression in more right-wing responses, which are superficially anti-capitalist but essentially focused on symptoms of the problem and on blaming perceived "others," like immigrants.

*D&S:* A half century ago, the most influential radical view of economic "underdevelopment" focused on the dominance of industrial-manufacturing "core" economies over raw-materials-producing "periphery." Has that story changed in the current era of neo-liberal globalization, with many developing countries moving out of mineral and agricultural exports and into export-oriented manufacturing (often "offshored")?

**JG:** Geographical and locational changes in productive structures do not negate the idea of "core" and "periphery" operating within capitalism. Global capitalism has, throughout its history, experienced such shifts.

First, despite the so-called shift in economic power between developed and "emerging" nations, the material differences between these countries remain very large. Second, the big engine of global manufacturing growth in the developing world, China, has emerged on the basis of a very different economic system, in which market forces have been shaped by the prevailing political and institutional relations, the control of a central party and the advantages of a broadly egalitarian system bequeathed by the Communist revolution. China's engagement with global markets therefore was on very different terms, unlike those of most primary product exporters. This has certainly enabled some productive relocation—but the idea that all other developing countries can follow a similar trajectory is misplaced. Even insertion into global value chains at lower levels can have the effects of perpetuating the unequal relations that propelled such insertion in the first place. Third, the production of underdevelopment is unfortunately not a process that has ended—it still persists, though sometimes in unlikely and unexpected ways. The core and periphery within the eurozone provides a striking example.

**D&S:** Another major aspect of radical economists' thinking about development in the "Third World" centered on the problem of the unequal distribution of wealth—especially the unequal ownership of agricultural land. Does the distribution of land remain a central issue in the global South? Has it declined in importance in more urbanized and non-agricultural regions?

**JG:** The idea that the distribution of wealth (including land) has become less important in contemporary capitalism is completely wrong. The talk of capitalism generating a new kind of productive system that relies on "knowledge" to transform material reality is similarly misleading. The rapacious exploitation of nature remains a central requirement of the capitalist system, and that in turn means that the need to control nature, to privatize it and make its ownership concentrated. This is actually true in all parts of the world, but in developing countries it is most directly evident.

Unequal control over land, water, and other resources is a huge impediment to real development for many reasons. Of course it has an adverse impact on agricultural productivity and the expansion of the home market, thereby impeding industrialization—but that is only one problem. It is significant that all the developing countries that have progressed in terms of industrial transformation, South Korea and China, for example, are those that experienced far-reaching land reforms including land redistribution at the start of the development project. Otherwise, landlordism creates not just economic obstacles but also socio-political impediments to industrialization and modernization, and allows the persistence of reactionary social features. India is a good example of this.

**D&S:** The ways that capitalism has linked together economies all over the world—trade in goods, international investment, international migration—directly pose the need for labor internationalism. Is it possible to develop the necessary kinds of labor solidarity when that means reaching across divides, say, between native and immigrant, or the workers of one country and with those of another country half a world away?

**JG:** It is obviously necessary for such bonds to be forged—it is even essential, because global forces cannot be fought only within nation states. But clearly such bonds are getting harder to forge. However, that is not only because of the material reality of physical differences and geographical distances. It is also—and possibly more crucially—because of changing perceptions of community, identity, oneness, and difference among various social groups. So workers from different countries see themselves as competing against one another in the struggle to keep their jobs and prevent their wages from falling.

A major role in this division across workers is unfortunately played by media, which wittingly (and sometimes unwittingly) transmits and disseminates a discourse in which workers of one country, region, or type are pitted against other workers, and in which they are then seen as the enemy that must be fought. This obfuscatory role played by the corporatized media is of course extremely useful for capitalism, for the agents of global finance and other large capital, because it succeeds in diverting and distracting from the real problems. Obviously, the left in different parts of the world has not just to express clearly the fallacies associated with such a position, but to think creatively about how to give that critique the widest possible traction and publicity.

**D&S:** How can we square development objectives—including a dramatic increase in standards of living in lower-income countries—with environmental sustainability? Is there a way to sustainably bring the entire world up to rich-country levels? Or should we also be imagining a massive global redistribution of income and wealth, equalizing per capita incomes of global North and South somewhere in the middle?

**JG:** In developing countries, the most important goals are to help people adapt to climate changes that we already see and to find ways of mitigation without burdening the poor or preventing their access to essential goods and services. This is important because, even in "emerging" economies, the development project is far from complete, with many millions—the majority of the people—excluded from the minimum conditions for a decent and secure life that ensures dignity and allows creativity. Bringing the vast majority of the developing world's population to anything resembling a minimally acceptable standard of living will involve extensive use of global resources. It will necessarily imply more natural resource use and more carbon emissions. So we have to reduce resource use and emissions elsewhere and in other activities, and re-orient growth in cleaner and greener directions.

In terms of economic strategy, this probably requires policies at several different levels. To start with, the orientation of economic policies and public perception must shift away from the single-minded obsession with GDP growth. For this to happen, it is necessary to develop a set of quantifiable measures of genuine human progress, based as far as possible on objective criteria describing conditions of life (not GDP), which can be regularly estimated and monitored to hold governments and other agents accountable.

Ways of production must change. In agriculture it would be necessary to promote actively the viability of sustainable food production with small holder cultivation that can cope with the greater incidence of climate variability. It is also necessary to reduce and regulate corporate power in food and other productive industries, as well as in finance, so that undesirable forms of consumption and production are not promoted or perpetuated. For all production, the shift from carbon-based production to renewable energy-based activities needs to be encouraged.

The ways in which we organise our physical conditions of life and work also need to change. This can include focussing on urban planning and management that reduces resource use and deals better with waste of all kinds; and emphasising clean, efficient and affordable public transport systems rather than allow polluting and congesting private transport systems. Clearly, protecting and nurturing dwindling water resources and preventing privatized over-exploitation of this and other key gifts of nature is essential.

This is not possible without a simultaneous attack on the growing inequality evident in most societies. Income and asset inequalities generate unsustainable consumption patterns among the privileged and create the desire for them among others. This has to be reduced by using explicitly redistributive measures, fiscal incentives such taxes and subsidies, patterns of public spending more directed to improving conditions of worse-off groups, and improvement of the conditions of work through better regulation and protection of wage workers and the small self-employed.

At the global level, this also requires fighting the monopoly of knowledge and control over technology created by the regime of intellectual property rights and ensuring greater access to relevant "green" technologies to developing countries. And this in turn is part of a broader need to resist and control international trade and investment patterns that create incentives for over-exploiting people and nature.

**D&S:** The problems we face are not going to be solved overnight, and certainly the world is not going to be transformed overnight. What do you think are the most important changes that we need to start making now, though, to see a world more like the one we want—more egalitarian, democratic, cooperative, and sustainable—forty or fifty years from now?

**JG:** For me, the desired goal for an ideal society would be one in which some things that you cannot control—where you are born, what you are born as, the family into which you are born—do not affect your basic conditions of life—having a secure home; peace and security; access to nutritious food and other basic requirements for good health; access to education; opportunities for work, leisure, self-expression, and social participation.

This would not mean putting an end to all social and cultural differences, because after all, that is what makes life interesting. But it would mean that your life chances are not fundamentally different because of accidents of birth. So if you are born as a girl of a minority ethnic group in a rural area of a poor region, you would still have access to minimum conditions of life and opportunities for developing your capabilities that are not too different from a boy born in a well-off household of a dominant social group in an affluent society. This would obviously require a certain organization of both economy and society.

To begin with, it would mean that economic arrangements would not be oriented around the simple expansion of aggregate incomes and profits as the most significant goals. It is actually irrational to be obsessed with GDP growth. Consider just one example: a chaotic, polluting, congested, and frustrating system of privatized urban transport generates much more GDP than a clean, efficient, affordable, and "green" system of public transport. This in turn means that other goals would matter: reasonable living conditions for all, development of people's capabilities and space for their creativity, decent employment opportunities, safe and clean environments.

Access to the essentials of life—food, water, basic housing, and so on—would not be determined by the ability to pay but treated as human rights, made available to all in an affordable way. Ensuring this does not mean eliminating market forces altogether. Rather, market forces that help in achieving these goals would be encouraged, while those that operate to reduce standards of living and quality of life of ordinary people would be regulated, restricted, or even abolished.

Extreme inequalities would not be tolerated. Systems of taxation and distribution, as well as methods of monitoring and regulating pay and other returns, would ensure that material differences between people did not grow too large. Social discrimination and exclusion of all kinds would be actively discouraged and sought to be done away with. In addition, in these economic and social arrangements there would be much greater social respect for nature. Economic activities would be monitored and assessed for the damage they do to nature, with a focus on reducing this as much as possible.

All this means that governments would obviously be much more important. So they would have to be more genuinely democratic, transparent, and accountable, and adjust policies to changing conditions. There would be more people's voice and participation in the decisions that affect their lives. Governments would respect both the collective rights and concerns of groups and communities as well as the individual rights of all citizens. For these to be possible within one country, it would be necessary for international political and economic arrangements to support the possibility of such societies emerging and being sustained, without the threat of destabilizing trade and capital flows or military aggression.

At least some of these goals are not so hard to achieve, after all. And for the more ambitious goals, it only requires more people everywhere to share them and strive to achieve them. ❑

*Article 13.2*

# RESPONDING TO COVID-19
*A Review of Cuba's Strategy*

## BY ZAEEM HASSAN MEHMOOD
*June 2020,* Modern Diplomacy

The Republic of Cuba is an archipelago that is home to 11.27 million inhabitants and is located in the Caribbean. The country's universal health care system is considered one of its greatest achievements. It was borne out of a socialist ideology which envisioned health care accessibility as a fundamental right for all Cuban citizens. In 2014, during an official visit to Cuba, United Nations Secretary General Ban Ki-moon described the country's health care system as "a model for many countries" to follow. The Latin American School of Medicine (Escuela Latinoamericana de Medicina) is one of the largest medical schools in the region, and each year hosts thousands of students from over 100 different countries, including those from the United States and Europe. As a result, a number of low-income families from across the world have benefited from Cuba's medical schools. In the past, Cuban health workers have contributed to the elimination of polio, tuberculosis, typhoid fever, and diphtheria. During the coronavirus pandemic, health care workers were sent to at least 21 countries by the government, most notably to Italy and South Africa. President Miguel Díaz-Canel of Cuba has recently declared Covid-19 as "under control in the country." In light of the above developments, this article provides an analysis of the policies adopted by Cuba to contain Covid-19.

## Strategies Adopted to Contain Covid-19

Before Cuba closed its borders last spring, the country increased monitoring at ports, airports, and marinas. During this period, travelers arriving with symptoms were hospitalized and placed in isolation for at least 14 days. The people who were most prone to be carrying Covid-19 were identified and government health agencies created a database to keep track of individuals coming from high-risk countries. They were then placed in isolation centers for diagnosis and the use of real-time polymerase chain reaction (RT-PCR) tests. Health professionals also carried out post-mortems of people who died with respiratory or diarrheal symptoms to identify virus circumstances and patterns. For the broader Cuban population, the health system launched a case-detection strategy that combined door-to-door screenings and testing by RT-PCR. Tens of thousands of doctors, nurses, and medical students went door-to-door on a daily basis to actively screen all Cuban residents for Covid-19 symptoms. It was reported that up to 2.5 million people were screened each day. When a case was confirmed, contact tracing was used to identify people who had come into contact with the person who was infected with Covid-19. These policy steps resulted in the early identification of cases. Patients who tested positive for Covid-19 were hospitalized for at least 15 days, and if they were declared symptom-free by the end of this period, they were once more tested by RT-PCR. If the results were negative, they were discharged and allowed to return to their home and required to limit their activities for another 15-day period. After this time, the patient would receive another RT-PCR test, and if the test was negative, they could return to their normal activities. However, if the test was positive, it was repeated again in five days and if it was still positive the patient was readmitted to the hospital until the test was negative.

An intense media campaign was also initiated by the Cuban government to inform the public about the dangers of Covid-19 and necessary precautions to prevent the spread of the virus. Scientists and medical practitioners affiliated with various organizations teamed up with BioCubaFarma, a Cuban biotechnology company, to develop a Covid-19 vaccine. Work was also carried out to develop digital applications that allow people with Covid-19 symptoms to communicate with health professionals and receive medical instructions. The success of these policies has been a direct a result of collaboration between local communities and national government agencies.

Cuban policymakers continue to be critical of the decades-old U.S. trade embargo, which poses a serious problem for Cuban biotechnology's efforts to develop a vaccine. Nevertheless, Cuba was able to upgrade its diagnostic lab facilities in Havana so that the National Civil Defense Scientific Research Center now has the capacity to process 1,000 RT-PCR tests daily. The first shipment of RT-PCR test kits came through the Pan American Health Organization (PAHO), and additional shipments were later received from China. In order to address the supply shortage of personal protective equipment, Cuba has also started domestically producing specialized gowns, aprons, masks, goggles, and face shields in order to ensure that people working in health care services are protected.

## Cuba's 'Anti-Covid-19 Cocktail'

Cuba's success in responding to Covid-19 has largely been a result of the country's universal health care system. Cuba also has a notable history of innovative medical research. In 1985, it created the first and only vaccine against meningitis B. Cuban scientists have also developed new treatments for hepatitis B, diabetic foot, vitiligo, and psoriasis. A lifesaving lung cancer vaccine was developed by Cuba that was subsequently imported by the United States. Cuba was also the first country to eliminate the transmission of HIV and syphilis from mother to child, an achievement recognized by World Health Organization (WHO) in 2015.

It is reported that Cuban biotechnology has developed drugs that have already been effective in fighting Covid-19 in China and other countries. According to the Director of Epidemiology at Cuba's Ministry of Health, Francisco Durán, drugs are in development stage "to improve innate immunity." These include Interferon Alpha

2B, which was created in the 1980s in collaboration with scientists in Helsinki to combat a dengue outbreak. It is currently being produced through a joint venture with a Chinese company. Cuba is also developing new varieties of Interferon in order to improve its effectiveness against Covid-19. Cuban institutes are also producing another domestically manufactured drug, CIGB 258, which was already under development prior to the pandemic for the treatment of rheumatoid arthritis. Duran stated, "These and other drugs, almost all manufactured and patented in Cuba, are components of the island's anti-Covid-19 cocktail." According to John Hopkins University, Cuba has had a case-fatality rate of just 1.7%, compared to 2.1% in the United States and 2.7% in Spain, according to Johns Hopkins University. ❑

**Sources**: Trading Economics, "Cuban Population: 1960-2019 Data," (tradingeconomics.com); WION, "Cuba's 'El Comandante': Castro's revolutionary mark on history," (wionews.com); The Editors of Encyclopaedia Britannica, "Cuban Revolution," *Encyclopedia Britannica*, July 19, 2020 (britannica.com); MEDICC, "UN Secretary-General Applauds Efforts of Cuban Medical School to Improve Health Worldwide," February 7, 2014 (medicc.org); Tom Phillips and Angela Giuffrida, "'Doctor diplomacy': Cuba seeks to make its mark in Europe amid Covid-19 crisis," *The Guardian*, May 6, 2020 (theguardian.com); Nelson Acosta and Sarah Marsh, "Closing in on all sides: Cuba nears declaring coronavirus victory," Reuters, June 8, 2020, (reuters.com); Ed Augustin, "Cuba sets example with successful programme to contain coronavirus," *The Guardian*, June 7, 2020 (theguardian.com); Jessie Yeung, Adam Renton, and Rob Picheta, "May 20 Coronavirus News - Cuba goes a week without a single coronavirus death," CNN, May 21, 2020 (cnn.com); The Caribbean Council, "Cuba's biopharma sector increasing production to meet coronavirus challenge," (caribbean-council.org); M. Barrry, "Effect of the U.S. embargo and economic decline on health in Cuba," *Annals of Internal Medicine*, January 18, 2020; Our Hannah Ritchie, Esteban Ortiz-Ospina, et al., "Statistics and Research: Coronavirus (COVID-19) Testing," World in Data, November 16, 2020 (ourworldindata.org); Nereida Rojo Pérez, Carmen Valenti Pérez, et al., "Science and technological innovation in health in Cuba: results in selected problems," *Pan American Journal of Public Health,* Dec. 2018; Sally Jacobs, "Cuba has a lung cancer vaccine. Many U.S. patients can't get it without breaking the law," *USA Today*, January 9, 2018 (usatoday.com); Sivlvia Ayuso, "Cuba becomes first nation to eliminate mother-to-child HIV transmission," *El País*, July 1, 2015 (elpais.com); Gillian Mohney, "3 of Cuba's Major Medical Achievements," ABC News, November 29, 2016 (abcnews.go.com); Xhinhua Net, "Cuba supports WHO in fighting COVID-19 pandemic: health minister," May 18, 2020 (xinhuanet.com); Qiong Zhou, Virgina Chen, et al., "Interferon-a2b Treatment for COVID-19," Frontiers in Immunology, May 15, 2020 (frontiersin.org); Beyza Binnur Donmez, "Cuba's potential virus vaccine has good results: expert," Andalou Agency, April 6, 2020 (aa.com.tr); Sarah Marsh, "Cuba credits two drugs with slashing coronavirus death toll," Reuters, May 22, 2020 (reuters.com); James McWhinney, "The Impact Of Ending The U.S. Embargo On Cuba," Investopedia, January 10, 2020 (investopedia.com); Ioan Grillo, "Cuba has had a lung cancer vaccine for years," The World (pri.org); Michael Gross, "Biotechnology: the second Cuban revolution," Chemistry World, October 31, 2004 (chemistryworld.com).

*Article 13.3*

# AFTER HORROR, CHANGE?
*Taking Stock of Conditions in Bangladesh's Garment Factories*

## BY JOHN MILLER
*September/October 2014*

> "I believe Bangladesh is making history as it creates new standards for the apparel industry globally."
> —Dan Mozena, U.S. Ambassador to Bangladesh
> "After the collapse of Rana Plaza, there has been an unprecedented level of cooperation, good will, and practical action toward better and safer places to work in Bangladesh."
> —Srinivas B. Reddy, Country Director, International Labor Organization (ILO) Bangladesh
> "It is fair to say that neither the government, nor the brands, is dealing adequately with the rising crescendo of employer-sponsored violence."
> —U.S. Rep. George Miller (D-Calif.)
> Statements made at the International Conference on Globalization and Sustainability of the Bangladesh Garment Sector, Harvard University, June 14, 2014

On April 24, 2013, the Rana Plaza factory building, just outside of Bangladesh's capital city of Dhaka, collapsed—killing 1,138 workers and inflicting serious long-term injuries on at least 1,000 others.

While the collapse of Rana Plaza was in one sense an accident, the policies that led to it surely were not. Bangladesh's garment industry grew to be the world's second largest exporter, behind only China's, by endangering and exploiting workers. Bangladesh's 5,000 garment factories paid rock-bottom wages, much lower than those in China, and just half of those in Vietnam. One foreign buyer told The Economist magazine, "There are no rules whatsoever that can not be bent." Cost-saving measures included the widespread use of retail buildings as factories—including at Rana Plaza—adding weight that sometimes exceeded the load-bearing capacity of the structures.

As Scott Nova, executive director of the Worker Rights Consortium, testified before Congress, "the danger to workers in Bangladesh has been apparent for many years." The first documented mass-fatality incident in the country's export garment sector occurred in December 1990. In addition to those killed at Rana Plaza, more than 600 garment workers have died in factory fires in Bangladesh since 2005. After Rana Plaza, however, Bangladesh finally reached a crossroads. The policies that had led to the stunning growth of its garment industry had so tarnished the "Made in Bangladesh" label that they were no longer sustainable.

But just how much change has taken place since Rana Plaza? That was the focus of an International Conference at Harvard this June, bringing together government officials from Bangladesh and the United States, representatives of the Bangladesh garment industry, the international brands, women's groups, trade unions, the International Labor Organization (ILO), and monitoring groups working in Bangladesh.

## How Much Change on the Ground?

Srinivas B. Reddy of the ILO spoke favorably of an "unprecedented level of ... practical action" toward workplace safety in Bangladesh.

The "practical action" on the ground, however, has been much more of a mixed bag than Reddy suggests. In the wake of massive protests and mounting international pressure, Bangladesh amended its labor laws to remove some obstacles to workers forming unions. Most importantly, the new law bars the country's labor ministry from giving factory owners lists of workers who want to organize.

But formidable obstacles to unionization still remain. At least 30% of the workers at an entire company are required to join a union before the government will grant recognition. This is a higher hurdle than workers face even in the not-so-union-friendly United States, where recognition is based at the level of the workplace, not the company. Workers in special export-processing zones (the source of about 16% of Bangladesh's exports), moreover, remain ineligible to form unions.

The Bangladesh government did register 160 new garment unions in 2013 and the first half of this year, compared to just two between 2010 and 2012. Nonetheless, collective bargaining happens in only 3% of garment plants. And employers have responded with firings and violence to workers registering for union recognition or making bargaining demands. Union organizers have been kidnapped, brutally beaten, and killed.

After protests that shut down over 400 factories last fall, the Bangladesh government raised the minimum wage for garment workers from the equivalent of $38 a month to $68. The higher minimum wage, however, fell short of the $103 demanded by workers.

The government and the garment brands have also set up the Rana Plaza Donor Trust Fund to compensate victims and their families for their losses and injuries. But according to the fund's website, it stood at just $17.9 million at the beginning of August, well below its $40 million target. Only about half of the 29 international brands that had their clothes sewn at Rana Plaza have made contributions. Ineke Zeldenrust of the Amsterdam-based labor-rights group Clean Clothes Campaign estimates that those 29 brands are being asked to contribute less than 0.2% of their $22 billion in total profits for 2013.

## The Accord and the Alliance

Following Rana Plaza, a group of mostly European retail chains turned away from the business-as-usual approach of company codes that had failed to ensure safe working conditions in the factories that made their clothes. Some 151 apparel brands and retailers doing business in Bangladesh, including 16 U.S.-based retailers, signed the Accord on Fire and Building Safety in Bangladesh. Together the signatories of this five-year agreement contracted with 1,639 of the 3,498 Bangladesh factories making garments for export.

The Accord broke important new ground. Unlike earlier efforts:

- It was negotiated with two global unions, UndustriALL and UNI (Global).
- It sets up a governing board with equal numbers of labor and retail representatives, and a chair chosen by the ILO.
- Independent inspectors will conduct audits of factory hazards and make their results public on the Accord website, including the name of the factory, detailed information about the hazard, and recommended repairs.
- The retailers will provide direct funding for repairs (up to a maximum of $2.5 million per company) and assume responsibility for ensuring that all needed renovations and repairs are paid for.
- Most importantly, the Accord is legally binding. Disputes between retailers and union representatives are subject to arbitration, with decisions enforceable by a court of law in the retailer's home country.

But most U.S. retailers doing business in Bangladesh—including giants like Wal-Mart, JCPenney, The Gap, and Sears—refused to sign. They objected to the Accord's open-ended financial commitment and to its legally binding provisions.

Those companies, along with 21 other North American retailers and brands, developed an alternative five-year agreement, called the Alliance For Bangladesh Worker Safety. Some 770 factories in Bangladesh produce garments for these 26 companies.

Unlike the Accord, the Alliance is not legally binding and lacks labor-organization representatives. Moreover, retailers contribute a maximum of $1 million per retailer (less than half the $2.5 million under the Accord) to implement their safety plan and needed repairs, and face no binding commitment to pay for needed improvements beyond that. The responsibility to comply with safety standards falls to factory owners, although the Alliance does offer up to $100 million in loans for these expenses.

Kalpona Akter, executive director of the Bangladesh Center for Worker Solidarity, told the U.S. Senate Foreign Relations Committee, "There is no meaningful difference between the Alliance and the corporate-controlled 'corporate social responsibility' programs that have failed Bangladeshi garment workers in the past, and have left behind thousands of dead and injured workers."

## Historic and Unprecedented?

Dan Mozena, U.S. Ambassador to Bangladesh, believes that, despite facing significant obstacles, "Bangladesh is making history as it creates new standards for the apparel industry globally."

While the Accord may be without contemporary precedent, joint liability agreements that make retailers responsible for the safety conditions of their subcontractor's factories do have historical antecedents. As political scientist Mark Anner has documented, beginning in the 1920s the International Ladies Garment Workers Union (ILGWU) began negotiating "jobber agreements" in the United States that held the buyer (or "jobber") for an apparel brand "jointly liable" for wages and working conditions in the contractor's factories. Jobber agreements played a central role in the near-eradication of sweatshops in the United States by the late 1950s. In today's global economy, however, international buyers are once again able to escape responsibility for conditions in the far-flung factories of their subcontractors.

Like jobber agreements, the Accord holds apparel manufacturers and retailers legally accountable for the safety conditions in the factories that make their clothes through agreements negotiated between workers or unions and buyers or brands. The next steps for the Accord model, as Anner has argued, are to address working conditions other than building safety (as jobber agreements had), to get more brands to sign on to the Accord, and to negotiate similar agreements in other countries.

That will be no easy task. But, according to Arnold Zack, who helped to negotiate the Better Factories program that brought ILO monitoring of Cambodian garment factories, "Bangladesh is the lynch pin that can bring an end to the bottom feeding shopping the brands practice." ❑

*Sources:* Arnold M. Zack, "In an Era of Accelerating Attention to Workplace Equity: What Place for Bangladesh," Boston Global Forum, July 8, 2014; Testimony of Kalpona Akter, Testimony of Scott Nova, Senate Committee on Foreign Relations, Feb. 11, 2014; Mark Anner, Jennifer Bair, and Jeremy Blasi, "Toward Joint Liability in Global Supply Chains," *Comparative Labor Law & Policy Journal*, Vol. 35:1, Fall 2013; Prepared Remarks for Rep. George Miller (D-Calif.), Keynote Remarks by U.S. Ambassador to Bangladesh Dan Mozena, Remarks by Country Director ILO Bangladesh Srinivas B. Reddy, International Conference on Globalization and Sustainability of the Bangladesh Garment Sector, June 14, 2014; "Rags in the ruins," *The Economist*, May 4, 2013; "Bangladesh: Amended Labor Law Falls Short," Human Rights Watch, July 18, 2013; Rana Plaza Donor Trust Fund (ranaplaza-arrangement.org/fund).

*Article 13.4*

# UNDERSTANDING FRANCE'S *GILETS JAUNES*
*Macron's centrist party collides with the yellow vest protests.*

## BY AARTH SARAPH
*January/February 2019*

France—a country where taking to the streets and demanding change is part of a broad political culture—is no stranger to protest, and citizens have a deep understanding that democracy isn't a singular event confined to a rendezvous at the ballot box every few years.

French protests have historically been organized and led by unions, student groups, or political movements. But beginning in mid-November, a different kind of protester began taking to the streets. The *gilets jaunes*, named for the bright yellow vests carried by motorists as a safety measure, are in many ways unique—a horizontal movement driven by the rural grassroots of the country, rather than by any centralized leadership or organized political force.

The initial rallying cry of ellow vest protesters was a hike in fuel taxes, announced by the French government as one of their measures towards a long-term ecological transition and greening of the transportation sector. However, the symbolism of this fuel tax hike, in the wake of both lowered corporate taxes and the elimination of a tax on wealth by the Macron administration, was not lost on the French public, already sharply divided between the urban Paris and rural *la province*.

Many of these protesters come from a diverse range of political opinions and had never taken to the streets or participated in any form of direct action. However, every Saturday since November 17, the yellow vests have flooded the streets of France, calling for social and economic justice—at a time when France's unemployment rate stands at 9.2% and youth unemployment is even higher at 21.8%. At a recent demonstration, most protesters spoke about their declining purchasing power and their inability to make ends meet under a heavy tax burden. Many expressed their frustration at a perceived loss of power and the impotency of political leaders that had come and gone over the years, from the center-right President Nicolas Sarkozy to center-left President François Hollande, without any change in the system.

The yellow vest protesters also highlighted how members of the ruling class are disconnected from the lives and concerns of ordinary people, and how they view politicians as both aloof and arrogant. President Emmanuel Macron didn't ameliorate this perception last September when he responded to a plea for help by an unemployed gardener by telling him he could easily find work if he applied for a restaurant or construction job. In a statement reminiscent of the ruling aristocracy during the French Revolution, French Budget Minister Gérald Darmanin reflected on the difficulties of the poor living on 950 euros a month, especially when a meal for two at a Parisian restaurant cost him 200 euros—without wine! In another faux pas, during a televised debate with some yellow vest protestors, a member of parliament from Macron's Republic on the Move Party, Elise Fajgeles, revealed that she was unaware of the level of the minimum wage in the country.

When the "neither left nor right" Macron came to power in July, he enjoyed a relatively high approval rating of 66%, on the back of his second-round victory against the far-right National Front's Marine Le Pen, portraying himself as a candidate outside of the political establishment. However, merely a year-and-a-half into his presidency, his approval rating has plummeted to 21%, while national approval of the yellow vests stands at 62%.

While both domestic and international critics of the yellow vest movement have described the protesters as revanchist forces opposed to the environmental actions of the French government, the yellow vests are simply wary of being asked to further tighten their belts while large businesses and the wealthy see tax cuts and subsidies. A vast swath of rural France relies on their vehicles for their day-to-day mobility, and the increase in the cost of an inelastic good—fuel—without the availability of clear alternatives, was perceived as an attack on the working class. Indeed, many yellow vests marched in solidarity with climate activists on December 8, staging a parallel march for the climate.

Much as the Occupy Movement sometimes struggled to get a clear message across, given its horizontal and leaderless approach, the yellow vests have also faced difficulties presenting their message and creating a coherent list of demands. Distrustful of both corporate media and political parties on the left and right, protesters have organized largely over social media, their initial demands including but not limited to a moratorium on the fuel tax and raising the minimum wage.

A broader list of demands now includes: eliminating homelessness; a more layered and progressive income tax; favoring taxation of multinational corporations over small businesses; salaries and pensions indexed to inflation; ending austerity; ending privatization; a maximum salary of 15,000 euros a month; and a constitutional reform to allow for any legal proposition gaining 700,000 signatures to be debated in parliament and subsequently put to the French people as a referendum.

Responding to the growth of the protests and opprobrium over the previous weeks, Macron announced a series of measures on December 10, including an increase to the minimum wage that would be paid by the state, a moratorium on the fuel tax hike, tax-free overtime hours, and cancelling the government's planned 2019 tax increase on pensioners—although stopping short of walking back the repeal of the wealth tax and concessions to corporations. While some of these measures were positively received, most of the yellow vests viewed these measures as too little and too late, and promised to continue their protests, characterizing the presidential offering as "crumbs."

Nonetheless, even these few measures from Macron elicited an immediate response from the European Commission's Economic Affairs Commissioner Pierre Moscovici, worried about the impact of increased spending on France's budget deficit. Under the terms of the Stability and Growth Pact, France, and other member states of the European Union, are expected to keep their budget deficits to under 3% of the gross domestic product, an agenda that has hitherto been championed by Macron as part of his political program.

Given the yellow vest's frustration with electoral politics, it is unclear whether the movement will become a political coalition, similar to the Five Star Movement in Italy, or coalesce into one of the existing political parties, either on the populist left or right. What is clear, however, is that the protesters are fed up—and past the tipping point. While their anger is now directed towards Macron, the yellow vests are aware that their fight is not with an individual, but with a system that has let them down for decades and a technocratic establishment that has replaced the political institutions of the past. While participation in the protests dipped during the holiday season, the first protests staged in 2019 have seen growing involvement. The demand for a constitutional amendment enabling citizen-proposed referendums has increasingly taken center stage. The yellow vests insist that greater direct democracy is the only counterbalance to the actions of their political representatives, whom they see as representing the rich, powerful, and predominantly Parisian elite.

In February 2015, during the Greek debt crisis negotiations, Wolfgang Schäuble, now president of the Bundestag, and then the finance minister of Germany, responded firmly to his Greek counterpart, Yanis Varoufakis—"Elections cannot be allowed to change an economic program of a member state!" In 2018, as the effects of prolonged austerity and growing inequality are increasingly felt across Europe, it is no wonder that movements like the yellow vests are growing in magnitude, as anger with the ruling elites continues to mount.

With European parliamentary elections scheduled for May, progressives would be well served to learn from these lessons and heed the message shared by the yellow vests—the alternative is to surrender this space to right-wing demagogues taking democracies by storm. There can be no ecological transition that isn't linked to economic and social justice; and any measures that subscribe to a top-down approach placing the interests of corporations above people will fail. The uprising of the yellow vests underlines the failure of this segregationist approach. As Europe, and the world, faces unprecedented environmental, social, and economic crises, it is time to turn away once and for all from the politics of austerity and invest in a green-energy economy that creates jobs and better lives for all. ❑

*Article 13.5*

# THE BUENAVENTURA CIVIC STRIKE

## BY PATRICIA M. RODRIGUEZ
*November/December 2017*

The people don't give up, dammit! *"¡El pueblo no se rinde, carajo!"* That was the chant that rose up from the Civic Strike of the city of Buenaventura, in the department of Valle del Cauca, Colombia, in May and June 2017. The Civic Strike, supported by 114 organizations and hundreds of thousands of people who barricaded access roads to the port, was according to some residents the strongest mobilization in Buenaventura's history. Paralyzing port activities and leading to millions in losses for multinational corporations, it was the result of years of civil-society organizing— spurred by the build-up of frustrations over the violence, historical neglect, and extreme poverty levels that plague a majority of the population in this city. The Strike ultimately led to the introduction in Congress of a law to establish an autonomous fund for Buenaventura, which includes mechanisms of collective decision- making about development plans for the city.

On July 17, 2017, about 40 community and labor leaders from Buenaventura met with a dozen members of international organizations like the World Organization against Torture, the U.S.-based Witness for Peace, and the Colombian-based NGO Inter-Ecclesiastic Commission of Justice and Peace, to testify about the precarious living and working situation of thousands of labor-union members, Afro-descendant community leaders, fisherfolk, and many others in and around this port city. The leaders took turns describing the vast reach of systemic violence and poverty, and the massive failures by national and local government officials to address these problems.

Speaking out against injustice was not an easy decision for the women and men gathered at this meeting, and at the various sites of resistance during the Civic Strike. The meeting took place in the Punta Icaco Humanitarian Zone of Buenaventura, a proclaimed safe-space established in October 2016 after local residents (who largely earn a living from small-scale local lumber operations) sought help from human-rights groups, after deeming it impossible to continue to suffer intimidation and extortion by illegal armed groups. Punta Icaco lies adjacent to the Puente Nayero neighborhood of Buenaventura, which in 2014 formed the first urban Humanitarian Space in Colombia, after a series of deaths by dismemberment were discovered in nearby "chop houses" run by local paramilitary groups. Today, the threats and attacks by paramilitary groups like AGC (Gaitanista Self-Defense Forces of Colombia) against community leaders still happen almost daily, in spite of the heavy presence of public security forces that are supposedly there to protect the population, and military presence in the nearby Bahía Málaga military base (also a U.S. Navy base since 2009). AGC is a paramilitary group that has terrorized communities in the Pacific Coast region since their supposed demobilization after the

2005 Justice and Peace Law. In fact, within nine days of the meeting with international organizations, one of the leaders at the meeting was held at gun-point in his home, allegedly by AGC operatives, and told "not to meet with the gringos or he would be killed."

But in Buenaventura, desperation has obviously surpassed the fear of speaking out; the living conditions of many who live and work in the port area are absolutely desolate. According to official figures, 80% of the population of Buenaventura lives in poverty, 21% are illiterate, and the unemployment rate is 62%. Residents complain of having little or no access to water; what little is available is often not safe enough to drink.

But the people of Buenaventura are, as their chant proclaims, not giving up.

## The Port as a 21st-Century Enclave Economy

At the Punta Icaco Humanitarian Space meeting, leaders spoke of labor abuses, forced displacement, torture, death threats, and killings practiced by a variety of powerful actors: paramilitary groups, guerrillas, and port officials. But the stories also implicate elites such as politicians and heads of national and multinational corporations, including Sociedad Portuaria de Buenaventura (SPB). SPB is a port-operations company majority-owned by a dozen billionaires from Colombia, the Philippines, Spain, China, and South Korea. SPB operates the biggest port in Colombia's Pacific Coast, which 60% of all Colombian exports go through, including 80% of coffee exports, and high percentages of palm oil, coal, steel, petroleum, grains, sugar, banana, and other products. The port brought in $5.8 billion (U$2 million) pesos in national customs revenue in 2016.

The port itself has an operating capacity of more than 12 million tons of cargo per year in its five terminals. *The Guardian* reported in 2011 that China had proposed building a rail link connecting the port of Cartagena with Colombia's Pacific Coast as well as a $7.6 billion plan for the expansion of the Buenaventura port, in order to increase Chinese exports into the Americas and to facilitate the export of coal and other raw materials from Colombia to China.

Though the port has indeed expanded, an even more telling sign of the importance of port access is the March 2017 inauguration of the new $550-million Port of Agua Dulce, owned and operated by two large Asian companies, ICTSI (International Container Terminal Services, Philippines) and PSA (World's Port of Call, Singapore). Agua Dulce is advertised as the most modern port on South America's Pacific Coast, yet it is swiftly leading to environmental destruction and the forced, violent displacement of Afro-descendant and indigenous communities in the area. In the Afro-descendant community of El Cruzero, for instance, leaders complain of violent displacements and the vast clearing of ancestral lands for mining and other purposes by companies that operate in Agua Dulce. In this sense, the ports' importance to a wide portion of the local population is quite reminiscent of the dependency produced during the era of expansion of enclave export based economies in the 1900s.

## The *Paro Cívico*: Labor, Ethnicities, Civic Organizations Hold their Ground

The contrast between the technological and infrastructural capacity of the port itself and the levels of poverty and displacement among the people living nearby is stark, revealing the essence of residents' long-term drive to organize. The city's crisis reached a climax during the 22-day Civic Strike, but the problems of extreme poverty, drug-trafficking, and violence in Buenaventura span many decades. Initially, the Civic Strike leaders called on the Colombian government to declare an economic, social, and economic state of emergency. Their demands included, among others, an increase spending on housing, healthcare, basic sanitation, infrastructure, and education at all levels, as well as an accountable and collective rights-based legal system that protects rather than victimizes marginalized populations. The organizations also asked for monetary and symbolic reparations for victims of violence by state- and non-state armed actors, and a commitment of funds for the strengthening of local economy, creating jobs and increasing salaries, as well as increased public expenditures on the recovery and conservation of degraded ecosystems, including rivers and biodiverse areas.

As the Civic Strike gained strength, more than a hundred civic organizations began working together at different strategic meeting points (or *puntos de encuentro*) in the city. Hundreds of thousands of residents of the region occupied entire areas, calling for transformative peace in the territories. By this they meant one that touches on structural changes and the right to live in dignity, and which goes beyond the cease-fire agreements, being negotiated between the Colombian government and guerrilla groups like FARC (Revolutionary Armed Forces of Colombia) and ELN (National Liberation Army), to end a civil conflict that has lasted more than fifty years. The strike was met with brutal attacks by police and the Escuadrón Móvil Antidisturbio (Mobile Anti-Riot Squad, known as ESMAD) forces, resulting in several deaths, and thousands injured. Security officials threw (U.S. manufactured) tear gas grenades and shot rubber bullets blindly toward the crowds, but the demonstrators who gathered at the strategic points held their ground.

La Delfina, one of the *punto de encuentro* communities, was selected by the Civic Strike Committee for its strategic location, at the entrance of the main highway leading into the island-port of Buenaventura, and its inter-ethnic profile, with indigenous and Afro-descendant groups coexisting but largely living and defending their separate territories. Having nearly always fought for their own interests, the groups were united by calls for mass non-violent resistance and by the brutal repression just four days into the strike. Two weeks into the road blockages and strike, the loss to the export sector was already $20 billion pesos ($7 million). As a leader of the Afro-descendant community explained: "We had an experience that merits being replicated elsewhere. We were able to interact and coordinate with the nearby indigenous leaders from the Nasa- Embera communities for the first time. We were attacked indiscriminately, but this just united us. If we did it alone, this would be impossible." Though the state of economic emergency was not called, allegedly due to the national government's fear of a domino effect, the idea of the autonomous budget has brewed from this unity.

The fifty-plus years of armed conflict are undoubtedly a source of the state's failure to implement more just economic plans and address human-rights violations. Despite the seeming advance in formal peace negotiations between the FARC and the Colombian government since 2012, peace is not at all felt on the ground. The problems in Buenaventura also have deeper structural sources, revealed most visibly in the labor situation in the Buenaventura Port itself.

## Privatization and Corporate Labor Abuse

Buenaventura has operated officially as a port city since 1827, but fast-paced modernization began with the creation of state-owned Empresa Puertos de Colombia (Colpuertos) in 1959. At its peak in the 1970s, Colpuertos directly employed about 10,000 workers. At that time, the port of Buenaventura consisted of a single dock. Throughout Colpuertos' decentralization (the process of decreasing the decision-making role by state managers of public enterprises) in the 1980s, jobs and salaries remained relatively stable, but its eventual privatization in 1991 and the concomitant end of collective bargaining agreements represented a drastic change in labor standards and protections. For instance, average salaries of port workers decreased from 6.3 times the minimum wage, in the 1980s, to just 1.8 times by 2002. During the 1980 and 1990s, Colombia's governments adhered to neoliberal economic policies, spurring the "flexibilization" of labor relations and the creation of hundreds of subcontracting firms of all sizes. These firms moved swiftly to hire low-paid temporary workers.

With new technology and a culture of antiunionism behind the economic model, the number of port-related jobs in Buenaventura declined, by 2008, to only about 3600, with only 200 being part of the SPB. As Daniel Hawkins (2013) states, "Buenaventura appears to have been the laboratory for labor intermediation in the Colombian port industry ... [it] was the port of most frenetic entrepreneurial activity." But in 2007, a handful of port workers in Cartagena decided to create a new, more representative union (Unión Portuaria, UP) to fight labor outsourcing (tercerización) and reestablish formal contracts with SPB in all the ports of Colombia. In August 2012, following years of labor conflict with SPB and subcontracting firms like TECSA (Terminal de Contenedores, S.A., responsible for loading and unloading of cargo containers), a strike by key UP workers led to 110 workers obtaining direct contracts with SPB, but this left another 3500 workers still in insecure indirect jobs with TECSA. Meanwhile, TECSA's net profit was 11.6 billion pesos ($3.7 million) in 2012.

The labor abuses continued, and in May and June 2015, Unión Portuaria organized another strike. This one ended with a direct contract with SPB for 376 workers, and with TECSA for another 523 workers. Again, another 3,000 workers remained without a direct collective bargaining agreement that would guarantee an eight-hour work day, increased wages, and other protections for them and their families. J.R., a leader from Unión Portuaria notes, "[2012-2015] were years of many violent mass displacements of people living in neighborhoods in and near the Buenaventura port, which in turn spurred many of us [in UP] to denounce forced displacement, and to organize actions to return to our territories [near the port]."

Labor abuses in Colombia were supposedly to be addressed as part of the 2011 U.S.-Colombia Free Trade Agreement Labor Action Plan (LAP), hailed by the Obama administration as a roadmap to improving labor rights in Colombia. Under its LAP commitments, the Colombian government would prioritize key economic sectors—including palm oil, sugar, mines, flowers, and ports—for increased labor inspections. Yet, by 2015, the failure of LAP was evident in a low number of inspections and weak enforcement of labor standards. In addition, labor leaders continued to be targets of threats and assassinations: Between 2011 and 2015, 105 labor leaders were killed, allegedly by right-wing paramilitary members or thugs paid by secret "intellectual authors" who are rarely identified.

The government of President Juan Manuel Santos (in office since 2010) has put in place socalled "integral development" schemes such as Plan Pacífico (2014), which would target infrastructure building all along the Pacific coast. In Buenaventura, the government hired a Spanish engineering and architecture consulting firm, Esteyco, to develop a multimillion master plan to modernize the port city and create biodiversity and ecotourism projects. But the plan was largely developed without consulting civil society organizations. As Senator Alexander López-Maya declared during a Congressional hearing in 2017, "This is basically a plan for clearing of the population from the island-port to the inland. It is a scene of frequent terror, fear, persecution so that people abandon their lands, and go wherever, and this is most worrisome. We have a total of 140,000 people displaced, six thousand just last year, in the Bajamar port-structure zone."

## The Autonomous Budget

Because Buenaventura has such a history of labor, indigenous, and Afro-descendant resistance to exploitation, the negotiations around the creation of (and mechanisms for) an autonomous budget (FonBuenaventura) takes on added importance. It shows the growth of collective methodologies and long-term thinking on the part of the movements. A member of the Civic Strike Executive Committee calls it "an acceptable resolution to problems that the government never intended to resolve." An autonomous budget involves a 10 billion peso (US$3.3 million) trust fund established by law (on July 26, 2017), to be gathered and used over a span of 10 years, and which forms an integral part of municipal development plans. The fund will be based on an allocation of 50% of local tax revenue each year and additional national funds and external loans.

The agreement includes an immediate infrastructure investment of 1.5 billion pesos ($500,000), which will include the construction of a sewage system for the port area, an emergency wing of a hospital, and other public projects. The fund, when approved in Congress, will be administered by a FonBuenaventura council, composed of five members of the community, seven national and local government officials, plus the mayor of Buenaventura and the governor of Valle del Cauca. Although lopsided in favor of the government, decisions will supposedly be made through participatory roundtable dialogues (*Cabildo Abierto*, or "open council") around issues such as land, housing, infrastructure, jobs and productivity, water and public services, education, reinvigoration of cultural expressions of Afro-descendant and indigenous groups, greater accountability of the justice system and protection for victims, and human rights. In addition, the agreement includes government recognition of right to social protest, the implementation of collective rights (like free prior and informed consent before any major infrastructural or mining project can begin), protection mechanisms for movement leaders who are threatened for mobilizing, monitoring of poststrike compliance by the state, and the creation of a truth commission to investigate ESMAD and other armed actors' violence during the strike.

According to one of the UP labor representatives speaking at the *Cabildo Abierto*, the future of Buenaventura lies in continuing to build a "culture" of organized popular resistance and struggle for social change. In addition, this requires the creation of a public enterprise of sorts—or at least one that more closely represents the interest of the population of Buenaventura, rather than private interests—continued actions for formalization of labor contracts, the creation of new jobs, and the increase in incomes for ordinary workers.

The unity built over years of organizing, culminating with the Civic Strike, is now reflected in the collective demands being pressed by the people of Buenaventura. These demands promise continued resistance against the exploitative model of labor relations being defended by global capital. Change will not come from entrepreneurs or politicians. It will come from grassroots organizations themselves, as labor and ethnic communities continue to deconstruct systems of power, exploitation, and racism—through continued mobilization, legislation at national and international levels (i.e,. the rights-based framework pushed by organizations like the International Labor Organization or the above-mentioned World Organization against Torture) or both. There is hope that the era of freereign by elite and state actors might end one day soon. If one thinks about the roots of problems in Buenaventura, it is not hard to imagine that it could be so much different, with a hint of ethical spirit by those in positions of power, and a lot of popular "not giving up, dammit!" ❑

*Sources:* Tania Branigan, "China goes on the rails to rival Panama canal," *The Guardian*, Feb 14, 2011 (theguardian.com); Daniel Hawkins, "The Formalization and Unionization Campaign in the Buenaventura Port, Colombia" (2013) (lser.la.psu.edu); Nayibi Jimenez and Wilson Delgado, "La política pública de privatización del sector portuario y su impacto en la organización del trabajo en el puerto de Buenaventura," *Revista científica pensamiento y gestión*, v. 25 (2008); Alexander López-Maya, Colombia Senate hearing, 2017 (youtube.com); Alonso Valencia, "Los orígenes coloniales del Puerto de Buenaventura," *Historia y Memoria* (July-December 2014).

Article 13.6

# THE FIGHT AGAINST MINING COMPANIES GOES GLOBAL
*Can an Historic Victory Over Irresponsible Mining in Central America Spur a Win in Asia?*

## BY ROBIN BROAD AND JOHN CAVANAGH
*December 2017, Triple Crisis Blog*

In March 2017, the small nation of El Salvador took a huge step towards protecting its environment for present and future generations when its legislature passed a law outlawing all metals mining. It was a momentous vote — a vote heard round the world.

Indeed, that vote ricocheted across the Pacific to the Philippines, which has emerged as one of the hot spots in the global fight of "water protectors" to end destructive industrial mining. In November 2017, Philippine President Rodrigo Duterte surprised many by listening to the call of strong peoples' movements as he declared that a ban on new open pit-mining in that country would remain in place. This, despite a concerted campaign by the country's mining interests to end that ban.

The open pit ban is a significant victory for communities across the Philippines, especially in the southern island of Mindanao where groups have waged a decades-long battle to block the construction of what would be one of the largest gold and copper mines in Southeast Asia. And it gives a boost to groups fighting to shut down the destructive mining activities of the very same Australian-Canadian mining giant, OceanaGold, that sued El Salvador in an effort to mine gold there. As a result, OceanaGold has become a symbol of irresponsible mining around the world and a prominent target of global anti-mining movements.

OceanaGold operates the highly profitable and environmentally devastating Didipio open pit mine in the northern Philippine province of Nueva Vizcaya. Since 2013, OceanaGold has funneled some of those profits into its expensive and nasty battle to kick-start mining in the environmentally fragile nation of El Salvador. It was actually OceanaGold that first publicly linked the two countries—through its public relations campaigns that claimed its "green" and "responsible" mining in the Philippines demonstrated it would be a responsible miner in El Salvador.

Instead, that El Salvador-Philippine connection proved part of OceanaGold's downfall in El Salvador. To counter OceanaGold's claims of "responsible" mining, water protectors in El Salvador brought Nueva Vizcaya's governor Carlos Padilla to their country in March 2017. Since we, the authors, have worked for years in both countries, one of us accompanied Padilla and witnessed the power of his recounting the Philippine story of OceanaGold to Salvadoran audiences. Padilla organized his presentations around a visually-arresting power point that featured before-and-after photos of his province's once lush Dinkidi mountain, a scene strikingly similar to hills of northern El Salvador. Salvadoran audiences gasped as Dinkidi disappeared and was replaced by a giant open pit that empties into a long dirty grey "tailings pond" with over one hundred ghostly, dead trees.

Padilla testified before the relevant Salvadoran legislative committee, met with El Salvador's president, and shared the Philippine OceanaGold saga to an audience of nearly one thousand in the province where OceanaGold desperately desired to mine in El Salvador.

In various audiences, the combination of economic, social and environmental violence wrought by mining in the Philippine clearly hit home. As one participant said in response to the Governor's speech to a large, high-level, multi-sectoral gathering convened by the Salvadoran government, "there should be a worldwide movement with Dinkdi as a symbol." Others assembled voiced agreement: "No more, Dinkidis!"

Padilla's visit climaxed on March 29, 2017 with the vote in El Salvador's legislature for what the *New York Times* called "El Salvador's Historic Mining Ban." The vote was the culmination of a lengthy battle by a Salvadoran coalition of local and national groups, backed by hundreds of allied groups in other countries. Reliable sources informed one of us that when one Congressperson wavered before the vote, another bolstered his "no" vote with "remember what the Governor told us." Hence, El Salvador became the first country in the world to ban metals mining, both open-pit and underground.

In a meeting with Salvadoran President Sanchez-Ceren right after the vote, Padilla congratulated El Salvador for being ahead of the Philippines on banning mining.

Now, Padilla is bringing the lessons of the Salvador victory back to the Philippines, where a broad range of Philippine groups, led by two national coalitions—Alyansa Tigil Mina (ATM) and Kalikasan—are strengthening their efforts to evict OceanaGold. We revisited the Philippine mine site in July 2017 (we had been there in 2013 with construction ongoing) to talk to community members about El Salvador's decisive move to save its key watershed and to witness what had happened to the once verdant Dinkidi area since OceanaGold operations had moved into full gear. Community leaders reminded us that the Didipio mine sits at the headwaters of the longest river system in the entire country. Indeed, that river system provides water to millions and key agricultural areas through four northern provinces ending in the vast Cagayan River.

Part of the OceanaGold Didipio horror is visible and audible outside the window of the one room meeting place of a local water protector group. When we visited in 2013, the noise from the round-the-clock machines was deafening. Community members described the torment to them and their children trying to sleep or work or simply live beside the constant noise of crushing and blasting rock.

In 2017, with the mine operational, we heard shocking stories of water sources drying up in some areas and becoming unsafe to drink in others. Farmers downstream from the mine told us of dead fish, fish losing scales, and of skin diseases on themselves and on the water buffalo they use to farm. As for Dinkidi, it was— as in the Governor's "after" photos—a gaping wound in the once-fertile earth.

Community members chronicled human rights abuses, including the death of at least two community members that reminded us eerily of the assassinations of anti-mining activists in northern El Salvador. We travelled to three of OceanaGold's so-called "reforestation" projects where the dying, non-endemic saplings made a mockery of the company's reforestation boasts and awards.

As the global fight against OceanaGold shifts to the Philippines, farmers and government officials are gathering evidence to build the case that OceanaGold has violated not only provincial laws and laws regarding mining in indigenous lands, but also the precise terms of OceanaGold's mining concession agreement. This last point is key as OceanaGold's 25-year Didipio concession agreement is up for renewal in 2019—a date which offers an important time-frame to eject the company from the Philippines.

But the fight of water protectors in the Philippines faces a large hurdle that did not exist in El Salvador: vested domestic interests. The domestic mining lobby in El Salvador shrank as mining operations largely ground to a halt during its bloody civil war (1980-1992). The Philippines, on the other hand, has a strong business elite tied to mining with roots going back to the construction of mines during the U.S. colonial period over 100 years ago. Hence, mining interests in the Philippines are powerful and tightly linked to top economic and political families. Case in point: the brother of the current Finance Minister is involved in the consortium behind the would-be Tampakan open pit mine in Mindanao.

Despite these obstacles, the anti-mining movement got a shot in the arm with President Duterte's surprising 2016 appointment of Regina "Gina" Lopez, a well-respected environmentalist, to be his Secretary of the Department of Environment and Natural Resources (DENR). Before her official confirmation, Lopez moved quickly to open a broad national debate on mining's devastating impacts. With her motto of "justice delayed is justice denied," she took decisive steps to audit the 41 large-scale mines across the archipelago to see which were out of compliance with their legal obligations under their mining agreements.

By early 2017, she earned the ire of the mining industry by announcing the ban on new open-pit mining, along with the closure of 22 mines and suspension of operations in four more. OceanaGold—already desperate in El Salvador—was among those on the suspension list. All affected mining companies, including OceanaGold, appealed these decisions; all were able to continue operations while their appeal is being considered. But, still, the momentum seemed to be moving against mining.

Philippine environmentalists received a harsh blow in May 2017 when Congress, where several members have mining connections, made its move against Lopez. The Congressional Committee on Appointments voted against Gina Lopez's confirmation to the DENR post.

Despite this setback, the national anti-mining coalitions and local groups have continued the fight against OceanaGold, against the giant Tampakan mine in Mindanao, and against other mining ventures. And these coalitions, working with local groups and provincial officials, understand that part of the challenge in the

Philippines is to prove that viable and sustainable alternatives exist, alternatives that can be environmentally, socially and economically superior to mining.

As in El Salvador, such alternatives focus on agriculture and eco-tourism. Exciting economic alternatives are thriving in Governor Padilla's province of Nueva Vizcaya. Indeed, just north of where Dinkidi once stood, we toured the fertile Malabing Valley where citrus farmers have blockaded roads every time OceanaGold tries to move its machinery to expand its operations. The farmers shared with us their work for an economic future free of mining, building on the province's "green gold" of citrus—and we sampled an array of fresh fruit and citrus wine. We also visited other organic farms producing tomatoes, lettuce, and a wide variety of other vegetables. We spent time at an expanding eco-tourism resort that is creating good jobs while conserving the environment, and we saw the provincial government plans to ramp up such endeavors.

OceanaGold has been stunningly defeated in El Salvador, at least for the time being. The months to come will determine whether it can be defeated in the Philippines by 2019. But however long it takes to win the fight against environmentally, socially and economically destructive mining, El Salvador has demonstrated that the good guys can win.

No more Dinkidis. ❑

# CONTRIBUTORS

**Frank Ackerman** was one of the founders of *Dollars & Sense*, and was a senior economist at Synapse Energy Economics in Cambridge, Mass. He died in July 2019.

**Francisco J. Aldape** is completing his Ph.D. in Economics at the New School for Social Research. His research interests include political economy, social justice, economic development, and financial and environmental economics.

**David Bacon** is a journalist and photographer covering labor, immigration, and the impact of the global economy on workers.

**Dean Baker** is co-director of the Center for Economic and Policy Research in Washington, D.C.

**James K. Boyce** is professor emeritus at the University of Massachusetts-Amherst and co-director of the Political Economy Research Institute (PERI) Program on Development, Peacebuilding, and the Environment.

**Sasha Breger Bush** is a lecturer at the Josef Korbel School of International Studies at the University of Denver and author of *Derivatives and Development* (Palgrave Macmillan, 2012).

**Robin Broad** is a professor of International Development at the School of International Service, American University.

**John Cavanagh** is the director of the Institute for Policy Studies in Washington, D.C.

**Anis Chowdhury**, an adjunct professor at Western Sydney University (Australia), has held senior United Nations positions in New York and Bangkok.

**Mateo Crossa** is a doctoral candidate in the Doctoral Program in Development Studies, Universidad Autónoma de Zacatecas, Mexico.

**James M. Cypher** is an emeritus research professor at the Universidad Autónoma de Zacatecas, Mexico.

**Nina Eichacker** (co-editor of this book) is an assistant professor of economics at the University of Rhode Island.

**Gerald Epstein** is a professor of economics and co-director of the Political Economy Research Institute (PERI) at the University of Massachusetts-Amherst.

**John Bellamy Foster** is editor of *Monthly Review* and a sociology professor at the University of Oregon.

**Kevin P. Gallagher** is director of the Global Development Policy Center at Boston University's Pardee School of Global Studies and the co-chair of the G20 task force for An International Financial Architecture for Stability and Development.

**Armağan Gezici** (co-editor of this book) is an associate professor of economics at Keene State College.

**Jayati Ghosh** is a professor of economics at the Centre for Economic Study and Planning at Jawaharlal Nehru University.

**Jörg Haas** is head of the department of international politics at the Heinrich Böll Foundation.

**Elizabeth T. Henderson** (co-editor of this book) is co-editor of *Dollars & Sense*.

**Marie Kennedy** is is professor emerita of Community Planning at the University of Massachusetts, has been a visiting professor of urban planning at the University of California, and is on the Venice Community Housing Board.

**Arthur MacEwan** is a founder of *Dollars & Sense*, a professor emeritus of economics at the University of Massachusetts-Boston and a *Dollars & Sense* Associate.

**Zaeem Hassan Mehmood** is an alumnus of National Defence University, Islamabad. He is serving as Research Associate at National Centre for Maritime Policy Research (NCMPR).

**John Miller** is a member of the *Dollars & Sense* collective and teaches economics at Wheaton College.

**Jeannette Mitchell** (co-editor of this book) is an associate professor of economics at the Rochester Institute of Technology.

**William G. Moseley** is a professor of geography at Macalester College in Saint Paul, Minn.

**Jawied Nawabi** (co-editor of this book) is a professor of economics and sociology at CUNY Bronx Community College and a member of the *Dollars & Sense* collective.

**Immanuel Ness** is a professor of political science at Brooklyn College.

**Evita Nolka** is a political theorist from Thessaloniki, Greece.

**Thomas Palley** is an economist and the author of *Financialization: The Economics of Finance Capital Domination* (Palgrave Macmillan, 2013).

**Vijay Prashad** is an Indian historian, editor and journalist. He is the chief editor of LeftWord Books and the director of Tricontinental: Institute for Social Research. He is a writing fellow and chief correspondent at Globetrotter, a project of the Independent Media Institute.

**Prabir Purkayastha** is the founding editor of Newsclick.in, a digital media platform. He is an activist for science and the free software movement.

**Smriti Rao** is a professor of economics and Global Studies at Assumption University in Worcester, Mass., and is a resident scholar at the Women's Studies Research Center at Brandeis University in Waltham, Mass.

**Alejandro Reuss** is a former co-editor of *Dollars & Sense* and an instructor in labor studies at the University of Massachusetts-Boston.

**Patricia Rodriguez** is an assistant professor of politics at Ithaca College.

**Aarth Saraph** works on enabling access to climate finance at the U.N. Environment Programme's Paris-based Economy Division and was a *Dollars & Sense* intern in the summer of 2013.

**Geoff Schneider** is a professor of economics at Bucknell University and co-author of *Introduction to Political Economy*, 8th ed. (*Dollars & Sense*, 2016).

**Jomo Kwame Sundaram**, a Malaysian economist, is senior adviser at the Khazanah Research Institute and a visiting fellow at the Initiative for Policy Dialogue at Columbia University.

**Intan Suwandi** is an assistant professor of sociology at Illinois State University and the author of *Value Chains: The New Economic Imperialism* (Monthly Review Press, 2019).

**William K. Tabb** is an economist and author of *The Restructuring of Capitalism in Our Time* (2012) and other books.

**Chris Tilly** is a professor and chair of urban planning at UCLA and a *Dollars & Sense* Associate.

**Esra Uğurlu** is a Ph.D. student at UMass-Amherst. Her research explores the effects of credit expansions on economic growth in developing countries.

**Ramaa Vasudevan** is an assistant professor of economics at Colorado State University.

**Matias Vernengo** is a professor of economics at Bucknell University.

**Timothy A. Wise** is Senior Researcher in the Land and Food Rights Program, Small Planet Institute, and Researcher at the Global Development and Environment Institute at Tufts University.

**Richard D. Wolff** is a visiting professor at the Graduate Program of International Affairs at New School University.

CPSIA information can be obtained
at www.ICGtesting.com
Printed in the USA
JSHW012029030822
28864JS00006B/130

9 781939 402479